Praise for *Lords of the Sea*

"With something for almost everyone, *Lords of the Sea* tells an important story and imparts to him who wants to learn important lessons. It's well worth the read."
—*The Washington Times*

"Dr. Hale's sparkling creation, that rare history so brilliantly told that, like the Athenian democracy, it is truly for all people."
—*The Courier-Journal* (Louisville)

"Historian and archaeologist Hale brings both skill sets to bear in this account of an Athens whose golden age and democratic institutions depended on its navy."
—*Publishers Weekly*

"Students of ancient history, broadly construed, will find *Lords of the Sea* to be a pleasurable, and edifying, experience."
—*History News Network*

"The dazzling moment of Golden Age Athens was built on democracy, silver, reason, and power. It was arguably the most creative moment in history, when Western architecture, philosophy, drama, and politics were all given their fundamental form. Behind it all was the Athenian navy, its life and fortunes described here with exemplary clarity and a vivid engagement with the visceral realities of battle and the sea. John Hale combines fluent readability with up-to-date scholarship and a sense that in these pages you are witnessing not only a driving collective enterprise, but the foundation-level struggles of our own world. This is a tour de force of historical imagination."
—Adam Nicolson, author of *God's Secretaries: The Making of the King James Bible* and *Seize the Fire: Heroism, Duty and Nelson's Battle of Trafalgar*

"To provide a new angle from which to view and understand the experience of the Athenians of the classical age is a remarkable achievement, but *Lords of the Sea* accomplishes just that. Nobody knows more about the history of oared ships around the world than John Hale, and he combines it with a knowledge of and love for the ancient Athenians that helps explain their achievement. The writing is utterly captivating and makes the reader feel he is back in ancient Athens among the great poets, historians, sculptors, architects, soldiers and sailors, all of whom were connected in important ways to the Athenian navy." —Donald Kagan, author of *The Peleponnesian War*

PENGUIN BOOKS

LORDS OF THE SEA

An Indiana native, John R. Hale studied at Yale and Cambridge universities before embarking on an archaeological career that has included extensive underwater searches for ancient warships. He has written for *Antiquity*, *Journal of Roman Archaeology*, and *Scientific American*; has been profiled by National Public Radio and *The New York Times*; and has been featured in documentaries on the Discovery and History channels. He is currently director of liberal studies at the University of Louisville.

LORDS
OF THE SEA

*The Epic Story of the
Athenian Navy and the
Birth of Democracy*

JOHN R. HALE

PENGUIN BOOKS

PENGUIN BOOKS
Published by the Penguin Group
Penguin Group (USA) Inc., 375 Hudson Street, New York, New York 10014, U.S.A. • Penguin Group
(Canada), 90 Eglinton Avenue East, Suite 700, Toronto, Ontario, Canada M4P 2Y3 (a division of Pearson
Penguin Canada Inc.) • Penguin Books Ltd, 80 Strand, London WC2R 0RL, England • Penguin Ireland,
25 St Stephen's Green, Dublin 2, Ireland (a division of Penguin Books Ltd) • Penguin Group (Australia), 250
Camberwell Road, Camberwell, Victoria 3124, Australia (a division of Pearson Australia Group Pty
Ltd) • Penguin Books India Pvt Ltd, 11 Community Centre, Panchsheel Park, New Delhi – 110 017,
India • Penguin Group (NZ), 67 Apollo Drive, Rosedale, North Shore 0632, New Zealand (a division of
Pearson New Zealand Ltd) • Penguin Books (South Africa) (Pty) Ltd, 24 Sturdee Avenue, Rosebank,
Johannesburg 2196, South Africa

Penguin Books Ltd, Registered Offices:
80 Strand, London WC2R 0RL, England

First published in the United States of America by Viking Penguin,
a member of Penguin Group (USA) Inc. 2009
Published in Penguin Books 2010

10 9 8 7 6 5 4 3 2 1

Copyright © John R. Hale, 2009
All rights reserved

Maps by Jeffrey L. Ward
Diagrams by Sam Manning; ancient images on p. 41 by Sam Manning after John S. Morrison and R. T. Williams,
Greek Oared Ships, 900–322 B.C., Arch. 50 (A), Clas. I (B), and Geom. 43 (C); diagram on p. 257 by Sam
Manning based on an image by B. Klejn-Christensen

THE LIBRARY OF CONGRESS HAS CATALOGED THE HARDCOVER EDITION AS FOLLOWS:
Hale, John R., 1951–
Lords of the sea : the eic story of the Athenian navy and the birth of democracy / by John R. Hale
p.   cm.
Includes bibliographical references and index.
ISBN 978-0-670-02080-5 (hc.)
ISBN 978-0-14-311768-1 (pbk.)
1. Athens (Greece)—History, Naval.   2. Democracy—Greece—Athens—History—To 1500.   I. Title.
V37.H355 2009
359.00938—dc22   2009001796

Printed in the United States of America
Designed by Carla Bolte • Set in Granjon

For my father

THOMAS FARRIS HALE

veteran of the United States Air Force,
who crossed the Pacific Ocean in a troopship when he was twenty-four
and later told his seven children their first stories of war and seafaring

The world before you has two realms open to human enterprise,
land and sea,
and over the whole of the sea you are lords.

—Pericles to the Athenians

CONTENTS

Part Three

EMPIRE

Part Four

CATASTROPHE

Part Five

REBIRTH

LIST OF MAPS AND DIAGRAMS

MAPS

DIAGRAMS

PREFACE

THE ATHENIAN NAVY FIRST FLOATED INTO MY CONSCIOUSNESS
on a winter afternoon in 1969, when I encountered Donald Kagan walking
down College Street in New Haven. Across the snowbound expanse of the
Yale campus his prizefighter's stance and rolling gait were instantly recognizable. I knew him well as the formidable professor of my Introduction to
Greek History course but had never worked up the courage to speak to him.
On the first day of class Kagan had marshaled the front row of students into
an improvised phalanx of Greek warriors, with notebooks for shields and
pens for spears, to demonstrate military maneuvers. Though like me a new
arrival, Kagan already ranked as a colossus among the faculty. I tacked
across the icy sidewalk to let him pass, but he stopped, asked my name, and
inquired what I was doing at Yale. I stammered a few words about major-
ing in archaeology and rowing for the freshman crew. Kagan lit up at once.
"Ha! A rower. Now you can explain something to me. In autumn 429, after
Phormio beat the Peloponnesians in the gulf, they sent their crews overland
to launch a sneak attack on the Piraeus. Thucydides says each rower carried
his own oar and cushion. But why on earth should they need cushions?
They certainly didn't have very far to row."

We talked for an hour of ships and oars and naval heroes, oblivious to
the cold. I fished up a recollection of rowing pads that had been used by
nineteenth-century American rowers so that they could work their legs
during the stroke. Kagan enlarged upon the tactical genius of the little-
known Athenian commander Phormio. He went on to speak of the many
unexplored issues that obscured the story of the mighty navy of Athens,
bulwark of liberty and engine of democracy. As the great man got under
way again, he told me that I should investigate Athenian history from the
vantage point of a rower's bench. It was an assignment, I found, for life.

Over the next four years I delved into the evidence for ancient rowing techniques, hoping to explain the phenomenal speed of ten knots over a full day of rowing that was attested for Athenian triremes. I also became immersed in Phormio's extraordinary career, and his string of naval victories against seemingly impossible odds. As a counterpoint to these marine interests, during my last semester the students of the Yale Drama School produced an extravaganza in the swimming pool of the Payne Whitney Gymnasium: an updated version of Aristophanes' *Frogs*. The ancient original featured many comments on the Athenian navy, some satirical, some patriotic. Most were cut in this new version, with songs by Sondheim and a cast that included the young Meryl Streep and Sigourney Weaver. But the high point of the comedy was still the chorus of noisy Frogs, now played by the Yale swimming team, who shouted the old rowing chant *Brekekekex ko-ax ko-ax!* as the god Dionysus rowed a little boat across the River Styx. Those were heady days.

At Cambridge in England, during doctoral research into the evolution of the Viking longship, I was drawn deeper into the world of the Athenian navy by a meeting with John Morrison. At that time his classic *Greek Oared Ships* was my bible. Morrison had been diverted from his early studies of Plato when he learned that nobody could explain various naval terms that punctuated the philosopher's dialogues. Ultimately he produced the first working model of an Athenian trireme with its complex three-tiered array of rowers. Morrison's reconstruction achieved nationwide notoriety when it was cited in the longest-running correspondence ever to appear in the letters column of *The Times*. The subject of the hot debate was the maximum speed of an ancient trireme.

Enthusiastic backers decided to build a section of a trireme in Morrison's garden. I had the good fortune to be among the Cambridge rowers who cycled out to Great Shelford and pulled an oar in this trial model. We dipped our blades into a plastic swimming pool set up next to the hull. There I also met John Coates, a royal naval architect who was devoting his retirement to the trireme project. Eventually the Greek navy made the vision a reality by constructing a full-scale replica according to Morrison's theories and Coates's plans. It was a happy day when, years later, I clambered aboard the trireme *Olympias* in dry dock near Athens, sat down on one of its 170 rowers' thwarts, and gazed across the shining bay to Salamis.

Even after Cambridge, when I returned home and took up a post as archaeologist at the University of Louisville, the siren song of the Athenian navy continued to haunt me. Digging at an ancient villa in Portugal, I saw Roman mosaics depicting the mythical hero Theseus, legendary slayer of the Minotaur and founder of the Athenian navy. When I was surveying the site of the Delphic Oracle in Greece, the dark tunnels through which I squeezed brought me close to the spot where the famous "Wooden Wall" oracle had been pronounced—the cryptic prophecy that foreshadowed the rise of Athenian naval power and the Greek victory over the Persian armada at Salamis. Lecturing in Finland, I encountered modern Vikings who seemed to have reinvented ancient Greek rowing technique complete with rowing pads. They had matched the legendary feats of Athenian triremes by crossing the Baltic Sea in a single day at—yes—an average speed of ten knots.

Nothing might have come of these sporadic reminders had it not been, again, for Don Kagan. In the spring of 2000 he invited me to lecture with him on the subject of "great battles of antiquity" during a Yale alumni cruise. Kagan tackled the land battles when we went on shore at Marathon, Thermopylae, or Sparta, re-creating his unforgettable classroom drills. I recounted the naval battles on the deck of the *Clelia II* as we voyaged through the home waters of the Athenian navy—cruising through the straits at Salamis, passing the Sybota Islands near Corfu (site of the battle that precipitated the Peloponnesian War), and forging at sunrise up the Hellespont, the strategic waterway that the Athenians had once expended so many men and ships in order to control.

On the long flight back home I told Kagan that he should do the world a favor and publish his history of the Peloponnesian War in a version for the general reader. The suggestion bore fruit for both of us. Some months later I received the message that led to the writing of this book. It came from Wendy Wolf, an editor at Viking Penguin in New York. "We are going to publish Don Kagan's *The Peloponnesian War.* He says that we should also publish a book on the ancient Athenian navy, and that you are the man to write it. Are you interested? I think it could be a blast."

Yes, I was interested. I had been interested for over thirty years. But if by "blast" Wolf envisioned something rocketlike and soon over, she was sadly misled. At a meeting in August 2001 I assured her that the research was complete and that I could finish the book within a year. Wolf prudently recommended that I plan on two. In the event, she has had to wait for seven years. It seemed that the more I looked, the more there was to learn.

Thanks to my editor's patience, I was able to visit the site of every Athenian naval battle and amphibious operation for which a detailed description survives, from Syracuse in Sicily to the Eurymedon River in southern Turkey, and to identify for the first time the location of Aegospotami ("Goat Rivers"), site of Athens' most terrible naval disaster. At the Piraeus, headquarters of the ancient Athenian fleet, I looked on as a team of young Danish and Greek archaeologists led by the indomitable Bjørn Lovén mapped the submerged slipways of the shipsheds where the triremes had been drawn ashore when not in use.

Finally, I went in search of triremes on the floor of the sea with my esteemed friends and colleagues Shelley Wachsmann and Robert Hohlfelder. In partnership with Greek oceanographers and underwater archaeologists, our Persian Wars Shipwreck Survey made four expeditions to sites in the Aegean Sea where, according to the ancient historian Herodotus, triremes had sunk in storms or naval engagements during campaigns of the Persian kings Darius and Xerxes to conquer Greece. From the Greek research vessel *Aegaeo* we scoured the search areas with side-scan sonar, the remote-operated vehicles *Achilles* and *Max Rover,* and the submersible *Thetis,* a real "Yellow Submarine." The quest turned up items that had probably spilled from triremes, along with a number of ancient wine freighters and even a lost cargo of marble blocks from the time of the Roman Empire. On the island of Euboea we had a mystical encounter with villagers, known locally as the "Whistlers," who claimed descent from Persians who had succeeded in swimming to shore in 480 B.C., when high winds in the Hollows had wrecked their squadron.

We did not, however, realize our dream of finding the remains of a trireme. The classic warship of the Athenian navy remains as elusive now as it was in 1881, when French classicist Augustin Cartault reflected on the highly perishable trireme and its enduring legacy in his book *The Athenian Trireme: A Study in Nautical Archaeology.* "The grand monuments that bear witness to the power of Athens, the temples on the Acropolis, the Propylaea, the theatre of Dionysus, still survive; architects and scholars have measured and reconstructed them. But the trireme, without which they would not have existed, was more fragile and has disappeared. It was swallowed up by the sea, broken open by enemy rams, or perhaps demolished in the dockyards after glorious exploits."

The Athenians in their years of greatness were first and foremost a people bound to the sea. This book is a tribute to the builders and rowers of those long-lost triremes, to the crucial role that they played in creating their city's Golden Age, and to the legacy they bestowed on the world.

—The Piraeus, June 24, 2008

INTRODUCTION

AT DAWN, WHEN THE AEGEAN SEA LAY SMOOTH AS A BURNISHED shield, you could hear a trireme from Athens while it was still a long way off. First came soft measured strokes like the pounding of a distant drum. Then two distinct sounds gradually emerged within each stroke: a deep percussive blow of wood striking water, followed by a dashing surge. *Whumpff! Whroosh!* These sounds were so much a part of their world that Greeks had names for them. They called the splash *pitylos,* the rush *rhothios.* Relentlessly the beat would echo across the water, bringing the ship closer. It was now a throbbing pulse, as strong and steady as the heartbeat of a giant.

Soon other sounds would become audible, always in time with the oar strokes: the reedy skirling of pipes, the rhythmic shouts of the coxswain as he urged the crew onward, and in answer the deep chant of the rowers. The ship's own voice joined the din, with tons of timber and cordage creaking and groaning. As the trireme hurtled forward, the steering oars and the bronze ram hissed like snakes as they sliced through the water. In the final moments, as the red-rimmed eyes set on the prow stared straight at you, the oar strokes sounded like thunder. Then the ship either ran you down or swerved aside in search of other prey.

This fearsome apparition, black with pitch, packed with men, and bristling with oars, was an emblem of liberty and democracy but also of imperial ambition. It was a warship of Athens, one vessel in a navy of hundreds that served the will of the Athenian people. At the height of their power they ruled a great maritime empire, almost forgotten today. This vast realm embraced more than 150 islands and coastal city-states and extended from the southern Aegean to the far reaches of the Black Sea. To patrol its seaways and defend its frontiers, the Athenians required fast and formidable ships. The answer was the trireme.

Built for speed, this torpedolike wooden ship measured some 120 feet from the nose of the ram at the bow to the curve of the upward-sweeping stern. The trireme was so slender and its construction so light that it had to be held together with gigantic girding cables that served it as tendons. When the winds were fair, the mariners unfurled the big square sail, but the prime means of propulsion was oar power. The Greek name *trieres* means "rowed by three," a reference to the three tiers in which the 170 oarsmen were arrayed. Rowing crews could maintain an astounding ten knots over a full day, a speed unknown to anything else that moved on the sea. Greeks classified the trireme as a *naus* or long ship. From that linguistic root we derive an entire constellation of marine terms: navy, navigator, nautical, astronaut ("star mariner"), chambered nautilus, and even nausea—the Greek word for the "feeling of being on a ship."

Athenians were a people wedded to the sea or, as one blustering Spartan crudely put it, "fornicating with the sea." The city staked its fortunes on a continuing quest for sea rule. Greek historians coined a term for this type of power: *thalassokratia* or thalassocracy. Throughout history fleets have clashed repeatedly on the enclosed sea that stretches from the coast of Lebanon westward to the Rock of Gibraltar. As Alfred T. Mahan observed in *The Influence of Sea Power upon History:* "Circumstances have caused the Mediterranean Sea to play a greater part in the history of the world, both in a commercial and a military point of view, than any other sheet of water of the same size. Nation after nation has striven to control it, and the strife goes on."

Athenians were early and eager contestants in the struggle. For more than a century and a half their city-state of some 200,000 inhabitants possessed the strongest navy on earth. Athenian thalassocracy endured, with ups and downs, for exactly 158 years and one day. It began at Salamis on the nineteenth day of the month Boedromion (roughly equivalent to September) in 480 B.C., when Athenians engineered the historic Greek naval victory over the armada of King Xerxes. It ended at the Piraeus, within sight of Salamis, on the twentieth of Boedromion in 322 B.C., when the successors of Alexander the Great sent a Macedonian garrison to take over the naval base. Between those two dates stretched the Golden Age of Athens.

Without the Athenian navy there would have been no Parthenon, no tragedies of Sophocles or Euripides, no *Republic* of Plato or *Politics* of Aristotle. Before the Persian Wars Athens produced no great traditions of philosophy, architecture, drama, political science, or historical writing. All these things came in a rush after the Athenians voted to build a fleet and transform themselves into a naval power in the early fifth century B.C. As for the cities of their maritime empire, they may have resented Athenian rule at times, but they also took part in the dynamism of the age. Herodotus of Halicarnassus invented history as we know it with his vast work on the Persian Wars. Hippocrates of Cos established a medical tradition that still flourishes today, along with the "Hippocratic Oath" attributed to the founder. Hippodamus of Miletus established a reputation as the world's first known urban planner. His most famous project was the Piraeus, and one can still trace his street grid throughout much of the modern port.

The Golden Age of Athens was also the age of the trireme. In their quest for sea rule the Athenians manned their triremes and fought many rivals: Persians, Phoenicians, Spartans, Sicilians, Macedonians, and even pirate fleets. A naval battle or *naumachia* had to be fought on a calm sea, in conditions that would have left a sailing vessel helplessly becalmed. Masts and sails were so useless in a trireme battle that they were unloaded and left on the beach before the ships were launched to meet the enemy. Smooth water was absolutely essential, since a trireme's lowest tier of oars lay just above the waterline. Early morning was the time for naval battles. Combat would be broken off if the wind began to blow. The crews always spent the night ashore, so all trireme battles were fought within sight of land. To be effective, Athens had to control not only the sea lanes but hundreds of landing places with sandy beaches and sources of fresh water.

Unlike round ships such as the *holkas* or freighter, a heavily ballasted sailing vessel with a deep keel and a capacious hold, triremes spent as much of their time on shore as at sea. Aside from meeting the needs of the enormous crew, the hulls had to be dried out on an almost daily basis to keep the destructive teredo or shipworm at bay. (Freighters could be sheathed with lead for the same purpose, far too heavy for a *naus*.) A trireme from Athens was thus an amphibious monster, thrashing its way through the seas by day, spreading its sail to the wind like a wing, yet drawn to shore as the sun went down. In the circular harbors at their home port, the Piraeus, the weary crews hauled their triremes up stone slipways into the shelter of colonnaded shipsheds. There the ships slept, stabled like racing stallions, until orders from the Assembly sent them to sea again.

Contrary to popular belief, the rowers in these warships were not slaves chained to their oars. This widespread misconception began with Lew Wallace's novel *Ben-Hur* and caught a second wind in Rudyard Kipling's "The Finest Story in the World," the tale of an ancient galley slave reincarnated as a London clerk. Ultimately it achieved immortality through a thousand popular cartoons. As with horns on Viking helmets, the error has now taken on a life of its own. But the stereotype of the emaciated, half-naked galley slave belongs not to classical Greece but to European, Ottoman, and Arab fleets of the Middle Ages and Renaissance. Jack Kerouac was memorably poetical but historically off-base in *Desolation Angels* when he traced his concept of "beat" back to the forced labor of ancient oarsmen.

> *Everything is going with the beat. It's beat. It's the beat to keep. It's the beat of the heart. It's like being beat and down in the world and like old time lowdown and like in ancient civilizations the slave boatmen rowing galleys to a beat.*

Nor did the experience of Athenian crews have much in common with the shipboard life known to modern readers through the annals of the British navy, whether historical (Horatio Nelson) or fictional (Hornblower; Aubrey and Maturin). Winston Churchill allegedly summed up British naval tradition as "nothing but rum, buggery, and the lash." With regard to the lash, at least, Athenian rowers would have promptly pitched overboard any officer who tried to ply a whip. Triremes were not pressure cookers of hostility between high-handed officers and resentful crews. There were no press-gangs, and mutinies were almost unheard of.

When the Athenian Assembly manned a fleet for a naval battle, the rowers were free men. Most were, in fact, citizens. They took pride in their navy and welcomed the steady pay and political equality that it offered. At times of supreme crisis, *all* free adult males in Athens—rich and poor, citizens and aliens, aristocratic horsemen and common laborers—would board the triremes and row to save their city. On one desperate occasion, when the main fleet was blockaded in a distant harbor, the Athenians freed thousands of their slaves so that a new fleet could row to the rescue. All these former slaves received citizenship.

The ancient Greeks knew that building a navy was an undertaking with clear-cut political consequences. A naval tradition that depended on the muscles and sweat of the masses led inevitably to democracy: from sea power to democratic power. Athens was Exhibit A in this argument, and radical democracy would indeed be the Athenian navy's greatest legacy. In Aristotle's *Politics,* written during his years at the Lyceum in Athens, the philosopher classified the constitution of Athens as "a democracy based on triremes." He traced its origins back to the Persian Wars: "The Athenian democracy was strengthened by the masses who served in the navy and who won the victory at Salamis, because the leadership that Athens then gained rested on sea power."

The navy was thus the origin of Athens' extreme form of democracy. It was also a force that fostered new democracies throughout the Greek world and defended Athens against attack by the enemies of democracy at home and abroad. In his *Rhetoric* Aristotle recorded that a politician named Peitholaus once made a speech in which he called the *Paralos,* the flagship of the Athenian navy, "the People's Big Stick." (Peitholaus was apparently an avatar of Teddy Roosevelt.)

Naval power naturally stimulated and protected commerce. Maritime trade, then as now a field dominated by Greek shippers, helped make ancient Athens the richest city in the Mediterranean. The Piraeus, Athens' port city, was the hub of an international web of commerce that spanned the eastern Mediterranean, Adriatic, Tyrrhenian, Aegean, and Black seas. At stalls in the Agora sellers offered African ivory, Baltic amber, and Chinese silk. Peacocks from Persia seem to have been strictly diplomatic gifts, like pandas today. Alongside the exotic luxury items ran a large-scale traffic in commodities such as wine, salt fish, building stone, and timber. Thanks to Athens' seaborne grain trade, the wheat in Socrates' daily bread was more likely to have grown in Russia, Sicily, or Egypt than in the fields of Attica, just outside the city walls. The far horizons opened up by the navy allowed Socrates himself to say, "Do not call me an Athenian. I am a citizen of the world."

A life linked to the sea bred an open spirit of experimentation and free inquiry. Unlike many of its neighbors Athens eagerly welcomed foreigners from overseas, whether Greek or "barbarian," and encouraged them to settle down as residents. So tolerant did the Athenians become that they permitted foreign merchants to build shrines to their own gods within the walls of the Piraeus. Such liberal thinking was rare. Among land powers like Sparta and Thebes the dominance of the hoplite phalanx exerted a stultifying effect. Military regimes in Greece were typically xenophobic, anti-intellectual, and chronically suspicious of change. Sparta was the antithesis—and likewise the sworn enemy—of Athens in its Golden Age

In the long run the Athenian spirit proved more resilient and enduring than the Spartan. Ten years after the so-called Fall of Athens in 404 B.C. and a Spartan victory in the Peloponnesian War, Athenian naval heroes had restored the city's independence, democratic government, and naval tradition. Within a generation Athens became the leader of a second maritime league and drove the Spartans from the seas. The renewed Golden Age launched by the navy's revival produced Xenophon's historical writings, Praxiteles' sculptures, Plato's philosophical dialogues, Demosthenes' orations, and Aristotle's scientific works. As an institution, the navy itself prospered in the fourth century B.C. as never before. During the final conflict with the Macedonians, when the power of Sparta had been permanently broken by Athens and other Greeks, the tally of triremes in the resurrected Athenian Navy Yard reached almost four hundred—far more than during the Persian or Peloponnesian wars.

In the Golden Age most well-known Athenians were directly involved with the naval effort. Among those who commanded fleets and squadrons of triremes were the statesman Pericles, the historian Thucydides, and the playwright Sophocles, whose election to the post of general was said to have been a public reward for the success of his tragedy *Antigone*. Aeschylus, a veteran of Salamis, wrote an account of the historic naval battle in his *Persians,* the oldest surviving play in the world. The orator Demosthenes served the navy both as a ship's commander at sea and as a political champion in the Assembly. Even Socrates, Athens' first homegrown philosopher, who is usually pictured with his feet planted firmly in the Agora, led a life touched at many points by the navy. He voyaged on a troop carrier to a distant war, presided over a trial of naval commanders, and enjoyed a long stay of execution while contrary winds prevented one of the sacred ships from returning to the city.

Athenians exposed their naval obsession even in the names they gave their children. You could meet men named Naubios or "Naval Life" and Naukrates, "Naval Power"; women named Naumache or "Naval Battle" and Nausinike, "Naval Victory." Pericles, architect of the Golden Age, identified himself so closely with the fleet that he named his second son Paralos after the consecrated state trireme *Paralos*. Another patriotic Athenian father named his son Eurymedon after the Eurymedon River in Asia Minor, where an Athenian naval force won a great victory over the fleet and army of the Persian king in about 466 B.C. It was as if a family in more recent times had named a child Trafalgar or Midway. Perhaps inevitably, young Eurymedon grew up to be a naval commander.

The sea penetrated every corner of Athenian life. Ships and seafaring formed a theme for poets, artists, dramatists, historians, politicians, philosophers, and legal experts. The people described their government as a "ship of state" and its leaders as steersmen. In the academies, scientific thinkers investigated the mechanics of oars and the movements of winds and stars, and the political theorists deplored the navy and its effects on Athenian morals. In the theater of Dionysus nautical scenes cropped up in both tragedies and comedies. (The theatrical properties included a miniature ship on wheels for rowing scenes.) In private houses drinking symposia held in the evenings were described as voyages upon a dark sea of wine, mirror images of actual voyages upon the wine-dark sea. And in the bedroom, nautical terms for rowing and ramming quickly became Athenian slang for sexual foreplay and penetration.

Many "firsts" helped give a peculiarly modern texture to Athenian daily life. Among them were the first maritime courts, the first shipping insurance, and the first recorded political cartoon. (Its target was the naval hero Timotheus in the mid-fourth century B.C.) The first mention of a traveler who passed the time on board ship by reading books comes from Aristophanes' *Frogs*. And one of the first known projects in historic preservation required the city's carpenters to conserve a little sacred galley, claimed by Athenians to be the actual vessel in which the legendary hero Theseus voyaged to Crete to kill the Minotaur.

The wealthiest Athenians took it in rotation to serve as "trierarchs" or trireme commanders, providing gear and acting as captains while the ships were at sea. Their financial contributions to the fleet were the tax required of them by the democratic majority, along with sponsoring dramatic festivals and choral performances. Just as common citizens enlisted willingly for service at sea, many rich Athenians competed to outshine their rivals in the number of their annual trierarchies, the lavish fittings of their ships, and the speed of their crews.

The glories of the Acropolis dominate our modern view of Athens. Ancient Athenians saw their city differently. In terms of civic pride, the temples of the gods were eclipsed by the vast complex of installations for the navy. Near Zea Harbor at the Piraeus stood the largest roofed building in Athens, indeed in all of Greece. It was a naval arsenal, four hundred feet in length. The Athenian architect Philo designed it to house the linen sails, rigging, and other "hanging gear" of the fleet. Philo was so proud of his storehouse or *skeuotheke* that he wrote a book about it, and the Assembly voted to inscribe its specifications on a marble stele. The Parthenon received no such attention at the time of its construction. Only one contemporary literary reference to the Parthenon has survived to our time, in fragments of an anonymous comedy. Even here the Parthenon takes second place to nautical monuments. "O Athens, queen of cities! How fair your Navy Yard! How fair your Parthenon! How fair your Piraeus!"

The great naval enterprise provided Athens with its unifying principle and cohesive spirit. Like the Vikings and Venetians, Athenians built a civilization on seafaring. Only the Phoenicians and the Polynesian islanders surpassed them in the totality of their maritime enterprise. While the ancient Spartans militarized their entire society, the Athenians navalized theirs. Alongside Athena they revered Poseidon as a patron god.

The odyssey of seafaring Athenians stands as one of history's great maritime epics. The tale abounds in hard-won victories against overwhelming odds, in crushing defeats, in battles decided sometimes by raw courage, sometimes by tactical genius, stratagems, and surprise. At times Athenian fortunes hung upon a bold escape from a blockaded port, or a desperate daylong chase across the open sea. The shallow draft of triremes encouraged amphibious actions as well. In these exploits marines poured off their ships onto hostile coasts, horsemen launched attacks on enemy soil from seaborne horse carriers, and engineers battered the walls of seaside towns with siege engines mounted directly on the triremes' decks. Storms and shipwrecks claimed many ships as mariners braved high winds and rough seas. On one extraordinary occasion a tidal wave triggered by an earthquake picked up a trireme and tossed it over a city wall like a toy.

The trireme ushered in a new era of warfare. For the first time battles were being fought where the majority of combatants never fought hand to hand with the enemy—indeed, never even saw the enemy. Sitting behind their protective screens of hide or within the wooden hull, the rowers could see nothing of the battle. They could only sit in silence, waiting for the word of command or the signal from the piper. Raw courage counted less than technique and the orderly execution of mechanical maneuvers. The goal of the fast trireme in battle was to disable, destroy, or capture entire enemy ships with, ideally, a single blow of the ram. Thus the attack was aimed at a piece of equipment rather than at individual fighting men.

In actions between trireme fleets the skill of the steersman was vital to success. Athenians called him a *kubernetes*. The term was echoed by the Romans in the Latin *gubernator* and is ancestral to both *gubernatorial* and *governor*. The Greek title is also embedded in the acronym of Phi Beta Kappa. *Philosophia Biou Kubernetes:* "Philosophy, life's steersman." One of Plato's many complaints against the navy was its reliance on the skill and technique of individual steersmen to win battles rather than the virtuous bravery of citizen soldiers fighting in the phalanx.

Athenian naval tacticians favored maneuvers intended to fool the enemy: the use of art and cunning rather than brute force. The same approach to war was being developed during this time at the far end of the Silk Road, in the "Warring States" of China. "Warfare is deception," declared the Chinese military sage known as Sunzi or Sun-tzu. Athenian naval commanders subscribed wholeheartedly to this creed. Themistocles lured the Persian armada into the narrow straits at Salamis with a false message. Cimon disguised his ships and marines with Persian insignia to take the enemy by surprise. Thrasyllus yoked his triremes together in pairs so as to make his squadron appear a small and tempting target. As Sunzi would have said, "Lure the enemy with a small advantage." Socrates commented on the practice among leading Athenian families of compiling books of stratagems and handing them down from father to son.

From the beginning the navy was a school for great leaders. The Athenian view of history focused on leaders and attributed both glorious victories and catastrophic disasters to the policies and actions of individual generals, commanders, and demagogues. Ancient writers might at times invoke the powers of destiny, national character, natural forces, or just plain chance. They nevertheless put individuals, especially leaders, at the center of unfolding history. Certainly the Athenian Assembly held its elected leaders fully responsible for the outcomes of their decisions.

Two forces within Athens itself sabotaged the city's naval adventure. First, the democratic Assembly had a fatal tendency to treat its elected leaders unreasonably and even vindictively, driving many promising commanders to pursue private enterprises rather than public service. Second, a cabal of antidemocratic citizens finally betrayed the fleet and the naval base at the Piraeus to the successors of Alexander the Great. Some Athenian aristocrats had secretly opposed the navy almost from the beginning. Among them was Plato, whose famous myth of the lost continent of Atlantis was an elaborate historical allegory on the evils of maritime empire.

Yet the fires of innovation and genius, even Plato's own, were fueled by sea power. In legendary times the Delphic Oracle had foretold that Athens would be unsinkable, a city destined to "ride the waves of the sea." So long as it had ships, commanders, strong crews, and the iron will to take risks and make sacrifices, Athens weathered every storm and recuperated from every disaster. In the end, weakened by a dearth of leaders and undermined by the disaffected upper classes, the Athenian navy and Golden Age ended together in 322 B.C., as abruptly as if someone had put out a light.

Athens was the first truly modern society, ruled not by kings or priests or nobles but by a sovereign democratic Assembly. The Athenians had to wrestle with the same polarities that confront the democratic nations of the modern world. Like us, they were caught up in conflicts that pitted West against East, liberal against conservative, and scientific inquiry against religious faith. They too confronted insoluble political paradoxes. The same navy that made Athens a democracy at home made it an imperialistic power abroad and at times an oppressor of the very cities that it had helped to liberate from the Persians. The Golden Age was funded in part by payments of tribute that Athens demanded of its maritime subjects and allies. As for the Parthenon, that iconic ruin in pure white marble makes today's world imagine a serene ancient Athens of lofty visions and classical balance. In fact, at the time of its building the Parthenon was a bitterly controversial project, paid for in part with what Pericles' opponents considered to be misappropriated naval funds.

Time and winter rains have washed the original gaudy colors of scarlet, azure, and gold off the Parthenon. Passing centuries have also washed the blood and guts, sweat and struggle, from the modern conception of Athens. In losing sight of the Athenian navy, posterity has overlooked the vital propulsive force behind the monuments. A living sea creature, all muscle and appetite and growth, generated the glistening shell of inspiring art, literature, and political ideals. Today we admire the shell for its own beauty, but it cannot be fully understood without charting the life cycle of the animal that generated it. The beat of oars was the heartbeat of Athens in the city's Golden Age. This, then, is the story of a unique and gigantic marine organism, the Athenian navy, that built a civilization, empowered the world's first great democracy, and led a band of ordinary citizens into new worlds. Their epic voyage altered the course of history.

LORDS OF THE SEA

Part One

FREEDOM

The greatest glory is won from the greatest dangers. When our fathers faced the Persians their resources could not compare to ours. In fact, they gave up even what they had. Then by wise counsels and daring deeds, not fortune and material advantages, they drove out the invaders and made our city what it is now.

—Pericles to the Athenians

CHAPTER 1

One Man, One Vision

[483 B.C.]

"So you tell your dream."
"Oh, mine is great—all about the city and the ship of state."
"Tell the whole thing now, ends and means, from the keel up."

—Aristophanes

ALL THE GLORY OF ATHENS—THE PARTHENON, PLATO'S
Academy, the immortal tragedies, even the revolutionary experiment in
democracy—can be traced back to one public meeting, one obstinate citizen,
and a speech about silver and ships.

On the day of the meeting Themistocles awoke well before dawn. Athenians tended to be early risers, but for him this was no ordinary morning.
The Assembly of Athens met on a rocky hilltop near his home about three
times each month. The published agenda for today's meeting included a
proposal to share out silver from a rich strike recently made in the mines of
Attica. Themistocles intended to make a counterproposal. In near darkness
he got up from the bed that he shared with his wife, Archippe, put on his
tunic and sandals, and went downstairs.

Breakfast was a simple affair of bread dunked in wine. Many others were
astir besides Themistocles. The house was full of children: three sons and
two daughters. Even so there was an empty place at the table. The oldest
boy, Neocles, had died young, killed in an accident with a horse. As Themistocles prepared for his speech, his younger sons made ready for their
daily round of lessons. The sky was brightening over the enclosed courtyard.
Themistocles donned his wool cloak, opened the door, and stepped outside.
If all went well, by the time he came home for dinner he would have mended
his own fortunes and changed his city's future as well.

The house was modest even by Athenian standards. It stood on an unpaved street near a city gate that led to the sea. As Themistocles climbed the rocky hill to the place of the Assembly, Athens gradually came into view: a huddle of some ten thousand flat housetops divided by twisting lanes and by the open space of the Agora, the marketplace and civic center. Smoke rose from ovens, potters' kilns, foundries, and forges. Hemming in the mass of shops and houses was an irregular city wall, mud brick on a stone footing. In the center rose the Acropolis, citadel of Athens.

Athens was in those days a humble place. Many city-states overshadowed it in military strength, religious prestige, or commercial success. Arts and sciences flourished elsewhere. Athens could boast no famous monuments, no remarkable philosophical schools or feats of engineering, no world-famous sculptures. Even the temples on the Acropolis were outclassed by those in other Greek cities and sanctuaries. Yet Themistocles cherished a vision in which Athens would surpass its rivals. "I cannot tune a harp or play a lyre," he would say, "but I know how to make a small city great."

He had no illusions about the rough yet slippery path that led to civic leadership. From their close-knit ranks the blue bloods of Athens looked down on him as an upstart and outsider. His father, Neocles, was neither very rich nor very famous; his mother was not even an Athenian citizen. When Themistocles was a young man, his father had taken him for a walk on the seashore, hoping to deter his son from seeking a career in politics. The two came to a place where old triremes had been hauled up on the beach and left to rot. "Look!" Neocles said, pointing to the abandoned hulks. "See how the people cast off their leaders when they have no more use for them."

Themistocles reached the topmost ridge of the Pnyx, the hill where the Assembly met, with its wide view of Attica, territory of the Athenian city-state. The surrounding countryside was flat and fertile: good farmland ran right up to the city walls. Humpbacked hills surrounding the plain were clad with timber or scarred with stone quarries. To the south lay Phaleron Bay, the port of Athens, and beyond it the sea. Most painful in Themistocles' eyes were the unfinished port installations at the Piraeus, four miles away to the southwest, toward the island of Salamis. The city had undertaken the construction project on the rocky promontory at Themistocles' own recommendation ten years earlier. He had intended these walls to transform Athens into a sea power and to protect the citizens in case of an invasion—an invasion that Themistocles believed to be inevitable.

In the time of Themistocles' grandfather, the distant Persians had begun to build the largest and most powerful empire that the world had ever seen. Themistocles had believed, and still believed, that the Great King of Persia meant to conquer Athens just as he had already conquered Greek cities in Asia Minor and the Aegean islands. Ten years earlier there had been warning signs that the Persians would invade Attica with an army coming overland and a fleet attacking by sea.

As archon or chief magistrate for the year, Themistocles persuaded the Assembly to fortify the Piraeus promontory with its three natural harbors. The walled port would provide a safe refuge for Athenian families while the citizens manned their ships and repelled the Persian fleet. Trusting his foresight, the Athenians had expended much money and effort to raise a massive wall of stone blocks clamped together with iron and lead, a wall so thick that two oxcarts could pass along it. But within a few years the Persian threat seemingly evaporated, and the costly project was left unfinished. The wall and the stumps of towers at the Piraeus now stood to only half the height that Themistocles had envisioned, a constant reminder of his poor powers as a prophet.

Athens had incurred the wrath of the Persians when Themistocles was still in his impressionable twenties. At one of the most memorable meetings ever held on the Pnyx, Aristagoras of Miletus had asked the Athenians to support a rebellion of Ionian Greeks against their overlord, King Darius of Persia. With Athenian help, the revolt might grow from a limited fight for freedom to a war that would reach all the way to the Persian capital at Susa, beyond the Tigris River. The Athenians voted to aid their kinsmen in Asia Minor and sent twenty ships filled with troops across the Aegean Sea. These men joined the Ionians in attacking the Persian provincial capital at Sardis. A fire broke out during the sack of the city, burning most of the houses along with the temple of the Mother Goddess Cybele.

Retribution was swift. A Persian army caught the Athenians as they marched back to the coast and beat them in battle. When the twenty ships limped home and the defeated troops told their story, the Assembly voted to have nothing more to do with the Ionian rebellion. The struggle lasted for six years. Shortly before Themistocles was elected archon, the Great King's navy defeated the fleet of the Ionian rebels near an island called Lade. Themistocles was convinced that Athens' turn would be next: hence the fortification of the Piraeus.

As Themistocles prophesied, Darius did send an army and fleet to conquer Athens. That first Persian attempt ended when a violent north wind drove the Great King's triremes onto the rocky coast of Mount Athos in the northern Aegean, where the Persians lost hundreds of triremes and thousands of men. The second Persian invasion came to grief at Marathon, in the northwestern corner of Attica. Led by the charismatic Athenian general Miltiades, Athens' phalanx of heavily armed soldiers called hoplites defeated a seaborne expeditionary force on a plain that lay just over twenty-six miles from Athens. King Darius' third attempt to conquer the Athenians was in preparation when he died, three years after Marathon. Since then, rebellions within the empire had kept the Persians at home. Themistocles looked like the boy who cried wolf in Aesop's fable. The city was still safe and free. After so many false alarms Athenians stopped believing in the Persian threat and stopped working on Themistocles' folly at the Piraeus as well.

Yet the man himself had never lost his conviction. At today's meeting he still intended to strengthen Athens' power to resist Persia, but by oblique means. The Assembly would have no patience if he predicted a Persian invasion yet again. No, Persia would not even be mentioned. There would be no direct attack on public opinion. Themistocles would use *mêtis* instead.

This distinctively Greek quality was virtually untranslatable into other languages. Indeed it ran contrary to the values of many nations, most notably the Persians. *Mêtis* embraced craft, cunning, skill, and intelligence, the power of invention and the subtlety of art. It was the weapon of the weak and the outnumbered. Athenians knew that no physical force was mightier than the mind. In the world of myth, Mêtis was the ancient goddess from whom Athena derived her own wisdom. Not brawn but *mêtis* was the special attribute of Athena's favorite hero, Odysseus, whose stratagem of the Trojan Horse succeeded where ten years of direct assaults had failed. Every educated Athenian knew the famous lines in Homer's *Iliad* on the uses of *mêtis*.

> *To win the prize, keep* mêtis *well in mind.*
> *By* mêtis, *not brute force, men fell great oaks.*
> *By* mêtis *steersmen on the wine-dark sea*
> *Steady their swift ships through the tearing gale.*
> *By* mêtis *charioteer beats charioteer.*

As a fervent advocate of naval power, Themistocles saw further than other Athenians of his time. There was more at stake than the Persian threat. Athens' future, he believed, lay with the sea. The projected fortification of the Piraeus had been just one step toward transforming his city into a maritime center with a commercial emporium and a strong fleet of warships. Over the past decade those hopes had been repeatedly frustrated. But when the agenda for the upcoming Assembly meeting was posted a few days earlier, listing a proposal concerning income from the Athenian silver mines at Laurium, he realized that fate or luck had finally turned in his favor.

Laurium ("Place of Silver") was a rugged knot of hills near the southern tip of Attica, about twenty-five miles from Athens. Prospectors had been working the Laurium lode for a thousand years. They had first dug out the greenish ore from surface deposits, then followed the glittering veins deep underground. By Themistocles' time there were shafts that reached depths of three hundred feet. Miners, most of them slaves, were lowered into the shafts armed with iron picks and clay lamps that held enough oil for an eight-to-ten-hour shift. Ropes and winches lifted the ore to the surface, where it was crushed, washed, sieved, and smelted. In Athens the mint master received the silver and used his iron anvils and punches to manufacture the city's coins or "owls," stamped on one side with the helmeted head of Athena, and on the other with the goddess's owl and an olive sprig.

Other Greeks had to procure their precious metals from the Aegean islands or the mountains of the north. The Athenian people owned the Laurium mines collectively, but the actual investment and operations were

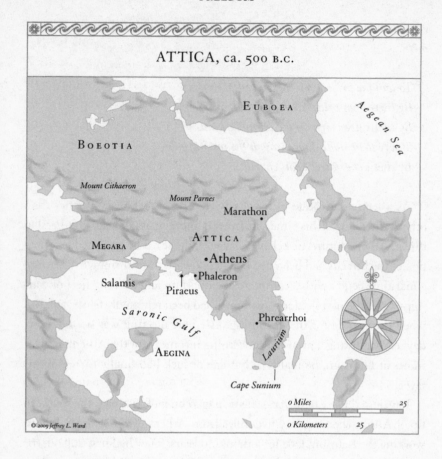

ATTICA, ca. 500 B.C.

EUBOEA

Aegean Sea

BOEOTIA

Mount Cithaeron

Mount Parnes

Marathon

ATTICA

•Athens

MEGARA

•Phaleron

Salamis

Piraeus

Saronic Gulf

Phrearrhoi

AEGINA

Laurium

Cape Sunium

0 Miles   25

0 Kilometers   25

© 2009 Jeffrey L. Ward

privatized. Mine leases were auctioned off at the start of each year to the highest bidders, and the Athenians also collected a percentage of each mine's yield at the end of the annual lease.

The lands of Themistocles' family lay at a township called Phrearroi ("Wells"), on the edge of the mining district. He knew that in recent years the miners had unexpectedly broken through to a zone where the ore lay in a vast subterranean reef. The annual trickle of silver from Laurium soon swelled to a mighty stream. Inspectors reported the increase in silver to the Board of Mines, which passed the news on to the councilors. The lucky strike at Laurium created a surplus big enough for a public distribution. The Council was submitting a proposal to keep half the silver in the treasury but to divide the rest in equal portions among all thirty thousand citizens. According to the draft resolution on the notice boards, ten drachmas would be the amount of the dole. Themistocles, however, had other ideas.

That morning a flag had been hoisted at daybreak to remind citizens of the Assembly meeting. Before Themistocles arrived at the Pnyx, officials had climbed to the hilltop and purified the place with prayers and sacrifices. Soon the ground in front of the speaker's platform began to fill as citizens came up from the Agora. The noise increased: an irrepressible Athenian hubbub of greetings, comments, arguments, obscenities, and jokes. At the rear of the talkative and straggling procession walked a line of slaves. They carried a rope dripping with dye and herded the slow-moving citizens toward the meeting place. Any laggard found with a red stripe on his tunic would be marked down for a fine.

The nine archons took their seats, led by the eponymous archon who gave his name to the year. Ten years ago Themistocles had held this post; now it was a man named Nicodemus. Places were also reserved for the fifty Council members whose tribe happened to be presiding that day in the annual rotation. The secretary prepared his stylus and wax tablets. At a signal from the president, the herald stepped up to the speaker's platform and spoke the invocation. There was no separation of religion and state in Athens: the government had no higher duty than propitiating the gods through almost constant rites and sacrifices. After the invocation the herald read out the first draft resolution on the Council's agenda and cried, "Who wishes to speak?" The Assembly of Athens was open for business.

The thoughts of most citizens that morning were pleasantly occupied with the question "What shall I do with ten drachmas?" The sum was enough to buy a new riding cloak, an exceptionally fine painted cup, or even an ox. It was a negligible bonus for men in the city's upper three citizen classes—the three or four hundred richest landowners, the twelve hundred horsemen, and the ten thousand hoplites who donned their bronze armor to fight in the phalanx. But for the great mass of Athens' landless workers, the citizens who were known as thetes, ten drachmas represented a major supplement to their scanty incomes.

These men of the fourth and lowest class numbered about twenty thousand. Most worked for hire in agriculture, manufacturing, or transport. Individually they lacked wealth or influence, but as a mass they were the *demos,* the "people" at the heart of Athenian democracy. Though the thetes constituted a clear majority of citizens, the city's laws still barred them from holding any elected office. This nondemocratic restriction was likewise placed on the hoplites. Unlike hoplites, however, thetes were excluded even from membership on the Council of Five Hundred. Thus the agenda for Assembly meetings rested firmly in the hands of the wealthy, and the thetes could only vote yea or nay to proposals that seemed good to members of the upper classes. At the time when Themistocles stepped forward to make his speech, Athens may have called itself a democracy, but in some ways it was a democracy in name only.

In anticipation of the Assembly's favorable vote on the silver dole, the mint had struck thousands of silver coins for distribution. One side of each coin was stamped with the head of a smiling Athena, wearing a helmet and a pearl earring, while the other displayed the goddess's owl, emblem of her wisdom. Unlike the Spartans, who claimed to scorn private wealth and did not even have a coinage or currency of their own, Athenians were hard-headed men who knew the value of a drachma. They were not likely to pass up such a windfall.

In response to the herald's cry, Themistocles came forward and mounted the speaker's platform or bema. He was a robust man of forty, with a wide challenging gaze and a neck like a bull. His hair was cropped short in the style of a workingman, not a noble. Along with an infallible memory for names and faces, he possessed one other prerequisite for a political career in Athens: a loud voice.

No one read from notes while addressing the Assembly: speeches were either memorized or extemporized. Themistocles had to keep in mind a number of rules while speaking. He must not wander from his point or address more than one topic. He was not permitted to slander a fellow citizen, step off the bema while speaking, or assault the president. Most important, he could not speak twice on the same proposal unless ordered by the Assembly to do so. Before stepping down from the platform Themistocles would have to provide every detail of his plan, explain all its benefits, and rebut in advance every possible argument against it. It was most unwise to incur the Assembly's impatience, usually expressed with hooting, booing, and other verbal abuse. But so long as a speaker broke no rules, he could not be interrupted.

Without flamboyant gestures or theatrical tricks Themistocles faced his fellow citizens and presented his proposal. The Council had reported the surplus of silver and proposed a dole. He believed that there was a better use for the silver. Rather than break up the enormous hoard, he urged the Athenians to devote the year's mining revenue, all six hundred thousand drachmas of it, to a single project: the building of a navy. With the full amount Athens could provide itself with one hundred new warships, fast triremes designed for naval warfare. In combination with the existing fleet of about seventy and some modest annual additions, the total would quickly climb to two hundred. This was about the maximum number of ships that the city could hope to man from its own population. At a stroke, Athens would become the greatest naval power in Greece.

This was no quixotic request: the fleet would protect the Athenians from a very real and immediate threat to their security. Themistocles aimed his revolutionary proposal at an enemy visible to all. From where he stood Themistocles could point across the sea to the dark heights of Aegina, an island that dominated the southern horizon. For generations an aristocracy of merchant princes had ruled Aegina, lording it over the Athenians in both naval power and maritime trade. Athenian "owls" competed in foreign markets with Aeginetan "turtles," silver coins stamped with the image of a sea turtle. Aegina, not Athens, set the common standards for weights and measures. An Egyptian pharaoh had granted Aeginetan merchants a trading post in the Nile delta, and fleets of grain ships from the Black Sea made Aegina their destination each summer. The island had become the greatest maritime emporium in Greece, while Athens still lacked a protected harbor where a freighter could dock and unload its cargo. The Aeginetans had once even humiliated Athens by placing a trade embargo on Athenian pottery.

Commercial dominance had not been enough for the Aeginetans. For the past twenty years they had been waging an undeclared war against the Athenians. It was the kind of running conflict that the Greeks called a *polemos akeryktos* or "war without a herald." One day, out of the blue, Aeginetan warships struck the coast of Attica and swept like a pirate fleet through

Phaleron and other coastal towns. Their next target was a sacred ship bound for the sanctuary of Poseidon at Cape Sunium. The Aeginetans ambushed the Athenian ship and kidnapped the priest and other dignitaries on board. After this act the Athenians had retaliated and scored a hard-won victory in a naval battle. Most recently, however, the islanders had taken an Athenian flotilla by surprise and seized four galleys with their crews. Athenians seemed incapable of parrying these lightninglike attacks.

At the time of the Aeginetan war, Athens' fleet was for the most part a disorganized mass of galleys. Since Themistocles' ambitious project at the Piraeus remained half-finished, some of the ships were drawn up on the open beach at Phaleron while others were scattered among ports and villages all around the Attic coast. To this ragtag force the Athenians had recently added seven Persian warships captured at Marathon during the fighting on the shore, and twenty triremes purchased from Corinth for a token payment of five drachmas apiece. These Corinthian ships had arrived in Athens just one day too late to provide support for a democratic revolution on Aegina, and in fact the revolution failed for lack of Athenian aid. Had it succeeded, the hostilities with the islanders would probably have ended.

Themistocles envisioned a fleet built by private citizens for the common good. According to his proposal, one hundred of Athens' richest citizens would each be allotted a talent of silver (that is, six thousand drachmas). Each man would then use the money to buy raw materials and organize the building of a warship. Themistocles even included an escape clause. Should the Athenians in the end disapprove of the plan, each wealthy citizen would pay back his one talent to the treasury—but keep the ship. Thus, in the case of a change of heart, the citizens would not have lost their ten-drachma dole but only deferred it for a few months. They had nothing to lose and much to gain. Having appealed to his fellow citizens' patriotism, pride, common sense, and self-interest, Themistocles stepped down from the bema and made his way back to his place among the ranks of citizens.

One important aspect of his proposal may have remained unspoken. One hundred new triremes would call for seventeen thousand men to pull the oars. Athens already had a fleet of seventy ships. Only by conscripting the citizens of the lowest class, the thetes, could Athens fight a naval battle with the large fleet that Themistocles was proposing. His navy would empower the city's masses while preserving its freedom of the seas.

Before the president could put the matter to a vote, another citizen asked to speak. The herald called forward Aristides from the *deme* or township of Alopeke, a fellow townsman of Themistocles' wife. This noble Athenian had earned a reputation as a fair and incorruptible arbitrator; hence his popular nickname, "Aristides the Just." He was about Themistocles' age, and the two men were political rivals. Seven years earlier both had fought at the battle of Marathon as generals in command of their respective tribal regiments. After the victory, when most of the army began its twenty-six-and-a-half-mile quick march to fend off a Persian counterattack on Athens, Aristides had been entrusted with the task of guarding the booty and prisoners. The following year he had been elected the city's eponymous archon. Now he put himself forward to lead the opposition to Themistocles' plan.

No record of his speech survives. As an arbitrator, Aristides may have wanted to see Athens resolve its quarrels with Aegina through arbitration. Why in any case should the war effort against Aegina be raised to this new level? If Aegina were truly the target, only a small increase in the number of Athenian ships would be needed to give Athens the advantage at sea. If on the other hand Themistocles still feared a Persian invasion, the victory at Marathon showed that the Athenians could best meet the Persians on land. Themistocles had led the citizens astray in the past and might do so again.

The president of the Assembly was an ordinary citizen who had been chosen by lot to act as the city's chief executive for that one day only. Now that Themistocles and Aristides had finished their speeches, it was time for the president to exercise virtually the only power granted to him and put the proposal to a vote. At Athens the citizens indicated their choice by a show of hands. Except in the case of a very close count, the president and the other officials simply looked out over the mass of citizens and then announced whether the majority had voted yea or nay. On this momentous occasion, despite the plea of Aristides, the Athenians first voted nay to the Council's proposed ten-drachma dole, then yea to Themistocles' proposal that one hundred citizens each be given a silver talent for a project that would benefit Athens. One man's vision had at last become the mission of an entire city.

Themistocles had made his proposal in the very nick of time. Almost two thousand miles to the east, beyond the Tigris River, plans were being laid for an invasion of Greece. Athens would be the prime target. But now, thanks to a chance discovery of silver ore at Laurium, a barricade of wooden ships and bronze rams would stand between the Great King and his goal. Themistocles saw himself as commander of that fleet, the key force in the struggle against the Persian invaders. And after the threat to liberty had passed, Themistocles envisioned a time when Athens would take its rightful place as the first city in Greece—small no longer, but made great by *mêtis,* bold action, and a navy.

CHAPTER 2

Building the Fleet

[483–481 B.C.]

Come! Haul a black ship down to the shining sea for her first cruise.

—Homer

ATHENIANS HAD BEEN SEAFARERS SINCE EARLIEST TIMES, BUT their ventures were always overshadowed by maritime powers from Asia Minor, the Near East, and the rest of Greece. Legend claimed that even in the days of the first king of Athens, Cecrops, the people of Attica had to contend with raiders who terrorized their coasts. Several generations later King Menestheus led a fleet of fifty ships to Troy as Athens' contribution to the Greek armada, twelve hundred strong. The city's record in the Trojan War was undistinguished, outshone even by the contingent from the little offshore island of Salamis under the leadership of Ajax. After the end of the Bronze Age the royal citadels throughout Greece gave way to Iron Age communities, and they in turn grew into prosperous city-states. New currents in overseas commerce and colonization left Athens behind. Cities like Corinth, Megara, Chalcis, and Eretria took the lead.

Meanwhile the noble clans of Athens were pursuing their own initiatives and policies with private warships, armies, trading contacts, royal guest-friends, and religious rites. Some of the most powerful Athenian families even seized and held strategic sites around the northern Aegean and Hellespont as private fiefdoms. The one thing they seem never to have done was to unite their ships and efforts into a state navy. Even the conquest of Salamis, the Athenian state's first nautical mission since the Trojan War, was said to have been carried out by a single thirty-oared galley and a fleet of fishing boats. But the spirit of free enterprise that ran strong in the ship lords

ATHENIAN TRIREME

of Attica was to remain a vital force within Themistocles' new trireme fleet.

Actual naval battles were rare events in early Greek history. Homer knew nothing of fleet actions on his wine-dark sea, though in his *Iliad* and *Odyssey* he often cataloged or described ships of war. Their operations were limited to seaborne assaults on coastal towns (of which the Trojan War itself was just a glorified example) or piratical attacks at sea. As the centuries passed, two sizes of sleek, fast, open galley eventually became standard among the Greeks: the triakontor of thirty oars and the pentekontor of fifty. The traders, soldiers, or pirates who manned these galleys (often the same men), thirsting for gain and glory overseas, usually pulled the oars themselves

It was the Phoenicians of the Lebanon coast who literally raised galleys to a new level. These seagoing Canaanites invented the trireme, though exactly when no Greek could say. Enlarging their ships, the Phoenician shipwrights provided enough height and space to fit three tiers of rowers within the hull. Their motives had nothing to do with naval battles, for such engagements were still unknown. The Phoenicians needed bigger ships for exploration, commerce, and colonization. In the course of their epic voyages, Phoenician seafarers founded great cities from Carthage to Cádiz, made a three-year circumnavigation of Africa (the first in history) in triremes, and spread throughout the Mediterranean the most precious of their possessions: the alphabet.

The first Greeks to build triremes were the Corinthians. From their city near the Isthmus of Corinth these maritime pioneers dominated the western seaways and could haul their galleys across the narrow neck of the Isthmus for voyages eastward as well. The new Greek trireme differed from the Phoenician original in providing a rowing frame for the top tier of oarsmen, rather than having all the rowers enclosed within the ship's hull. Some triremes maintained the open form of their small and nimble ancestors, the triakontors and pentekontors. Others had wooden decks above the rowers to carry colonists or mercenary troops. Greek soldiers of fortune, the "bronze men" called hoplites, were in demand with native rulers from the Nile delta to the Pillars of Heracles.

Like the Phoenician cities of Tyre and Sidon, Corinth was both a great

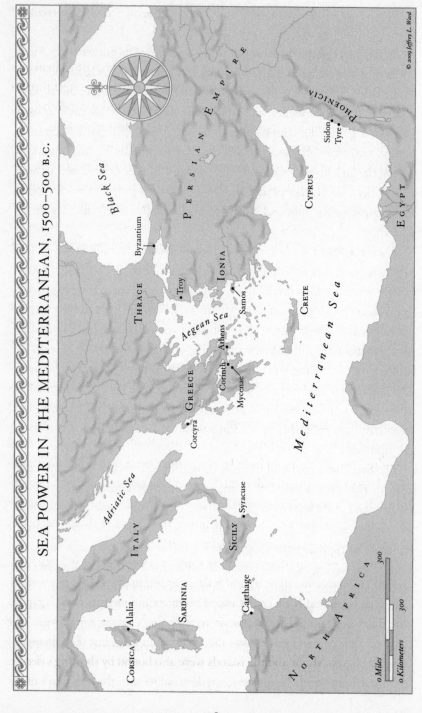

SEA POWER IN THE MEDITERRANEAN, 1500–500 B.C.

Black Sea

Byzantium

THRACE

Troy

Aegean Sea

IONIA

Samos

GREECE

Corcyra

Corinth
Athens
Mycenae

CRETE

PERSIAN EMPIRE

PHOENICIA

Sidon
Tyre

CYPRUS

EGYPT

Mediterranean Sea

Adriatic Sea

ITALY

SARDINIA

CORSICA
Alalia

SICILY
Syracuse

Carthage

NORTH AFRICA

© 2009 Jeffrey L. Ward

0 Miles   300
0 Kilometers   300

18

center of commerce and a starting point for large-scale colonizing missions. Triremes could greatly improve the prospects of colonizing ventures, being able to carry more of the goods that new cities needed: livestock and fruit trees; equipment for farms and mills and fortifications; household items and personal belongings. For defense against attack during their voyages through hostile waters, or against opposition as the colonists tried to land, the large crew and towering hull made the trireme almost a floating fortress.

The earliest known naval battle among Greek fleets was a contest between the Corinthians and their own aggressively independent colonists, the Corcyraeans. Though the battle took place long after the Corinthians began building triremes, it was a clumsy collision between two fleets of pentekontors. The outcome was entirely decided by combat between the fighting men on board the ships. Naval maneuvers were nonexistent. This primitive procedure would typify all Greek sea battles for the next century and a half.

Then, at about the time of Themistocles' birth, two landmark battles at opposite ends of the Greek world brought about a seismic shift in naval warfare. First, in a battle near the Corsican town of Alalia, sixty Greek galleys defeated a fleet of Etruscans and Carthaginians twice their own size. How was this miracle achieved? The Greeks relied on their ships' rams and the skill of their steersmen rather than on man-to-man combat. Shortly afterward, at Samos in the eastern Aegean, a force of rebels in forty trireme transports turned against the local tyrant and crushed his war fleet of one hundred pentekontors. In both battles victory went to a heavily outnumbered fleet whose commanders made use of innovations in tactics or equipment. Ramming maneuvers and triremes thus made their debut in the line of battle almost simultaneously. Together they were to dominate Greek naval warfare for the next two hundred years.

Now everyone wanted triremes, not just as transports but as battleships. Rulers of Greek cities in Sicily and Italy equipped themselves with triremes. In Persia the Great King commanded his maritime subjects from Egypt to the Black Sea to build and maintain trireme fleets for the royal levies. The core of Persian naval power was the Phoenician fleet, but the conquered Greeks of Asia Minor and the islands were also bound by the king's decree. All these forces could be mustered on demand to form the huge navy of the

Persian Empire. Themistocles believed that Athens' new trireme fleet might soon face not only the islanders of Aegina but the armada of the Great King as well.

While many cities and empires jostled for the prize of sea rule, ultimate success in naval warfare called for sacrifices that few were willing or able to make. Only the most determined of maritime nations would commit the formidable amounts of wealth and hard work that the cause required, not just for occasional emergencies but over the long haul. With triremes the scale and financial risks of naval warfare escalated dramatically. These great ships consumed far more materials and manpower than smaller galleys. Now money became, more than ever before, the true sinews of war.

Even more daunting than the monetary costs were the unprecedented demands on human effort. The Phocaean Greeks who won the historic battle at Alalia in Corsica understood the need for hard training at sea, day after exhausting day. In the new naval warfare, victory belonged to those with the best-drilled and best-disciplined crews, not those with the most courageous fighting men. Skillful steering, timing, and oarsmanship, attainable only through long and arduous practice, were the new keys to success. Ramming maneuvers changed the world by making the lower-class steersmen, subordinate officers, and rowers more important than the propertied hoplite soldiers. After all, a marine's spear thrust might at best eliminate one enemy combatant. A trireme's ramming stroke could destroy a ship and its entire company at one blow.

Themistocles had specified that Athens' new ships should be fast triremes: light, open, and undecked for maximum speed and maneuverability. Only gangways would connect the steersman's small afterdeck to the foredeck at the prow where the lookout, marines, and archers were stationed. The new Athenian triremes were designed for ramming attacks, not for carrying large contingents of troops. By committing themselves completely to this design, Themistocles and his fellow Athenians were taking a calculated risk. For many actions, fully decked triremes were more serviceable. Time would tell whether the city had made the right choice.

The construction of a single trireme was a major undertaking: building one hundred at once was a labor fit for Heracles. Once the rich citizens who would oversee the task received their talents of silver, each had to find an experienced shipwright. No plans, drawings, models, or manuals guided the builder of a ship. A trireme, whether fast or fully decked, existed at first only as an ideal image in the mind of a master shipwright. To build his trireme, the shipwright required a wide array of raw materials. Most could be supplied locally from the woods, fields, mines, and quarries of Attica itself. Many local trades and crafts would also take part in building the new fleet.

First, timber. The hills of Attica rang with the bite of iron on wood as the tall trees toppled and crashed to the ground: oak for strength; pine and fir for resilience; ash, mulberry, and elm for tight grain and hardness. After woodsmen lopped the branches from the fallen monarchs, teamsters with oxen and mules dragged the logs down to the shore. The shipwright prepared the building site by planting a line of wooden stocks in the sand and carefully leveling their tops. On the stocks he laid the keel. This was the ship's backbone, an immense squared beam of oak heartwood measuring seventy feet or more in length. Ideally this oak keel was free not only of cracks but even of knots. On its strength depended the life of the trireme in the shocks of storm and battle. Oak was chosen for its ability to withstand the routine stresses of hauling the ship onto shore and then launching it again. Once the keel was on the stocks, two stout timbers were joined to its ends to define the ship's profile. The curving sternpost rose as gracefully as the neck of a swan or the upturned tail of a dolphin. Forward, the upright stempost was set up a little distance from keel's end. The short section of the keel that extended forward of the stempost would form the core of the ship's beak and ultimately support the bronze ram.

Between the stern- and stemposts ran the long lines of planking. In triremes the outer shell was built up by joining plank to plank, rather than by attaching planks to a skeleton of frames and ribs as in later "frame-first" traditions. For the ancient "shell-first" construction the builders set up scaffolds on either side of the keel to support the planking as the ship took shape. They cut the planks with iron saws or adzes. Because the smooth lengths of pine were still green from the tree, it was easy to bend them to shape. Along the narrow edges of each plank the builders bored rows of holes: tiny ones for the linen cords, larger ones for the *gomphoi* or pegs. The latter were wooden dowels about the size of a man's finger that acted as tenons. Starting on either side of the keel, the shipwright's assistants secured the rows of planks by matching the row of larger holes to the tops of the pegs projecting from the plank below, then tapping the new plank into place with mallets. The pegs, now invisible, would act as miniature ribs to support and stiffen the hull. No iron nails or rivets were used in a trireme.

Once the planks were in place, the shipwright's assistants spent days squatting on the inside of the rising hull, laboriously threading linen cords through the small holes along the planks' edges and pulling them tight. Greek farmers sowed *linon* or flax in autumn, tended and weeded the fields over the winter, and harvested the crop in spring when the blue flowers had faded. The stems were cut, soaked, and allowed to rot. After beating and shredding, lustrous white fibers emerged from the decayed husk and pith. Twisting these fibers into thread produced a substance with near-miraculous properties. Linen cloth and padding were impenetrable enough to serve in protective vests or body armor for hoplites on land and for marines on board ship, while a net of linen cords could hold a tuna or a wild boar. Yet linen could be spun so fine that one pound might yield several miles of thread. Unlike wool it would not stretch or give with the working of the ship at sea. Linen also possessed the very proper nautical quality of being stronger wet than dry.

The system of construction made a strong hull that could withstand severe shocks. Only after the hull was pegged and stitched with linen—or, as an Athenian would have said, *gomphatos* and *linorraphos*—did the builder insert the curving wooden ribs. And should a rock or an enemy ram punch a hole through the planking, a wooden patch could be quickly stitched into place to close the breach.

On top of the long slender hull the shipwright now erected the structure that set Greek triremes apart from their Phoenician counterparts: the wooden rowing frame or *parexeiresia* (that is, a thing that is "beyond and outside the rowing"). Sometimes referred to as an outrigger, the rowing frame was wider than the ship's hull and in fact performed multiple functions.

First, the rowing frame carried the tholepins for the upper tier or thranite of oars, and its wide span allowed for a long rowing stroke. Second, side screens would be fastened to the rowing frame when the ship went into

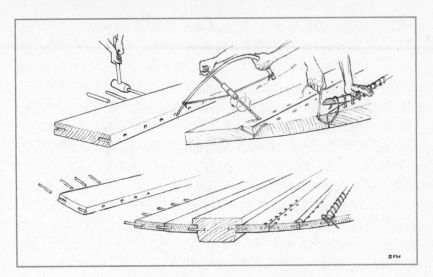

PLANKS PEGGED AND SEWN

FITTING THE RAM

battle to protect the thranite rowers from enemy darts and arrows. And third, the top of the frame could support a covering of canvas or wood. On fast triremes such as Themistocles had ordered, white linen canvas was spread above the crew to screen them from the hot sun while rowing. On a heavy trireme or troop carrier, wooden planking would be laid down on top of the rowing frame to make a deck on which soldiers or equipment could be transported. Finally, the stout transverse beams that crossed the ship at the end of the rowing frame served as towing bars to tow wrecked ships or prizes back to shore after a battle.

As the great size of the rowing frame suggests, oars were the prime movers of the trireme. At two hundred per ship (a total that included thirty spares), Themistocles' new fleet required twenty thousand lengths of fine quality fir wood for its oars. The long shaft had a broad, smoothly planed blade at one end, and at the other the handle ended in a round knob to accommodate the rower's grip. One man pulled each oar, securing the shaft to the upright tholepin with a loop of rope or leather. The 62 thranite oarsmen on the top tier enjoyed the most prestige. Inboard and below them were placed the wooden thwarts or seats for the 54 zygian oarsmen and the 54 thalamians. The latter took their name from the ship's *thalamos* or hold since they were entombed deep within the hull, only a little above the waterline. All the rowers faced aft toward the steersman as they pulled their oars.

Once all these wooden fittings of the hull were complete, it was time to coat the ship with pitch, an extract from the trunks and roots of conifers. Once a year pitch-makers tapped or stripped the resinous wood of mature trees. In emergencies they cut down the firs and applied fire to the logs, rendering out large pools of pitch in just a couple of days. Carters conveyed thousands of jars of pitch to the shipbuilding sites in their wagons. The poetical references to "dark ships" or "black ships" referred to the coating of pitch.

More than hostile rams or hidden reefs, the shipwrights feared the *teredon* or borer. Infestations of this remorseless mollusk could be kept at bay only by vigilant maintenance, including drying the hull on shore and applications of pitch. In summer the seas around Greece seethed with the spawn of the teredo, sometimes called the "shipworm." Each tiny larva swam about in search of timber: driftwood, dock pilings, or a passing ship. Once fastened to a wooden surface, it quickly bored a hole by wielding the razorlike edge of its vestigial shell as a rasp. From that hiding place the teredo would never emerge. Once inside the hole it kept its mouth fixed to the opening so as to suck in the life-giving seawater. The sharp shell at the other end of the teredo's body continued to burrow deeper. As the burrow extended into the timber, the animal grew to fill its ever-lengthening home.

Within a month the sluglike teredo could reach a foot in length. Now it was ready to eject swarms of its own larvae into the sea, starting a new cycle. Once planking and ribs were riddled with their holes, a ship might suddenly break up and sink in midvoyage. Even when a wreck reached the bottom of the sea, the teredo would continue its attacks. In a short time no exposed wood whatever would be left to mark the ship's resting place. Through conscientious maintenance—new applications of pitch, drying out and inspection of the hulls, and prompt replacement of unsound planks—an Athenian trireme could remain in active service for twenty-five years.

The trireme's design approached the physical limits of lightness and slenderness combined with maximum length. So extreme was the design that not even the thousands of wooden pegs and linen stitches could prevent the hull from sagging or twisting under the stresses of rough seas or even routine rowing. On Athenian triremes huge *hypozomata* or girding cables provided the tensile strength that the wooden structure lacked. A girding cable weighed about 250 pounds and measured about 300 feet in length. Each ship carried two pairs. Looped to the hull at prow and stern, the cables stretched around the full length of the hull below the rowing frame. The ends passed inside where the mariners kept them taut by twisting spindles or winches. Just as pegs and linen cords formed the joints of the hull, the girding cables acted as the ship's tendons.

The trireme required many other ropes as well. Made of papyrus, esparto grass, hemp, or linen, ropes supplied the rigging for the mast and sail, the two anchor lines, the mooring lines, and the towing cables. The ship's tall mast and the wide-reaching yards or yardarms that held the sail were made from lengths of unblemished pine or fir. For the sail, the women of Athens wove long bolts of linen cloth on their upright looms. Sailmakers then stitched many such bolts together into a big rectangle. Despite their great weight—and their great cost—the mast and sail were secondary to the oars and, when battled threatened, were removed from the ship altogether and left on shore. Some triremes also carried a smaller "boat sail" and mast for emergencies.

The ship's beak had already been fashioned in wood as part of the hull. To complete the trireme's prime lethal weapon, the ram, metalworkers had to sheathe the beak with bronze. The one hundred rams needed for Themistocles' triremes required tons of metal—a gigantic windfall for the bronze industry. Bronze, an alloy of nine parts copper to one part tin, does not rust and is more suitable than iron for use at sea. Some of the bronze poured into the rams of the Athenian triremes was recycled, melted down from swords that had been wielded in forgotten battles, from keys to vanished storerooms, images of lost gods, and ornaments of beautiful women long dead. Master craftsmen made the rams with the same lost-wax method that they used to cast hollow bronze statues of gods and heroes for the temples and sanctuaries.

The form of the ram was first modeled in sheets of beeswax directly onto the wooden beak, so that each would be custom made for its ship. As the artists worked the wax onto the beak, it warmed up and softened, becoming easier to handle. At the ram's forward end the wax was built up into a thick projecting flange, triple-pronged like Poseidon's trident. When every detail of the ram had been modeled, the wax sheath was gently detached from the wood and carried over to a pit dug in the sand of the beach.

The next step called for clay, the same iron-rich clay that went into Athens' red and black pottery. With the wax model turned nose downward in the pit, clay was packed around its exterior and into its conical hollow to create a mold. Thin iron rods forged by the blacksmiths were pushed through the wax and the two masses of clay. When the wax was entirely encased in the clay except for its upper edge, the massive mold was inverted and suspended over a fire until all the wax was melted out. A hollow negative space in the exact shape of the ram had now been formed inside the packed clay. It remained only to fill the mold with molten bronze. But this was a complex and difficult undertaking.

Wood fires could not produce the necessary heat; the process required charcoal. A trireme's ram had to be cast in a single rapid operation. First the bronze workers erected a circle of small upright clay furnaces around the rim of the pit. A channel led from the foot of each furnace to the edge of the mold. Broken bronze, whether from ingots or scrap, was divided among the furnaces. With the lighting of the charcoal, the metal in each furnace quickly became a glowing, molten mass. At a signal, the bronze workers and their apprentices removed the clay stoppers from all the furnaces. Simultaneously the bright hot streams poured down the channels and filled the hollow in the clay mold left by the melting of the wax. The casting happened with a rush, and the bronze cooled and hardened quickly. When the clay mold was broken (never to be used again), the bronze ram itself, smooth, dark, and deadly, saw the light for the first time. After cutting away the iron rods, finishing off the back edge, and polishing the surface, the bronze workers slid the new ram into place over the trireme's wooden beak, fastening it securely with bronze nails.

Quarrymen and stone workers provided fine white marble from Mount Pentelicus near the city, and from thin slabs of this marble the sculptors carved a pair of *ophthalmoi* or "eyes" for each trireme. A colored circle painted in red ochre represented the iris. The eyes were fixed on either side of the prow. Athenians believed that these eyes allowed the ship to find a safe passage through the sea, completing the magical creation of a living thing from inanimate materials. In Greek terminology, the projecting ends of the transverse beam above the eyes were the ship's ears, and the yardarms were its horns; the sail and banks of oars were its wings, and the grappling hooks were its iron hands.

Blacksmiths fashioned a pair of iron anchors for each trireme, to be slung on either side of the bow. They would prevent the ship from swinging while its stern was grounded on the beach. Tanners and leatherworkers provided the tubular sleeves that waterproofed the lower oar ports. From the same workshops came the side screens of hide for the rowing frames. Pads of sheepskin would enable the trireme's oarsmen to work their legs as they rowed, thus adding to the power of each stroke.

Finally goldsmiths gilded the figurehead of Athena that would identify each ship as a trireme of Athens. The goddess wore a helmet as well as the famous breastplate or aegis adorned with the head of Medusa, the gorgon that could turn a mortal to stone with a single glance. As patron deity of arts and crafts, a goddess of wisdom and also of war, Athena had been presiding over the entire project from beginning to end.

From the mines of Laurium the silver had flowed through the city's mint, where it was transformed into the coins that bore the emblems of Athena. Then as Themistocles had planned, the river of silver broke into a hundred separate streams, passing through the hands of the wealthy citizens who organized the great shipbuilding campaign. During the months of shipbuilding the silver was disbursed to all those workers, from loggers to shipwrights to bronzesmiths, whose efforts made Themistocles' vision a reality. In the end, the money returned to many of the same citizens who had voted to give up their ten drachmas for the common good. By the time one hundred new triremes gleamed in the sunlight at Phaleron Bay, the Athenians were already a changed people. In the great contest that lay ahead, as they hazarded their new ships and their very existence in the cause of freedom, their sense of common purpose would grow stronger with every trial and danger.

CHAPTER 3

The Wooden Wall

[481–480 B.C.]

These are the right questions to ask, in winter around the fire,
As we sit at ease over our wine: Who are you, friend? What is
  your land?
And how old were you when the Persians came?

—Xenophanes

THE ATHENIANS LOVED TO TELL HOW KING DARIUS OF PERSIA
had reacted when he learned that they had helped burn Sardis. He called
for his bow, fitted a shaft to the string, and shot an arrow high into the air.
In this nation of archers, it was a ritual action to seal an oath. While the
arrow was in flight, Darius swore that he would one day avenge the attack
on his empire. Turning to the royal cupbearer, he commanded him to repeat
every day the words "Master, remember the Athenians." When Themistocles made his proposal to build a fleet, Darius was already dead. His son
Xerxes inherited both the throne and the oath of vengeance.

The Athenians had been building ships for three years when Xerxes
launched his attack. At thirty-eight he already ruled an empire that stretched
from the Sahara Desert to the Caspian Sea, and from the Balkans to the
Hindu Kush. At the corners of his realm ran the four great rivers of the
known world: the Nile, the Danube, the Oxus, and the Indus. Through its
heart ran the Tigris and Euphrates, rivers that had nurtured kingdoms and
empires for centuries. The new king saw more in his expedition to the west
than pious fulfillment of a vow. When the Athenians burned the temple of
the Mother Goddess at Sardis, they provided the Great King with a justi-
fication for a holy war. The punishment of Athens would inevitably lead to

the conquest of the other Greeks and then Europe all the way to the Atlantic. Great empires must grow, and Xerxes had inherited an empire at its zenith.

The Persians believed that God, or in their case the all-powerful deity Ahura Mazda, fought on the side of the big battalions. Having first dealt with rebellions in Egypt and Babylonia, Xerxes levied troops from all parts of his empire for the invasion of Greece. The resulting horde was so elephantine that it took six months to make its way from the capital at Susa to the coast of the Aegean Sea. The king's relays of mounted couriers took only thirteen days to cover the same sixteen hundred miles. The motto of these riders was remembered through the ages: "Neither snow nor rain nor heat nor dark of night keeps these couriers from the swift completion of their appointed course."

Like his mail carriers Xerxes was inexorable, but at a walking pace. The royal field pavilion, which had to be pitched anew at every night's stopping place and struck every morning, was the size of a concert hall. Magi carrying portable fire altars marched beside the king's chariot. To keep his brothers and other kinsmen out of trouble at home, Xerxes brought them along with him. His own attendants, including concubines, cooks, pastry chefs, musicians, bath attendants, astrologers, keepers of the wardrobe, and baggage handlers were an army in themselves. Close to Xerxes were the two royal intelligence officers known as the Great King's Eye and Ear. Important Greek exiles also accompanied the king: these turncoats would guide the army's course after it entered Europe and looked forward to ruling their native lands on Xerxes' behalf once the Persians restored them to power. From Sparta came a banished king named Demaratus; from Athens, sons of the old tyrant Hippias. After spending half a year on the Royal Road, the grand army settled down in Sardis to pass the cold and rainy winter months. Poised at the eastern edge of the Greek world, the Persians would launch their invasion at the beginning of spring.

Even before then Xerxes intended to dazzle his puny antagonists with two amazing feats. The first would allow his army to walk into Europe. His corps of engineers spanned the Hellespont with a pair of pontoon bridges, connecting Asia to Europe with gigantic cables of papyrus and esparto grass. The hulls of more than six hundred galleys would be anchored

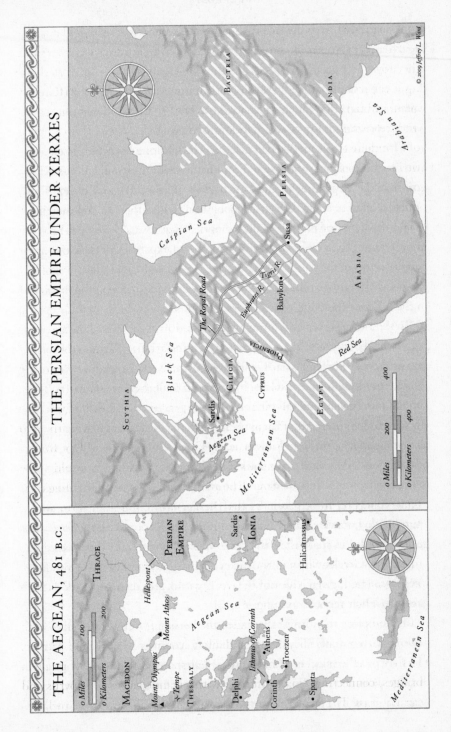

THE AEGEAN, 481 B.C.

THE PERSIAN EMPIRE UNDER XERXES

© 2009 Jeffrey L. Ward

31

in the stream to carry the two roadbeds. The second marvel would enable the triremes of Xerxes' fleet to cut through dry land. For almost three years other royal engineers had been directing huge gangs of workmen as they dug a canal through the peninsula at Mount Athos. By entering Greek waters through this canal, the armada would bypass the dangerous cape where stormy winds once wrecked Darius' fleet.

With these two superhuman achievements Xerxes hoped to shock and awe his enemies into submission. From his winter quarters the Great King sent heralds to the Greeks in his path, demanding earth and water. This symbolic offering showed that the people had yielded their land to the king. When the heralds finally returned, months later, it was clear that the war of nerves had been well worth the trouble and expense. All the cities and peoples north of the pass at Thermopylae capitulated. Only a few in central and southern Greece refused. They would join the Spartans and Athenians in the fight for freedom, regardless of the odds.

By the time Xerxes and his army appeared in Asia Minor, the Greeks had at last begun to take united action. The Spartans, traditional leaders and arbiters of Hellenic affairs, called a council at the Isthmus of Corinth. All the cities who meant to resist the Persians sent representatives. The council met beneath the tall pine trees in the sanctuary of Poseidon, god of the sea and lord of horses. That autumn, with the Great King sitting in state at Sardis and his canal and bridges nearing completion, the newly convened council decided to send three spies across the Aegean to ascertain the size of the enemy forces. It turned out to be an unexpectedly dangerous mission. While collecting information in the Persian camp, the three spies were apprehended, tortured, and sentenced to death. Xerxes himself, however, gave the order to spare their lives. He was delighted with this chance to provide the Greeks with up-to-date, eyewitness accounts of his army. The spies were freed, given a tour of the entire camp, and then sent back to the Isthmus. Their report was a shock to all.

In attempting to estimate the size of the Persian forces, the Greeks were dealing with numbers beyond their ability to count or comprehend. In the end they put the number of fighting men at somewhere between one and three million, and the number of triremes at over twelve hundred. The ships were not actually Persian, since the Persians were not a maritime people.

Instead the Great King levied triremes from the seafaring nations within his empire—Phoenicia, Egypt, Syria, Cyprus, Cilicia, Caria—and from eastern Greek cities. Four royal Persians, kinsmen of the king, had been appointed as admirals of the monstrous naval force, but local rulers commanded the various contingents of the fleet. One of these leaders was a woman: Artemisia, queen of the Greek city of Halicarnassus in Asia Minor and the lone female combatant among all the hundreds of thousands of men who followed Xerxes to Greece.

The Greeks may have been deceived about the exact tally of triremes in Xerxes' armada, but it was no illusion that the Persians held an overwhelming advantage in numbers of ships, not to mention wealth, engineering, communications, siegecraft, and unified command. Whether his forces numbered in the millions or the thousands, Xerxes had paid the Athenians and the rest of the Greeks the compliment of attacking them with the largest combined army and navy ever assembled up to that time.

After receiving the spies' report, the council voted to seek more allies within the Greek world. They sent an embassy to Sicily to solicit help from Gelon, the powerful tyrant of Syracuse. Originally a colony of the Corinthians, Syracuse had become one of the richest and strongest Greek cities. For this prestigious mission, Themistocles saw to it that an Athenian envoy accompanied the Spartans. During the negotiations at Syracuse the Athenian envoy put forward the idea that his city might lead the resistance at sea while the Spartans took charge on land, an idea that the Spartans seemed initially to accept. They had fewer than a dozen warships of their own, and the hostile masses of helots in the Spartan countryside made them always reluctant to send troops overseas. However, the diplomatic mission to Syracuse was a failure. The western Greeks had troubles of their own. Inspired by Xerxes' example, Phoenician colonists at Carthage in North Africa were planning their own attack on the Greek cities in Sicily.

The council's other appeals for help were also fruitless. In the end, out of hundreds of Greek city-states and islands scattered throughout the Mediterranean, only about thirty joined the alliance against the Persians. Given the odds, the wonder was not that there were so few but that there were any. What made the Spartans, Athenians, and others willing to fight?

Part of the answer lay in a raw Greek spirit of independence, a fierce and fanatical zeal for liberty. Their rough and rocky land had bred a race of tough, self-reliant people. Greek cities were as obstinate as individual citizens in jealously guarding their freedom. For centuries this spirit had kept the Greeks divided against one another. Now at last it helped them unite against a common enemy.

Certain rational and strategic calculations, too, made resistance more than a forlorn hope. The man who saw them most clearly was Themistocles. Each city-state had sent one deputy to the council at the Isthmus. The life-or-death nature of the emergency forced the cities to grant decision-making powers to these deputies, powers that in peacetime they would never have possessed. No arrangement could have given Themistocles greater influence. Back home at Athens, in the Assembly or the Agora, he was merely one of the ten generals elected for the year, criticized and challenged daily (as were all Athenian leaders) by his colleagues and fellow citizens. At the Isthmus he suddenly became the voice of Athens. The Spartans were the nominal leaders, but even they soon acknowledged Themistocles as the mastermind behind the allied strategy.

In Themistocles' judgment, the most vulnerable element in Xerxes' forces was the navy. Seemingly an invincible fleet of unprecedented size and grandeur, the huge armada was in truth a shambling giant. While the land army of cavalry, spearmen, and archers had a solid core of Persians and Medes, the empire's power at sea lay entirely in the hands of subject peoples. Below the level of the four royal Persian admirals the fleet was a hodgepodge of nationalities, languages, and nautical traditions (or lack thereof). It was unlikely that the various contingents would be capable of any coordinated maneuvers. Their loyalty to Xerxes was questionable too. And Themistocles, moved by cunning *mêtis* rather than noble heroism, believed that the Greeks should aim their strongest blow at the enemy's weakest link.

In the meetings at the Isthmus, wily Themistocles was waging two campaigns at once. Behind his public efforts to devise a winning strategy lurked a second and covert goal: to stake out a position for Athens as joint leader with Sparta. Luckily for him, Spartans seemed by nature slow to act. This slowness gave quicker-witted men, whether friends or enemies, plenty of opportunities to seize the initiative. Themistocles began by urging that all the allies give up hostilities among themselves, beginning with the long-standing feud between his own city and Aegina. The vision of Athens as peacemaker and unifier made a compelling image. With it Themistocles launched his undeclared campaign.

Next, he brought the council over to his idea of meeting the barbarian "as far forward as possible." In early spring the alliance undertook its first military action: an expedition to block the Persian army at the narrow Tempe gorge in Thessaly. A Spartan named Euainetus led his country's contingent, and Themistocles himself in a seemingly equal role led the Athenians. With ten thousand troops to ferry northward, the expedition launched Athens' new fleet of triremes on its maiden voyage. Within a few days of arriving at Tempe, however, Euainetus and Themistocles learned that the Persians would have a choice of several passes through the mountains, and the Greeks could not hope to guard them all. Equally demoralizing was the discovery that Xerxes had not yet even crossed into Europe and might not reach Thessaly for months. So Tempe was abandoned. The Greeks boarded their ships and rowed home.

After this fiasco Themistocles rejoined the council at the Isthmus, where a new plan was devised for the defense of central Greece. When the Persians came, the Greeks proposed to divide their forces. The Greek army would block Xerxes' army at the narrow pass called Thermopylae or the "Hot Gates," while the Greek fleet would oppose the Great King's armada in the nearby Artemisium channel. The new plan suited Themistocles very well. With the enemy still so distant, however, he made no headway against the allies' reluctance to actually send their troops and ships northward.

Where were the Persians? As the Athenians and other Greeks were rowing home from their misbegotten expedition to Tempe, the Persians had still not entered Europe. Xerxes was holding reviews and regattas for his ships on the Asiatic shore of the Hellespont. The boat races were a diversion to pass the time while the army prepared to cross the two new pontoon bridges. An unexpected disaster had disrupted the royal plans. Before anyone had crossed the bridges a violent storm broke the huge cables and swept the original spans downstream. Furious at the delay, the king beheaded the overseers and ordered his men to beat the unruly waters of the Hellespont with whips. After a new engineering team rebuilt the bridges in record time, Xerxes marched grandly across to the European shore in the midst of his army. It took a month for the entire horde to cross.

In the rough country beyond the Hellespont, the army trekked overland while the ships coasted along toward Mount Athos. They avoided the deadly cape by rowing through the newly dug canal. With numbers increased by galleys levied from Greek cities along the way, the fleet rejoined the army at Therma on the Macedonian coast. Here Xerxes called a halt. His troops and rowers rested as the engineers smoothed a road through the mountains. From his new base Xerxes could gaze south toward the high peak of Mount Olympus. Its snowcapped summit was the dwelling place of Zeus and the other Greek gods. On a whim, Xerxes cruised down the coast on his fastest trireme, a Phoenician ship from the city of Sidon, to view Mount Olympus and the vale of Tempe from the sea. The holy mountain was now part of his empire, and it seemed inevitable that all the lands ruled by those gods would soon be his also.

Once the Persian forces had entered Europe, the desperate Athenians sent two envoys to consult the oracle of Apollo at Delphi. Though only a small village on the slope of Mount Parnassus, Delphi was venerated by the Greeks as the center of the world and the navel of Mother Earth. Its famous temple was sacred to Apollo, god of light, inspiration, and prophecy. Enclosed within its crypt was a fault in the rock, and through this fissure emerged a sacred spring and a mysterious vapor. The Greeks believed that the Delphic Oracle had been a source of wisdom and guidance throughout history, from the time of the universal deluge through the heroic age of the Trojan War and on down to the present. Apollo delivered his oracles through the mouth of a local woman called the Pythia, who sat atop a bronze tripod above the fissure. The exhalation rising from the fissure in the inner sanctum endowed her with prophetic power. In her trances she spoke as the medium of the god.

At dawn on the seventh day after a new moon, the two Athenian envoys climbed the switchback trail up the mountainside and took places of honor near the head of the long line. On the front of the temple were written the words "Know Thyself." The oracles were often cryptic—not straightforward predictions but tests of self-knowledge and insight. As Xerxes was approaching Greece, the Delphic Oracle had warned the Spartans that their country could be saved but that a Spartan king must die. Now it was the turn of the Athenians. The two envoys passed through the tall doorway into a shadowy space lit by the glow of an eternal flame. Descending a ramp, they plunged into the perpetual twilight of the inner sanctum, seemingly deep within the earth. Straight ahead gleamed the gold cult statue of Apollo; to their left they could dimly see the Pythia in her alcove. The envoys recited the question from the Assembly: What course of action should the Athenians take at this time? The woman's deep voice answered, chanting in verse like a Homeric bard.

Apollo was angry. Why were these Athenians lingering at Delphi? They must abandon their city and flee to the ends of the earth. Ares, god of war, was advancing toward Athens in an Asiatic chariot, with fire and destruction. He would bring down towers and temples. Images of the gods would sweat and shake. Black blood would run down the rooftops. At the end of the nightmarish prophecy, the god ordered the wretched Athenians out of his shrine. Climbing back into the daylight the envoys debated what they should do. While they hesitated, their Delphian sponsor urged them to enter the temple again, this time as suppliants carrying olive branches, to ask for a better prophecy. The Athenians took his advice, and their persistence was rewarded with a second oracle that held out a glimmer of hope.

> Athena cannot appease Olympian Zeus
> With her pleading words and shrewd mêtis,
> Yet I speak this word, firm as adamant.
> Though all else within Attica's border shall be taken
> Even the secret places on divine Mount Kithairon,
> Far-sighted Zeus will grant to Athena a wooden wall.
> It alone shall come through uncaptured: good fortune for you and your
>   children.
> But do not wait for the host of foot and horse coming overland!
> Do not remain still! Turn your back and retreat.
> Someday you will yet oppose them.
> O divine Salamis, you will destroy many women's children
> When Demeter is scattered or gathered in.

Demeter was goddess of wheat, and according to the Greek farmer's almanac, her times of scattering and gathering would be either autumn or early summer. Salamis was, of course, an island off the coast of Attica, but it was also the name of a Greek city in Cyprus where the Ionians had won a sea battle against the Phoenicians during the Ionian revolt. Did Apollo mean to guide the Athenians to Salamis, or to warn them away? As for a "Wooden Wall," such a structure was typically a palisade erected around a military camp, but there were other possibilities. The second prophecy at least contained some hopeful ambiguities to counteract the dire warnings of the first. Somewhat encouraged, the envoys secured a transcript of the Pythia's words and departed.

Back in Athens, the words of the two oracles were made public and an Assembly was convened to debate them. If the Athenians obeyed the oracle to the letter, they would flee their land, avoid all contact with Xerxes' forces, and found a new city far away, at "the ends of the earth." Some professional diviners and older citizens indeed urged the people to abandon hope and emigrate. According to their interpretation, the gods had promised to protect their own temples behind the thorny hedge that encircled the Acropolis. This, they claimed, was the Wooden Wall of the prophecy.

The Pythia had given no prediction of ultimate victory, no reference to the sea or ships, no suggestion that the Athenians should fight as far forward as possible or indeed fight at all. Nothing could have been more disastrous for Themistocles and his aggressive naval policy than a sudden Athenian resolution to "turn their backs" on the Persians. It would be up to Themistocles himself to bend the prophecy to his purpose.

And when the Assembly met to debate the oracle's meaning, he did just that. The Wooden Wall was not the palisade around the Acropolis, Themistocles said, but the navy. Its triremes, by now numbering two hundred, would be a wooden bulwark for the people's defense. Apollo had revealed that this floating Wooden Wall would endure and bring benefits for generations to come. The Athenian citizens should man their ships, not to flee, but to face the Persians at sea.

His interpretation won over the majority. Seizing the moment, Themistocles pushed through the Assembly a series of emergency measures. All citizens regardless of class would man the triremes, most of them as rowers. The Athenians would not wait for the vote of the other allies but would act on their own. At Themistocles' urging, they voted to send their own ships north to Artemisium, inviting all other Greeks to share the danger with them. The navy's mission would be to keep the Persian fleet from reaching Attica and the interior of Greece for as long as possible. This bold communal decision set the capstone on all Themistocles' efforts.

Evacuation of noncombatants was an essential condition for mobilizing the fleet. Themistocles could not expect all the the men of Athens to confront the Persians far from Attica if they were leaving defenseless hostages to fortune behind them. So at Themistocles' recommendation the Assembly accepted the invitation of the city of Troezen in the Peloponnese to send their families there for refuge. Troezen claimed to be the birthplace of the Athenian hero Theseus and felt close ties to Athens. Meanwhile the flocks and herds of Athenian landowners and herdsmen would be shipped to offshore islands.

Once the able-bodied citizens were packed together within the Wooden Wall and their families safely evacuated to Troezen, the Athenian elders would set up a government-in-exile on the island of Salamis. This base, while still on Athenian territory, would remain secure so long as Athenian triremes could hold off the Great King's armada. As for Salamis, Themistocles managed to convince the Assembly that the oracle would not have called the island "divine" if it were going to bring harm to Athenians.

Athenians lived lightly upon the land. Their homes were simple, their possessions few and mostly portable. With Attica in a turmoil of triremes and ferries, tears and farewells, uprooted households and migrating livestock, Themistocles returned to the Isthmus. There he informed the Spartans and the other allies of his city's decisions and challenged them, on behalf of Athens, to "share the danger" of a naval campaign.

One class of Athenians obstinately opposed the naval mobilization: the horsemen. They balked at the idea of serving alongside lower-class citizens at the oars of the triremes. Athens' horsemen had officers of their own, namely the two hipparchs or cavalry commanders, and they were ready to defy Themistocles and the Assembly itself. The crisis was resolved by the son of Miltiades, a patriotic young Athenian named Cimon. Though he was not yet thirty, his winning character had already made him a leader among the horsemen. Cimon felt no loyalty to Themistocles, but he loved his city. Roping in a band of friends, he led them on foot up to the Acropolis. At the great altar on the summit, Cimon ceremonially dedicated his bridle to Athena and left it in the goddess's safekeeping. Then he and his comrades joined the rank and file down at Phaleron. Inspired or shamed by their example, the rest of the horsemen followed them to the ships.

Meanwhile Themistocles' efforts at the Isthmus were not prospering. The allies refused outright to serve in a fleet led by Athenians. To the Dorians of Aegina, Corinth, Megara, and Thebes—and of course to the Spartans most of all—the Athenians and their fellow Ionians seemed a lesser breed of Greek: dangerously volatile, restless, and presumptuous. In the face of these sullen antagonists, Themistocles' dream of an Athenian naval command melted away. Athens would contribute more than two-thirds of the ships, but the admiral of the Greek fleet would have to be a Spartan.

More than a month after midsummer, as the sour debates dragged on, messengers from the north arrived at the Isthmus. They reported that Xerxes was on the move at last. The Persian army was marching south past Mount Olympus while the fleet prepared to cruise down the coast. In less than half a month the Persians could be expected to reach the gates of central Greece at Thermopylae. If the Greeks intended to oppose the Persians anywhere north of the Isthmus, they must take immediate action. The news succeeded where Themistocles' arguments had failed. Quickly they resurrected the plan to hold the invaders at Thermopylae and Artemisium. On land, they would avoid the risk of a major battle in open terrain. At sea, the Greek ships would make an all-out effort to destroy Xerxes' fleet.

In keeping with this strategy, the council of allies accepted Athens' unprecedented and unilateral decision to commit all of its manpower to the navy. No Athenians would fight on land, though their ten thousand hoplites would have been a welcome addition to the Greek phalanx. King Leonidas of Sparta led a small advance force to hold Thermopylae until the main Greek army arrived. Meanwhile a Spartan named Eurybiades was appointed *navarchos* or admiral of the allied fleet, even though Sparta had practically no navy. At once the deputies at the Isthmus notified their cities of the plan

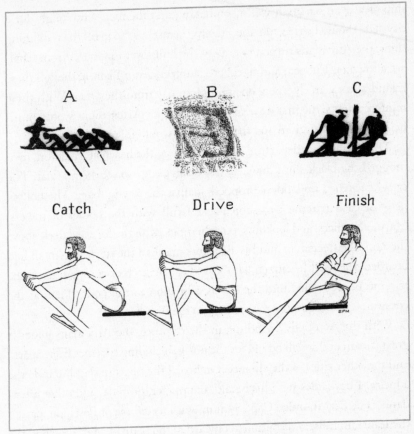

ROWING THE TRIREME

and instructed their fellow citizens to send ships to join the fleet under Eurybiades and men to join Leonidas. The main Peloponnesian army, however, would first muster at the Isthmus.

Back at Athens, Themistocles broke the news to the Athenians that they would not after all lead the naval effort. For the sake of the cause of liberty as well as survival, the Athenian people yielded to Themistocles' persuasion and waived their claim for the time being. Another difficulty now arose, for only part of the fleet was ready to launch. Athens' shipbuilding had outstripped its manpower, and the city could not man its two hundred triremes. Had it been conceivable to conscript slaves as rowers, the ships could all have been filled, for there were thousands of slaves in Attica. But on a ship of war an oarsman was a combatant, and the men who fought for a city-state should be free, like the citizens themselves. So to fill the remaining ships, the Athenians turned twenty of the hulls over to Greeks from Chalcis, a town on Euboea, and to eager volunteers from Plataea, though these inland allies scarcely knew one end of an oar from the other. With these reinforcements, the first wave of ships bound for Artemisium would number almost one hundred and fifty. The rest would follow later.

The morning of departure came. All along the beach at Phaleron, men dragged the black ships down to the water's edge to set them afloat. The crews swarmed up ladders propped against the towing bars. The hollow belly of each trireme was soon packed full with the bodies of rowers. Marines, archers, and lookouts took their places on the forward deck above the ram; the steersman and his assistants manned the stern. When all had boarded, the wealthy citizen who served as trierarch or commander of the trireme poured wine into the sea as a libation to the gods. Then at the coxswain's command the rowers bent to the first stroke.

With the Acropolis dwindling in the distance, the Athenians joined a great stream of ships all bound for the north, including triremes from Sparta and the other cities of the alliance. On board the Spartan flagship rode the admiral Eurybiades with his herald, trumpeter, prophet, and other attendants. The fleet rounded Cape Sunium with its temple of Poseidon, passed the Laurium hills, and continued onward to the plain of Marathon and the frontier of Attica. Ten years had elapsed since an Athenian army had succeeded in driving King Darius' forces back to their ships at Marathon Bay. The men in the fleet hoped for the same success in facing the Persians now. Leaving the historic battlefield astern, the Greeks entered the long winding gulf that separates the island of Euboea from the mainland. Ahead lay Thermopylae and Artemisium. The great adventure, the greatest that any Athenian would ever know, had begun at last.

CHAPTER 4

Holding the Pass

[SUMMER, 480 B.C.]

Pindar rightly called the battle of Artemisium the place where the sons of Athens laid the shining cornerstone of freedom; for courage is the beginning of victory.

—Plutarch

THREE FAST TRIREMES HAD GONE AHEAD TO ESTABLISH A guard post on Skiathos, an island at the entrance to the Artemisium channel. The traditional lookout point on the westernmost heights of Skiathos commanded a view of the seaway to the north that would shortly be filled with the ships of Xerxes' armada. The Greeks set up a chain of beacons from Skiathos across the hilltops of Euboea so that the watchers from the three triremes—one from Athens, the others from Aegina and Troezen—could flash news by fire signal to the main Greek fleet.

While the lookouts on the island were scanning the northern approaches, an advance squadron of ten fast Phoenician triremes managed to take them by surprise. Running for their lives, the hapless Greeks scrambled into their ships and tried to escape. The triremes from Troezen and Aegina had no chance, though one of the Aeginetan marines put up such a heroic fight that the admiring Phoenicians bandaged his wounds and kept him with them as a sort of talisman. Only the Athenian trireme managed to break through to the open sea. Hotly pursued by the enemy, the trierarch Phormos and his crew raced northward along the mountainous Magnesian coast, outrowing Xerxes' fastest ships for half a day. At last, with Mount Olympus in view, the Athenians risked a landing. They jumped out at Tempe and fled up the narrow gorge of the Peneus River. The Phoenicians captured only the empty hull abandoned at the water's edge. It was the first Athenian trireme to fall into enemy hands, but Phormos and company reached home safely after a long trek overland.

Once the Phoenician scout ships returned to Therma, the entire Persian armada began its cruise southward. The fleet could reach Thermopylae in just three days of rowing, while the army's march through Thessaly would require fourteen. So Xerxes had told his naval commanders to wait eleven days after his departure before setting out. In their anxiety to reach the rendezvous on time, the commanders unwisely bypassed the long strand south of Mount Ossa, the last haven that could accommodate all their ships. Instead they pushed forward down the rocky Magnesian coast as long as daylight lasted. Nightfall caught them below the heights of Mount Pelion, where only a few short beaches lay between slopes that plunged steeply into the sea. On this hostile shore the armada had to disperse among many small mooring places. At some beaches the triremes tied up eight deep, with the outermost ships swinging at anchor far out from land.

Earlier that summer the Delphic Oracle had advised, "Pray to the winds." Next morning those prayers were answered. A violent northeasterly gale, known locally as a "Hellesponter," struck the Magnesian coast. For three days Xerxes' triremes were helplessly smashed against the rocks while the Magi offered prayers to quiet the storm. The winds wrecked many of the Great King's triremes and supply ships, scattering the shattered hulks far and wide. The dwellers along the Magnesian coast later combed the beaches for gold cups and other Persian treasure that washed up in the surf.

The allied Greek fleet spent the three days of the storm safely sheltered in the lee of Euboea. They learned of the disaster to the Persians from watchers on the hills and the seaward coast. When the gale finally blew itself out, the Greek fleet resumed its voyage toward Artemisium, fervently hoping that the winds had cut Xerxes' navy down to size. As the Greeks rowed past Thermopylae, they stopped to confer with Leonidas, whose army of four thousand was busy repairing the ancient fortifications in the pass. All were confident that the main Greek army would appear any day to reinforce Leonidas' small contingent. Before proceeding on to Artemisium, the commanders of the fleet left a galley at the Hot Gates to carry dispatches from

Leonidas if need arose. They chose for this mission an Athenian triakontor commanded by a citizen named Abronichus. At the same time a local boat from a town near Thermopylae joined the Greek fleet. It would observe the naval actions at Artemisium and report to Leonidas. These slender links would connect the Greek efforts to hold the Persians by land and by sea.

Several more hours of rowing brought the Greeks to their destination. Artemisium was a long curving beach on the northern shore of Euboea, facing the channel that had been since time immemorial the maritime gateway to central Greece. A temple of Artemis, the virgin huntress, overlooked the golden sands. Themistocles venerated this goddess, calling her Artemis Aristoboule or "Artemis of Best Counsel." Religious conviction as well as strategy had marked out Artemisium as the right place to block the passage of Xerxes' armada.

The Greek fleet approached Artemisium late in the day, as the battered Persian survivors of the storm were rounding Cape Sepias and entering the channel from the other end. On the northern coast there was no long beach such as the Greeks would occupy at Artemisium. Instead the contingents of Xerxes' fleet occupied widely separated stations at a string of little beaches known as Aphetai ("Starting Places"). From one of these beaches Jason and his Argonauts had launched the legendary *Argo* on their quest for the Golden Fleece. Themistocles' calculations proved correct: the huge number of the Persian ships was a weakness, since few harbors or beaches could hold them all.

Then through the afternoon haze appeared fifteen Persian ships rowing directly across the channel toward the Greeks. Was it a mad challenge? Or an attempt at a parley? Before the ships reached them, the Greeks realized the truth. These late arrivals, overlooking the disorganized Persian fleet at Aphetai, had mistaken the Greek fleet for their own and were attempting to join it. The newcomers were immediately surrounded and escorted back to Artemisium. Among the captured crews was a commander from Cyprus who had lost eleven of his ships to the storm. He was now losing the twelfth and last to his own carelessness. After questioning, the prisoners were shackled and sent off to the Isthmus.

That night some fifty thousand Greeks camped at Artemisium. Grateful

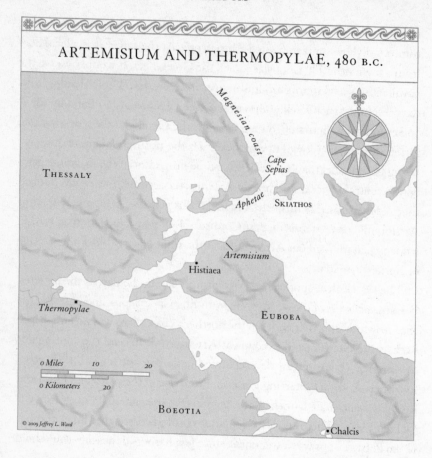

ARTEMISIUM AND THERMOPYLAE, 480 B.C.

Magnesian coast

Cape Sepias

THESSALY

Aphetae SKIATHOS

Artemisium

Histiaea

Thermopylae

EUBOEA

0 Miles   10   20

0 Kilometers   20

BOEOTIA

© 2009 Jeffrey L. Ward

•Chalcis

for the fleet's protection of their island, the Euboeans who lived at Histiaea and other neighboring towns brought livestock, firewood, and other provisions to feed the crews and fighting men. The Athenian division of the camp covered the eastern half of the waterfront. There were 271 Greek triremes drawn up at the water's edge that night, more than half of them Athenian. In recognition of their great contributions, the Spartan admiral had awarded them the coveted post of honor on the right wing. Eleven other city-states contributed the remainder of the Greek ships. Highest in prestige were the ten Spartan triremes. From elsewhere in the Peloponnese came triremes from Corinth, Sicyon, Epidaurus, and Troezen. Central Greece was represented only by triremes from Megara and old-fashioned pentekontors or fifty-oared galleys from Opuntian Locris. The fleet also included ships from the islands of Aegina, Euboea, and Keos. At the west end of the beach camped the Corinthians, whose forty triremes would hold the left wing in the Greek battle line.

Athens alone had mobilized its entire citizen body for the naval effort. Young Cimon and his fellow horsemen were now riders to the sea. The hoplites of Athens had traded their shields and spears for rowing pads and oars. As for the thousands of common citizens, the naval expedition had given them for the first time a feeling of true equality with horsemen and hoplites. Oars were great levelers. Rowing demanded perfect unison of action, and the discipline inevitably generated a powerful unity of spirit. Rich and poor shared the same callused palms, blistered buttocks, and stiff muscles, as well as the same hopes and fears for the future. A new unified Athens was being forged on the decks and rowing thwarts of the fleet.

Across the water glimmered other fires, clusters of twinkling lights that stretched for miles. There was no danger that the Persians would slip by them in the night—Xerxes had ordered his admirals to annihilate the Greeks down to the last fire-signaler. They had not expected the Greeks to confront them but were happy to take advantage of their rashness. The ten miles of open water in the Artemisium channel would be the arena for the coming contest.

That evening a deserter from Xerxes' armada reached the Greek camp in a small boat. He was a famous diver named Skyllias of Skione. For centuries divers around the Aegean Sea had fished for sponges, pearls, coral, and valuables from sunken wrecks. Over the generations they developed the skill and stamina to work for long periods at depths of one hundred feet or more. The trade ran in families, though girls usually gave up diving after marriage. As protection from the dangers of the deep the divers smeared their bodies with olive oil and carried knives. In time their eyes became bloodshot and their bodies bent, but the treasure recovered from a single shipwreck could make a family rich.

War fleets used divers for reconnaissance, salvage, and clandestine operations. Skyllias had been pressed into Persian service as Xerxes passed through his home territory in northern Greece, and he had helped salvage some of the Persian treasure lost during the recent storm off the Magnesian coast. Seeing the campfires of fellow Greeks across the water, he seized the chance to warn them of a new danger. The Persians had sent a squadron of triremes south along the seaward coast of Euboea, hoping to outflank the Greeks' position. No one had anticipated such a move. Whether this roving squadron circled back to Artemisium or pressed ahead to Attica and the Saronic Gulf, the success of the Greek naval mission was now in jeopardy.

Eurybiades called a meeting of the allied commanders to debate strategy. Most voted to keep their ships ashore and let the enemy make the first move. Themistocles disagreed. In his view, everything favored a bold move. The Greeks, though few, were united. The Persian forces were divided among many mooring places and were further depleted by the absence of the division that was making its way around Euboea. With sublime confidence Themistocles told the other commanders that he wanted to test Persian seamanship. Were Xerxes' steersmen and crews adept at breaking through the line with the *diekplous* or "rowing through" maneuver? Or at encircling an enemy with the simpler *periplous* or "rowing around"? These were the lethal maneuvers that could expose the vulnerable sterns and flanks of the Greek triremes to the Persian rams.

Themistocles proposed to use science and skill to overcome the Greeks' disadvantage in numbers. He expected no close coordination among the various squadrons in the enemy armada. It also seemed likely that the Phoenicians, Egyptians, and the rest would count not on their steersmen but on their marines. In that case they would fight in the old-fashioned way, with ships locked together and armed men using their decks as a battleground. True, the Persian ships outnumbered the Greeks' by more than three to one, and in open water such as the Artemisium channel the larger fleet usually won by simply enveloping the smaller. But Themistocles had devised a maneuver that he believed would protect the Greeks from defeat.

On the following day the crews rested on shore till well after the midday meal. When only a few hours of daylight remained, the Greeks launched all their ships and rowed north toward Aphetai. The customary hour for a naval battle was early morning, the time of calm winds and flat water. A late-afternoon attack would take the enemy by surprise. More important, Themistocles had realized that the approach of darkness would ensure that, even if the fighting went against the Greeks, the battle would be too short for the Persians to win a decisive victory.

When the Persians saw the enemy fleet rowing toward them, they decided that the Greeks must be insane. Communication among the scattered beaches at Aphetai was difficult, but before long the Persian ships in their hundreds were bearing down on the Greek line. As they neared the enemy, the Persians began to fan out. The enveloping movement was not carried out in order but at varying speeds. Bolder commanders spurred their crews as they strove to be first to take a Greek ship and thus secure a reward from the Great King. All were eager to capture an Athenian.

Before the two fleets came close enough to engage, the trumpeter on the Spartan flagship blew a signal. In response the Greek line began to bend like a bow, curving back in an immense convex arc as the Athenians on the right wing and the Corinthians on the left reversed their oar strokes and backed away from the advancing Persians. They kept their bronze rams constantly pointed toward the enemy, who were now prowling around them like wolves around a herd. Frustrating the Persian attempt at a *periplous,* the Greek line finally contracted into an immense ring. The ships that had occupied the extreme ends of the original line were now side by side at the rear of the *kyklos* or circle, facing south. All the sterns and steering oars were drawn together in the center, while the outer rim of the vast circle presented a continuous array of rams. It was as if a hedgehog had curled into a ball with all its spines pointing outward.

Themistocles was counting on the defensive appearance of the *kyklos* to make the enemy overconfident. With the Persian fleet milling around the circle's perimeter, carelessly exposing their ships' sides, Eurybiades had his trumpeter blow another call, this time the familiar signal for an attack. At the sound the Greek rowers pulled their hardest, and the triremes lurched from a standstill to a sprint. Bursting from the protection of the circle, each Greek steersman targeted an enemy hull or oar bank in the disorganized throng that surrounded them. The Persians were caught completely off guard. Ship after ship was immobilized as the Greeks smashed hulls or sheared off oars with their rams. The disabled triremes were left to drift in the melee, until their attackers could come back and tow them off. Elsewhere in the crush some Greek marines leaped across to the decks of enemy triremes. They killed or captured the fighting force on board and then claimed the ship as a prize, with its rowing crew intact.

Once the Persians recovered from the shock of the initial Greek charge, they began to counterattack, but nightfall put an end to the battle before they could turn the tide. The demoralized crews of Xerxes' grand armada returned to their havens. A current from the straits carried after them the debris of battle: wrecked ships, broken oars, floating corpses. The Greeks' performance had been so impressive that one trireme from the Aegean island of Lemnos deserted from the Persian side. The Athenians were so grateful to the Lemnian trierarch for joining the resistance that they awarded him a grant of farmland on the island of Salamis.

Acting like judges at a musical or athletic contest, the Greek commanders voted to honor those who had contributed most to the victory. The Athenians received the group prize for valor, and one of their own, Themistocles' kinsman Lycomedes, won the individual prize. He had been the first trierarch to take an enemy ship.

The following day at Artemisium the Greeks spotted a large squadron of triremes rowing toward them from the west. It was not the encircling Persian squadron that the diver had foretold, but the fifty-three Athenian triremes that had been left behind in Attica. They were welcome both as reinforcements and as bearers of good news. Violent storms had wrecked the southbound enemy squadron on the dangerous stretch of coast called the Hollows of Euboea. As the Delphic Oracle had predicted, the winds still seemed to be fighting for the Greeks.

Late in the afternoon, as on the previous day, the Greeks put out to sea. This time they engaged just one isolated division of Xerxes' navy. The target was the contingent from Cilicia in Asia Minor, one hundred strong. The javelins and cutlasses of the piratical Cilicians proved to be no defense against Greek rams, and they lost many triremes in the fighting. Few Asiatics knew how to swim, so the sinking of a ship inevitably caused many deaths. By the time the skirmish ended, the Cilicians had been virtually destroyed.

The Persians in the fleet at Aphetai were well aware that they were keeping their royal master waiting and as yet had nothing to show for the delay. On the third day Xerxes' naval commanders finally took the initiative, launching their entire force at about noon and bearing down on the Euboean shore. The crews yelled their battle cries, flaunted their insignia, and shouted encouragement from ship to ship. The competitive scramble of the first day's attack was gone: the various contingents kept good order as they crossed the channel. The Greeks awaited the charge in silence. They planned to hug their own coast, leaving as little sea room as possible to their rear so as to hamper any enemy attempt at a *diekplous* or *periplous*.

The Persians began with an enveloping movement. Their left and right wings stretched forward in two curving prongs menacing the ends of the shorter Greek line, like the horns of a bull or a crescent moon. At last Eurybiades gave the order to attack. The two fleets collided all along the line. The Persian order broke with the collision. In the chaos that followed, their ships fouled one another as much as they injured the Greeks. Still they did not retreat, and the Egyptians among others began to perform with success. Ships were lost on both sides, but in the end Xerxes' mighty navy once more got the worst of it. After three successive engagements at Artemisium, Themistocles' interpretation of the Delphic Oracle still held true. The Wooden Wall had endured.

The retreating Persians left the Greeks in control of the sea. They carried out the sacred duty of picking up the floating corpses of their comrades and towed the wrecked vessels back to Artemisium. After the heavy ramming action on that third day of fighting half the Athenian triremes needed repairs. Given their small numbers, the Greeks could ill afford to lose any ships. Yet they had survived and had refused to let the enemy drive them from the sea. At the victory celebration on the beach they again voted to award the prize for valor to the Athenians. This time the individual prize went to a noble Athenian named Cleinias. His ship had not been built with public money from the silver strike but was a trireme of his own, as in the buccaneering days of old, furnished with a crew of followers in Cleinias' pay.

While the Greeks were taking their evening meal, the lookouts caught sight of a vessel coming in fast from the west. It was the Athenian galley from Thermopylae. As soon as it reached shore, Abronichus made his report. There was no message from Leonidas: the king was dead. For two days the Spartans and other Greek allies had succeeded in repelling wave after wave of Persian attacks, even though the main Peloponnesian army had still not arrived. That morning, however, scouts had come running down from the hills with the news of a Persian breakthrough.

In the night a local Greek turncoat had led the dreaded spearmen whom the Greeks called "The Immortals" around Thermopylae by a path running along a high mountain ridge. Within a short time Leonidas was trapped between two fires. The Spartan king now had only three options: flight, surrender, or death. Xerxes would have been only too delighted if his opponent had agreed to terms, but Leonidas, achieving true heroism in his final hours, resolved that he would fight to the death in the pass. His courage inspired the three hundred Spartans and a thousand men from the town of Thespiae to follow his lead. Leonidas sent the bulk of his army away toward the south and dispatched Abronichus and his Athenian crew to their triakontor at the same time. By staying behind, Leonidas and his thirteen hundred meant to hold the Persians long enough for the other allies to escape. They, at least, would live to fight another day.

Marshaling his hoplites for the last time, Leonidas led them to the end of the pass in battle array. He had to defend himself from enemies in front and to the rear, as "The Immortals" were now clambering down from the hills into the narrow roadway behind him. When it became clear that the Greeks would not surrender, Xerxes responded with such an avalanche of men that some Persians on the edge of the mass were pushed into the sea and drowned. The Greeks fought like men possessed. When their spears broke, they went on fighting at close quarters with swords and finally with their bare hands. Even after Leonidas fell, the Greeks would not surrender. In the end Xerxes had to send in his light-armed troops to finish the job with a hail of missiles. The road to the south now lay open. Powerless to help, the Athenians had watched until they could no longer doubt the outcome. Then they set off as fast as they could row to warn the fleet.

The news from Thermopylae changed everything. Exhausted after a full day of rowing and fighting, the Greeks had no choice but to retreat from Artemisium immediately. If they waited until daylight, they would have the Persian fleet dogging their tails. Their foresight in posting the Athenian galley at Thermopylae had bought them a few hours' head start on the Persians. Xerxes had no boats at Thermopylae to carry a message to his naval forces, and it would take at least a day for any of his mounted couriers to reach Aphetai.

Themistocles did what he could to improve their chances of escape and raise the morale of the men. He proposed a plan to provision the ships at once for the long row ahead and recommended heaping more fuel on the campfires along the beach. With extra wood the fires would burn through the night and perhaps convince the enemy at Aphetai that the Greek fleet was still at its battle station. Themistocles also heartened the men with a novel scheme to induce the eastern Greek contingents to defect from the Persian fleet. He would inscribe messages on the rocks at the watering places on the way south, appealing to the Ionians to join their fellow Greeks in the fight for freedom.

It remained to settle on their destination. Knowing that Xerxes' army and navy would converge as rapidly as possible on Attica, Themistocles persuaded Eurybiades that the Greek fleet should fall back not to the Isthmus of Corinth but to Salamis. On that island the Athenian elders had established their headquarters in exile. They could help provision the Greek fleet, just as the Euboean islanders had done at Artemisium. And in the protected waters of the Salamis channel, the Greeks might hold Xerxes' armada at bay until the onset of bad weather closed the seaways for the winter. Thermopylae had given the resistance its first heroic martyrs. The spirit of Leonidas and his men could already be seen in the Greek fleet's decision to seek and hold another pass.

Nothing, however, altered the discouraging fact that their struggle at Artemisium had been in vain. With every stroke of the oars they would now be drawing Xerxes' armada after them into the heart of Greece. At that dark hour no Athenian could have predicted that a poet would one day hail Artemisium as the place "where the sons of Athens laid the shining cornerstone of freedom."

As the full moon rose, casting a glittering silver path down the channel, the Greek crews pushed off from shore and began the retreat. Behind them the campfires burned brightly on the deserted beach. Themistocles went first with a squadron of the fastest ships. Then came the Corinthians at the head of the main fleet, followed by the other allied contingents and last of all the long line of Athenian triremes. Several hours later the vanguard reached the westernmost cape of Euboea, pointed like a dart toward the Greek mainland. Fifteen miles ahead of them, across a wide stretch of water and alluvial flats, lay Thermopylae.

At the Hot Gates the distant coast appeared lit by an unearthly glow. In and around the pass shone the myriad flames of the Persian camp: victory bonfires, watch fires, fires for roasting meat, and the blazing fire altars of the Magi. Xerxes' army was celebrating its first taste of Greek blood. Somewhere amid the eerie wisps from the hot springs stood Xerxes' proudest trophy: the head of Leonidas, cut from his body and stuck on a pike. Out at sea, hidden by darkness, the ghostly line of ships made its way past the scene of revelry and vanished southward into the night.

CHAPTER 5

Salamis

[END OF SUMMER, 480 B.C.]

Go, sons of Greece! Free your fatherland! Free
Children, wives, your forefathers' graves,
Shrines of ancestral gods. Fight now for all!

—Aeschylus

FOR HOURS THAT NIGHT PERSIAN SENTRIES ON THE BEACHES
at Aphetai watched the distant fires of the Greek camp while the crews and
fighting men slept. Sometime after midnight the quiet was broken by the
sound of oars approaching from across the channel. A small boat appeared
on the moonlit water, rowing fast for shore. Out of the darkness a voice
hailed them. A Greek on board the boat claimed to have a message for the
Persian commanders. The boat landed, a Greek-speaking translator was
roused from among the thousands of sleeping rowers and soldiers, and the
man poured out his story to the officers in charge of Xerxes' armada.

He told them that he came from Histiaea, a town on the Euboean coast
west of Artemisium. Earlier that evening he had heard or seen the ships of
the Greek fleet rowing past, headed west. Instantly the man had realized
that they were retreating homeward, leaving the islanders to their fate. After
the last trireme disappeared into the night, the watcher from Histiaea gathered a crew and crossed the channel with the news, hoping for a reward
or at least favorable treatment for his town. If the Persians launched a pursuit at once, they might attack the fleeing Greeks from the rear and destroy
them all.

To the Persians, the story seemed incredible. Only a few hours earlier they
had watched the defiant Greeks rowing back to Artemisium, diminished
but still dangerous after three days of fighting. Their blazing campfires were

still plainly visible. Greeks were notorious for tricks and deceit: the tale was likely to be a trap. Were the Greeks hoping to lure them away from the safe havens at Aphetai, or to exhaust their crews with a night spent at the oar? Ignorant of Xerxes' breakthrough at Thermopylae and fearful of making a mistake, the Persian commanders put the Histiaean under guard and sent a few ships south to check the truth of his story. Dawn was in the sky by the time the scouts returned with their report. They had found Artemisium abandoned: the only sign of life was the untended fires.

Themistocles' deception was now exposed, but it seemed too late to pack up camp, marshal the scattered armada, and give chase. Far from destroying the Greeks down to the last fire-signaler, the Persian naval commanders had let the entire fleet slip through their fingers. Even worse, their mistrust of the nocturnal visitor had cost them a last chance of victory. How, exactly, would Xerxes punish them? The grim possibilities ranged from demotion to decapitation. Determined to have something to show for the days spent on their own, the Persians took the fleet across to the northern shore of Euboea, captured the helpless town of Histiaea, and pillaged the surrounding countryside.

They were still collecting loot when a royal messenger from Thermopylae finally caught up with them. He brought an invitation from Xerxes to cross over to the mainland for a tour of the battlefield, so that they could witness the fate of those who resisted the Great King. The mariners enthusiastically accepted the invitation and commandeered every available boat for the crossing, since the triremes could not land in the muddy shallows off Thermopylae. At the Hot Gates they saw no Persian casualties, only the corpses of the massacred Spartans and other Greeks. The centerpiece of the bloody display was the head of King Leonidas. Luckily Xerxes was so elated by his victory that he took little notice of the fleet's dubious performance. The battlefield tour cost the Persians a day, and more days passed as the king's forces gathered momentum for their next target: Athens.

Xerxes' leisurely advance gave the Greeks time to catch a second wind. In the few precious days between the retreat from Artemisium and the arrival of the Persians, Themistocles set out to complete the evacuation of Attica. The Spartan admiral Eurybiades granted permission for the Athenian ships to detach themselves from the main fleet. They proceeded to ferry the remainder of the populace across to Troezen and other places of refuge. In the end, out of tens of thousands, only about five hundred stubborn souls refused to leave their homes.

Themistocles' original bill before Artemisium had called for leaving the temples on the Acropolis to the care of Athena and the other gods. Xerxes would have found only the priestesses and temple officials on the citadel, along with some poor citizens who were willing to take their chances behind that other "wooden wall," the thorn hedge. Matters looked different after the disaster at Thermopylae. Themistocles decided that the priestesses and the ancient wooden statue of the goddess should also be moved to safety. To overcome the opposition of religious conservatives, he persuaded the guardian of the sacred snake on the Acropolis to announce that the snake had abandoned its lair—a sign that the gods had departed and all others should follow. When the evacuation was complete, the Athenian crews rowed back to rejoin the Greek fleet, well entrenched in a seemingly impregnable position within the Salamis channel.

The rugged island of Salamis, legendary home of the hero Ajax, had been conquered by Athenians more than a century earlier in that epic action involving a fleet of fishing boats and one thirty-oared galley. A long waterway stretched between the northern coast of Salamis and the mainland, and the eastern reach of this channel formed the strait of Salamis. The island's principal port lay between two natural harbors at a dogleg bend within the strait. Here the Athenian elders had been presiding over the city's government and treasury ever since the evacuation began. Here too the Greek fleet would await the arrival of the Persians. Now that the original defensive line at Artemisium and Thermopylae had fallen, the Greeks had drawn a new line across the heart of Greece. One end lay at the Isthmus of Corinth, where the Peloponnesian army was toiling to block Xerxes' land forces with a newly erected wall. The other end lay in the Salamis strait. All land north of this line had been yielded to the Persians.

Most Greeks were inclined to criticize Themistocles' strategy. They argued that the fleet should withdraw to the Isthmus of Corinth and the protection of the army. To them, the straits looked like a potential death trap for the Greeks. But in Themistocles' eyes the strait was a watery version of Thermopylae, a constricted space where natural features could nullify the overwhelming Persian advantage in numbers. There was still a hole at the center of his vision, however, for in one crucial point Salamis differed from Thermopylae. King Leonidas had needed no stratagems to bring Xerxes to the Hot Gates: the narrow pass was the only entry to central Greece. No such compulsion would force the Persian navy into the Salamis strait, since the main sea route to southern Greece lay across the open waters of the Saronic Gulf. Somehow Themistocles would have to lure the Persian ships into the strait.

At summer's end the Persian hordes finally reached Attica, pushing their way through the passes of Mount Cithaeron and spreading across the deserted countryside like a river in flood. They quickly captured the local residents who had dodged Themistocles' evacuation decree and shipped them off to distant Samos as prisoners of war. Athens was Xerxes' for the taking, except for the Acropolis. There an Athenian garrison held out behind the old palisade, now reinforced with other timbers. The garrison rejected the blandishments of the Athenian exiles when the latter came to the foot of the Acropolis and called on them to surrender. They likewise defied a hail of flaming arrows from the Persian archers and rolled big stones down on anyone who tried to scale the slopes. Nature had barricaded the Acropolis with sheer cliffs and supplied its defenders with a spring of fresh water deep in the rock. Stymied by their resistance, Xerxes postponed tackling either the Greek fleet at Salamis or the Greek army at the Isthmus. Instead he pitched his royal pavilion at Athens and settled down to a siege of the Acropolis.

Meanwhile on Salamis, Themistocles faced a new crisis. The common citizens of Athens, the twenty thousand thetes, were running short of money on this, their first campaign on behalf of their city. Themistocles' expanded navy called for the enlistment of all citizens, rich or poor. The horsemen and hoplites were men of means, who could afford to buy their own provisions while on campaign. But after almost a month of naval service the poorer citizens had exhausted their scanty savings. The city had no funds to help them and no stockpiles of food to dole out to relieve the shortfall.

In this time of need the rich Athenians who sat on the ancient council of the Areopagus or "Hill of Ares" came to the rescue. The council included Themistocles, who like all former archons was a member for life. In answer to the navy's need, the Areopagites contributed enough from their private funds to provide a stipend of eight silver drachmas for each thete among the rowing crews. The crisis was averted, and the aristocratic council of the Areopagus earned itself a fund of goodwill from the democratic citizens that would endure for a generation.

A few days before the autumnal equinox the Greeks at Salamis saw a column of black smoke rising from the direction of Athens. Xerxes' assault had succeeded at last, and the temples on the Acropolis were being put to the torch. Vengeance was taken for the burning of Sardis, and Darius' vow that he would "remember the Athenians" was at last fulfilled. Xerxes had done what his father had failed to do. In the three months that had passed since the Great King crossed the Hellespont into Europe, he had killed a Spartan king, conquered Athens, and added all of northern and central Greece to his empire. The expedition was already a success. At once royal couriers were dispatched to carry the glad tidings back to Susa.

At about the time that the Acropolis fell, the sky watchers and diviners among the Greek and Persian armies observed the star Arcturus in the east just before dawn, visible for the first time since the beginning of summer. The rising of Arcturus marked the end of the seafaring season in the eastern Mediterranean and the Aegean. Soon it would be time to draw boats and ships up on beaches and secure them against the winter storms. Should Xerxes miss the last of the fair days, his fleet would be weather-bound in Greece. He would then have more than a hundred thousand idle mariners eating their heads off at his expense for months. If his navy could not destroy the Greek fleet immediately, it would be better for the Great King to send his armada back across the Aegean to spend the winter in Asia. By spring the united Greek resistance at sea might well have disintegrated.

Though Xerxes could not know it, a violent conflict was already threatening to shatter the unity of the Greek fleet. As the days of waiting dragged on, the steady undertow of resistance to Themistocles' strategy grew stronger. The Greeks were caught in the demoralizing position of sitting in full sight of an enemy that was concealed from them. A conical knoll on the mainland gave Persian scouts a bird's-eye view of the Greeks' every move. Xerxes' fleet at Phaleron, on the other hand, was screened from Greek view by the heights of the Piraeus promontory at the eastern end of the strait.

When the Peloponnesian commanders saw the smoke from the Acropolis, they called for Eurybiades to abandon Salamis and fall back to the Isthmus while there was still time. The Spartan admiral called a council, and Themistocles impetuously began to argue against a withdrawal. The Corinthian leader angrily reminded him that at the games, runners who started too soon were beaten with rods. "Yes," retorted Themistocles, "but those who start late do not win." The Athenian then considered their odds of survival if they retreated. At the Isthmus, any naval battle would have to be fought in open water, where the huge Persian fleet could surround and destroy them. They were safer at Salamis. The strongest arm of the Greek resistance, Themistocles said, was the navy. And he reminded them again of the oracle of the Wooden Wall, which had named Salamis as a place of destiny.

To stop this impassioned flow of argument, the Corinthian commander declared that Themistocles should no longer be allowed to speak in the council. He was now a man without a country, a mere refugee. The insult goaded Themistocles to state, in the clearest terms, his belief in the Athenian navy. He told the Corinthian, a man named Adeimantus, that the Athenians had a greater city and a greater land than Corinth or any other Greek state as long as they had two hundred ships filled with their men. If the other Greeks abandoned Salamis, the Athenians would collect their families and voyage in their floating city to a new home in the west, far from Persians and Peloponnesians alike. Faced with this ultimatum, the allies agreed to stay where they were. Themistocles had won this skirmish, but time was running out. By what trick or contrivance could Xerxes be persuaded to fight in narrow waters that favored the Greeks? At last the great idea came. Themistocles shared it privately with the Spartan admiral and then, with his permission, put it into action.

Among Themistocles' slaves was a daring and resourceful Greek named Sicinnus. His regular duties called for him to serve as pedagogue to the sons of the family, overseeing their education and leading them to and from their lessons. That night Themistocles put Sicinnus in a small boat and sent him down the channel to Phaleron, where the shore was crowded with the hundreds of triremes that Xerxes had brought to Attica. Sicinnus attracted the attention of some of the Persian naval officers and then called out the message that Themistocles had told him to deliver. The future of Athens, and

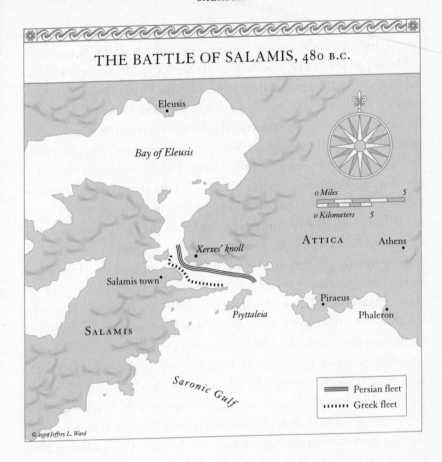

THE BATTLE OF SALAMIS, 480 B.C.

Eleusis

Bay of Eleusis

ATTICA

Athens

o Miles 5
o Kilometers 5

Xerxes' knoll

Salamis town

Piraeus

Psyttaleia

Phaleron

SALAMIS

Saronic Gulf

══ Persian fleet
...... Greek fleet

© 2009 Jeffrey L. Ward

possibly the freedom of Greece, depended upon how well Themistocles had judged Xerxes' reaction.

Sicinnus identified himself as a secret envoy from Themistocles, leader of the Athenians. His master was eager to win the Great King's friendship, as the Athenians were about to be betrayed. On the following night, Sicinnus said, the other Greeks planned to withdraw from Salamis and row away to their own cities. Yet the king could still have his victory if he prevented the would-be runaways from escaping. The allies were quarreling among themselves. Some already favored submission to Xerxes. As soon as the Persian navy appeared at Salamis, the Athenians and other disaffected Greeks would change sides. It was of course a barefaced lie, but like all good lies it had the virtue of incorporating many elements of the truth. Without giving the Persians a chance to ask troublesome questions, Sicinnus slipped away as soon as he had delivered the message and returned to Salamis.

History seemed to be repeating itself. Xerxes' naval commanders had received just such a nocturnal message from the Greek turncoat at Artemisium. To their regret they had refused to believe the man, and so the Greeks had escaped. The Persians did not intend to make the same mistake twice. When told of the message, Xerxes agreed. He gave orders to prepare for an advance on Salamis the next evening. He also instructed his staff to have his chariot ready to convey him to the hilltop that looked down on Salamis. The king was convinced that his mariners would not have performed so poorly at Artemisium if he had been present to keep an eye on them. At Salamis he meant to watch the battle in person.

Next morning there was an earthquake. Xerxes, unshaken by the portent, ordered his fleet to sea. In battle array the Persians waited outside the strait, but no Greek ships ventured forth to answer the challenge. At midday the armada returned to the beach at Phaleron, and the crews climbed down the ladders to eat their dinners. Anticipating the movement into the strait that night, however, the rowers left their oars in place, looped tightly to the tholepins. At sunset Xerxes' admirals called the men back to the ships.

The entire Persian fleet was to join in the unparalleled night maneuver. Some triremes would circle the southern coast of Salamis in order to block the narrow channel at the western end, near Megara. The main fleet, however, would row directly into the Salamis strait. Echoing his own command before he dispatched his fleet to Artemisium, Xerxes ordered that not one Greek rower or marine should escape. The men felt confident. As they settled into their places, the crews cheered one another on.

The Persian plan called for surrounding the Greeks under cover of darkness, either capturing or turning back any Greek ships that tried to break out into the open water. Dawn would find their fleet arrayed against the north shore of the Salamis channel, ready to pounce upon what promised to be a divided and disheartened Greek naval force. Thanks to Themistocles' message, the Persians believed that the large Athenian contingent would desert their side. Victory seemed foreordained, as was only right when the Great King watched his subjects fight in person.

As the sunset faded in the western sky, only faint starlight illuminated the sea. The triremes moved slowly offshore and eased into line, three ships abreast. Knowing that they outnumbered the Greeks more than three to one, the commanders had decided that the main fleet would file into the strait in a triple formation. At midnight the moon soared up over the shoulder of Mount Hymettus, brilliantly attended by the planet Zeus, as the Greeks called Jupiter. The moon was four days past the full but still bright enough that the lookouts in the ships' prows could guide the course of the triremes. The Phoenician ships that headed the three long files now began to row slowly westward. They rounded the curve of the Piraeus promontory, then passed the island of Psyttaleia to enter the Salamis channel. There was no more cheering. All were silent. In the wake of the Phoenicians came the rest of the fleet, an ever-rolling stream that flowed for miles along the Attic coast. Only the muffled beat of the oars and the glittering ripples of the wakes marked their passing.

The last to enter the strait, hours after the leaders, were the triremes of the Ionian Greeks, outnumbered in Xerxes' fleet only by the Phoenicians. Most of the Ionian ships had come from the Greek cities of Asia Minor or the islands along the Asiatic coast. Only seventeen had been mustered from the Cyclades, the archipelago of rocky islands that dotted the Aegean Sea. In this squadron that brought up the rear of the mighty procession, one ship's crew was fired with a desperate resolve. They were reluctant subjects of Xerxes from Tenos, an island east of Attica. The men from Tenos had privately agreed at this ultimate hour to desert the Great King and join the Greek side. They knew the odds; they knew what the Persians expected the morning to bring. Even so, the steersman swung his steering oars over and bent his course gently away from the steadily advancing column. The lone Tenian trireme then headed straight for the lights of the Greek camp at Salamis, and a few hours of honor and freedom before the end.

In the last hours of the night, transports ferried four hundred elite Persian troops, the pick of the army, across to Psyttaleia. The Athenians held this island to be sacred to the great god Pan, lord of goats, of wilderness, and of that irrational terror known as a "panic." To the Persians it seemed no more than a strategic post for an auxiliary force. Should there be a battle, these soldiers would offer aid to any fellow warriors who fetched up on the island, and a quick death to shipwrecked Greeks.

The leading Phoenician triremes had by this time reached the point where the channel turns north toward Eleusis. As each set of three triremes reached its station, the ships swung around until their prows pointed toward the Salamis shore, a mile off and still invisible in the dark. The seemingly endless column in three files heading west was thus transformed into a compact battle line in three ranks facing south. The rear ranks were expected to reinforce the front line and prevent a *diekplous* on the part of the Greeks. Triremes could cruise by moonlight, but they could not attack. Lookouts and steersmen needed daylight to aim their ramming strikes and to distinguish friends from foes.

That night no one in the king's armada was allowed to sleep. The Persians remained on the alert for any Greeks who might try to flee from Salamis. But the night wore away, and they saw no ships in motion but their own. Xerxes' crews had already been rowing ceaselessly for hours. Even after they reached their stations, the cramped quarters within the triremes prevented any real rest for their weary limbs.

In the darkness before dawn Xerxes himself rode in his chariot to the knoll opposite Salamis harbor. The king's servants had erected a seat for him on the crown of the hill. From this natural grandstand Salamis and the strait were spread out before him like a scene at a play. Members of the court surrounded him, and royal scribes were in attendance to record the day's events. In his supreme confidence, the king had brought them along to write down the names of commanders who especially distinguished themselves in the course of destroying the Greek fleet.

As for the Greeks on the far side of the channel, their rowers and soldiers rested ashore through the night. It was a different story with the commanders. Themistocles still had no idea whether Sicinnus' mission had succeeded. The possibility that the Persians would enter the strait, though known to Eurybiades, had been kept from the rank and file in the fleet. Confirmation came at last from an unexpected source. In the middle of the night Aristides (his ten-year ostracism cut short because of the crisis) arrived by boat from Aegina, bringing with him sacred images from the island. He had seen the Persian ships by moonlight as they entered the strait and had in fact almost been caught by the blockaders at the mouth of the channel. Aristides first took Themistocles aside to give him the news. He then joined the allied council and broke the news. Shortly afterward the trireme from Tenos arrived to confirm that the Greeks were surrounded. The Tenians could also recount all the Persians' expectations for the day ahead.

After welcoming the Tenians and enrolling them in the alliance, the Greek leaders made a hasty battle plan. They decided to array their ships in a single line against the Salamis shore to prevent a Persian *diekplous* or *periplous,* just as they had done on the last day at Artemisium. The Greek trierarchs and steersmen would be instructed to keep good order in the line until gaps opened in the Persian formation. At that point they would use their rams to cripple as many enemy ships as possible. After that the outcome depended on the help of the gods. But thanks to Themistocles, the Greeks had already done everything possible to help themselves.

One last stinging disappointment awaited Themistocles. By order of Eurybiades, the post of honor on the right wing fell this time to the islanders of Aegina, bitter rivals of the Athenians, accompanied by the Spartans with the admiral's flagship. From the Tenians' report, the Greeks now knew that their right wing would face the Ionians at the eastern end of the battle line, nearest to the Piraeus and the mouth of the channel. The Athenian fleet was relegated to the left wing—indeed it would occupy the entire western half of the Greek line. Their principal antagonists would be the Phoenicians. Once the order of battle had been decided, the commanders dispersed to their own divisions to rouse the crews.

In the dawn light the fighting men assembled on the beach, clustering around their commanders for the inspirational speech that preceded every battle. Themistocles spoke to the Athenian trierarchs and marines, almost two thousand strong. That day, the nineteenth of Boedromion, was one of the holiest days in the Athenian calendar. If Xerxes had not driven them from their land, these men would have been making a fourteen-mile pilgrimage from Athens to the shrine of Demeter and her daughter at Eleusis. Sacrifices and mystical rituals would have ensured that a new harvest would grow from the dry seeds of the old; the pilgrims too underwent a life-changing rebirth of the spirit. It was not lawful to talk of these mysteries, but as Themistocles stood on the beach, he called on his fellow Athenians to think of the best that human nature and fortune could offer, and the worst. And he challenged them to take their destinies into their own hands that day and choose the best. Then he offered sacrifices for victory and sent them to their ships.

The triremes were already afloat, with only their sterns grounded in the shallows. The crews filed aboard and felt their way through the hulls until each man reached his own rowing thwart. The rowers of the lower tiers seemed enveloped in a well of darkness. As the side screens of tough hide were spread down the length of the rowing frames, the upper thranite tier too was blacked out. Fresh from Themistocles' oration, the trierarchs and marines made their way to the forward decks above the rams. The mariners raised the ladders and anchors, the rowers pulled the first light strokes, and the ships began to move slowly away from shore.

The Persians were still as invisible to them as they were to the Persians. In any case, the rowers, now pulling away from Salamis with their backs to the enemy, would see nothing of the battle unless their ship was wrecked. The stars were fading as they left the shelter of the bays, though the channel still lay in shadow. Soon the light would be strong enough for the ships to burst out of their huddle and extend their battle line along the shore. As they waited, some of the marines began the war chant. Their song was the ancient paean that preceded every battle: *Ie, ie Paian! Ie, ie Paian!* "Hail, hail, healing Lord!" If by some miracle the Greeks were victorious that day, they would sing the paean again at battle's end. The chant spread from ship to ship until the echoes came back from the hills, and the strait was filled with the sound of singing.

Amid the chanting, the trumpeter on the flagship turned the flaring bell of his instrument upchannel toward the distant Athenians. Lifting the bronze to his lips, he listened for the command from Eurybiades, who was waiting for daylight. At last the moment came when dawn spread right across the sky, and the lookouts could see the rocky coast. A deep breath, and—"Now!" from the admiral—the trumpet blew, and the Greek ships burst out into the open. At a sprint they raced along the Salamis shore. Frothing white water spurted from the oar banks at every stroke. For the first time the Persians saw them clearly. This was not the disorderly mob they had been led to expect. But Xerxes' admirals did not hesitate. Each was desperately eager to shine in the eyes of the watching king. They too swept forward after the trumpet signal, the front line forging into the wide strip of unruffled water that still separated the two fleets.

Before the Persian onset could reach them, the Greeks broke off their dash along the shore and turned their rams toward the enemy. Then came the coxswains' urgent orders for the crews to back their oar strokes and reverse the triremes away from the enemy and toward the rocky coast of Salamis. Up and down the line the steersmen adjusted their positions, each holding his trireme level with the ships on either side while leaving as little open water as possible astern. Beyond the onrushing enemy ships, the officers and marines could now see Xerxes enthroned in splendor on his hill.

The charge across the open channel broke the uniformity of the Persian front. As it neared Salamis, the line became ragged, toothed like a saw blade with gleaming bronze rams. Observing that one Phoenician ship had pulled clear of the rest, an Athenian trierarch named Ameinias ordered a ramming attack, the first action of the battle. His rowers dug their oars into the water, propelling Ameinias' trireme out of the Greek line. At the last possible moment the steersman shifted his steering oars so that the ship veered into the oncoming Phoenician. The Athenian ram hit so hard that it smashed through the enemy hull and lopped off the entire stern section. Ameinias' own ship was caught in the wreckage. The Athenians on either side surged forward to his aid, closing up their ranks, and battle was joined all along the line. Off to the east the Greek right wing engaged at the same time after an Aeginetan trireme struck an Ionian.

From his hilltop Xerxes found himself looking down on more than a thousand ships locked in a struggling mass that writhed like a monstrous snake along the Salamis shore. His fleet could not recover from the initial disorder of that first charge, when the fastest crews had outstripped the pack. Each commander was now fighting his own battle. In the narrow waters Xerxes' ships did as much damage to one another as to the Greeks. Oar banks shattered, and rowers were thrown from their thwarts. There were even accidental rammings between ships of the armada. These collisions further weakened the Persian line. The two rear ranks feared that the king might accuse them of cowardice if they held back. Instead of maintaining open zones of water between the ranks, they pressed forward. Preoccupied with maintaining their own reputations, they gave no thought to the consequences for the forward line, now helplessly pinned against the Greek rams. Crippled triremes fought to back away and escape from the mayhem but found they could not avoid the Greeks. Gaps in the Persian line were multiplying, and the Greeks darted forward wherever they saw an opening.

Throughout the morning the thin Greek line held, resilient and unbroken. Like soldiers in the shield wall of a hoplite phalanx, the Greeks kept level with the ships on either side, whether stemming an enemy attack or shoving forward. The skill of the steersmen was critical, but when a trireme was at a standstill, the steering oars became useless. Then only the rowers, responding quickly to orders, could direct the ship to one side or another. Making a sharp turn in tight quarters called for the oarsmen on one side to row harder than their counterparts on the other, or even to row alone. Here the Greek crews with their long powerful strokes had the advantage.

Toward midday, when the sun climbed high enough to blaze down into the densely packed hulls, watchers on shore perceived a change in the configuration of the fleets. It began on the Greek left wing, where Themistocles commanded the Athenians. Since early morning there had been a steady seepage of damaged Persian ships toward the eastern exit as they sought shelter at Phaleron. With each departure, the pressure that the Phoenicians had been maintaining against the Athenians slackened. The time came when the westernmost Athenian triremes were able to push away from the shore and swing out into the open channel. With this move they outflanked the Phoenicians and began to force them into what remained of the Persian center. It was the turning point.

Now at long last the Greek line broke up. One Athenian trireme after another gave chase to fleeing Persians, and the allies followed suit. Eagerly they threaded their way through the roiling mass of ships, hunters seeking prey. The Persians moved sluggishly, their crews exhausted from lack of sleep and hours of hard rowing. Many evaded the Athenians only to encounter the Aeginetans who hovered near the mouth of the channel. As the battle disintegrated into a rout, even undamaged Persian ships crowded toward the exits on either side of Psyttaleia, like herd animals running from a pride of lions. The Greeks did all they could, but inevitably most of Xerxes' ships slipped by them and escaped.

As sea room opened up in the strait, the battle entered a new phase. It became a series of duels, like the Homeric contests between Greek and Trojan heroes on the plains of Troy. This was the time of greatest danger for the Greeks. Once free of the line, every trireme had to look to its own defense. In open water even a successful ramming attack made the aggressor vulnerable in turn to the rams of passing enemies. In the course of these ship-to-ship actions, Xerxes' scribes were kept busy. Now it was easier for a courageous and skillful commander to score a success. Two Ionian trierarchs from the island of Samos distinguished themselves for bravery in capturing Greek ships. Queen Artemisia of Halicarnassus was also entered in the list after the king's attendants saw her ram and sink a ship. Once they had assured Xerxes that the attack had really been made by Artemisia, whom they recognized by her insignia, the Great King exclaimed, "My men have turned into women, my women into men!"

The true story of Artemisia's exploit would not have earned her a place on the king's honor roll. Finding her trireme the target of an Athenian ship, Artemisia tried to escape through the crowded battlefield. She could not shake off her pursuer. The Athenian trierarch was the same determined Ameinias who had destroyed the first Phoenician ship that morning. Had he known that the ship ahead of him was Artemisia's, he would have redoubled his efforts, for the Athenians had put a price on the queen's head. As Ameinias closed in for the kill, Artemisia found herself blocked by a ship that lay broadside across her only path of escape. This obstacle was the flagship of the King of Calynda, an Asiatic ruler who served Xerxes and who was a local rival of Artemisia. Without hesitating, she ordered the steersman to maintain his course straight ahead, and the rowers to give her full speed. Artemisia's ship rammed the hapless Calyndian so hard that it destroyed the ship and the entire crew drowned, leaving no one to tell Xerxes what had really happened. The queen was doubly lucky: Ameinias assumed from her attack on a Persian ship that she must be an ally, and let her go.

By late afternoon the collapse of the Persian battle line brought the Athenians and Aeginetans into contact, although they had started the morning on opposite wings. One spectacular action involved triremes from both Athens and Aegina. Looking east down the channel, Xerxes saw one of his ships, a Greek trireme from the island of Samothrace, ram an Athenian.

As often happened, the bronze ram of the Samothracian ship was caught and stuck in the timbers of its victim. A passing Aeginetan then rammed the immobilized ship from Samothrace, so that all three were locked together. Trapped between the heavily armored marines from Athens and Aegina, the islanders appeared doomed. To Xerxes' joy, however, the Samothracians fired a hail of light missiles at the Aeginetan foredeck to clear it of defenders. They then jumped across from the railing of their own sinking ship. In the fight that followed, they wielded their javelins so ferociously that the Aeginetan crew abandoned ship. Claiming the enemy trireme as a prize, the victorious islanders cruised off in search of further adventures.

At about this time a group of unhappy Phoenician commanders climbed up Xerxes' hill for an audience with the king. All these men had lost their ships, and they blamed their misfortunes on the perfidious Ionians and other eastern Greeks, saying that they had betrayed the Persian cause. The Phoenician commanders had the bad luck to make their accusations just as the Greeks from Samothrace were simultaneously sinking one enemy ship and capturing another. Furious with the Phoenicians for criticizing such heroes, Xerxes made them scapegoats for the entire disaster and had them beheaded.

Themistocles was close to an Aeginetan trireme when it captured one of the Phoenician ships from Sidon. On board the Phoenician ship the Aeginetans discovered a fellow countryman. He was the soldier whom the Phoenicians had kept as a trophy ever since their engagement with the Greek scout ships at the island of Skiathos. For the men of Aegina, the liberation of this lonely prisoner was the greatest moment of the entire battle. Seeing Themistocles nearby, the commander shouted across the water to ask if he still claimed that the Aeginetans were friends of the Persians.

As Greek marines boarded enemy ships brandishing swords and spears, or simply pitched the Persians into the water, the Salamis strait became a killing ground. Among the victims was the king's brother Ariaramnes, one of the four admirals. Most of the Persians who died simply drowned, spilling into the sea as their ships sank or swamped. Casualties were light among the Greeks. They all knew how to swim and simply stroked their way to the Salamis shore. Any Persians who clung to floating wreckage died also; as the crush of ships cleared the narrows, the Greeks rowed about the battlefield like fishermen circling a school of tuna, spearing survivors with weapons or even broken oar shafts. Wrecked and capsized triremes littered the sea; corpses covered the rocks and reefs.

Once the last Persian ships had been chased from the channel, the Greeks turned their attention to the troops on the islet of Psyttaleia. The hard-pressed Persian ships had been unwilling to risk their own survival to pick up these men. Four hundred of Xerxes' best troops were now stranded, and the Greek navy prepared to avenge the massacre at Thermopylae. Led by Aristides, a Greek force made a landing on Psyttaleia. They rounded up the Persians with a barrage of arrows from the archers and a shower of stones from enthusiastic rowers who had jumped ashore to join the fight. When the lightly armored Persians were penned close together on the island's central ridge, Aristides and the hoplites charged into the mass and butchered them all. The golden rays of the setting sun gilded the struggle, visible afar in the clear evening light. The tragedy at Salamis had now reached its final scene and, for the Persian king, its bitter climax. Xerxes tore his robe in grief, stepped into his chariot, and departed.

Themistocles' strategy had succeeded. Fast and maneuverable Greek ships and the narrow waters of the Salamis channel had been the keys to victory. At battle's end a west wind was carrying the wreckage past Psyttaleia, but the Greeks dared not follow it into the open sea. The main body of the Persian fleet still held Phaleron, and they still outnumbered the Greeks. Except for the minor losses on Psyttaleia, Xerxes' army remained untouched. That evening the Greeks towed the salvageable wrecks back to their station at Salamis. On shore they built funeral pyres and burned the bodies of comrades who had died that day. Amid the mourning and uncertainty, however, rose the irrepressible joy of victory. After dedicating an offering of thanks to Zeus, the Greeks danced to celebrate their triumph with shouts and stamping feet.

For the next two or three days the fleet at Salamis remained in suspense as to the enemy's next move. The Persians had not given up the struggle after their first loss at Artemisium, and there was no reason to think that they would be any less relentless here at Salamis. Unknown to the Greeks, however, on the day after the battle in the strait the Phoenicians—the backbone of the armada—had in fact slipped away to their home cities. The rest of the fleet left Phaleron shortly afterward under cover of darkness, bound for the Hellespont or for ports in Asia Minor and distant isles. Xerxes sent some of his illegitimate sons back to Asia under the protection of Artemisia. He himself retreated overland with part of his army. A large number of troops were left behind under the command of Mardonius, with orders to complete the conquest of Greece the following spring.

When word reached Salamis that the Great King's ships had left for home, the Greeks immediately set out in pursuit. Out of the strait that had held them for so long, past the deserted beach at Phaleron Bay, and down the Attic coast they rowed, till Cape Sunium loomed up ahead of them. The ruined temple of Poseidon stood starkly atop the cliffs, burned by the vengeful Persians like the temples on the Acropolis. Still they caught no sight of the enemy. Nightfall overtook them near the island of Andros.

Themistocles urged that they row on to the Hellespont and break the bridges. He was overruled by Eurybiades, who expressed the majority view of the Peloponnesians: the sooner Xerxes was out of Europe, the better. Nothing should be done to impede his departure. Eurybiades' decision was later confirmed by a dramatic omen at the Isthmus. At the moment when the Spartan commander Cleombrotus, brother of the fallen Leonidas, was offering a sacrifice for victory, an eclipse hid the sun. The omen was interpreted as a warning against taking the proposed action, so Cleombrotus and the rest of the Spartans abandoned their plan to pursue Xerxes.

It was high time for the Greeks to commemorate the glorious naval victory. Among the trophies were three intact Phoenician triremes. One of these they dragged up to the shrine of Poseidon on Cape Sunium. Another was sent to the Isthmus and dedicated in the sanctuary of Poseidon there. The third captured trireme stayed on Salamis, an offering to the hero Ajax. Other spoils from the sea battles at Salamis and Artemisium were divided among the cities, once they had first set aside a tenth of the bronze from the enemy rams and weapons. From this metal they cast a statue of Apollo eighteen feet tall and erected it in the sanctuary of the oracle at Delphi. Without the prophecy of the Wooden Wall, Themistocles might never have persuaded the Athenians to face the Persians at sea.

Before the Greeks left the Isthmus, the allied naval commanders cast votes to decide who had displayed the greatest merit in the war with the

Persians. There were ballots for first and second choices. The matter was considered so important that they laid their votes on the altar of Poseidon. Every man felt honor bound to vote first for himself, so there was no winner. But when they counted the votes for second place, it was found that most had voted for Themistocles. With this last rite, united in their disunity, the Greeks launched their ships and rowed away to their homes.

Themistocles went south with Eurybiades to Sparta. There he received a crop of honors for his value as a loyal ally and architect of victory. The Spartans placed a crown of wild olive on his head as a prize for wisdom and cunning. They also assigned to Themistocles an honor guard of three hundred Spartan soldiers, thus treating him like another Leonidas. And as a more tangible token of respect, they gave this Athenian lover of horses the best chariot in the country.

While Themistocles was being lionized in Sparta, the rest of the Athenians returned thankfully to their own land. Someone climbed the hill where Xerxes had sat to watch the battle of Salamis and found the gilded footstool on which the Great King had stepped to mount his chariot. In their haste to pack up and return to the royal pavilion, the king's attendants must have overlooked it. This most cherished relic—something touched by Xerxes himself!—was carried up to the scorched and desolate Acropolis and presented to Athena as an offering. The Athenians also held a victory celebration of their own with song and dance. The boy chosen to lead the dance was a handsome and talented youngster named Sophocles, at that time about sixteen years old. The great poet Simonides wrote memorable verses as epitaphs for the fallen and eventually composed odes on the naval battles at Artemisium and Salamis. These may have been performed at the dedication of a new temple to Boreas the North Wind, a hitherto neglected god who had earned the gratitude of the Athenians for his repeated attacks on the fleets of the Great King.

It was now autumn, season of chilly showers and mild blustery winds. At peace after so many trials, the Athenians returned to their beloved countryside. The time for planting crops was well advanced. From overhead in the clouds came the clacking of migrating cranes, southward bound for the lakes of Africa. Soon those misty sisters, the seven Pleiades, would vanish from the constellations of the evening sky, and winter would put an end to sowing. All over Attica farmers were camping out in their homesteads, yoking their oxen, and beginning the seasonal round once more. Callused hands that had pulled oars at Artemisium and Salamis now gripped the handles of plows.

The seeds sown that autumn would sprout and grow in a new world. For a little space of time, scarcely more than a month, the citizens of Athens had abandoned their ancestral land and compacted themselves, one and all, into the wooden hulls of their newly built triremes. Never had they been more of a city than when they had no city. Never had they been more formidable than when they set aside their shields and spears and submerged their differences of class and politics into one common effort—the navy. They had risked everything they possessed on one throw, and their daring had been rewarded a hundredfold. Above all, they had fulfilled Themistocles' dream. Guided by his vision, the Athenians had raised their small city to stand among the most powerful on earth. The Athens that rose from the bare fields and ruined walls would be fired by their spirit for generations to come.

Part Two

DEMOCRACY

Our constitution is called a democracy because power is in the hands not of a minority but of the whole people. When it is a question of settling private disputes, everyone is equal before the law; when it is a question of putting one person before another in positions of public responsibility, what counts is not membership of a particular class, but the actual ability that a man possesses.

—Pericles to the Athenians

CHAPTER 6

A League of Their Own

[479–463 B.C.]

Seamanship, just like anything else, is an art. It is not something that can be picked up and studied in one's spare time. Indeed, it allows one no spare time for anything else.

—Thucydides

AFTER THE VICTORY AT SALAMIS, TWO AMBITIOUS RIVALS challenged Themistocles' sole leadership of Athens. Both men had been recalled from ostracism during the national emergency. When the war effort resumed in the spring, the Assembly appointed Aristides to command the army and Xanthippus the navy. Themistocles was passed over. His political opponents were well organized, and he himself soured public opinion with his vanity, his itching palm, and his courting of Spartan favor. In future the hero of Salamis would devote himself to Athens' defenses, not its wars abroad.

The war was by no means over. Persians were famed for their persistence, even after suffering disastrous setbacks. To guard against a return of the armada from Asia, the Spartans announced that the Greek fleet would assemble at Aegina under the admiralship of the Spartan king Leotychidas. The decision to pass over Athens and Salamis as naval bases was another blow to Athenian prestige. In any case, Athens could not commit as many triremes as before. Eight thousand citizens of the hoplite class would follow Aristides in the campaign against the Persian army that Xerxes left behind, thus depleting the pool of Athenian rowers. Xanthippus joined the allies at Aegina with only 140 triremes. Even so the Athenians were still contributing the majority of ships and crews.

The summer days passed, and no Persian fleet appeared. The Greeks might have remained at Aegina indefinitely if a ship had not arrived from the island of Chios with an appeal for aid. The Chians were still subjects of the Great King and had risked their lives on this secret mission to Greece. They assured Leotychidas that the cities and islands of Ionia were eager for liberty. The arrival of the allied fleet of 250 ships in the eastern Aegean would be enough to spark the rebellion. Reluctantly the Spartan king left Aegina and advanced as far as Delos, but he refused to go farther. The coast of Asia lay only one hundred miles farther east, but to a land-bound Spartan it seemed "as far away as the Pillars of Heracles."

At Delos a fresh appeal came from the Ionians of Samos. They reported that the Persian armada was at that moment stationed in their harbor, a prize ripe for the picking. The chance to eliminate Persian sea power once and for all was too tempting to resist. Leotychidas ordered the fleet forward. At his approach the Persian admirals, still traumatized by memories of Salamis, abandoned Samos for a safer haven on the mainland of Asia Minor. At Samos the Athenians and other Greeks equipped their ships with wooden gangways for boarding enemy ships. Then they cruised east in search of the enemy. They did not have to search long.

Half a day's row beyond Samos the lookouts spotted their quarry on a beach below the rugged heights of Mount Mycale. One look at the Persian camp convinced the Greeks that there would be no battle at sea that day. The Persians had hauled their fleet ashore and constructed a stockade of stones, timber, and pointed stakes around the precious ships. But the Greeks had come too far to give up without a fight. Leotychidas' flagship steered for a landing place beyond the stockade. As they rowed past the fortified camp, the Spartan herald shouted a message to the Ionians still in Xerxes' service, urging them to join in the fight for freedom.

The Greek rowers backed the triremes onto the beach, and the fighting men leaped onto the sand. With about ten marines on each ship, the Greeks could field an army of more than two thousand hoplites. Arrayed eight deep in the traditional phalanx, their line stretched along a front about three hundred yards in length: too long to fit on the flat land between the mountain and the sea. Honor required the Spartans to hold the right wing, though this placement forced them off the beach altogether and onto the rough and rocky base of the mountain. The center, held by Peloponnesian allies from Corinth, Sicyon, and Troezen, stood on level ground, while the Athenians under Xanthippus were assigned the left wing near the water's edge. The Athenians were cheered by the presence in their ranks of an athletic champion named Hermolycus, a notable celebrity. He had been crowned for victories at the Panhellenic Games in the *pankration* or kickboxing event, and to march beside such a hero from the world of sports came close to walking in the aura of a divine hero.

It was late afternoon by the time Leotychidas gave the order to attack. So began an extraordinary naval battle, with both fleets on shore and the Greek rowers watching from their triremes as if from a grandstand. To keep the Greek phalanx as far as possible from their ships, the Persians sallied out from the stockade and marshaled their archers and light-armed troops behind a wall of close-set wicker shields. As the Greeks advanced, the Spartans on the right wing were gradually separated from the rest of the line, swallowed up by a ravine, and lost to sight. Meanwhile the forward motion had brought the other Greeks within range of Persian arrows. As zealous for Athenian preeminence as Themistocles had ever been, Xanthippus decided to go on with or without the Spartans. After telling the men to pass the word down the line, he led a charge that broke through the enemy shields and carried the Greeks to the stockade. At first the Persians resisted, but their lack of defensive armor put them at a disadvantage in hand-to-hand combat. Abandoning the battle line, they turned and fled inside the stockade.

But the Greeks were at their heels. Led by Xanthippus and his Athenians, they burst into the camp and attacked the disorganized pockets of resistance. Now the Persians fought alone: the Ionians and other subject peoples had begun to aid the enemy. It was the long-lost Greek right wing that delivered the final blow. Having struggled over the uneven ground, the Spartans finally worked their way around to the slope above the beached ships, then came pouring over the landward side of the stockade. Many Persians were killed; the rest surrendered or escaped over the passes to Sardis. There they had the unenviable task of reporting the catastrophe to Xerxes himself.

That evening the triumphant Greeks awarded the prize for valor to the Athenian contingent and the individual prize to Hermolycus the *pancratiast*. The Peloponnesians of the center were recognized next, but the Spartans not at all. The larger issue was the fate of the Persian ships. The Greeks did not have enough crews to man them all, yet it was imperative to keep them out of enemy hands. So after stripping the captured triremes of their money chests and other valuables, the Greeks lit a titanic victory bonfire. Timber and pitch flared like torches until the fire consumed even the stockade. The glow against the dark side of Mount Mycale that night was a beacon of victory and liberty for the Greeks of Asia.

Within a few days messengers arrived from Greece to report that the allied army had won a decisive victory over Xerxes' grand army on the plains near Plataea. The great invasion was over: Greece was free. As news spread, envoys from the Greeks in Asia descended on Leotychidas to seek admission to the alliance led by Sparta. If granted, these requests would have embroiled Sparta in overseas wars for years to come, for the Great King would certainly not give up his rich satrapy of Ionia without a bitter fight. Leotychidas therefore made a counterproposal: the Ionians should abandon their cities in or near Asia and immigrate over the sea to their original homeland. The port cities of traitorous Greeks who had surrendered to Xerxes could be cleared out and handed over to the Ionians. Xanthippus and the Athenians opposed the proposal. They stated that Ionia had been colonized long ago from Athens and that no one should rob the Ionians of the cities that they had founded in those far-off days. At their demand, the Greeks of Samos, Lesbos, Chios, and other islands were all sworn into the alliance.

Though late in the season, the Greek fleet, now reinforced by Ionians, set out from Samos on a final mission. Despite the onset of contrary winds they voyaged northward to break Xerxes' bridges. They were too late— storms had already swept the pontoons away. Local informants told Leotychidas that the big cables now lay in Sestos, a city on the European shore of the Hellespont. The high walls of Sestos were also sheltering all of the Persians left in the area. Unwilling to storm the place, Leotychidas declared that the fleet would return to Greece.

Xanthippus and the Athenians parted company with the admiral. Supported by contingents of the new Ionian allies, they remained at the Hellespont after the departure of the Spartans and Peloponnesians. Lacking siege equipment, they settled down to starve the defenders into submission. At last the desperate Persians slipped over the walls by night and escaped into the countryside. Some fell into the hands of Thracian tribesmen, who sacrificed the Persian commander to one of their gods. The Athenians caught most of the rest near a beach called Aegospotami ("Goat Rivers"), about twelve miles from Sestos. Among the prisoners was a Persian governor who had desecrated a Greek sanctuary by having sex with his concubines on sacred ground. Though the Persian offered a king's ransom of three hundred silver talents for himself and his son, Xanthippus had him crucified as if he had been a pirate. As the Athenians voyaged homeward, they carried in the holds of their triremes the immense bridge cables that had for a short time yoked Europe to Asia.

The Athens to which they returned was scarcely recognizable. The Persians had destroyed everything except the houses where their officers were billeted, so the city had to be reconstructed from the ground up. In this vast undertaking Themistocles moved once more to the forefront of Athenian life. The Spartans discouraged the Athenians from rebuilding their city wall on the grounds that it might serve as a Persian stronghold if Xerxes came back. Themistocles had to use all his cunning to distract the Spartans while the entire population of Athens rushed to complete the job. After the victory at Plataea the Greeks had sworn not to rebuild the temples burned by Xerxes: their scorched ruins would forever bear witness to Persian sacrilege. There was no ban, however, on raising new temples. Themistocles dedicated a new sanctuary in the Piraeus and built a temple to Artemis, truly the goddess of best counsel, near his own house in Athens. On the banks of the Ilissus River the Athenians raised their new temple to the god they had not previously worshipped: Boreas the North Wind, destroyer of Persian ships. In these and other holy places they hung the cables from Xerxes' bridges as offerings of gratitude to the gods.

With the city in ruins, Themistocles tried to persuade his fellow citizens to abandon the old site around the Acropolis and rebuild Athens directly on the coast. He failed, but the Assembly did vote to finish constructing a fortified port at the Piraeus, a project that had lain dormant for more than a decade. They also voted to build twenty new triremes each year and offer incentives to attract skilled craftsmen from other cities to immigrate to Athens. All of these initiatives originated with Themistocles.

When the time came to launch the triremes for the second campaigning season after Salamis, the Athenians allotted command of their squadron to Aristides the Just. Four years earlier he had been ostracized after opposing Themistocles' proposal to build a fleet with the silver from Laurium. Now, like most of his countrymen, Aristides embraced the idea that Athens' future lay with the sea. He had won glory in the fighting on Psyttaleia island at Salamis and at the battle of Plataea the previous summer. The Spartans assigned the admiralship of the allied fleet to Pausanias, supreme commander at Plataea, who was acting as regent for Leonidas' young son. Pausanias was a tactician of genius and a dangerous megalomaniac, though that did not become clear till later.

Expanding the range of naval activity, Pausanias first led the fleet to Cyprus and then, having stirred up a rebellion against the Persians throughout the island, cruised around the entire western end of Asia Minor to Byzantium, a Greek colony lying at the gateway to the Black Sea. After capturing Byzantium, the Spartan admiral became increasingly tyrannical and inaccessible even to his own allies. Eventually some of the allied contingents mutinied. The Ionians begged the Athenians to take over the leadership of the fleet. Such an act would ratify the informal arrangement of the previous autumn, when Xanthippus had led a united Athenian and Ionian fleet at Sestos. In addition to sharing a common ancestry, the Ionians put more trust in the Athenians to protect them from reconquest by Persia. Athenians were energetic and adventurous; Spartans (with the exception of the volatile Pausanias, of course) tended to be stolid and earthbound. The universal respect inspired by Aristides also played a part in their decision.

When the government in Sparta sent a new admiral to Byzantium to replace Pausanias, the Ionians refused to take orders from him. The die was cast. The frustrated admiral went home to Sparta, and the Peloponnesian triremes also abandoned the expedition. Aristides remained behind with the fleet of Athenians and Ionians to lay the foundations of a new world order in which Athenians would lead a league of their own.

The Ionians proposed that they and the Athenians form a new naval alliance patterned after the Spartan-led alliance that had won the war against Xerxes. The Spartans had convened their councils at the Isthmus; the Athenians and Ionians would meet on the island of Delos, in the heart of the Aegean. Within the alliance Athens would play the role of hegemon (literally "the one who goes in front") or leader. Athenian generals would command the allied fleet, and Athens would take the lead in all decisions, with the council of allies serving in an advisory capacity. Their mission was simple: perpetual war against the barbarian. The new Athenian alliance would exact revenge on the Persians for all the injuries that they had done to the Greeks.

Because this new alliance was dedicated to naval warfare, it needed something that Sparta's alliance had never required: regular contributions of money and ships. The huge crews of rowers would have to be paid; new triremes would have to be built and old ones repaired. A standing fleet was far more costly than an army to maintain, and it remained a heavy financial burden even when the ships were in port.

To ensure that each ally shouldered a fair share of the burden, the Athenians proposed a system much like the annual tribute of the Persian Empire. Each city or island would be assessed a yearly contribution based on its resources and would pay either in cash or in kind (that is, by sending triremes) as Athens determined. Aristides himself was to make the assessments. Contributions of silver would be sent each spring to Delos, and entrusted to ten Athenian citizens bearing the grandiloquent title of *Hellenotamiai* or "treasurers of the Greeks." The proper name of the new alliance was The Athenians and Their Allies. Later historians dubbed it the Delian League.

Aristides made an initial assessment of tribute that yielded 460 silver talents each year. The amount would grow as more Greeks joined the alliance. The Athenians decreed that those with large fleets, such as the islanders of Samos, Lesbos, Chios, Naxos, and Thasos, would contribute quotas of ships. Other allies possessed only small and antiquated galleys; they paid in silver from the start. When all were in accord, the representatives on Delos swore oaths of allegiance to the new Athenian alliance on behalf of their cities. Then they ceremonially cast iron bars into the sea. This act symbolized their intention that the oaths would endure until the iron rose again. It was a heady moment. Gazing east from Delos, they must have thought the Persian Empire looked big enough to sustain an eternity of pillage and plunder.

To lead the new allied expeditionary force, the Athenian Assembly appointed none of the successful naval commanders of the previous three years—Themistocles, Xanthippus, Aristides—but Cimon, a newcomer to the generalship. It was he who had rallied the city's young horsemen to the naval effort before Salamis. Cimon was a tall, athletic man with a crop of curly hair and a genial, gregarious manner. His father was Miltiades, his mother a Thracian princess. Part of his youth had been spent in his family's fiefdom on the northern shore of the Hellespont, watching the rich argosies sailing downstream from the Black Sea to the Mediterranean.

Now just thirty-one years old, Cimon launched the new alliance on its first campaign. The most pressing target seemed to be Eion, a walled city on European soil that was still in Persian hands. Eion lay on the Strymon River in Thrace, the native land of Cimon's mother, and commanded access to the Thracian gold fields. Cimon's allied forces disembarked and defeated the enemy in a battle outside the city; but then the surviving Persians defied the Greeks from behind Eion's strong fortifications. Cimon promptly imitated the Persians' own penchant for engineering feats. He turned the course of the Strymon so that the river flowed against the city's walls. As they were made of mud brick, the walls began to melt. In despair, the Persian commander committed suicide, and Cimon was able to take the town. Those who had collaborated with the Persians were sold into slavery, and the proceeds were divided among the cities and islands of the alliance. Cimon turned the collaborators' rich farmlands over to Athenian settlers.

This dramatic success brought the first campaigning season of the new alliance to an end. The grateful Athenians set up a war memorial at the main entrance of the Agora. Its inscribed verses compared Cimon and his troops to the Athenians who fought in the Trojan War, "masters of warlike arts and leaders of valiant men." Pleased with their choice of general, the Assembly continued to send Cimon out to lead allied expeditions for fifteen seasons. As his tally of victories mounted, so too did membership in the alliance, which eventually reached a total of about 150 cities and islands.

Cimon's most popular exploit involved him in a quest for sacred relics: the bones of the hero Theseus. The Athenian navy had established itself as a force in the world: it was time to endow it with a patron hero and a creation myth. Theseus—voyager, liberator, slayer of monsters—seemed the right hero. In his youth Theseus had entered the Labyrinth at Knossos and killed the Minotaur, a fearsome beast that was half-man, half-bull. By this daring exploit he had freed Athens from its bondage to King Minos of Crete, who had demanded a regular tribute of Athenian youths and maidens to feed the Minotaur. During his long life Theseus took part in so many other quests and adventures that the phrase "Not without Theseus!" became proverbial. He was supposed to have died on the island of Scyros, but no one knew his burial place.

Several years after the founding of the Delian League, the Delphic Oracle announced that the Athenians must retrieve Theseus' bones and worship him as a divine hero. Cimon undertook the mission. After a long search on Skyros, he happened to see an eagle tearing at a mound of earth. Recognizing the omen, Cimon ordered his men to dig. They uncovered a sarcophagus containing a sword, a spear, and the skeleton of a very big man. With elaborate ceremony Cimon conveyed the bones back to the Piraeus in his flagship. The Athenians welcomed the relics with parades and sacrificial offerings and laid the bones to rest in a sanctuary in Athens devoted to Theseus' cult. An annual festival by the sea commemorated the date when Theseus was supposed to have begun his epic voyage, just as a second festival in the autumn celebrated his return. Each year the steersmen of Athens held a festival in honor of the man from Salamis who had piloted Theseus' galley to Crete and back.

Athenians inherited many myths from the remote past, but when current developments, such as the rise of the navy, seemed to cry out for mythical precedents, they readily invented new ones. Cimon abetted the process. Among the creative artists whom he patronized was a genealogist and mythographer named Pherecydes. He had already traced Cimon's family tree back to the hero Ajax of Salamis. Now Pherecydes rewrote the Theseus myth. In this exciting new account, a desperate Theseus rushes back to the harbor near Knossos after killing the Minotaur and ensures a safe escape by ramming the hulls of the Cretan ships so that they cannot pursue him. A later mythographer named Demon improved the tale by transforming the Minotaur into a Cretan general named Taurus and claiming that

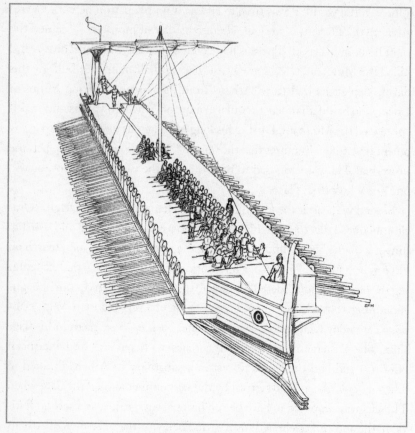

ATHENIAN TROOP CARRIER

Theseus defeated him in a naval battle—the first naval battle in Athenian history!—at the mouth of the harbor. Thus Theseus metamorphosed into a true naval hero, with exploits that foreshadowed naval warfare of Cimon's own day.

In addition to the bones, Athens laid claim to a second tangible relic of Theseus. The little triakontor called the *Delias* was the city's oldest ship. Each spring it conveyed a sacred embassy to Delos, birthplace of Apollo, where the Athenians and other Ionian Greeks honored their ancestral god at a sort of family reunion. In one of the earliest recorded acts of historic preservation, the city's carpenters continually replaced worn-out or rotting timbers in the sacred galley with new wood. The *Delias* had the typical

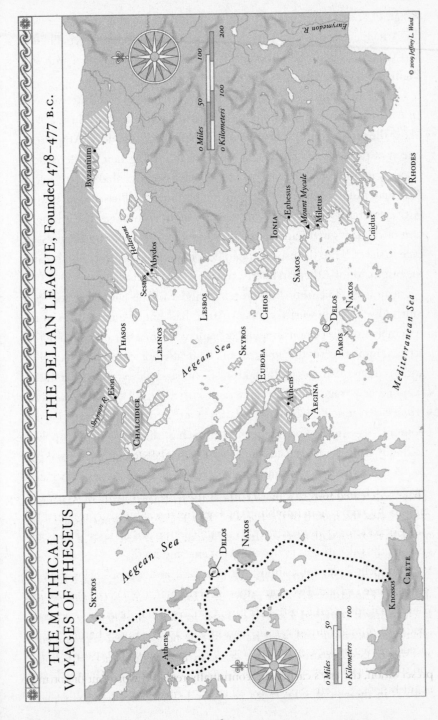

THE DELIAN LEAGUE, Founded 478–477 B.C.

© 2009 Jeffrey L. Ward

Byzantium

Hellespont

Sestos
Abydos

Thasos

Strymon R.
Eion

CHALCIDICE

LEMNOS

LESBOS

Aegean Sea

SKYROS

EUBOEA

Athens

AEGINA

PAROS
NAXOS

DELOS

CHIOS

SAMOS

IONIA

Ephesus
Mount Mycale
Miletus

Cnidus

RHODES

Mediterranean Sea

Eurymedon R.

0 Miles   50   100   200
0 Kilometers   100

THE MYTHICAL
VOYAGES OF THESEUS

SKYROS

Aegean Sea

DELOS

NAXOS

Athens

CRETE

Knossos

0 Miles   50   100
0 Kilometers

design of an Iron Age galley, complete with ram, but that did not prevent the Athenians from identifying it as the very same vessel in which Theseus had voyaged to slay the Minotaur. It was another relic, another link in a chain that bound Athens to an imagined heroic past.

One of the paintings that decorated Theseus' temple was the creation of an Athenian artist named Mikon. The mythical scene showed Theseus deep under the sea, surrounded by tritons and dolphins. The goddess Amphitrite, queen of the sea, was handing a crown to the young hero while Athena stood by as witness. Other additions to Theseus' myth enhanced his role in Athenian history. It was said that during his kingship Theseus had unified Attica, established the first democratic assembly, encouraged the immigration of resident aliens, and stood as champion to the poor and oppressed, even to slaves. Thus the primeval founder of the city's sea power also became the originator of Athenian liberty, unity, and democracy.

Meanwhile Themistocles, the real founder of the navy, was still very much alive. The powerful clans of Attica had united against him in the Assembly, and his personal reputation suffered from a smear campaign that accused him of corruption and treason. In an attempt to restore his standing and to counter Cimon's mythmaking, Themistocles sponsored the production of a new tragedy by the playwright Phrynichus. The play, *Phoenician Women,* recounted the battle of Salamis as a tragedy seen from the Persian point of view. In the opening scene a eunuch of the Persian court spoke a soliloquy while arranging cushions in the council chamber of the royal palace. A chorus of wailing women, the grieving widows of Xerxes' Phoenician mariners, lamented their fate. Themistocles thus reminded his fellow citizens of his own role in humbling the Persians at sea. He also presented the story of Salamis on a stage that was usually dominated by tales of gods and heroes, thus elevating it to the realms of epic and myth.

Phrynichus' play sank almost without trace, and Themistocles' political career shared its fate. Two years after the performance of *Phoenician Women,* the Athenians voted to ostracize him. Ostracism did not always mean the end of a man's political career: Xanthippus and Aristides had both succeeded in regaining power after returning to Athens from ostracism. But no such happy future awaited Themistocles. Midway through his ten-year banishment, vengeful Spartans and envious Athenians stirred up accusations against him that led to formal criminal charges of treason. The Assembly summoned Themistocles back to Athens to stand trial.

Rather than face a jury of his fickle fellow citizens, Themistocles fled over land and sea, pursued by Athenian officials across the Peloponnese and then to Corcyra, eastward through the mountains of northern Greece to Macedon, and finally by ship to the territory of the Persian Empire, the only haven where he could feel safe from the long arm of the Athenian law. To save his life, Themistocles surrendered himself to the Great King. The victor of Salamis and father of Athenian naval power thus ended his days as a trophy of a Persian monarch, whom he served as a semicaptive governor of a few Greek cities in Asia Minor.

Themistocles died an outlaw, still under a charge of treason. His children were therefore refused permission to bring his bones back to Athens. No monument was raised or funeral oration spoken in his native land. Many years passed before an Athenian finally wrote a proper eulogy for the founder of the navy: "It was he who first ventured to tell the Athenians that their future was on the sea. Thus he at once began to join in laying the foundations of their empire." The writer was Thucydides, a historian born within a few years of Themistocles' death. "He was particularly remarkable at looking into the future and seeing there the hidden possibilities for good or evil. To sum him up in a few words, it may be said that through force of genius and speed of action this man was supreme at doing precisely the right thing at precisely the right moment."

With Themistocles gone, Cimon dominated Athenian affairs unchallenged. Year after year he held the generalship, campaigning with the fleet during the summer months and keeping open house for distinguished visitors and common citizens alike when he came home from the wars. Despite his easy sociability, Cimon cherished his own ambitious vision of his city's future. And his model, strange to say, was Sparta.

Alone among the Greeks, Spartan citizens remained in a perpetual state of military readiness throughout their adult lives. In order to control hostile helots and other subject peoples, Spartans of all ranks right up to the kings had become permanently militarized. Their constant training made them the most feared fighting force in the Greek world. Cimon admired the Spartans without reserve: he even named one of his twin sons Lacedaemonius or

"The Spartan." He also perceived in Sparta a way of life—the city as armed camp—that the Athenians would have to emulate if they meant to remain leaders of the Delian League.

Under Cimon's charismatic leadership, Athenian society became "navalized" from top to bottom. Before Salamis, citizens of the lowest census class, the thetes, had never been compelled to train for military service at all. Now they took to the sea in thousands every spring, pulling the oars or learning the craft of lookouts, coxswains, or steersmen. The hoplites were also brought into the rotation, serving as marines on the triremes or transported overseas to fight on foreign soil. The richest Athenian citizens joined the naval effort as trierarchs—the commanders and financial sponsors of the triremes.

To make the process of navalization complete, it became customary for the Athenians to choose as political leaders, not lawgivers or orators, but generals. Though power rested ultimately with the popular Assembly, executive authority at Athens was in the hands of ten annually elected generals or *strategoi*. They were true general officers, overseeing all matters pertaining to war: the navy, the army, the fortifications, and at times even diplomacy. At the controversial dramatic festival when young Sophocles first competed against Aeschylus, the generals led by Cimon even served as judges in the theater.

Ten generals were elected each year, one from each Attic tribe. Themistocles had been elected by his fellow citizens of the fourth tribe, Leontis; Xanthippus and Pericles by the fifth tribe, Akamantis; and Cimon by the sixth tribe, Oineus. These men, like Miltiades before them, had brought immense prestige to the generalship, and it was only through military or naval command that an ambitious citizen could be sure of gaining influence in Athens. Thus a political "rule by generals" was established that was to endure for a century.

While Athens and its navy prospered, enthusiasm for the alliance began to ebb here and there among the member states. For some, the endless running war with the Persians seemed an unreasonable burden. No Persian ships had been seen in the Aegean for years. The outcome of this discontent was a reluctance to serve or contribute in the timely, enthusiastic manner that Athens expected and that their oaths required.

Some Athenian generals handled the recalcitrant allies harshly, but Cimon took a different tack. He was always friendly and encouraged allied cities to choose the kind of contribution that best suited them. Most voluntarily withdrew from active service in the annual naval campaigns and turned the empty hulls of their triremes over to Athens; from that time forward they paid a tribute of silver each year to the allied treasury. Cimon was affable where his colleagues were severe, but in both cases the result was the same. As campaigning seasons came and went, the tradition of military service and competence waned among the allies, while growing ever stronger in Athens.

Keeping the alliance together and the treasury filled required an iron will. Almost from the beginning the Athenians found it necessary to wage war not only on the Persian Empire but also on other Greeks. Their argument was a simple one: all those who reaped the benefits of the Athenian alliance—freedom of the seas and freedom from Persian aggression—should join and contribute. Some islands and cities were forced to join against their will. Others, such as the rich island of Naxos, tried to withdraw from the alliance after a number of years, only to have the allied fleet descend upon their shores, blockade their port, and treat them as dangerous rebels. The Athenians took full advantage of these conflicts. On Skyros they expelled the original piratical inhabitants and resettled the island with colonists drawn from Athens' own booming population. On Thasos the Athenians fought with their allies for control of local mines. By the end of the war the islanders were forced to surrender both their fleet and their mining rights to Athens. The annual yield was a staggering eighty silver talents.

Some Athenians were undoubtedly troubled by these brutal campaigns against fellow Greeks, the very people whose liberty they had pledged to defend. A new threat in the eastern Mediterranean, however, seemed to justify the strong measures that kept the alliance unified. Fourteen years after Salamis the Persians began to assemble another huge fleet and army for a new expedition against the Greeks. Xerxes could no longer ignore the successes of the Delian League and the erosion of his western frontier. He would mount a Persian naval offensive to check the advance of the Athenians and their allies. Rousing himself temporarily from his preoccupation with harem intrigues, Xerxes gave the word. The mustering point for men and ships was to be a plain beside the Eurymedon River, on the southern coast of Asia Minor.

To forestall a Persian advance into the Aegean, Cimon assembled the allied fleet at the southwestern cape of Asia Minor near the ancient Greek city of Cnidus, sacred to Aphrodite. He intended to carry an army of fighting men in his triremes and decided to modify the vessels so that the troops could fight more easily from the decks during any naval battle that might lie ahead. Thanks to painstaking maintenance, many triremes from Themistocles' shipbuilding campaign were still in service. Their light, open construction made them fast and maneuverable, but they were ill adapted for carrying large numbers of troops. Under Cimon's instructions, the shipwrights spanned the hulls with overall decking across the tops of the rowing frames. Now a full complement of rowers could ply their oars below deck, while dozens of hoplites and javelin throwers could be accommodated above.

When the alterations had been made, Cimon started eastward for the Eurymedon River with an Athenian and allied fleet of 250 triremes. After cruising through the turquoise-blue waters off Caria and Lycia, the fleet skirted the little chain of Chelidonian Islands and passed beyond the realm of Athenian influence. Ahead of them loomed the mysterious mountain of the Chimera, home to a mythical fire-breathing monster, where by night mysterious flames could be seen spouting from the rocky heights. Learning that the Persians at the Eurymedon were expecting a fleet of reinforcements any day, Cimon prepared for an immediate attack. After capturing the city of Phaselis, the allied fleet crossed the Gulf of Antalya and camped for the night within striking distance of the Persian base.

Xerxes' fleet was moored at the mouth of the Eurymedon River, a broad stream fed by the melting snows of the Taurus Mountains. The Great King had appointed his own son Tithraustes as admiral. While he was still awaiting the arrival of reinforcements, the horizon suddenly filled with the black hulls and white spray of an approaching fleet: not friendly Phoenicians but Greeks. In a panic, the admiral first ordered his Cyprian and Cilician triremes to crowd into the river mouth for safety. Realizing that the fleet was now forced into a trap of his own making, Tithraustes reversed his decision and ordered all the ships to sea. So the hundreds of vessels rowed out into open water and formed a battle line.

As the leading ships in the two fleets collided, the shock proved too much for the inexperienced Persians. Most turned and dashed for shore. The Greeks chased them into the shallows. The first Persian crews to reach land spilled out of their vessels and ran. Piling up hull against hull, the entire mass of ships fell prey to their attackers. By one estimate Cimon captured two hundred triremes over and above the vessels that escaped or sank.

Meanwhile the Persians had marshaled their army and marched down to the beach. Cimon's men were hot and tired from their struggle across the ships' decks, but the hoplites made it clear that they were ready for more. At Cimon's command the Greeks jumped down onto the sand and ran toward the Persians, just as an earlier Athenian army had followed Cimon's father Miltiades across the plain at Marathon. Now Cimon's foresight in bringing as many troops as possible reaped its reward. Little by little the Greeks gained ground, and in the end the battle became a rout. The Athenians and their allies pursued the Persians all the way back to their camp. The haul of booty from the pavilions and baggage train was immense.

In Cimon's eyes, however, the fight was not over. Leaving some troops at the camp to guard the plunder, he ordered the rest back to the ships, rallied the crews, and rowed east in search of the last remnant of Persian naval power, the eighty ships from Phoenicia. Cimon moved so quickly that he outstripped the news of his victory at the Eurymedon. He caught the unsuspecting Phoenicians at sea and captured or destroyed them all.

When the Athenian fleet arrived back at the Piraeus, towing the captured enemy triremes behind their own, the city gave Cimon a hero's welcome. His achievement that summer rivaled the victory at Salamis and in some ways surpassed it. Cimon had carried the fight against the Great King through Persian waters and onto Persian soil. He had performed the unparalleled feat of winning two battles on the same day, one at sea and another on land. And while a large part of Xerxes' royal navy had survived Salamis, Cimon's destruction of the Persian fleet had been complete. Sweetest of all, none of the credit had to be shared with the Spartans or other Peloponnesians.

Xerxes did not long survive the humiliation of his army and fleet at the Eurymedon River. That winter Persian ministers assassinated the king in his own palace. Xerxes' son Artaxerxes succeeded to the throne. The new Great King was an able administrator but not a conqueror. His reign began a period of conservative retrenchment in place of perennial wars and expansion.

With the treasure won during the campaign, Cimon and the Athenians beautified their city as never before. In the Agora they planted majestic plane trees with rich green foliage and spreading boughs dappled white and brown. The deep shade gave the once-barren market and civic center the airy coolness of a royal Persian pleasure park. Also in the Agora a new colonnaded portico or stoa was built to house paintings of historic Athenian battles: the world's first public art museum. The painted stoa became a popular gathering place and ultimately gave rise to the term "Stoics" for a school of philosophers who met under its colonnade.

On the Acropolis engineers and masons raised a magnificent buttressed wall to fortify the south slope of the rock and uphold a broad flat terrace on the summit, fit site for a future temple. At the Academy or grove of Akademos outside the city walls, Cimon improved the training grounds for Athens' young athletes with aqueducts, fountains, shady groves, and running tracks. At the Piraeus a new temple was erected to honor a divine hero just added to the Athenian pantheon. His name was Eurymedon.

Appropriating Themistocles' naval vision, Cimon began the task of joining Athens to the sea with long walls. Ultimately these massive fortifications would run from the city gates right down to the Piraeus and the beach at Phaleron, almost four miles away. Cimon paid for the foundations, laying down tons of rubble in marshy areas between the city and the sea.

The Persians had razed Athens to the ground, but within two decades the city was reborn. Xerxes' attempt to crush the Athenians had the paradoxical effect of spurring them to new heights of achievement. Cimon presided over the transformation of a small city-state into the leader of a mighty maritime league. The astonishing transformation of character in the ordinary Athenian was an outcome that he had not foreseen. The city was becoming a vast urban stage decorated with sumptuous scenery, and the men of the *demos,* veterans of many successful campaigns at sea, were at last ready to take the direction of the drama into their own hands.

CHAPTER 7

Boundless Ambition

[462–446 B.C.]

I assert that the poor and the common people are right to prevail against the well-born and the rich, since it is the common people who propel the ships and empower the city.

—Xenophon the Orator

THE OAR AND ROWING PAD OF THE COMMON CITIZEN OF ATHENS might seem less poetical and glorious than the hoplite's shield and spear, but all the world now knew that the city's power rested on swift triremes and strong crews. Abroad, the Athenian commoner ruled the seas. At home, he was still a second-class citizen. The law allowed to him a vote in the Assembly, but he was barred from holding public office. The pressures of his daily work often kept him away from Assembly meetings. Athens was in fact less a democracy than a commonwealth governed by the richest citizens. All archons and generals came from the ranks of the wealthy, and the bar of property qualification was set so high that even the ten thousand hoplites were excluded. The common citizen could do no more than choose his leaders: leadership itself was denied him.

Ever since Salamis a council of aristocrats and wealthy citizens had been steadily encroaching on the power of the democratic Council and Assembly. It was called the council of the Areopagus or "Hill of Ares," an exclusive body of men who had previously served as archons. As members-for-life in the Areopagus, about three hundred of these upper-class citizens exercised what influence they could on Athenian politics. They held their meetings on a spur of the Acropolis sacred to the war god, and from their high perch they looked down in every sense on the rest of Athens.

In the years after the victory at Eurymedon, while Cimon was engaged in a war over the markets and mines of Thasos, the radical democratic element in Athens at last found an effective champion. He was Ephialtes, a citizen who had already established his credentials as a political leader by undertaking a naval command. As a general he had led a fleet to the eastern Mediterranean; as a public figure he had acquired an unassailable reputation for being upright and incorruptible.

Ephialtes was among the few Athenians who could find their own names in Homer's *Iliad* and *Odyssey*. These stories told how a giant named Ephialtes set out to scale Mount Olympus, piling Pelion atop Ossa in his ambition to dethrone the gods. The giant was a true son of the sea. His mother, a young maiden in love with Poseidon, had conceived twin sons by pouring sea water into her lap. Once they had grown to titanic size, Ephialtes and his brother started their revolt against the gods by capturing mighty Ares and binding him in chains. As had happened before with Cimon and Theseus, the ancient myths were again shedding a luster of divine prophecy on daily events in Athens. Once the contemporary Athenian Ephialtes began a political revolution, his challenge to the rulers who sat on the Hill of Ares must have seemed foreordained even to his opponents.

Ephialtes began by hauling individual Areopagites into court on accusations of official misconduct, using judicial procedures to achieve political ends. Having weakened the venerable council, he launched a broadside attack on its accumulated privileges and prerogatives. New laws reassigned them to the democratic Council of Five Hundred, the Assembly, or the jury courts. In the end the Areopagus was left with nothing but jurisdiction over two kinds of cases: homicides and injuries to the sacred olive trees. In a grand symbolic act, Ephialtes uprooted the tablets of the law from their traditional place of seclusion on the Acropolis and carried them down to a new site in the Agora, where they could be read and consulted by all.

Among the Greeks revolution usually meant *stasis,* violent civil strife between factions. But the radical changes precipitated by Ephialtes were carried through, not by armed mobs in the streets, but by an orderly show of hands in the Assembly. It was a bloodless revolution—until a lone assassin murdered Ephialtes himself. The killer was never caught, but it became known that he was a man from Tanagra in Boeotia, acting on behalf of parties unknown. In the ancient myth of the giants, the Olympian gods shot out Ephialtes' eyes with arrows and roped him with vipers to a pillar in hell. The Areopagites and their aristocratic sympathizers must have wished even worse torments on the man who had robbed them of their powers. But to most Athenians, Ephialtes died a hero.

The torch of radical democracy was passed forward to Pericles, the son of Xanthippus, who pressed ahead with the reforms. A decade earlier, when he was still in his twenties, Pericles had launched his public career by sponsoring the first production of Aeschylus' *Persians*. Like Phrynichus' *Phoenician Women*, Aeschylus' tragedy presented the battle of Salamis from the Persian point of view and made the Athenian victory seem part of a divine punishment of the Great King. Aeschylus was not only Athens' first playwright of genius but a veteran of Salamis, and he brought the battle to life with his vivid poetry. Two lines of the play hinted at Pericles' democratic convictions. Concerning the Athenians, the Persian queen mother asked, "Who shepherds them and rules their host?" And the chorus of Persian elders replied: "They are not called slaves or subjects to any man."

Now in his early thirties, Pericles had naval achievements of his own to celebrate. After the victory at the Eurymedon River he led a fleet of fifty Athenian triremes on an expedition to the eastern Mediterranean. As heir to Ephialtes' revolution, Pericles took advantage of Athens' brimming treasury to institute pay for jurors. Thanks to him, poor citizens were now able to leave their daily work to serve on immense juries of up to 501 that dealt out justice around the Agora. Thus the judiciary was democratized also. And six years after Ephialtes' death, the office of archon was officially opened to the citizens of the hoplite class. Eventually the archonship was even held by thetes.

One prominent opponent tried in vain to stem the onrush of radical democracy. Cimon made every effort in the Assembly to restore the status of the Areopagus. With his naval campaigns he had done even more than Themistocles to empower the lower classes, but he had not foreseen the consequences. Nor had Cimon anticipated the change in Athenian feeling that suddenly made his admiration for Sparta appear treasonous. A catastrophic earthquake had devastated Spartan territory and touched off a rebellion of the Messenian helots, but the Spartans had brusquely dismissed

Athenian efforts to aid them. Angered by Spartan mistrust and suspicion, the Assembly repudiated the alliance that Cimon held so dear. He had often told them that Athens and Sparta were in truth two horses yoked to the same chariot. Should either member of the team go lame, all Greece would suffer.

In opposing the city's spirit of revolution, Cimon suddenly seemed irreconcilably at odds with his fellow citizens. In the spring after Ephialtes carried his democratic reforms, a vote of ostracism sent Cimon into exile. Only six years had passed since the victory at the Eurymedon River had seemingly put Cimon at the summit of Athens' pantheon of heroes. His father, Miltiades, had suffered a similar fate within a year of his victory at Marathon. There was no question that the Athenians often dealt more harshly with their leaders than they did with their enemies.

The Assembly, now in an expansive mood, was willing to reconsider an alliance that had been offered some years earlier, an alliance that would embroil them in a war more distant than any Athens had yet undertaken. Shortly after the death of Xerxes a rebellion broke out in Egypt. Led by a Libyan king named Inarus, a descendant of the last native Egyptian pharaohs, the population of the Nile delta had driven out their Persian governors and tax collectors. Inarus sent envoys to beg the Athenians for aid. If they would send a fleet to support his war of liberation, he offered to give them a share in running the country and monetary rewards far greater than the cost of the expedition.

The possibility of an alliance with Egypt intrigued Aeschylus, who loved to make references to remote parts of the world in his plays. While the Assembly was debating Inarus' invitation, Aeschylus presented a tragedy called *The Suppliants* that intertwined a mythical plot with a specific political agenda and a general plea for helping foreigners in distress. Just as he had done in *Persians* ten years earlier, Aeschylus gave the Athenian audience a geography lesson. He reminded them of the Egyptian cities of Memphis and Canopus, the remote land of the Ethiopians, and the fabulous wheat harvests of North Africa.

From its opening lines, *The Suppliants* conjured up images of the Nile delta with its many streams, papyrus plants, buzzing insects, and sand dunes. The play even included a reference to nomadic women riding camels. The chorus sang of the sea voyage from Greece to Egypt, a simple matter of crossing the Aegean, passing Asia Minor, continuing onward to Cyprus, and then turning south. Aeschylus' plot hinged on the ancestral ties that linked Egyptians and Greeks as descendants of the mythical brothers Aegyptus and Danaus. On the surface the play seemed timeless, and it would in fact endure for ages to come. But like most Athenian art, *The Suppliants* also reflected the current topics of debate in the Assembly and Agora at the moment of its creation.

For two years after the democratic revolution the Assembly was engaged in creating new alliances with Argos, Thessaly, and Megara in case of Spartan aggression. Once these friendships were formalized, the people felt ready to undertake more distant ventures. With Egypt still on their minds, the Athenians fitted out a large number of ships, called for contingents from the maritime allies, and dispatched a fleet of two hundred triremes to Cyprus under a general named Charitimides. The island was still bitterly divided between Phoenician cities that paid tribute to the Persians, and Greek cities struggling to maintain their independence.

Soon after the Athenians arrived in Cyprus, messengers from King Inarus brought an appeal for immediate help against the Persian satrap and his army of occupation. The entire western delta was now in rebel hands, and a crisis seemed imminent. The Athenians broke off their campaign on Cyprus and headed south. The Nile River made its presence felt a full day out from their landfall. As the Greek lookouts cast sounding leads into the water, they brought up thick mud from a depth of about sixty-five feet. This silt had been pushed far out to sea by the river's annual floods. Soon they caught their first glimpse of the long sand dunes broken by gaps where the river channels flowed out to the sea. From here the two hundred triremes began to traverse the immense wedge of land on which Greeks had bestowed a name borrowed from the triangular fourth letter of their alphabet: delta.

To the Athenians, used to rocky hills and dry summers, this flat green world was intoxicatingly strange. Water mingled with black mud, teeming with life. The air was humid and fresh; the earth smelled like a garden. From the decks of their triremes the Greeks looked out over a boundless expanse of papyrus, hemp, sedge, and lotus: heavy vegetation never touched by snow or frost. Above the rippling water plants rose slender palms, their crests nodding in the steady northerly breezes. Flocks of wild ducks, geese, and ibises burst into view, startled by the passing of the ships. Squealing hippopotami ("river horses" to the Greeks), challenged their passage. Nile perch and other monstrous fish swam alongside the triremes in the froth stirred up by the oars. Mosquitoes tortured everyone who could not get a sleeping net.

The long line of triremes shared the narrow channels with local craft from a tradition immeasurably older than anything the Athenians knew. They saw cargo boats built of short planks laid together like bricks in a wall, rafts made of bundled papyrus, and flat-bottomed punts propelled through shallows with long poles. Strange, strange: a man leaned from a papyrus skiff to harpoon a crocodile; a calm bare-breasted woman squatted at the steering oar of a passing barge; funeral barques bore wailing mourners and mummified corpses. On shore the people drank mugs of frothy beer instead of wine. Strange.

In the delta the allies from Samos, Lesbos, and Chios came into their own. Many steersmen from those islands knew Egypt well. Their forefathers had been among the Greek "bronze men" who had served the pharaohs for more than two centuries as mercenary troops and later as traders. Like the Aeginetans, the Ionians had been granted an emporium on the Canopic branch of the Nile. The Greek merchants named their city Naukratis ("Ship Power"), and the Egyptians allowed the little expatriate community to build temples to their gods.

The Athenians and their allies were cheered by news from the rebel king Inarus, whose army had just won a great victory near Naukratis. Following the battle the Persian survivors had fled upriver toward the ancient city of Memphis. Soon afterward Charitimides arrived with his fleet; Inarus and the Egyptian troops boarded the Greek triremes and set off in pursuit. Up to now the Persians had cruised about at will with their own trireme fleet. The Nile was the highway of Egypt. Whoever controlled the river controlled the entire country.

The Canopic branch was too narrow for fleet actions. Above the delta, however, where all the branches were united in one stream, the great river broadened dramatically. Here the Greeks caught their first view of the Great

Pyramid, rearing up amid attendant tombs and temples on the western bank. Though two thousand years old, it was still the largest and tallest structure on the face of the earth. From Giza southward the river matched the monuments in majesty, spreading more than a mile from bank to bank. In some places and seasons the Nile was in fact wider than either the Hellespont or the Salamis strait. Much of it was shallow, but the triremes with their shallow drafts could navigate the river easily.

In one of the broad reaches upriver from the delta, Persian triremes at last came into view. Though only eighty in number, they had an initial advantage as they swept down on the Greeks with the force of the current behind them. But at Salamis the Athenians had been more than a match for the Egyptians in Persian service, and they faced them now with two additional decades of training behind them. In the final tally twenty Persian ships were sunk, thirty were captured, and the remaining thirty managed to escape, either passing through the delta to the sea or fleeing southward to Upper Egypt, where some Persian garrisons still held their ground.

Nearby lay the greatest prize of all: Memphis. There the Persians had maintained a royal navy yard called the House of Boats, staffed with thousands of workers. The harbor was crowded with ferryboats, fishing craft, cargo vessels, and transports, and the city walls rose almost from the water's edge. Memphis had fallen at least once before to an army in ships: an invading Nubian king had brought his tall-masted warships right up to the walls. Some of his men swarmed across to the battlements on the yardarms, while others reached shore on pontoons made of local boats.

Inarus and his Greek allies enjoyed the great advantage of having friends within the walls—most Egyptians resented the Persians just as they had resented other foreign rulers. In short order the rebel army liberated two-thirds of the city. The remaining Persians and their Egyptian collaborators retreated through the streets to a stronghold that the Greeks called the White Fortress. Except for this fortified place, all of Lower Egypt from Memphis to the sea was now in the hands of Inarus and his Greek allies. Not only was this the richest and most populous part of the country, but the Greek fleet at Memphis could act like a stopper in a bottle, taxing or impounding cargoes from higher up the Nile as they made their way to the sea.

The Athenians proudly considered themselves to be champions of freedom, but they had not undertaken the expedition solely for the cause of Egyptian liberty. In terms of wealth, Egypt stood third among the twenty satrapies of the Persian Empire. Only Babylonia and India surpassed Egypt's annual tribute of seven hundred silver talents, a greater amount than the Athenians collected each year from their entire maritime alliance. Egypt also provided 120,000 bushels of grain annually to feed the Persian army. And it was through Egypt that the Ethiopians had been accustomed to send their own tribute of ebony logs, elephant tusks, and unrefined gold. By wresting Egypt from the Persians, Inarus and his Greek allies had deprived the Great King of a fortune in annual income, some of which would now find its way to Athens.

But Egypt meant more to the Athenians than treasure. A century before the Persian Wars, the famous Athenian lawgiver Solon had voyaged in his own trading ship from Athens to Egypt and had brought back history and wisdom gleaned from priests in the cities of Saïs and Thebes. Generations later, when the Athenian philosopher Plato wrote his famous myth of Atlantis (in truth an allegory on the evils of maritime empire), he claimed that Egyptian priests were the keepers of the most ancient historical traditions. Egypt offered Athens wheat, papyrus, mathematics, medicine, and the world's richest tradition of stone sculpture and architecture.

Most of the Greek fleet returned to the Aegean at the end of its successful first year of campaigning, along with the first loads of booty that Inarus had promised. Charitimides stayed behind to command the Greek allied forces. The army of several thousand hoplites would besiege the White Fortress in Memphis, while the fleet of forty triremes controlled shipping and transported troops up and down the Nile.

In order to support its mission in Egypt, the Athenians needed a naval base on the coast of Lebanon or Palestine. They could avail themselves of well-known landing places as far as Cyprus, but as yet they had no secure way station where the crews could rest on the long haul from Cyprus to the delta. The success of any maritime empire built on oared ships depended on its control not of large tracts of territory but of strategically situated coastal sites that offered fresh water, provisions, and protection from bad weather and enemy attacks. The Phoenician cities of Sidon and Tyre held much of the mainland coast, and they were still loyal to Persia. Fifty miles south of these urban centers, however, the Athenians found an isolated and tempting target.

The ancient town of Dor stood atop a rocky promontory, protected on its landward side by a marshy swale that formed a natural moat. Beyond the coastal lowlands rose the majestic ridge of Mount Carmel. To the south of Dor a chain of islets enclosed a lagoon and a sandy beach. An unfailing freshwater spring welled up at the sea's edge. Taking advantage of Dor's distance from its rightful master, the King of Sidon, the Athenians came ashore and seized the place. As they settled into the little hilltop town of straight streets, with its Persian-built fortifications and Phoenician dye pits for the purpling of cloth, these adventurers were establishing on the Great King's doorstep the most remote outpost of the seemingly invincible Athenian navy.

After several years of Athenian engagement in Egypt, Aeschylus took notice of the great venture once again, this time in his famous trilogy the *Oresteia.* When his hero Orestes cried out to Athena for help, the goddess was imagined a long way off, fighting alongside her friends in North Africa. Aeschylus also meditated on justice and civil strife, on wars and wealth. His verses warned the Athenian audience to revere justice, comparing a prosperous but unjust man to a ship carrying a rich cargo through a stormy sea. Athena herself issued a commandment against civil strife at home: "Let our wars rage on abroad, with all their force, to satisfy our powerful lust for fame."

When news of the Egyptian rebellion reached Susa, King Artaxerxes considered how best to deal with the Athenians. It would be years before he could assemble a force big enough to drive them out of Egypt. In the meantime striking a blow closer to Athens itself seemed worth trying. Fitting out a royal embassy with chests of gold from his treasury, Artaxerxes sent an envoy from his court all the way to Sparta, with orders to bribe the Spartans into launching a war against the Athenians. An attack from the Peloponnese would surely force the Athenians to withdraw from Egypt. It seemed inconceivable to the Great King that Athens could wage war on two fronts at once.

The Spartans showed no interest in the Persian gold. Their naval allies, however, were ready to attack Athens with or without bribes. The Corinthians were angry that the Athenians had sided against them in a border war with Megara, while the islanders of Aegina bitterly resented the eclipse that their own navy and shipping had suffered. The Athenians aimed a preemptive strike at a Peloponnesian port called Halieis, but Corinthian hoplites drove them back to their ships. Then Sparta's maritime allies assembled a fleet and engaged the Athenians in battle near the rocky islet of Cecryphaleia in the Saronic Gulf. Fighting on their own element this time, the Athenians were victorious. After the battle they vengefully followed the Aeginetans back to their island stronghold. There the Athenian navy won an even greater victory, capturing seventy enemy triremes and setting up a blockade of Aegina Harbor. Crossing back to the Piraeus, the Athenian general Leocrates mounted siege machinery on the decks of his triremes and then returned to assault the Aeginetans' city walls.

The siege lasted for months, but neither Sparta nor the Peloponnesian allies could do anything to raise it. King Artaxerxes summoned his envoy back to Persia, his mission a complete failure. Nothing could check the Athenians. They were still entrenched in Egypt, and they now had a pretext for conquering their old rivals on Aegina. Never had Athens known such a year of fighting. Never before had there been such a heavy toll of dead and so many heroes to bury along the Sacred Way.

That year the monument over the common tomb was a long wall of names inscribed on stone slabs. Generals and even a prophet were listed democratically alongside the rank and file. Above the names, in a mixture of grief and pride, the people had set inscriptions to tell of the campaigns that had claimed the men's lives. "These died fighting in Cyprus, in Egypt, in Phoenicia, in Halieis, in Aegina, at Megara, in the same year." A few months earlier the men on those lists had crowded into the Assembly to hear the debates on the far-flung campaigns and to raise their hands in the voting. Their boundless ambition was equaled only by their readiness to pay the price.

Back in Athens, the hostilities with Corinth and Aegina made the completion of the Long Walls to the Piraeus seem an urgent matter. Before Cimon's ostracism, he had stabilized the wet ground west of Athens, preparing a solid base for the wall that would run to the Piraeus. A second wall would connect the city to the old port of Phaleron. With the wealth of Egypt and the Thracian mines filling the treasury, the Assembly was now in a position to vote the necessary funds for a building project greater than any other in Athenian history. The scale was heroic. Eight miles of walls were to be constructed, sixteen feet thick at the base and soaring to a formidable height. The vertiginous walkway along the top of the wall would be twelve feet broad. Stone blocks would form the lower courses, bricks the upper, and the plan also called for projecting towers. Once completed, the walls would make Athenian access to the sea as secure as if the city had been an island: the realization of Themistocles' dream.

The resumption of work on the Long Walls jolted Athens' oligarchs into action. A small group of upper-class citizens still hoped to destroy the radical democracy. These men feared that once Athens was permanently and inseparably linked to its navy by the Long Walls, the common people would never be unseated from their rule. Before the walls had been completed, the oligarchs sent secret messages to a Spartan army that was at that moment encamped not far from the frontiers of Attica. The oligarchs invited the Spartans to attack Athens, promising to assist in the overthrow of the current regime. In their own minds these men were patriots, pledged to restore the ancestral constitution.

Somehow the plot was betrayed, and the entire Assembly was warned of the danger. The hoplites were as eager to defend their democracy and the Long Walls as were the rowers in the fleet. The full army of Athens marched out and confronted the Spartans on a field near Tanagra in Boeotia. The Spartans won a narrow victory, but the Athenian citizens had not fought in vain. Discouraged by the unexpected resistance, the Spartans gave up any further idea of interfering with the Long Walls and marched home.

The Athenians wanted revenge. Their hotheaded general Tolmides (his name meant "Son of the Bold") proposed that an Athenian fleet should carry out a novel expedition around the Peloponnese to punish the Spartans and force them for once onto the defensive. Coasting along from one target to the next, the Athenians would destroy fortifications, collect booty, and spread terror. Before local defenders could reach the scene, the raiders would have boarded their ships and moved on. In short, Tolmides proposed that the Athenians act exactly like pirates. The Assembly voted Tolmides a fleet and a military complement of one thousand hoplites, but his scheme was so popular that many young citizens joined as volunteers. The trireme design

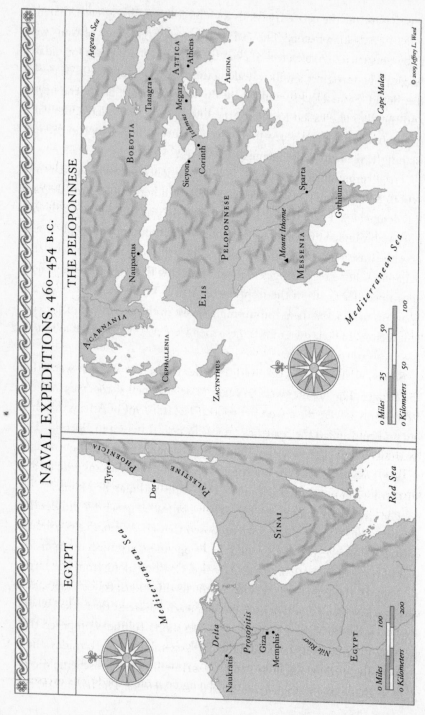

NAVAL EXPEDITIONS, 460–454 B.C.

THE PELOPONNESE

EGYPT

© 2009 Jeffrey L. Ward

that Cimon had introduced before the Eurymedon campaign allowed extra hoplites to be accommodated on the wide decks.

With fifty triremes Tolmides cruised south to Cape Malea. After rounding this dangerous promontory, the fleet descended without warning on the Spartan port of Gythium and set fire to the docks. The marauders then continued their hit-and-run tactics all the way around the Peloponnese. Before returning to Athens that autumn, Tolmides landed at the seaside town of Naupactus in the Corinthian Gulf and turned it over to a band of Messenian rebels. These men had been recently expelled from their homeland by the Spartans. From Naupactus the refugees would be a thorn in Sparta's side for years to come. Tolmides' expedition proved so profitable on so many levels that during each of the next two summers the Assembly sent Pericles west with a fleet to keep up the tradition.

Of all Tolmides' successes, none gave more happiness to Athenian shipwrights than the alliance he concluded with the islanders of Zacynthus, a little paradise of white cliffs and sandy coves. At the bottom of one of its lakes the island had a black treasure: tar. In the continual battle against rot, decay, and the teredo, a coating of tar could protect a trireme's planking even more effectively than pitch from pine trees. At Zacynthus the tar was dredged up from a depth of twelve feet in the lake using leafy myrtle branches tied to the ends of poles. After being collected in pots, it could be carried to the beach and swabbed directly onto the hulls, or shipped home for storage in the Navy Yard at the Piraeus.

Bad news from Egypt put a temporary check on Athens' campaigns in Greece. For six years the Athenians had shared the rule of the country with the rebel king Inarus. But Artaxerxes, though slow to act, felt that he could not afford to let Egypt go. A massive Persian counterattack overcame both the Egyptians and their Greek allies. The victorious Persians besieged the Athenian and Ionian troops on the island of Prosopitis in the Nile delta and, after Persian engineers drained the channels surrounding the island, captured or killed them all. Meanwhile the Great King's force of Phoenician triremes ambushed and annihilated a relief fleet from Athens as it was entering the easternmost mouth of the Nile.

After the unexpected failure of the Egyptian venture, Pericles and the other generals attempted for the time being no more expeditions overseas.

When Cimon returned from ostracism, he led an allied fleet of two hundred ships once again into the east, undaunted by the recent events on the Nile. One hundred forty triremes stayed with Cimon in Cyprus, while the remaining sixty went south to aid the continuing resistance to the Persians in the Nile delta. One Athenian trireme coasted westward from the delta on a sacred mission. Sent by Cimon himself, a deputation went ashore to consult the oracle of Zeus Ammon at the oasis of Siwa, eight or nine days from the sea. After their long journey, Ammon's prophetic voice ordered them to go back to Cyprus. Cimon, said the god, was already with him.

Rejoining the main fleet, the Athenians discovered that Cimon was indeed with the gods. He had fallen sick and died while they were away. Fired by the spirit of their dead commander, the allied fleet fought a battle against another large Persian fleet and succeeded in capturing one hundred Phoenician triremes. Coming quickly to shore after the victory at sea, the Greek hoplites disembarked and defeated the Persian army on land. It was a victory that echoed Cimon's own great double victory at the Eurymedon River, sixteen years before.

When the bitter news reached Susa, King Artaxerxes made a momentous decision. He could see no end to the vengeful attacks of the Athenians on his empire. Only four years earlier they had suffered heavy losses of men and ships in Egypt, yet now they were back, threatening to take Egypt from him once again. It was time to end the war that his forefathers had started. Artaxerxes sent riders along the Royal Road to the coast with a message for the Athenians. The Great King invited an embassy from their city to Susa, where his ministers would negotiate an end to hostilities.

When Artaxerxes' invitation was delivered to the Assembly, the people voted to send Cimon's brother-in-law Callias to Susa. As hereditary herald of Athens, he was given full powers to negotiate with the Great King. Months later Callias returned with a number of valuable items: golden bowls, a pair of peacocks, and a peace treaty. The Persians agreed to keep their naval forces east of the Chelidonian Islands in the Mediterranean and east of the Cyanean Rocks in the Black Sea. The Great King thus tacitly recognized the Aegean Sea, the Hellespont, the Sea of Marmara, and the Bosporus as Athenian waters. The Persian Wars were over.

While Callias negotiated peace with Persia, the most remarkable generation in Athenian history was passing into retirement. These citizens were members of the annual cohort who had now reached the age of sixty. The turning points of their lives had been turning points in Athens' fight against Persia as well. They had been the first crop of Athenian babies born into a free city in the year after the last tyrant was thrown out. At twenty they had fought the Persians at Marathon, the youngest Athenians on the field. At thirty they had boarded the triremes with Themistocles at Artemisium and Salamis. Before reaching the end of their active service at forty-five, they had followed Cimon to the Eurymedon River.

Now they would turn over to their sons the headship of their families and the governance of Athens. They themselves were embarking on the sheltered lagoon of old age, a placid round of family rites and jury duty. In the shade of Cimon's plane trees, their spears and oars exchanged for walking sticks, they would recount their own deeds and remember fallen comrades. As youths many had taken the traditional oath: "I shall hand on my fatherland not less, but greater." More than any other generation, these men had fulfilled that promise.

The hostilities with the Spartans and their allies still remained to be resolved. For years the Athenians had been aiding democratic factions in the cities of central Greece. As oligarchic rulers were expelled, these cities joined the Athenian alliance and received Athenian garrisons to ensure democratic rule and loyalty to Athens. By the time of the Peace of Callias an Athenian sphere of influence stretched from the northern Peloponnese almost to Thermopylae. When the forces of the exiled oligarchs finally struck back, the general Tolmides impetuously demanded that the Assembly give him an army to protect the land empire. Pericles opposed the expedition, but the Assembly voted in favor. The army lost a great battle at Coronea in Boeotia, Tolmides was killed, and many of the troops were taken prisoner. To ransom these hostages, the Athenians gave up their newly won territories and concluded a Thirty Years' Peace with the Spartans and their Peloponnesian allies. In the future the Athenians recognized the wisdom of Pericles and accepted rule of the sea as their destiny.

CHAPTER 8

Mariners of the Golden Age

We must add to our knowledge of the countryside, both animals and plants, knowledge of the sea, for we are in a way amphibious, no more land dwellers than sea dwellers.

—Strabo

AN ATHENIAN SERVING ON ONE OF HIS CITY'S TRIREMES commanded a wide view of the world, and the world teemed with wonders. Great fin whales forged through the Aegean, leviathans that were guided on their way (or so the Greeks believed) by cunning pilot fish. At the opposite end of the scale, the delicate paper nautilus scudded along by spreading a translucent membrane to the breeze, a miniature ship under full sail. Dolphins leaped and sported alongside the triremes, encouraged by whistling and singing from the mariners. Sailors believed that dolphins brought good luck and at times even carried castaways to shore. Solitary sea turtles basked on the surface or plied their powerful forelegs like pairs of oars. Elsewhere a migrating school of tuna might suddenly appear, snaking across the sea's surface in a turbulent stream of flashing fins and frothing water. These big blue and silver fish were worth a fortune. When fishermen spotted the migrating tuna, they would corral them within a ring of nets, then kill them with clubs or spears.

Steersmen navigated by the stars on clear nights and by landmarks during the day. The archipelagoes of the Aegean were drowned mountain ranges with peaks rising high above the sea, and the mainland coasts were mountainous also. In the watery realm of the Athenian navy, a lookout on a mast top was seldom beyond sight of land. The mountains brewed winds, however, and through most of the summer stiff northerlies ruffled the sea from midday till sunset. The Greeks called them etesian or "seasonal" winds. When they were blowing, the triremes plowed through choppy waves or stayed in port. Occasionally the mountains created violent downdrafts called katabatic winds, cold gusts that hit the sea and fanned out in a rushing wall of white spume. Then the rowers would hear a curse from the lookout followed by a shout of "Squall! Squall coming!"

At day's end the evening star Hesperus appeared above the western horizon, herald of the great wheeling pageant of moon, stars, and planets. Winds dropped after sundown, and triremes could make good time by rowing through moonlit nights. Sometimes the dark sea was lit by a phosphorescent glow, and balls of greenish-white fire burned at the ends of the yardarms. Like the dolphins, these lights meant good luck. They signified the presence of two divine guardians of seafarers, the twin heroes Castor and Pollux. As dawn approached, the celestial fires faded until only one remained. It was the morning star Phosphoros, the "Light Bearer," bringing up the sun to start another day.

During these years of peace Athenian ships ventured far beyond their home waters. A sacred trireme carried Athenian envoys to Libya, where they consulted the oracle of Zeus Ammon at Siwa in the Sahara Desert. In the north Athenian emissaries negotiated with the local Scythian and Thracian tribal chiefs for access to wheat, salt fish, and other resources. One diplomatic mission went west as far as the Bay of Naples in Italy and the famous Greek colony at Neapolis ("New City"). There the Athenian crews saw a high conical mountain called Vesuvius, quiet for so long that the world had forgotten it was a volcano.

The same voyage took them past the famous rocks of the Sirens off the Amalfi coast, where a pair of beautiful seductresses once tried to lure Odysseus from his ship with their irresistible song. The general in command of the mission to Neapolis was Diotimus. On another occasion Diotimus' service to his city took him two thousand miles east of Athens as an envoy to the Great King at Susa. Expeditions like these left their mark on the Athenian character, breeding citizens who were active, adventurous, restless, and proud of their exploits.

The experiences of the common Athenian in seafaring and fighting were beginning to rival those of the aristocrats. He might not know Homer by heart, or trace his ancestry back to a warrior who had fought in the Trojan War. But the average thete had now *seen* Troy with his own eyes, a small hill off to the south as one rowed into the Hellespont on the run to Byzantium. During his naval service the ordinary citizen would follow the sea routes hallowed by the legends of Odysseus, Theseus, Jason, and Cadmus to Asia, Africa, Europe, and the islands between. Although he cut a modest figure ashore in foreign parts, carrying his rowing pad as his only weapon instead of shield and spear, a mariner from Athens was the Odysseus of his time, widely traveled, many-minded, facing dangers on the deep in the struggle to bring himself and his shipmates safely home.

As winter approached and the seafaring season drew to its close, the widely scattered triremes returned like homing pigeons to the Piraeus. While still far out at sea, they were greeted by a flash of light on the summit of the Acropolis, four miles inland. It was the sun reflected on the shining spear tip and crested helmet of a colossal bronze statue of Athena, one of the first great masterpieces of the Athenian artist Phidias. The statue had been nine years in the making and stood thirty feet tall. As the triremes approached the end of their voyaging, the crews strove to look their best with perfect timing and oarsmanship. There was a popular saying, "As the Athenian goes into the harbor," for any task done with utmost precision. The mariners knew well that thousands of critical eyes were watching and judging their performance.

The two small harbors on the east side of the Piraeus promontory, Zea and Munychia, were entirely devoted to the navy, while the large Cantharus Harbor on the west was both naval and commercial. At the start of an expedition triremes from the other two harbors of the Navy Yard rowed around to the jetty at Cantharus for inspection before setting out, and at times of extreme urgency the Council actually moved down from Athens and held its meetings on the jetty until the fleet was at sea.

Around the rims of all three harbors curved long rows of shipsheds, built at a cost that would ultimately reach a thousand talents. Each returning trireme was assigned to a berth in one of these sheds and hauled up the sloping ramp till it rested high and dry for the winter. The ship was then stripped of its gear, and the sails and rigging were carefully dried before being put into storage. Trierarchs accused of losing naval equipment or mariners condemned for breaches of discipline might choose to slip away furtively through the streets and seek asylum in the sanctuary of Artemis on Munychia Hill. Strict security ruled at the Navy Yard, as hundreds of guards kept watch for everything from outbreaks of fire to the stealing or smuggling of pitch and cordage.

An Athenian mariner's first stop outside the gates of the Navy Yard was likely to be the barbershop. In Athens haircuts and hairstyles had social and political implications. Aristocratic horsemen still wore long braids and gold hairpins. The common man (and the politicians who spoke for him) preferred a short cut, though not quite a crewcut. The customer sat on a low stool, his body draped in a sheet to catch the shorn locks. The barber then cropped and curled the hair, anointed the head with scented oil, and trimmed the beard to a neat point. (At Athens any man with a long unkempt beard ran the risk of being mistaken for a philosopher.) Dyes were available to hide gray patches. Along with hairdressing and manicures, the barber dispensed a ceaseless stream of anecdotes and observations. The mariner just arrived in port could catch up on all the latest news and add an account of his own voyage to the barber's store of information. Greek barbers were notoriously talkative. On being asked how he wanted his hair cut, one wit was supposed to have told his barber, "In silence."

From the barbershop the Athenian mariner emerged neatly trimmed and fully up to date. Flush with pay, he was now ready to plunge into the roiling marketplace of the Piraeus, located just beyond the perimeter of the shipsheds at Zea Harbor. Here the returning mariner could indulge in the luxuries that had been denied him during months of hard service with the fleet. Athenians of the Golden Age never tired of enumerating the seaborne imports that flowed into the Piraeus. From Libya came ivory, hides, and the medicinal plant and dietary supplement called silphium. Egypt provided papyrus and sailcloth. Cretan cypress wood was good for carving images of the gods, and Syrian incense could be burned at shrines in thanksgiving for a safe return.

The food vendors provided fare fit for the Great King himself. An Athenian feast could include salt fish from the Black Sea, beef ribs from Thessaly, pork and cheese from Syracuse in Sicily, dates from Phoenicia, raisins and figs from Rhodes, pears and apples from Euboea, almonds from Naxos, and chestnuts from Asia Minor. The rounds of flat bread, often dressed with relish or fish sauce, were usually made from Russian, Egyptian, or Sicilian wheat. As they enjoyed these delicacies, Athenians could rest their feet or elbows on brightly colored carpets and cushions from Carthage. If the dinner lasted into the night, a bronze lampstand of Etruscan manufacture from central Italy might light the convivial scene. In the words of the comic playwright Hermippus, who wrote a catalog of imported goods to be found in the markets of Athens:

> Tell me, now, Muses dwelling on Mount Olympus
> Ever since Dionysus has sailed on the wine-dark sea,
> All the good things he has brought hither to men on his black ship!

Some unlucky Athenian seafarers, however, were seeking not a grocer but a doctor. Rowing and maritime service involved certain occupational hazards. Among the doctors who treated such conditions were disciples of a revolutionary medical practitioner named Hippocrates. He was born on the small island of Cos in the eastern Aegean, a member of the Athenian alliance, but his teachings had spread far and wide. Hippocrates created a school of medicine patterned after the schools of philosophy. His disciples and successors swore the sacred "Hippocratic" oath, but they based their scientific work not on piety but on observation of symptoms, experimentation with different treatments, and careful recording of case histories.

The journals kept by Hippocrates and his followers provide glimpses of the dangers that beset Greek mariners of their time. "On Salamis, the man who fell on the anchor received a wound in the belly. He had great pain. He drank a drug but there was no evacuation below, nor did he vomit." It was not merely blistered hands and sore rumps that afflicted the rowers of the navy. Despite the fleecy rowing pads that aided their legwork, Greek oarsmen suffered a particular occupational malady from the hard service on the wooden thwarts: fistula of the anus.

If the rower put off treatment, the fistula might penetrate the wall of the rectum. Now the matter was serious. Once the physician had taken the measure of the problem, the fistula was treated over a period of days with linen plugs and suppositories made of powdered horn. Other medicines included root of hartwort pounded fine, water mixed with honey (a good antibacterial agent), burnt flower of copper, fuller's earth, and alum. The rectum of the miserable rower was anointed continually with myrrh until the fistula healed over. Without a doctor's care the prospects were bleak: "Any patients that are left untreated die."

Hippocrates' disciples brought the same orderly, intellectual approach to medicine that was revolutionizing many other fields at that time, from history to urban planning. They studied the patterns of winds, rain, and stars as assiduously as any mariner, for it was a tenet of their belief that the weather and the seasons had a powerful influence on health and sickness. In eastern Greek cities the arts and sciences had withered under Persian rule. Now the liberal outlook of the Athenians was bringing about a scientific renaissance. Ease of travel throughout the maritime empire helped the rapid spread of new ideas and techniques.

As the role of the navy and maritime trade expanded, the Piraeus became a great city in its own right. To create a home worthy of the Athenian navy, the Assembly hired the world's first professional urban planner, Hippodamus of Miletus. He too was an eastern Greek, but Hippodamus' patrons were not individuals seeking cures; rather they were entire populations desirous of new cities. Athens was willing to pour out vast sums on such itinerant consultants, be they prophets, astronomers, architects, or engineers. Hippodamus' home city of Miletus had been rebuilt on a grid plan after Xerxes' troops razed it to the ground. The success of this huge reconstruction project encouraged Hippodamus to travel around the Mediterranean to spread the gospel of modern urban design. As befitted a pundit much in the public eye, Hippodamus cut a colorful and eccentric figure. His hair was long, his coiffure expensive. Even his clothing was peculiar. Winter and summer, he wore the same odd costume of cheap fabric.

No mere surveyor of streets, Hippodamus was in fact a utopian theorist. His quest led him in search of a physical setting for the perfect human community: social, spatial, and spiritual. Along with his own mastery of philosophy, meteorology, and architecture, Hippodamus seemed to see threefold divisions everywhere. In his ideal city the population would be divided into three classes: craftsmen, farmers, and warriors. Land should also have its tripartite division: sacred, public, and private. Hippodamus even proposed

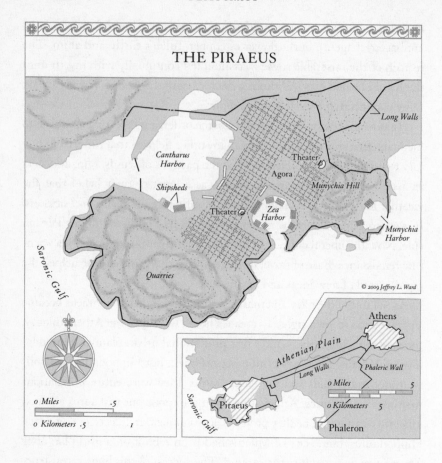

THE PIRAEUS

Long Walls

Cantharus
Harbor

Theater

Agora

Shipsheds

Munychia Hill

Theater

Zea
Harbor

Munychia
Harbor

Quarries

© 2009 Jeffrey L. Ward

Saronic Gulf

0 Miles   .5

0 Kilometers .5   1

Athens

Athenian Plain

Long Walls

Phaleric Wall

0 Miles   5

Saronic Gulf

Piraeus

0 Kilometers   5

Phaleron

that juries should be able to choose from not two but three possible verdicts: guilty, not guilty, and not sure. How his heart must have leaped when he caught his first glimpse of the three natural harbors at the Piraeus!

Behind the harbors, however, lay a difficult site, one with no springs and little flat land. It would be no easy task to impose order on the land within Themistocles' circuit of fortifications. In addition to the rough and waterless terrain, the site was already encumbered with various fortifications, shipsheds, shrines, roads, and an ancient fishing village that had stood on the Piraeus promontory for thousands of years. Extensive areas, however, were still virgin terrain. The site even provided its own building stone. Quarries at the seaward end of the promontory would provide porous yellowish-gray limestone and soft marl. It was not a glamorous stone like the white marble from Mount Pentelicus, but it was serviceable and convenient, like the Piraeus itself.

The old city of Athens had grown organically through the centuries, its streets and neighborhoods radiating out from the Acropolis like blood vessels from a heart. Private homes, shrines, public facilities, and industrial workshops all jostled side by side along its twisting lanes. The confusion had its defenders. Many Greeks believed that a town plan *should* be illogical and hard to follow. If the streets were straight and orderly, then enemy invaders who broke into the city would be able to find their way around as easily as the residents. Certainly the mass of Athenians had stoutly resisted Themistocles' suggestions for change when they rebuilt the city after Salamis. The Piraeus, child of modernity and enlightenment, would be different.

Hippodamus' assignment was described as dividing or cutting up the Piraeus. First he chose as his axis the long saddle of land that ran from the foot of Munychia Hill, the acropolis of the Piraeus, southwest to the Akte Hill and the quarries. On either side of this central spine Hippodamus marked out the boundaries of the sacred, public, and private areas. Inscribed boundary stones proclaimed the function of each zone. There were also markers for the sanctuaries of the gods, the quarters for foreign merchants, and even the station where one could catch a ferryboat to Salamis or one of the other islands.

In the center was the Agora, with its own council house and public offices. On the expanse of level ground north of Zea Harbor Hippodamus laid out this civic center, ever after known as the Hippodamian Agora. Near the edge of Zea Harbor the Agora widened out into an open area where the crews of triremes could assemble at the start of a naval expedition.

Cross streets connected the Cantharus port on one side of this ridge to the Zea naval harbor on the other. Marking off the streets, Hippodamus embedded a mathematical ratio of 3:5:9 into his grid. Alleys around blocks had a width of 15 feet, main streets around districts a width of 25 feet, while the major arteries were a majestic 45 feet wide. All were straight. The Athenians were so well satisfied with his work at the Piraeus that they later entrusted to Hippodamus the task of laying out a new colony called Thurii in southern Italy.

Uniformity of housing reinforced the message of democracy and equality. Hippodamus divided each residential city block among eight dwellings, all of which were only variations on a uniform "Piraeus house." The long and narrow lots, 40 feet by 70 feet, accommodated in one half a flagged courtyard equipped with outdoor ovens and a deep bell-shaped cistern to provide the household's water. The house itself included a family room with a hearth, with bedrooms on an upper floor above it. No one in the Piraeus was ever very far from the water. Thanks to the sloping terrain, the houses rose in tiers like the seats in a theater. Almost every roof or upper story commanded a view down to the nearest harbor and out to the blue sea beyond.

The *andron* or men's meeting room opened directly off the courtyard. Here the master of the house entertained his friends. The *andron* in a Piraeus house was designed to accommodate seven couches around its square perimeter: two couches on three sides and one sharing the fourth wall with the door, which was placed in the corner. After dinner, when the sun cast a shadow longer than a man was tall, was the time for wine. The *symposion* or drinking together was the crown of every Athenian feast. To accompany the flow of stories, speculations, and poetry, a fleet of earthenware pots were carried into the banqueting room. All had been fired a distinctive glossy black and red, and all were made in Athens of good Attic clay. Familiar mythical scenes were painted on the vessels. One cup showed Odysseus tied to the mast of his ship, listening to the songs of the Sirens. But there were contemporary scenes, too, celebrating the exploits of the men who would be drinking from these very cups: warriors rowing across the sea to battle; warships cruising in convoy; archers shooting from ships at sea; pirates stealthily attacking unsuspecting freighters. The most beautiful of these ship paintings showed long sleek galleys rowing around the inner surface of a pot. When the vessel was brimming with wine, the ships appeared to be floating on its surface: warships reflected in a sea of wine, reflecting the "wine-dark sea" of the beloved poet Homer.

Sometimes the host of the party provided sexual pleasures along with wine, music, and conversation. The men might also seek more straightforward relief, free from civilized frills, at one of the many brothels in the Piraeus. Exercising untrammeled sexual freedom carried few consequences for Athenian citizens. Sexually transmitted diseases were as yet unknown, and few societies in history have granted to free adult males such extremes of sexual license.

It was perhaps inevitable that Athenian men, who enjoyed thinking, talking, and joking about sex when they were not actually engaged in it, should have at times viewed sex organs and sex acts as extensions of their experiences at sea. A woman's vagina could be described as a *kolpos* or gulf, like the Corinthian and Saronic gulfs, where a happy seafarer could lose himself. As for the penis, a modest man could claim to have a *kontos* or boat pole, an average man a *kope* or oar between his legs, and a braggart a *pedalion* or steering oar. Inevitably too, the erection poking against an Athenian's tunic was referred to as his "ram." Sexual intercourse was likened to ramming encounters between triremes, but the men did not always take the active role. The popular Athenian sexual position in which the woman sat astride her partner gave her a chance to play the *nautria* or female rower, and row the man as if he were a boat. A man who mounted another man might claim to be boarding him, using the nautical term for a marine boarding a trireme. Sexual bouts with multiple partners were sometimes dubbed *naumachiai* or naval battles.

These were private pleasures. But with its lively market, religious festivals, and two open-air theaters (Athens itself only had one), the Piraeus also provided public entertainment throughout the year. A colorful element in the life of the port city was the presence of shrines and temples to foreign gods. Each one served as a religious center to a group of expatriate merchants who had come to roost in the Piraeus. In honor of their northern goddess Bendis the Thracians held relay races on horseback, with a burning torch passed from rider to rider. Egyptian merchants carried Isis with them from the banks of the Nile, just as the traders from Asia Minor brought Cybele the Mother Goddess and the Syrians imported Astarte. The Phoenicians introduced to the Piraeus not only the cult of Baal but also a mysterious divinity with the body of a man and a head like the prow of a warship, complete with ram. On the tombstone of a Phoenician resident of the Piraeus, this strange ship god was shown wrestling with a lion for possession of the corpse.

In the maritime world of the Piraeus a happy tolerance reigned among all religions, and the idea of killing a man for worshipping the wrong god was unknown. Only godlessness and impiety were condemned. In Athens ideological strife was a feature of the philosophical schools, not the temples. So popular were the foreign festivals that Athenians often walked the four miles down to the Piraeus to watch some new and exotic celebration in the streets.

The democratic spirit of Athens and its navy found its fullest embodiment in the sacred trireme *Paralos*. The name was mythical: the sea god Poseidon had fathered a hero called Paralos ("Man of the Shore") who was credited with inventing the galley or long ship. Each year the crew of the sacred trireme, who were known as the Paraloi, held a festival and offered sacrifices to his memory. The ship's name was continually passed on through the years as one sacred trireme retired and a new vessel took its place. It was also the only masculine name in the fleet: all other Athenian triremes had feminine names and were referred to as "she." Ardent democrats to a man, the crew of the *Paralos* opposed any proposals that smacked of oligarchy or tyranny. Pericles chose to show his commitment to the navy by naming his second son Paralos after the ship and the legendary hero.

The *Paralos* took on the role of flagship for the entire navy. At times the *Paralos* served as a ship of war, but it also carried important dispatches, conveyed embassies on diplomatic missions, provided scouting reports to the rest of the navy, or served as a sacred ship to take priests and celebrants to rites and festivals overseas. Every four years the ship transported the city's Olympic athletes and their entourage around the Peloponnese to Olympia for the prestigious games celebrated in honor of Zeus.

Closer to home the crew of the *Paralos* would row their ship southwest to the Isthmus, where the Corinthians sponsored games to honor Poseidon. The athletic events of the Isthmian games were held beside the pine trees in the sanctuary where Themistocles and the other Greek delegates had planned the resistance to Xerxes. At the stadium the Athenian contingent was traditionally allowed as much space in the grandstand as could be covered by the sail of the *Paralos,* set up as an awning. Unlike the Olympic games, the Isthmian games included races for ships, so the crew of the *Paralos* had the chance to compete against contenders from Corinth, Megara, Sicyon, and many other Greek cities. The victor's crown at the Isthmus was woven from twigs of pine, the wood most useful to shipwrights and therefore the sea god's special tree.

Every member of the *Paralos'* crew was an Athenian citizen. The ship had no trierarch: the democratic crew was in command. The highest-ranking officer on board was the treasurer, known as the *Tamias Paralou.* The selection of this treasurer was considered so important that the entire Assembly voted on it and also assigned to the treasurer the funds needed to keep the sacred ship in constant readiness. At times the Paraloi served in a body as Athenian ambassadors abroad. Crew members who performed exceptional services were rewarded with gold crowns, an honor normally reserved for the aristocratic trierarchs.

The experiment in democracy ensured that the fruits of naval victories were shared by all Athenians, transforming the life of even the poorest citizen. The age of the common man had dawned. For the first time anywhere on earth, a mass of ordinary citizens, independent of monarchs or aristocrats or religious leaders, was guiding the destiny of a great state.

Part Three

EMPIRE

No doubt all this will be disparaged by people who are politically apathetic. But those who, like us, prefer a life of action will try to imitate us. If they fail to secure what we have secured, they will envy us. All who have taken it upon themselves to rule over others have incurred hatred and unpopularity for a time. If one has a great aim to pursue, this burden of envy must be accepted, and it is wise to accept it. Hatred does not last long, but present brilliance will become future glory when it is stored up everlastingly in the memory of mankind.

—Pericles to the Athenians

CHAPTER 9

The Imperial Navy

[446–433 B.C.]

O Athens, queen of cities!
How fair your Navy Yard! How fair your Parthenon! How fair your
*   Piraeus!*
Your sacred trees—what other city can match them?
Heaven itself, they say, shines on you with a brighter light.

—Fragment of a lost comedy

IN GREEK MYTH, HUMAN HISTORY BEGAN WITH A GOLDEN AGE.
Cronus, father of Zeus, ruled the world. During this idyllic period our
ancestors enjoyed long life, perfect health, and food in abundance. As time
passed, the golden race declined through cycles of silver, bronze, and iron.
For Athens after the Peace of Callias, naval supremacy seemed to have
brought back the legendary age of gold. The people prospered. Art, architecture, philosophy, drama, historical writing, and scientific inquiry flourished as never before. Pericles was the architect of this new Golden Age,
and under his benign guidance the Athenians were justified in believing
that they were setting in motion a new cycle of human history.

Pericles built upon four mighty pillars: democracy, naval power, the
wealth of empire, and the rule of reason. In Pericles the Athenians had
found a leader whose genius for public affairs pervaded all these realms.
For more than three decades he was the city's leading politician, orator,
naval commander, administrator, and promoter of arts and learning. True,
he stood on the shoulders of giants. In the course of his long career Pericles
followed the precedents of Themistocles as a maritime proponent and sponsor of politically oriented plays, Aristides as an architect of empire, Ephialtes
as a democratic reformer, Cimon as a civic benefactor, Tolmides as a naval

strategist, and Anaxagoras as a scientific thinker. Yet as a visionary leader he surpassed them all. Partly in admiration, partly in jest, his fellow citizens called Pericles "the Olympian," or just Zeus.

In the Assembly Pericles made few speeches, reserving his appearances on the speaker's platform for momentous occasions. One wit compared him to the sacred state trireme *Salaminia,* which was launched only for important missions. He had a knack for coining phrases that stuck in the mind. He visualized Aegina as "the eyesore of the Piraeus," threats of conflict as "war bearing down from the Peloponnese," and the loss of young Athenian soldiers abroad as "the taking of the springtime from the year." The philosopher Socrates remembered to the end of his days that he had been in the Assembly when Pericles proposed the construction of a third Long Wall to secure Athens' link to the Piraeus. The comic playwright Eupolis compared Pericles' speeches to the work of bees: sweet as honey, but leaving a sting behind in the memories of his listeners.

Peace with Persia and the Peloponnesians did not diminish Athens' naval effort. Naval power demanded a constant investment of material, effort, and money. Like the boar in Aesop's fable, which spent all its leisure time sharpening its tusks, the Athenian navy could not relax in time of peace. Ships required time to build, large sums to maintain, and constant practice to operate. During Pericles' projected age of peace, Athens would devote itself to its fleet as much as during Cimon's time of perpetual war.

Pericles took it upon himself to set up a peacetime routine for the navy. Every spring sixty triremes would put to sea with crews composed entirely of citizens. Twelve thousand Athenians were regularly involved in these expeditions. The right to serve on board the triremes was reserved for men who could prove Athenian ancestry on both their father's and their mother's side. Athenian citizenship was a cherished prize, as was the pay that came with naval service, and the citizenship lists were jealously guarded against pretenders. Special naval judges or *nautodikai* heard accusations against men of suspect birth. They judged these cases each year during the month of Munichion, at the start of the seafaring season.

Even with these periodic purges, the Athenian population was experiencing an explosive period of growth. One of the greatest benefits of empire was the acquisition of new territory overseas that could be divided among the poor citizens of Athens, transforming them from urban masses to private landowners. Such allotments were called *klerouchoi* or cleruchies, meaning lands assigned by lottery. The Athenians who took possession of these parcels of land kept their Athenian citizenship rather than becoming citizens of a new colony. Tolmides established cleruchies on the islands of Euboea and Naxos, Pericles divided land in the Gallipoli peninsula among Athenian cleruchs, and certain tracts in Thrace were specifically reserved for citizens of the two lowest classes, the thetes and the hoplites. Thus the conquests of the Athenian navy provided land and livelihoods for thousands of commoners.

The triremes of Pericles' peacetime navy were launched in early spring. They remained in service for eight months, until the onset of winter storms brought them back to their shipsheds in the Piraeus. During those months the triremes of Athens performed many tasks. Twenty ships guarded the coasts of Attica and the approaches to the Piraeus. Ten collected tribute from allied cities and islands. Some triremes carried embassies to foreign lands or ran sacred missions to distant sanctuaries and religious festivals. Others hunted down pirates. Still others conveyed troops of Athenian hoplites to islands and cities where they would serve as garrisons, supporting local democratic factions against their oligarchic opponents. Whatever their orders, all Athenian crews used their time at sea to perfect the skills needed in naval battles. Athenians were talkative and self-willed by nature, but on board the triremes the common citizens learned the disciplines of silence and instant obedience. The Athenian navy depended upon their skills, and the people's political power depended on the navy.

The annual cost of Athens' peacetime navy of sixty ships was 480 talents for their eight months at sea. Lower-class citizens benefited greatly from the steady income, which was drawn from the tribute paid by the allies. At home more than twenty thousand Athenian citizens depended for their livelihoods on naval and maritime income. The city's swarms of jurors, archers, horsemen, councilors, Acropolis guards, prison guards, and orphans might have no direct connection with the naval effort, but they were all paid with wealth from the sea. There were five hundred guards in the Navy Yard, and seven hundred civil officials who were sent out annually to enforce compliance among the allies.

To regularize the annual tribute payments, the Athenians gradually organized the allies into five districts: Islands, Caria, Ionia, Hellespont, and "Thraceward." The districts had no independent political identity, nor did the Assembly appoint governors to rule the districts on the model of the Persian satraps. In time the Athenians introduced standardized coinage, weights, and measures and even required many judicial matters that arose in allied cities to be tried in Athenian courts. The Athenians took a hint from both the Persians and the Spartans and ordered the cities in their realm to dismantle their walls and fortifications. Thousands of troops were shipped out from Athens to serve on garrison duty, protecting Athenian interests and guarding subject cities and democratic factions throughout their realm. The true guarantee of their safety, however, was the Athenian navy. In an empire of coastal cities and islands, ships constituted the best defense. The Wooden Wall now safeguarded a frontier more than fifteen hundred miles long.

The empire's geographical extent more than doubled when the Athenians extended their thalassocracy into the Black Sea. This fathomless expanse of dark water, so unlike the aquamarine Aegean Sea, dwarfed the cities on its shores and the ships that plied its surface. In crossing the immensities of the Black Sea, a freighter could sail for nine days and eight nights and see nothing on the horizon but waves and water. With its storms, fogs, and wild currents the Black Sea seemed hostile to seafarers bred in the south. To ward off its dangers they called it the Euxine ("Friendly to Strangers") or simply Pontus ("The Sea"). Earlier Greek colonists had long controlled the shores of the Black Sea, but the hinterlands were inhabited by non-Greek tribes known for archery and horsemanship. These included the Thracians, the Scythians, and somewhere out on the steppes, the legendary Amazons. The riders had little interest in the sea, and the Greeks seldom attempted to penetrate far inland.

The Black Sea was a place of riches. The most venerable of all Greek seafaring sagas, the tale of Jason's quest for the Golden Fleece at Colchis, told of the voyage of the ship *Argo* to the eastern end of the Black Sea. In Pericles' day its waters teemed with tuna, sturgeon, and other fish that migrated in huge schools from their spawning grounds in the rivers Danube, Dnieper, and Don. The salt pans along the northern coast supported

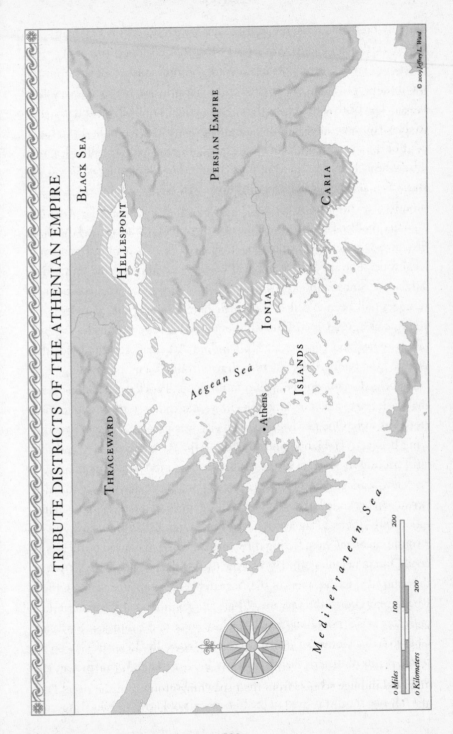

TRIBUTE DISTRICTS OF THE ATHENIAN EMPIRE

BLACK SEA

HELLESPONT

PERSIAN EMPIRE

CARIA

THRACEWARD

IONIA

Aegean Sea

ISLANDS

•Athens

Mediterranean Sea

0 Miles   100   200
0 Kilometers   200

© 2009 Jeffrey L. Ward

a highly profitable trade in salt fish. Along with horses the Scythians produced cattle and hides. Amber was transported along the rivers from unknown lands to the north; minerals and ores washed down from the mountains to the sea. The true gold of the Black Sea, however, was yellow wheat. The fields started near the mouth of the Danube River and stretched to the Crimea and beyond. In places the grain was sown right down to the edge of the sea, and flocks of black crows mingled with wheeling seagulls. The wheat, like the other precious commodities, was shipped across the Black Sea and down the Bosporus during the short sailing season of two months after midsummer.

After the Persian Wars the fame of Athens had spread around the Black Sea. Some of the Greek cities sent envoys to seek Athenian intervention in local wars. The appeal that initiated Pericles' expedition came from exiled citizens of Sinope, an old colony of Miletus on the southern coast. These refugees had been expelled from their homes by a tyrant. Pericles and a young colleague named Lamachus equipped a large fleet including both fast triremes and carriers for six hundred Athenian settlers. Once they defeated the tyrant, these colonists drawn from Athens' burgeoning population helped secure Sinope against future coups. Pericles' expedition opened the Black Sea to a host of Athenian envoys, merchants, settlers, and garrison troops as well. One newly established city was named "Piraeus"; another, lying between Trebizond and Colchis, "Athens." Between fifty and sixty cities around the margin of the Black Sea joined the Athenian alliance.

A few years after the Black Sea expedition, the golden west of the Mediterranean beckoned Athenians as well. Again, local conflicts led to an invitation for Athens to intervene. Two Ionian cities, Rhegium in Italy and Leontini in Sicily, were feeling threatened and overshadowed by their powerful Dorian neighbor, the city of Syracuse. At the height of Athens' power, they appealed to the rulers of the Aegean to enter into alliance with them. Rhegium occupied the very toe of Italy and commanded the eastern shore of the famous Strait of Messina, legendary home of the monsters Scylla and Charybdis in Homer's *Odyssey*. The other new ally, Leontini, lay on the fertile plains of eastern Sicily between Mount Etna and Syracuse, an area that, like the Black Sea coast, abounded in wheat.

Only one short war marred the fifteen years of Pericles' Golden Age, and it ended in a victory that enhanced Athenians' pride in their navy. The great island of Samos, along with Lesbos and Chios, had been furnishing ships rather than tribute ever since the founding of the Delian League. Of these three semi-independent allies, Samos was the most powerful. The Athenians did not interfere with the oligarchic regime on Samos until the Samians defied Athens' authority and attacked a neighboring city that was also a member of the Athenian alliance.

Pericles had a personal interest in countering the aggressive actions of Samos. Their target was Miletus, the home city of his beloved consort Aspasia. When attempts at arbitration failed, Pericles led an Athenian fleet to Samos and established a democracy. Soon after he departed, the unrepentant oligarchs overturned the fledgling democracy and imprisoned the soldiers of the new Athenian garrison. Pericles and the other generals mustered a fleet of forty-four fast triremes and set out for Samos. One of the generals was the playwright Sophocles, who had been elected to command after the success of his tragedy *Antigone.* Pericles considered Sophocles to be of little use in a battle, however, so the distinguished playwright was dispatched instead on a mission of goodwill, visiting the still-loyal maritime allies on Chios and Lesbos. Meeting his fellow poet Ion at Chios, Sophocles said, "Pericles told me that I may have mastered poetry, but I know nothing of generalship."

Near Tragia ("Billygoat Island") the Athenians came upon the big rebel fleet and defeated them. But the Samian War was not yet over. The Persian satrap at Sardis had summoned a Phoenician fleet, and Pericles voyaged east to head off these reinforcements. In his absence the Athenian squadron that had been left to blockade the main port was overcome by a sudden sortie. The Samian oligarchs controlled the seas around their island for half a month, until Pericles returned and forced them to surrender.

It was a proud moment. Pericles had often been elected general, but he had never matched the distinction that his father, Xanthippus, had won at Mycale, let alone that of Cimon at Eurymedon. A general should be known for feats of arms, not merely for prudence. Now Pericles could claim that he had achieved at Samos in nine months what it had taken Agamemnon ten years to accomplish against Troy. Samos lost its walls, its navy, and its privileged status within the empire. Moreover the readiness of the Persians to support rebellion in the Athenian Empire exposed the fragility of the peace and confirmed Pericles' wisdom in keeping the navy on alert.

The Athenian Golden Age was a time of power and prosperity, but it was also an age of reason. Confident that science must prevail over superstition, Pericles set out to enlighten his fellow citizens. On one occasion he boarded his trireme at the Piraeus and prepared to launch an expedition. At that moment the sky darkened with a solar eclipse. The steersman was too alarmed by the portent to get the ship under way. Pericles, however, had no fear of eclipses. His friend Anaxagoras, a Greek philosopher from Clazomenae in Asia Minor, had explained to him that the darkness was only a shadow cast across the face of the sun. His crew, however, regarded the eclipse as a divine warning against starting the expedition. Pericles promptly walked over to the steersman. Holding his cloak in front of the man's eyes, Pericles asked if he were frightened. "No," the steersman answered. "What difference is there between this and the eclipse," Pericles asked, "except that the eclipse was caused by something larger than my cloak?" After this the men consented to start, their fears dispelled by Pericles' arguments and perhaps also his air of Olympian calm.

The majority of Athenians believed in omens and divination. Prophets accompanied all Athenian expeditions of any importance. They read the signs for the generals at the morning sacrifices and interpreted the meaning of comets, eclipses, phases of the moon, the flight of passing birds, and even dreams. To counterbalance this religious intrusion into military and political affairs, Pericles welcomed natural historians, city planners, philosophers, military engineers, and astronomers to Athens. Debates over their ideas and teachings were far from abstract or academic. Some Athenians readily accepted innovations, but others found them shocking. Among the common people there was a widespread mistrust of scientists or philosophers whose theories seemed based on the theory of a universe without gods. Among Athenian crews, superstition often trumped common sense.

Yet through constant give and take, Pericles and Athens maintained a delicate balance between reason and tradition. The city provided almost free of charge a public education in political science, rhetoric, philosophy, and many other fields. So remarkable was the liberal intellectual life in the city that Pericles called Athens the "School of Greece." Every citizen was expected to engage in the discourse. As Pericles said, "We do not say that a man who takes no part in public affairs minds his own business; on the contrary, we say that he has no business here at all."

Pericles was eager to transform Athens into the imperial capital of his dreams. The treasury of the maritime alliance had gradually accumulated a surplus of several thousand talents, first on Delos and later at Athens. The sum could be expected to grow with every year of peace. Guided by his vision of a new Athens, Pericles proposed to the Assembly that they build new temples and public buildings to replace those destroyed by the Persians during Xerxes' invasion, about thirty years before. In particular, he wanted to raise a grand new marble temple to Athena on the southern side of the Acropolis. In time this temple would be known as the Parthenon. Surplus naval funds would help defray the costs of materials and construction.

At once there was an outcry, not from the allies who paid the tribute but from Pericles' aristocratic opponents. They denounced Pericles' proposal as an unseemly attempt to deck Athens out like a pretentious woman in finery and ornaments. Worse, this use of the tribute money would be a fraudulent misappropriation of naval funds and a betrayal of the allies. Pericles had his answer ready. "They do not give us a single horse, soldier, or ship. All they supply is money." In Pericles' view, so long as the Athenians protected their allies at sea, they could do as they wished with the rest of the funds.

All of Attica was then beautified and invigorated as new temples arose to the sea god Poseidon at Cape Sunium, to the vengeful goddess Nemesis at Rhamnous, and to the great goddesses Demeter and Persephone at Eleusis. On a hill above the Agora, overlooking the smoky kilns and casting pits, rose a temple to the craftsman god Hephaestus. Outshining all the other buildings were the new Parthenon and the Propylaea, gateway to the Acropolis.

These marble edifices were the crown of Pericles' ambitious building program and indeed of Athens as well: matchless in grandeur, poise, and harmony. The Parthenon dominated the artificial terrace on the south side of the Acropolis, rising above the massive retaining wall that had been constructed after Cimon's victory at the Eurymedon. To ornament the new statue of Athena inside the Parthenon, some of the city's haul of gold was hammered into sheets. These were then molded into elaborate folds to represent the goddess's robe, setting off the pieces of lustrous ivory that formed her face and arms. In the hand of Athena, Phidias placed an image of the winged goddess Nike ("Victory"), looking as if she had just descended from Mount Olympus to place a victor's wreath upon the brow of Athens.

For all its resplendent decoration and sacred images, the Parthenon had a practical side as well. Phidias' gold and ivory statue not only greeted visitors to the Parthenon but also guarded the hoard of tribute from the Athenian allies, now secured in a special chamber at the west end of the building. Pericles also directed that the gold plating should be removable so that in time of need the metal could be taken off and melted down to pay for ships and other armaments. The Parthenon combined the functions of a temple and a treasury, while serving also as a victory monument for all Athens' triumphs during the Persian Wars. Not far from the temple stood a massive marble stele inscribed with a record of the annual tribute payments from the allies or, more specifically, with a tally of the sixtieth part of each ally's tribute (one drachma per mina of silver) that was given to Athena as her share in the enterprise.

During the Golden Age the city fostered geniuses in many fields. Indeed, the field of history was actually invented at this time. While the Parthenon was under construction, a visitor to Athens named Herodotus was offering public recitations on the Persian Wars, that epic contest that led to the emergence of Athenian thalassocracy. Born at Halicarnassus in Asia Minor, Herodotus had been a young boy when Queen Artemisia returned with her triremes after the battle of Salamis. As a man he traveled widely, collecting stories from veterans on both sides.

In time Herodotus came to view the Persian Wars, and indeed all of Hellenic history, as a series of conflicts between East and West, Asia and Europe. The saga started when ancient seafarers from one continent kidnapped women from the other. The abductions of the Greek princess Io, the Phoenician princess Europa, the Asiatic sorceress Medea, and even Helen of Troy were hostile acts and reprisals in this age-old struggle. He then traced the conflict through the rise of the Persian Empire and its epic collision with the free cities of Greece. The impact of Herodotus' theorizing was so profound that it changed the meaning of the word *historia*. Before Herodotus it had meant no more than "inquiry" or "research"—the term that he himself applied to his epic work. After him it designated a new branch of human intellectual endeavor: the quest to compile a record of events that would uncover root causes and recurring patterns.

The stories recorded by Herodotus confirmed two controversial Athenian claims: their right to the leadership of the Greeks, and the justice of their maritime empire. Herodotus indeed concluded that the Ionians had been subjugated by the Athenians because they were unfit to maintain their own liberty. He exposed their flawed character in the tales of the great naval battle of Lade that ended the Ionian revolt against Persia, when the Ionian crews refused to submit to the arduous training in rowing and seamanship that might have granted them victory. In considering the rise of Athens, Herodotus expressed a view that he knew would fly in the face of popular opinion among many readers outside Athens. "If the Athenians, through fear of the approaching danger of Xerxes, had abandoned their country, or if they had stayed in Greece and submitted to the Persians, there would have been no attempt to resist the Persians by sea. In view of this, therefore, one is surely right to say that Greece was saved by the Athenians."

While Herodotus studied history and geography, Sophocles addressed himself to questions of ethics, morals, and human destiny. The son of a sword manufacturer, Sophocles had been in the public eye since his youth, when he led the victory dance for Salamis. In addition to commanding an Athenian naval squadron as a general in the Samian War, he had also held the position of *Hellenotamias,* one of the "treasurers of the Greeks" who supervised the tribute from the allies. Names were believed to hold great significance, so it is not surprising that Sophocles, whose name was a compound of "Wisdom" and "Glory," seemed the right man for almost any job.

Sophocles brought the sea and ships into his dramas. An unflattering description of a cowardly trierarch is so vivid that it seems drawn from his own experience as general with the fleet. "I've heard a man, a bully with his tongue, ordering his crew to put to sea in dirty weather. Aboard, and in the thick of the storm, you'd always find him speechless, hiding his head beneath his cloak, and letting any man walk over him." In other tragedies Sophocles charted the "sea of troubles" that overwhelmed his heroes and heroines, or compared a government to a "ship of state." He also dramatized the divine punishments meted out to men who were guilty of hubris. To a Greek, hubris was more than arrogance. It was arrogant, wanton violence against others, yet it seemed difficult to control an empire without it.

At the Dionysia festival in Athens, the staging of new plays was preceded by an imperial pageant. After the thousands of Athenians and their guests had taken their seats, a procession of porters emerged from the wings into the circular orchestra, the area where the chorus traditionally sang and danced. Each porter carried a portion of the annual tribute money that had arrived that spring from the allied cities. In a stately parade they carried the hundreds of silver talents in front of the citizens, a reminder of the great wealth that came to Athens over the sea. Only when the treasure had been shown to the people could the dramatic competition proceed.

The Athenian people celebrated the start of a new civic year at midsummer with a festival called the Panathenaea. By the time of Pericles this festival had become a citywide celebration of Athens, its maritime empire, and the goddess under whose aegis both had prospered. During the days of this festival the city was alive with processions, feasts, religious rites, displays of sacred regalia, and competitions for athletes and artists. All the pride that the Athenians felt in their achievements and their city was shown to men and gods during these days of summer.

Among the sporting events of the Panathenaea was a rowing race for triremes. Each of the ten Attic tribes entered its own tribal ship in the regatta, with a crew of young citizens to man the oars. The tribe whose trireme won the race received a prize of three hundred drachmas and two bulls from the organizers of the festival. An additional prize of two hundred drachmas was presented to the crew, one drachma per man, to cover the costs of the victory banquet.

The highlight of the Panathenaea was a grand parade. Young and old, men and women, Athenians and foreigners—all took part. The daughters of the resident aliens carried jars of holy water. Freed slaves carried oak branches. Envoys from the cities and islands of the empire led cattle that would be sacrificed to the goddess. They also brought shining panoplies of hoplite arms and armor as gifts to the city. The centerpiece of the procession was a little galley mounted on wheels that was called the Panathenaic ship.

Before the start of the procession many citizens joined in the symbolic ritual of grasping long ropes to raise the mast and hoist the yardarm.

The climactic moment came with the unfurling of the sail. For nine months young girls of old Athenian families had been weaving and embroidering a beautiful new robe or *peplos,* the city's birthday gift for their goddess. Now their handiwork adorned the sail of the sacred ship. The design, glowing with purple and saffron dyes, showed Athena triumphing over the giants in the great battle of gods and titans. The people caught their first glimpse of the new robe as the ship rolled through the Potters' Quarter and the Agora, billowing in the summer breeze. The sail with the *peplos* was suspended high in the air above a "crew" of priests and priestesses crowned with golden garlands. At the far side of the Agora the slope up to the Acropolis became too steep for this elaborate parade float. Here the sail was taken down, to be carried on foot up the long flights of marble steps to the sunlit summit. In a final act of reverence, the new robe was offered to the goddess, whose ancient wooden image was the holiest possession of the Athenian people. It was fitting that each year the Athenians presented their patron deity with a robe that was also a sail. With this act of devotion they reminded themselves, their maritime allies, and the world at large that Athens, from its harbors right up to its highest citadel, was a city wedded to the sea.

CHAPTER 10

War and Pestilence

[433–430 B.C.]

Here is the rock that strands me now:
With one side or the other it must come to war.
That's as sure as a ship's hull pegged tight.
Nowhere do I see safe, untroubled harborage.

—Aeschylus

ON A LATE SUMMER MORNING, AS WORK ON THE PARTHENON was drawing to completion, a squadron of ten fast triremes rowed out of the Piraeus bound for the west of Greece. Though small, the squadron was top-heavy with brass, as it carried no fewer than three Athenian generals. One was Lacedaemonius, the son of Cimon and grandson of Miltiades, victor of Marathon. With him were the generals Proteas and Diotimus, the latter of whom had visited in the course of his travels both the court of the Great King in the east and the Bay of Naples in the west. No practical military purpose could be served by putting three generals in command of ten ships. Their mission was not to make war but to prevent it.

As the little squadron pursued its course around the Peloponnese, Lacedaemonius and his colleagues had ample time to reflect on the difficulties that lay ahead. In their direst imaginings, however, they could never have predicted that their expedition to the island of Corcyra would renew dormant hostilities with the Spartans and ultimately embroil Athens in the most destructive of all its conflicts, the Peloponnesian War.

Pericles had just turned sixty, and Athens' maritime empire was basking in peace and prosperity. A seemingly insignificant cloud had appeared on the horizon a couple of years earlier, when a war blew up between Corcyra and Corinth. Athenian steersmen knew Corcyra well: its harbors were the last stations in Greek waters for ships bound northward into the Adriatic Sea or westward to Italy. Almost from the time the Corinthians established a colony on Corcyra, many generations earlier, the islanders had been at odds with their mother city. The earliest known naval battle in Greek history had in fact been fought between these two antagonists, and the Corcyraeans had won. That battle was now ancient history, but disputes between mother city and colony had flared up once more in the days of the Persian Wars. Themistocles himself was called upon to act as arbitrator.

Now hostilities had erupted again. Faced with the prospect of contending against not only the Corinthians but also other maritime cities of the Spartan alliance, the stiff-necked and friendless Corcyraeans unbent from their policy of isolation and asked the Athenians to accept them as allies. When the Corinthians got wind of the Corcyraean embassy, they sent envoys of their own to Athens. The deputation from Corinth urged the Assembly to turn down the Corcyraean alliance and adhere to the spirit of the Thirty Years' Peace. After the first day of debate the Assembly seemed ready to reject any involvement in this distant conflict. Afterward, talking over the question with friends and families, the Athenians began to envision the advantages of an alliance with Corcyra. That night many dreamed of extending their empire westward to Italy and Sicily or even into the realms of the Etruscans and Carthaginians.

Next morning the citizens climbed up to the Pnyx in a changed mood. They consented to a purely defensive alliance, promising to aid Corcyra in the event of an enemy attack on the island. The Assembly then voted to send a squadron of ten triremes to Corcyra. Three Athenian generals would act as observers of the conflict, and their presence would remind the Corinthians that the island was now an Athenian ally. Under no circumstances were they to launch an attack on Corinthians. Only if Corinthian ships attempted to land on Corcyra were the Athenian generals authorized to use force.

At Corcyra the three Athenian generals found that their new allies had assembled a fleet of 110 triremes. After some twenty days of suspense, messengers brought word that a large enemy fleet was approaching from the Gulf of Corinth. At once the Corcyraeans and Athenians launched their ships and moved southward to meet it. They planned to face the enemy in the opening of the gulf that divided the southern cape of Corcyra from the mainland, a wide and troubled stretch of water where the currents running up the coast met the winds that blew down the channel. The ten Athenian ships took up a position supporting the Corcyraean right wing at the southernmost tip of the island, where an expanse of shoals made navigation hazardous. To their left the line of Corcyraean triremes stretched away toward a pair of steep and rocky islets called the Sybota Islands.

Shortly after dawn triremes began to appear in the open sea to the south. The size of the enemy force was alarming. To their own ninety ships the Corinthians had been able to add sixty from their own allies and colonies. An army of barbarian warriors from tribes friendly to Corinth followed the fleet on the mainland shore. The lookouts on the Corinthian ships had no difficulty in picking out the Athenians, easily identified in the morning light by the gilded figures of Athena on their triremes. The Corinthians accordingly formed a battle line with their allies on the right wing, so that their own best ships would confront the Athenian "observers." If they induced Lacedaemonius and the other Athenians to attack them, then the Thirty Years' Peace could be considered broken. And if the Spartans could then be persuaded to make war on Athens with the full force of their Peloponnesian alliance, Athenian naval power would surely be humbled, leaving room for Corinth to recover its ancient position as mistress of the seas.

Except for the ten triremes from Athens, the ships on both sides were crowded with hoplites, archers, and javelin throwers. This use of galleys as mere floating platforms for soldiers struck the Athenians, holding aloof, as very primitive. They would see no sophisticated ramming maneuvers, no displays of skill from steersmen or rowers. As the two lines surged forward and collided, the ships became locked together in a great crush. The decks then became a floating battlefield. Amid a din of shouts and cheers the troops forged across onto the enemy ships that were caught alongside their own.

From their station the Athenians saw the Corcyraean triremes on the distant left wing making short work of the Megarians and the other allied contingents. After the first reverses most of the enemy ships broke free and fled south into the open sea. Nothing could prevent the jubilant Corcyraeans from abandoning their own line and giving chase. Discipline and tactical sense were thrown to the winds by these western Greeks, not giving a thought to the battle that still hung in the balance behind them.

On the other wing the fighting followed a different course, as the presence of the Athenian ships gave the advantage to the Corcyraeans. Initially the Athenians were able to keep the enemy at bay without actually striking a blow. As a Corinthian ship bore down on an opponent, one of the ten Athenian triremes would move up to threaten its flank. Frustrated and fearful, the Corinthians would veer off or back away from their targets. For all their skill and speed, however, the Athenians could not be everywhere at once. As the morning wore on, Corinthians beyond the reach of Athenian rams were able to engage and board Corcyraean triremes. Finding that their maneuvers no longer had any effect, the Athenian triremes were drawn one by one into actual contact. They made no more feints but now engaged in open attacks and hand-to-hand fighting. In the fury of battle, they forgot the Assembly's orders and the dictates of prudence. As if the two cities were already at war, the ships from Athens began to ram those of Corinth.

Had the Corcyraean left wing maintained order and turned their attack on the Corinthians, they might have saved the day. By now they were far away, however, chasing their prizes. Worse, it soon became clear that the Athenians had waited until too late to help the right wing. All moral and strategic advantage lost, the Athenians had to break off their attacks and join the fleeing Corcyraeans in the dash to shore and safety. From there they watched helplessly as the Corinthians rowed back and forth among the wreckage, spearing most of the men struggling in the water or clinging to floating timbers. Only when the enemy had finished this killing did they take in tow the abandoned ships, pick up their own dead, and row away to a cove on the mainland, beyond the Sybota Islands.

It was now afternoon. The crews had been at the oars since before dawn, and the struggle on the decks had exhausted the fighting men. The Corcyraeans on the right wing had lost most of their triremes, and even with the return of the renegade left wing they were no match now for the enemy. So it was with consternation that they saw movement on the opposite shore. The Corinthians were putting out again, rowing up the channel to attack a second time. Evidently they meant to finish the job that the morning's battle had begun: the complete destruction of Corcyraean naval power and the extinguishing of Athenian efforts to avoid all-out war. Doggedly the Corcyraeans and their Athenian allies, observers no longer, manned their ships once again and rowed out to face their attackers.

In the fading light the two lines approached each other, the Corinthian troops singing their paean as they rowed forward. Then the chant abruptly ceased. The Athenians awaited the attack. Yet after a short hesitation the Corinthians began to back away. Oars reversed, they retreated from the line of battle, keeping their rams toward the enemy as they moved off. The Athenians and Corcyraeans watched this strange maneuver, mystified, until their lookouts caught sight of the apparition that had motivated the Corinthian retreat. More triremes were coming up over the southern horizon, twenty in all: triremes of Athens, sent by the Assembly. Second thoughts had convinced the Athenians at home that the original squadron had been too small. Through a watery field of wreckage came these reinforcements, arriving at the end of their long voyage a few hours too late to rescue Athenian honor. Still, they had come in time to save the lives of their fellow citizens.

The next morning the remnant of the Corcyraean fleet and the squadron of Athenian ships, doubly shamed by the events of the day before, arrayed themselves in line of battle offshore from the Corinthian camp. The Corinthians launched their ships but did not advance, unwilling to attack a fleet that included even thirty Athenian ships in open water. Eventually the Athenians saw a small boat rowing across from the enemy line. When the boat was within hailing distance, a Corinthian on board called across to the Athenians, ignoring the Corcyraeans. He accused the Athenians of breaking the Thirty Years' Peace and thus putting themselves in the wrong. The Corinthians, the herald claimed, were only chastising rebellious allies of their own. If the Athenians intended to block their way to Corcyra or anywhere else, and if they meant to break the peace, then they could start by seizing the Corinthians in the boat as their first prisoners.

The Corcyraeans all shouted to the Athenians to take the Corinthians and kill them. The Athenians were more moderate. They told the Corinthians to take their ships anywhere that they wished, so long as they left Corcyra alone. The Corinthians and their allies then rowed away to the south, confident that the Athenians would not risk a further breach of the treaty by attacking their rear. Corcyra had been preserved, but at a cost of seventy Corcyraean triremes, a thousand prisoners now in Corinthian hands, and thousands more killed in the fighting or drowned. As the Athenians made their way home through autumn seas, they could add two other casualties to the list: the military and political career of Cimon's son Lacedaemonius, and the Thirty Years' Peace itself, now gravely wounded but not quite dead.

The Corinthians lost no time in descending upon the leaders of their alliance, the Spartans, to accuse Athens of breaking the peace. The Corinthian cause attracted others. Megarians complained that Pericles had barred them from the harbors under Athenian control. Islanders from Aegina bemoaned their lost autonomy. There were even Macedonians among the throng, fearful of Athenian power in the north. That winter Sparta hummed with angry allies demanding that Athens be attacked and humbled.

When the Athenians heard the generals' report on the battle of the Sybota Islands, they sent a peremptory order to the one and only Corinthian colony within their empire, the wealthy northern city of Potidaea. Though the Potidaeans had as yet done nothing wrong, the Athenians doubted their loyalty. To prevent the Corinthians from using Potidaea as a base, the Athenians ordered the Potidaeans to expel their Corinthian magistrates, pull down part of their fortifications, and send hostages to Athens. The Potidaeans delayed responding to the Athenian demands, while secretly they sent messages to Sparta, begging for aid.

On receiving a covert and unfounded assurance that the Spartans were prepared to invade Attica, the Potidaeans revolted openly from Athenian rule. Many neighboring cities followed their lead, creating a crisis for imperial Athens. Unmoved by these events, the Spartans took no action at all. A Corinthian force went by sea to defend its colony. Athens in turn sent fleet after fleet to recapture the city and the surrounding region. When the strong walls of Potidaea withstood their first attacks, the Athenians dispatched a fleet under the veteran general Phormio carrying sixteen hundred hoplites, the pick of Athens' land forces, to join the siege.

Among the troops who went north with Phormio were two citizens very much in the public eye: Alcibiades and Socrates. Alcibiades, a young kinsman and ward of Pericles, was setting out on his first military campaign. Only eighteen, wild and handsome, Alcibiades had already become notorious for escapades that not even the sober Pericles could keep under control. The young man had inherited martial courage from his father, who had been killed in action under general Tolmides' command, and political gifts from his mother, a great-niece of the lawgiver Cleisthenes. Alcibiades' ungovernable passions, however, seemed to be very much his own. His rich horse-breeding clan must often have dealt with rogues among their herds. Now they had one in the house, eager to make himself master of the family and then perhaps of all Athens.

The philosopher Socrates, the constant companion of Alcibiades, was in his late thirties. He reminded Athenians irresistibly of a satyr, or the potbellied, snub-nosed, wine-imbibing companion of Dionysus called Silenus. A familiar figure in the Agora, Socrates was the first native Athenian to vie intellectually with the many foreign-born philosophers who had made Athens their home, from Anaxagoras with his primordial elements to Zeno with his paradoxes. Socrates' father was a sculptor, his mother a midwife. Early training as a sculptor had given way to an interest in natural history. Now he bemused his fellow Athenians with theories about the origin of the sun and moon, and whether humans think with their blood. However rarefied his scientific pursuits, Socrates was a citizen of the hoplite class. When his name appeared on the call-up lists, it was his duty to appear bearing his arms and three days' rations to join the expedition.

As the troop carriers rowed north, the air grew cold, but Socrates wore only one cloak as usual. He seemed oblivious to physical discomfort. Alcibiades, universally attracted and attractive, fixed on the imperturbable philosopher as his next amorous target. Socrates for his part was interested in the challenge of educating a youth who promised, more than Pericles' own sons, to become a force—whether for good or evil—in the city's future.

Phormio's forces made a landfall nine miles south of Potidaea and advanced slowly toward the city, ravaging the farms in the countryside in the hope of provoking the citizens within the walls to come out and attack. When the Potidaeans declined the gambit, the Athenian troops launched a series of direct assaults. During one attempt to storm a defensive wall that ran from sea to sea across a narrow isthmus, Alcibiades battled alongside

Socrates. At length he exposed himself so rashly that he was struck by an enemy missile and fell. The Athenian line moved on and left the pair exposed. Socrates stayed on guard, shielding the wounded Alcibiades till a rescue party reached them. After the battle Phormio awarded Alcibiades the coveted prize for valor: a complete bronze hoplite panoply. Socrates was eager in approving their general's decision. Alcibiades just as eagerly insisted that by rights the prize belonged to Socrates.

While the Athenians in the north kept up their long and costly siege, Spartan envoys began to arrive in Athens. They declared that Athens had indeed broken the Thirty Years' Peace and must be punished with war if they did not redress the wrongs they had done to the Peloponnesians. The Spartans had formulated three demands. First, the Athenians must end the siege of Potidaea, where Phormio and other commanders were attempting to starve the rebels into submission. Second, they must restore the autonomy of Aegina. Finally, they must rescind the notorious proclamation known as the Megarian Decree, which excluded citizens of Megara from the Agora and the harbors of the Athenian empire. If not, there would be war.

It was—initially, at any rate—a war of words. In response to the Spartan demands Pericles posed a series of awkward questions. Why had the Spartans not asked to submit their complaints to arbitration? Athens was willing. Why did the xenophobic Spartans not open their own borders to the Athenians? The Athenians would allow the Megarians into their harbors as soon as the Spartans ceased to exclude foreigners from their own territory. Finally, when would Sparta permit its allies to choose their own governments, even if the choice was for a democracy? Athens would agree to free its allies as soon as Sparta led the way.

Pericles assured the Athenians that as long as they maintained their rule of the sea, they held an insuperable advantage over the Spartans. The Athenians had gained experience of land fighting through amphibious naval operations. He predicted that the Spartans would find seamanship difficult to learn. After half a century of practice, the Athenians had still not entirely mastered the subject. How could Spartans make much progress? They were landsmen, not seafarers.

It remained for Pericles to calm Athenian concerns that the Spartans could defeat them by invading Attica. Here again the great statesman assured the Assembly that the navy would prove their salvation. His strategy evoked the vision of Themistocles. "Sea power is of enormous importance. Look at it this way. Suppose Athens were an island, would we not be absolutely secure from attack? As it is, we must try to think of ourselves as islanders; we must abandon our land and our houses, and safeguard the sea and the city." With Athens linked to the sea by the Long Walls, and the navy ensuring that food and other supplies continued to reach the Athenians, no Spartan attack or siege could have any hope of succeeding.

The strategy that Pericles had devised was entirely based on the Athenian navy: its ability to control the seaways that brought food to Athens, and its power to keep the treasury full. He foresaw a war in which the Athenian army would never have to confront the Spartans on land, regardless of the temptations of honor and national pride. Instead, Pericles would voluntarily give up Attica and its farmlands to the invaders, just as Themistocles had once done. With the Peloponnese stripped of its troops, the Athenian fleet could attack the enemy's coasts with impunity. Yes, there would be war, or something very like a war, but it would be a war without battles. The combatants would be locked in mutual hostilities without ever actually confronting each other. Soon the fire-breathing Spartans, balked of a decisive battle and worn down by seaborne raids, would sue for peace. Pericles' strategy was as triumphantly scientific, as coolly calculated, as a mathematical formula or a medical prescription.

Young Athenians were eager for war, but Pericles' strategy made no demands on their enthusiasm, courage, or willingness to die for their city. Those hot emotions belonged to hoplite warfare. They would be a positive danger to Athens in the coming war with the Peloponnesians. Pericles called instead for naval virtues: self-control, timing, and silence. As steersman of the ship of state, he would devote himself to the plotting of courses and balancing of odds. So long as the Athenians could resist the natural urge to defend their land, they might wage and win a war without risk, indeed almost without inconvenience. It was for this that they had built the Long Walls. Athens was now an island, fed by its fleet, and as long as it remained so it was unconquerable.

As for the Spartans, they had confidence in their army but were acutely conscious of their inferiority in naval matters. While their envoys were visiting Athens, they were sending other messages to their seafaring allies in Sicily and southern Italy. The Spartans appealed to these fellow Dorian Greeks for aid against the despised Ionians led by Athens. The wealthy westerners could surely spare some money for the cause. The Spartans also requested, with almost stupefying naïveté, that the Sicilian and Italian cities assemble a fleet of five hundred triremes for the coming war against Athens.

After two years of provocations and planning, neither great power was willing to initiate hostilities. The spark was finally touched off by one of Sparta's hotheaded allies. The citizens of Thebes, a member of the Peloponnesian League, had long coveted the small but free city of Plataea, a loyal Athenian ally since before the Persian Wars. On a stormy night in early spring the Theban army launched a surprise attack. It failed to capture Plataea, but all parties recognized that the war had now begun. Just forty-nine years had passed since Xerxes' invasion, when a common danger had brought Sparta and Athens together for the good of all Greeks. The war between these two former allies would prove far more destructive to Greece than any disasters inflicted by the Persians.

Following the strategy laid down by Pericles, the Athenians who lived in the villages and farms of Attica prepared for evacuation. Abandoning their own countryside, they shipped their livestock across the channel to Euboea, just as their ancestors had done almost fifty years before in the face of Xerxes' invasion. This time, however, the people did not seek refuge across the water. At first they crowded into Athens itself, filling every available space except the sanctuaries. When that situation became intolerable, thousands of temporary dwellings were hastily constructed in the corridor between the Long Walls. These were allotted to the displaced population.

When the Peloponnesian army marched into Attica in early summer under the command of a Spartan king, Pericles prevented the Athenians from making any attempt to protect their farms and crops. Unopposed, the Peloponnesians fanned out across the deserted country, plundering and burning. Under the shock of seeing smoke rising from their fields, the people forgot all about the master plan. They turned on Pericles, blaming him for their losses. To keep their unreasoning anger from finding a vent, Pericles postponed all meetings of the Assembly. Democratic principles were thus sacrificed on the altars of two great gods: Expediency and Security.

In response to the Peloponnesian invasion by land, Pericles ordered the preparation of a large fleet to carry out reprisals on enemy territory. One hundred fast triremes were equipped, carrying a combined force of a thousand marines and four hundred archers. Leaving the scorched earth of Attica behind them, the fleet set out to capture enemy towns and raid enemy territory while the Peloponnesians were occupied in Attica, too far off to protect their own coasts.

Following the strategy that Tolmides had pursued with such success, the Athenians launched surprise attacks followed by speedy withdrawals, swooping down on undefended shores like birds of prey and departing almost as swiftly. When the fleet reached western waters, it was joined by fifty triremes from Corcyra, in accordance with the alliance. At the southwestern cape of the Peloponnese they attacked Methone and almost took the town. After squalls interrupted their assaults on Elis, the Athenians crossed over to northwestern Greece, capturing two cities and bringing the large wooded island of Cephallenia over to their alliance. Returning home, the expeditionary force found the Peloponnesian army gone and the Athenian army invading the territory of Megara in reprisal for the invasion of Attica.

During the war's first year Athenian triremes were also operating in home waters. One hundred of them were patrolling the seas around Attica. Another fleet attacked Aegina. The Athenians landed, forced the Aeginetans into exile, and distributed the island's territory among settlers from Athens. Thirty triremes were cruising the seas around Euboea to guard Athenian livestock and other property from privateers. Before the summer was over, they set up a small naval station on an islet called Atalante. From there the campaign against piracy could be kept up throughout the year.

Now that the war seemed certain to last for two or even three years, the Athenians took additional steps to secure their territory. Guard stations were created at strategic sites around the coast of Attica. One thousand talents were set aside on the Acropolis as a reserve, to be used only in the event of an enemy attack on the city by sea. Any proposal to expend these funds for

ATHENIAN HORSE CARRIER

a different purpose would be punishable by death. In addition to the reserve of silver, the Athenians voted to set aside one hundred of their best triremes every year and appoint one hundred trierarchs to keep them ready.

Over the winter Athenian shipwrights began work on a new project in the Navy Yard. They selected ten old triremes and converted each one into a *hippagogos* or horse carrier. To make the change, the interior of the trireme's hull had to be altered. The carpenters dismantled the rowing seats of the lower two tiers of oarsmen and sealed up the oar ports, leaving an enclosed space some eighty feet long by sixteen feet wide. The empty hold, formerly the domain of 108 zygian and thalamian rowers, would now accommodate thirty horses.

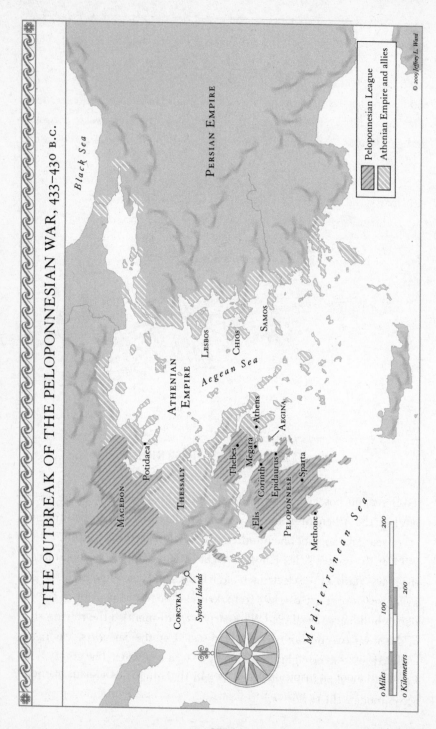

THE OUTBREAK OF THE PELOPONNESIAN WAR, 433–430 B.C.

Black Sea

PERSIAN EMPIRE

Aegean Sea

ATHENIAN EMPIRE

LESBOS

CHIOS

SAMOS

MACEDON

Potidaea

THESSALY

Thebes

Megara

Athens

AEGINA

Corinth

Epidaurus

Elis

PELOPONNESE

Sparta

Methone

CORCYRA

Sybota Islands

Mediterranean Sea

Peloponnesian League

Athenian Empire and allies

© 2009 Jeffrey L. Ward

0 Miles   100   200

0 Kilometers   200

Fifteen animals could be tethered along either side, spaced about five feet apart. Floor width was constricted at the waterline, but at head height the flaring sides of the trireme would provide additional room for the horses' forequarters. Storage spaces were then created for fodder and fresh water, saddles and bridles, and for the lances, shields, and helmets of the horsemen. The shipwrights refitted the sterns of the vessels with removable sections and gangways so that when the ships came to shore, the horses could easily be led or even ridden out onto the beach.

The creation of these horse carriers marked the first major innovation in Athenian naval architecture since Cimon introduced the fully decked troop carrier thirty-five years earlier. New ships called for new names: *Hippodromia,* "Horse Race"; *Hipparche,* "Queen of Horses"; *Hippocampe,* a mythical monster that was half horse and half fish. There were still Athenians alive who could recall the sight of King Darius' horse carriers and their equine cargoes landing on the beach at Marathon. For the first time the Athenian navy could transport cavalry to war zones overseas, just as the Persians had once done.

One year had passed since the Peloponnesian War began. As the signs of spring appeared, the Athenians seemed poised for success. They had survived a Spartan invasion, inflicted damage on the enemy's coasts, and brought over new allies to their side. Waging war from the northern Aegean to the western isles, Athens had proved again, as in the days of the Egyptian expedition, that it could fight on many fronts at once. The monetary reserves on the Acropolis would sustain three years of such operations. By then Pericles predicted that the Peloponnesians would be glad to end the futile struggle. Even with winds of war blowing all around it, the ship of state seemed to be cruising forward on an even keel.

At the start of the war's second summer, the Spartans led the Peloponnesian army into Attica to destroy crops and farms. And for the second year the invaders watched helplessly as an Athenian fleet rowed out of the Piraeus to attack their own coasts. The armada included ten of the new horse carriers and fifty ships from the Athenian allies on Lesbos and Chios.

To the Athenians, all seemed well, but there were in fact troubling signs at the Piraeus. Fatalities were reported from an unknown disease. In the heightened mood of suspicion brought on by the war, the Athenians blamed the enemy. The Peloponnesians, they said, must have somehow poisoned the water in the Piraeus reservoirs. When the fleet departed for that summer's cruise, the mysterious malady was still unidentified.

Pericles himself commanded the naval expedition, but the itinerary was much less ambitious than that of the first year. Perhaps the horse carriers slowed the fleet, or perhaps Pericles was reluctant to voyage too far from Athens. After assaulting a few cities on the Saronic Gulf and the eastern coast of the Peloponnese, the fleet turned back. Pericles reported that they had almost taken the town of Epidaurus by storm, but the expedition had achieved no solid success. At the Piraeus they discovered that the sickness they had left behind them had become a plague, and had already claimed hundreds of lives.

After a short time in port some of the triremes were handed over to new generals for yet another expedition to Potidaea, where the siege was still dragging on. Wooden siege machinery was loaded onto the ships, and the crews embarked again, this time heading north. The plague went with them. Within the cramped hulls of the triremes the explosive disease could not be controlled. When the fleet arrived at Potidaea, the plague spread from the ships to the entire Athenian camp.

An aristocratic young Athenian named Thucydides caught the plague that year but survived to write an account of the disease, from the burning head and eyes at the start on through the bleeding mouth, the chest pains, the bilious vomiting, the eruption of pustules on the skin, and the restless insomnia. Most victims died after seven or eight days.

By the time the new generals at Potidaea abandoned their effort and led the fleet home, more than a thousand of the expedition's hoplites had died of the plague. Arriving at the Piraeus, they found the plague everywhere. Starting around the harbors, it had spread through the crowded huts between the Long Walls and swiftly reached Athens itself. Corpses of rich and poor alike littered the temples and choked the water tanks. Pericles lost his two elder sons, Xanthippus and Paralos. As he was placing a wreath on Paralos' body before the lighting of the pyre, Pericles finally broke down and wept in public. Only Aspasia and their illegitimate son, young Pericles, were spared. Responding to an emotional appeal, the Assembly agreed to rescind Pericles' own citizenship law so that the boy could be recognized as an Athenian. One-third of the hoplites died of the plague—a number that could be determined exactly from the register of names kept by the generals and the tribal commanders. Other segments of the population probably perished in the same proportion.

The most famous of Sophocles' plays, *Oedipus Rex,* or "Oedipus the King," seemed to hold up a mirror to the tragic fates of Pericles and Athens. Like Pericles, the hero Oedipus insisted on the rule of reason and order, never suspecting that his own actions and destiny were bringing disaster on the city. Like the Athenians, the people in Sophocles' drama had been struck by a devastating pestilence and called on their leader to save them: "Better for you to rule a land with men than an emptiness. Walls and ships are nothing without men living together inside them." As events spiraled downward toward catastrophe, even Queen Jocasta admitted that the ship of state might be doomed: "Now we all feel fear, seeing the ship's steersman fail."

As for the real plague, the Athenians eventually learned that they could blame neither the Peloponnesians nor the water supply of the Piraeus. Ships, not Spartans, had brought the sickness to Athens. The epidemic had originated in Ethiopia and then spread down the Nile River to the ports of the delta. From there, a hidden cargo in holds and cabins, it crossed the sea to the Piraeus. When the Spartans and their allies destroyed the wheat harvest of Attica, they left the Athenians more dependent than ever on imported grain. The Peloponnesians grew much of their own wheat and were cut off from foreign supplies by the vigilance of the Athenian navy. The epidemic scarcely touched them.

The plague wrecked Pericles' grand strategy. He could not have foreseen or prevented such a calamity, but the people laid the blame on him. Athens could no longer assemble great fleets for the amphibious campaigns that were to have countered the annual Spartan invasions of Attica. The danger of contagion made it too dangerous to pack the crews together inside the ships. The crowded conditions created by bringing all residents of Attica inside the walls had in the end cost thousands of lives. Pericles' powers of reason seemed no match for the forces of nature. Not content with fining him, the angry Assembly voted to strip Pericles of his official powers as general. Athenian envoys traveled to Sparta seeking peace, but the Spartans rebuffed the offer. Instead they were negotiating with the Persians, hoping to bring the Great King into the war on their side. In that dark hour Athenians no longer thought of victory, only of survival.

CHAPTER 11

Fortune Favors the Brave

[430–428 B.C.]

"But tactical science is only one part of generalship," said Socrates. "A general must be capable of equipping his forces and providing for his men. He must also be inventive, hardworking, and watchful—bullheaded and brilliant, friendly and fierce, straightforward and subtle."

—Xenophon

THE ONLY GENERAL CAPABLE OF SAVING ATHENS WAS AT THAT moment living in poverty, disgrace, and dishonor, almost forgotten by his fellow citizens. Phormio had been a successful commander through almost three decades of service to the city, but like Pericles he had fallen victim to the people's hunt for scapegoats during the plague. Always ready to answer the trumpet's call even without pay, Phormio was Ares in the civic pantheon of celebrities, a counterpart to the Zeus of Pericles. Both Olympians had fallen from favor.

Though his ancestry was as noble as any Athenian's, Phormio was now a poor man. In the course of his honest generalship at Potidaea he had helped provide for his troops from his own personal funds. After his return to Athens the civilian scrutiny board censured him for his conduct of the campaign and fined him one hundred silver minai. Phormio was too proud to beg or borrow the money from friends. His failure to pay the punitive fine led to an official ban of *atimia* or dishonor. Until it was lifted, he could not set foot on consecrated ground, including the Acropolis, the Agora, and the Pnyx.

In this crisis Phormio left the city and retired to his ancestral home at Paiania on the far side of Mount Hymettus. The family farm lay in the heart of the broad plain called Mesogaia or Middle Earth and had been visited earlier that summer by the marauding Peloponnesian army. For forty days the Spartans and their allies had worked their way through Attica, spreading fire and destruction everywhere. Phormio had been a small boy when Xerxes' army had devastated the countryside. Just as the men of his father's generation had done, Phormio settled down to live off the blackened earth, work his fields, and plant his crops. His career as a naval commander seemed over.

Now almost sixty, Phormio was used to living rough. On his many campaigns he had shared the hardships and short rations of his troops. Every day he stripped down and exercised naked, like a boy toughening his body in the gymnasium at home. Phormio had kept up this regimen in all weathers, winter and summer. Exposure to sun and wind had burned his body dark brown, so the men gave him one of Heracles' nicknames, Melampygous or "Black Butt." At night he slept on the ground. His pallet was a reed mat so thin and poor that "Phormio's sleeping mat" became a proverb in Athens to describe anything of truly wretched quality.

His look of a simple, weatherbeaten campaigner was deceptive. He had stormed cities, won allies, enriched the public treasury, and even beaten fifty enemy triremes with an Athenian fleet of only thirty. Phormio's genius lay in quick improvisation on unexpected themes, and in his conviction that every situation, no matter how discouraging, offered a chance for victory. That chance had to be discovered and exploited through *mêtis*. Through cunning intelligence young Phormio had once tricked a city into opening its gates. On that occasion he borrowed techniques from the playwrights of Athens, including disguises and a dramatic messenger's speech that he wrote and recited himself in order to fool the enemy. In the case of the sea battle of fifty against thirty, Phormio used a standard cavalry formation to hide the true numbers of his ships, thus luring the foolish enemy into undertaking a hasty and disordered charge. For Phormio as for Themistocles, the general's *mêtis* was the decisive element in war.

His career had fallen in between the two supreme challenges to Athenian liberty, the Persian invasion and the Peloponnesian War. Phormio had been too young to fight against Xerxes and would soon be too old to participate further in the war against the Spartans. His antagonists had been unruly westerners, rebellious allies, and Corinthian colonists, with no chance to measure himself against the city's principal foes. Phormio's gifts had been squandered while he played minor roles in distant campaigns, and now, when Athens most desperately needed able commanders, it seemed his disgrace would keep him from coming to his city's aid until it was too late.

One day a party of men approached his farm through the desolate landscape. They were not Athenians but Acarnanians, distant allies who had come to beg Athens for protection. During that second summer of the war, when the plague cut short the Athenian naval expedition around the Peloponnese, enemy fleets had ventured to sea with more than a hundred ships. Corinthians and other Spartan allies had made landings on the territory of Acarnania and other western allies. It seemed clear that the Peloponnesian fleet would return the following year to complete the job unless Athens sent a force to prevent them.

As general of that force, the Acarnanians wanted Phormio. He had been a hero in their country ever since the day long before when he arrived with thirty triremes, stormed a hostile city, and handed it back to its rightful Acarnanian owners. Local families had even named their sons Phormio in honor of the liberator. This party of Acarnanian envoys had arrived at Athens at summer's end after a dangerous voyage, only to learn that the man whom they sought was now banned from office. So they had journeyed through Attica to Phormio's farm, hoping to persuade him to abandon the Athenians and come west with them as a general at large, an honored guest who would take into his own hands the defense of their country. If Athens did not want Phormio, Acarnania did.

Phormio declined the offer. He told his visitors that as a dishonored man and a debtor, he would feel ashamed to face his men. This reply was not completely open. He saw in this unexpected offer a lever that might move the Assembly to reconsider his case. Phormio had no intention of spending his declining years as a soldier of fortune in the wilds of western Greece. Time was running out if he wanted to render any last great service to his city.

Meanwhile back in Athens a strong reaction had emerged in Phormio's favor, perhaps simply because he was now in demand with other Greeks. To cancel his fine, the Assembly resorted to a ruse. The citizens appointed Phormio to decorate the sanctuary of Dionysus for an upcoming festival. One hundred minai of silver from public funds would be handed over to him to cover the cost. Of course Phormio took the money to the scrutiny board instead and paid his fine. He then fobbed off the god Dionysus with a cheap gift, inspiring a couple of comic verses from an anonymous playwright:

Phormio said, "I'll raise three silver tripods!"
Instead he raised just one—made out of lead.

With Phormio's debt cleared and his honor restored, the Assembly reelected him general in charge of a special mission: the defense of Acarnania and other western allies. His base would be Naupactus, a seaside town that had been given to a group of friendly Messenians during Tolmides' circumnavigation of the Peloponnese. From there Phormio could blockade the Corinthian Gulf in both directions, preventing enemy fleets from rowing out, and Sicilian or Italian grain freighters from sailing in. He would face a combination of Spartan allies that had mustered one hundred ships earlier that year. How many triremes would the Assembly assign to him? Twenty. The plague had left Athens incapable of more.

In the first year of the Peloponnesian War the Athenians had launched a war fleet of 180 ships; in the second year, even with the outbreak of the plague, 150. In the war's third year, Phormio's 20 triremes would be the sum of the Athenian naval effort. This squadron was smaller than the vanguard of an Athenian fleet in their days of glory, but with Phormio in command its chances of survival were not as desperate as the numbers suggested. His flagship would be the *Paralos,* pride of the Athenian fleet.

During the winter Phormio left the Piraeus and led his little force around the Peloponnese to Naupactus. The town faced south across a broad oval of water, the westernmost reach of the Gulf of Corinth. Cold streams tumbled down from the hills to the flat reedy shore. To the west the coast curved south toward the Peloponnese, a long finger reaching out as if to touch the opposite shore. The cape at the tip of this finger, Cape Rhium of Molycria, guarded the gulf's narrow entrance. The Messenian exiles at Naupactus gave a warm welcome to Phormio and his fleet. The harbor had room for twenty slipways but little more. The fortifications of Naupactus came right down to the beach and joined the harbor walls to create a complete defensive circuit.

The Athenians held their station unchallenged through the winter and spring. At about midsummer two messengers arrived at Naupactus almost simultaneously, both bearing bad news. From Acarnania came a desperate appeal: the Spartan admiral Cnemus had dodged Phormio's blockade and landed an army that was about to attack the cities that Phormio had been sent out to protect. From the opposite direction Phormio received a report that a large fleet was ready to put to sea from Corinth and other Peloponnesian ports.

Phormio was caught in a dilemma. Without his help Acarnania might fall. He had already failed his friends by letting the Spartan ships elude him. But it was his first duty to block the gulf. The fleet launched by Sparta's maritime allies was no doubt coordinated with the Spartan invasion under Admiral Cnemus. The close timing suggested an attempt to draw him away from Naupactus. Hoping that the Spartans would wait for their reinforcements before proceeding with their attack, Phormio told the unhappy Acarnanian messenger that he could not abandon his post.

The Athenians did not have long to wait. Within a few days they spotted enemy warships cruising westward along the gulf's opposite shore. At once Phormio launched his full force of twenty triremes and rowed south to observe them. A closer view revealed an assemblage of forty-seven triremes with a flotilla of small support vessels bobbing in their wake. Only a few were fast triremes; the rest were heavily laden troop carriers. Phormio had no intention of challenging them inside the gulf. Instead he shadowed them as they passed between the capes and entered the open sea to the west. That evening the Peloponnesian fleet camped at Patras. Instead of returning to Naupactus, Phormio chose to bivouac on the opposite shore. He suspected that the enemy would attempt a night crossing, and he was right.

Several hours before sunrise the Athenians were again at sea, feeling their way southward across the dark water. The sea was flat, the air still. Ahead they could hear the sounds of an approaching fleet. But the enemy was already aware of their presence. By the time the two fleets made contact, the Peloponnesians had arrayed their forces in the same *kyklos* or wheel formation that the Greeks had used with such good results at Artemisium. The troop carriers formed a wide circle with their rams pointing outward, protecting the support vessels like dogs around a flock of sheep. Five fast triremes were also stationed inside the circle, ready to attack any Athenian that dared to break through.

After studying the enemy's wheel, Phormio decided on an oblique and delayed attack. He intended to imitate the ploy used by Greek fishing boats when tackling a big run of tuna. Once alongside the huge fish, the fishermen would row quietly around the school, enclosing their prey within an ever-tightening circle of nets. Herded together, the jostling and terrified tuna inevitably started to leap from the water. As they landed in or near the boats, the fishermen clubbed them to death. Phormio had no nets, but he meant to go fishing nonetheless.

Following their general's lead, the twenty Athenian triremes formed a single line and began a leisurely encircling maneuver, rowing around and around the perimeter of the motionless *kyklos*. At times a single trireme broke from the line to make a ramming charge at a Peloponnesian troop carrier. Convulsively the threatened ship would retreat deeper into the circle, and its companions on either side would pull back to close the gap. At the last moment the Athenian steersman veered away and resumed his place among the prowling triremes in the line. Little by little the Peloponnesian circle contracted. At last the Athenians drew the noose so tight that the oar banks of the troop carriers became enmeshed in a tangled ring.

Even now Phormio held off. He was waiting for the dawn, and the stiff easterly wind that blew every morning out of the Corinthian Gulf. It came at last, catching the Peloponnesian hulls and driving them against one another. Long poles struck planking as mariners tried to fend off neighboring vessels. Choppy waves kicked up by the wind added to the confusion of the colliding ships. In the rough sea the raw Peloponnesian rowers could not lift their oar blades clear of the water, and without steerage way the steersmen were helpless. An uproar of shouts, warnings, and curses drowned the orders of the officers. In the center of the chaos lay the five fast triremes, trapped between small craft and troop carriers.

When the confusion reached its height, Phormio gave the signal to attack. Each of the twenty Athenian triremes aimed for an enemy ship on the outer edge of the struggling mass. The flagship of one Peloponnesian contingent was struck in the first charge. Others followed as the Athenians settled down to the business of ramming every ship within reach. As the mass of ships broke up, those Peloponnesians who could get free fled back toward Patras. Before the morning's work was over, the Athenians had captured twelve enemy triremes and most of their crews: more than two thousand men. At that point they abandoned the chase. With many more prizes they ran the risk of being outnumbered by their prisoners. Not one Athenian ship had been lost.

In Poseidon's sanctuary on Cape Rhium the Athenians raised their victory trophy and sang their paeans. The battle of Patras was Athens' first major success at sea since the beginning of the Peloponnesian War. An extra measure of thanks seemed due to the sea god, so Phormio ordered his crews to haul one of the captured triremes onto the consecrated ground. Near it a stone was inscribed with a dedication to Poseidon and the Athenian hero Theseus. Good news from Acarnania capped the celebrations. The invading army led by the Spartan admiral Cnemus, deprived of the reinforcements sent by sea, had been defeated. For the moment Athens' western allies were safe.

The contest for control of the western seas continued. It was not in the nature of the Spartans to yield so easily, however poorly their allies fought. Scouts brought Phormio word that in the harbors of the Peloponnese shore the troop carriers that had survived the battle of Patras were being refitted by the shipwrights as fast triremes. Sure that he would have to fight again, Phormio sent a messenger to Athens with an appeal for more ships.

The Athenians at home had their own preoccupations. Since the outbreak of the plague the previous summer, the greatest naval power in the Mediterranean had been unable to man a large fleet. Between two and three hundred triremes lay empty in the Navy Yard, lifeless pods of timber without their crews. The outlook on land was even bleaker. The Peloponnesian army was besieging Athens' closest ally, Plataea, yet the Athenians could do nothing to help. The treasury was at low ebb: a naval mission to collect tribute money in Asia Minor ended in the death of the commander. In this hour of crisis the entire city was held in suspense by the imminent loss of its wisest counselor. Pericles had contracted a lingering form of the plague and was slowly dying. Most citizens could not remember an Athens without that calm Olympian figure at the helm.

Phormio and his troubles in the Corinthian Gulf seemed small and far-off. The Assembly could do no more than send him another twenty triremes, and even those could not be spared immediately. On their way to Naupactus the squadron would have to stop at Crete and join with local forces in the assault of Cydonia. Only then could they proceed around the Peloponnese to their rendezvous with Phormio. It seemed uncertain that they could reach him before the Spartans launched another attack. Bearing nothing but bad news, the messenger returned to Naupactus.

At Sparta reaction to the battle of Patras was very different. Admiral Cnemus' report on the Peloponnesian defeat angered the ephors and other leaders who were directing the war against Athens. They could see only one explanation for the humiliating loss. *Malakia!* The allies had been soft! In their fury the Spartans sent out three distinguished commanders to advise Cnemus. The group included a valiant young soldier named Brasidas, who had already scored one victory against an Athenian expeditionary force. For the moment Acarnania was forgotten. Phormio and his blockaders must be destroyed. The advisers delivered new orders to the admiral: muster more ships; prepare the crews for battle; and this time do *not* let a few Athenian ships drive them off the sea.

Fresh levies of ships from league members soon raised the Peloponnesian total to seventy-seven. Phormio would face the combined naval forces of eight states: Sparta, Corinth, Megara, Sicyon, Pellene, Elis, Leucas, and Ambracia. The ships assembled at a place called Panormus, near the mouth of the Corinthian Gulf. From the high citadel at Naupactus, Phormio's lookouts had a clear view of Panormus, five miles to the south across the broad oval of open water. The enemy fleet outnumbered them almost four to one and was backed by a land army that had marched up to reinforce it. Almost overnight a city of mariners and armed men had sprouted on the coast of the Peloponnese.

It was contrary to Phormio's beliefs—and his orders from the Assembly— to yield control of the sea. He had been ordered to guard the entrance to the gulf, and like Leonidas at Thermopylae, he would make his stand where obedience to those orders required. Launching his twenty ships, Phormio moved down to Cape Rhium to show that he meant to fight. Pebbles and shingle covered the shoreline within the gulf, denying him a landing place. So he rounded the cape and set up camp on a sandy beach near the sanctuary of Poseidon, facing west toward the distant isles of Ithaca and Cephallenia. The twenty triremes sent from Athens had still not appeared. His only supporters were a few hundred Messenian hoplites from Naupactus.

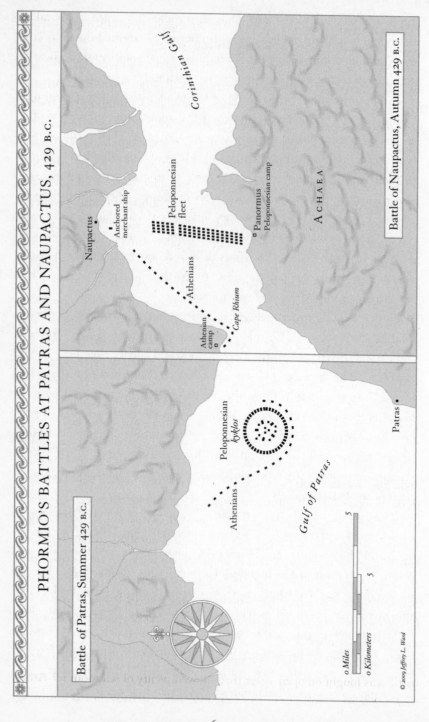

PHORMIO'S BATTLES AT PATRAS AND NAUPACTUS, 429 B.C.

Battle of Patras, Summer 429 B.C.

Battle of Naupactus, Autumn 429 B.C.

Corinthian Gulf

Naupactus

Anchored merchant ship

Peloponnesian fleet

Athenians

Panormus
Peloponnesian camp

A C H A E A

Cape Rhium

Athenian camp

Peloponnesian *kyklos*

Athenians

Gulf of Patras

Patras

0 Miles   5

0 Kilometers   5

© 2009 Jeffrey L. Ward

162

They would protect the camp while the Athenians were at sea and aid any Athenian trireme driven to shore during a battle.

Phormio held a near-mystical faith in the invincibility of the Athenian navy. He often exhorted his men to remember that they were Athenians and the equal of any enemy force no matter how great. Common sense should have convinced him to stay behind the strong walls of Naupactus until the winter storms dispersed the enemy fleet. But Phormio preferred his unprotected beach and an immediate challenge. Here the relief fleet from Athens could reach him most easily, should it ever arrive. Here too he could assert the Athenian rule of the sea on which Pericles had founded his grand strategy. And from here he might lure the Spartans and their allies into the open sea, where the superior skill of his crews and steersmen could be given full rein.

The Spartans' response to Phormio's bold challenge was quiet and ominous. Instead of attacking the Athenians, they began to drill their crews on the calm water of the gulf. Every morning the Athenians pushed off from their beach and formed a battle line outside the entrance to the gulf. From there they observed the enemy's steady improvement in maneuvers and oarsmanship. With each passing day Peloponnesian confidence rose as Athenian morale began to ebb.

After six or seven days Phormio saw signs of an impending mutiny. Normally Athenian citizens serving in the navy felt free to talk back to their officers; perhaps for that very reason actual mutinies were virtually unknown, either by a fleet against its general or by a crew against its trierarch. So it was alarming when knots of fearful men formed here and there in the camp at Cape Rhium, earnestly talking among themselves. Hoping to reverse the despondent mood, Phormio called an assembly by the ships. He spoke frankly about the enemy's advantage of numbers and the Spartans' belief that they held some sort of monopoly on bravery. But he observed that the Peloponnesian allies were unlikely to risk their lives for the cause of Spartan honor. Then he shared his vision of the coming battle: "Great forces before now have been beaten by small ones because of a lack of skill or daring. We lack neither."

Phormio promised that, if humanly possible, he would ensure that the battle was fought on open water that allowed plenty of sea room for Athenian maneuvers, full use of the *diekplous,* and carefully aimed ramming charges. He would keep out of the gulf, where they would have less room to back away if surrounded. In return, Phormio asked his men to play their part. They must stick to their posts, maintaining discipline and silence so that the commands could be clearly heard. Finally he reminded them that they had already won a victory over most of the men in this new fleet. "Beaten men never face danger again with the same resolve."

During the days of training the Spartans had forged the motley collection of allied contingents into a well-ordered line of battle. With almost eighty ships to pit against Phormio's twenty, they were able to array their triremes four deep yet still match the length of the Athenian line. The Peloponnesian right wing, center, and left wing were under the leadership of Brasidas, Lycophron, and the admiral Cnemus. The twenty fastest triremes, however, had been brought together in a special flying squadron posted beyond the right wing—that is, on the north end of the fleet as it faced the Athenians. The Spartan Timocrates commanded this special squadron. He had chosen for his flagship the finest and fastest vessel of all, a trireme from the island of Leucas.

Next morning the Peloponnesians were astir before first light. Whether they meant to train or to fight, the Athenians could not tell. They rowed out from shore four abreast, with Timocrates' squadron leading the way. As the Athenians watched, the fleet rowed north toward the center of the gulf. At any moment Phormio expected the enemy to start the daily exercises. But today was not like the other days. The fleet did not turn: drills and delay were over. This was a battle fleet advancing in quadruple column, ready for action, and it was aimed not at the Athenians at Cape Rhium but at Naupactus.

Phormio had told his men that he would not fight in narrow waters. Now he had no choice. He could not abandon his Messenian allies to a direct assault when all their hoplites had left the city to support him. Hastily and against his will he ordered his fleet to sea. As the Athenian crews poured onto the ships, the Messenians seized their arms and took off overland toward their homes and families. Phormio's triremes rowed in single file with the *Paralos* halfway down the line. Should they have an opportunity to turn and face the Spartans, the flagship would hold the center. As each ship rounded the point of the cape and entered the gulf, its steersman set his course north-northeast toward Naupactus, barely visible at the far end of its curving bay. The race was on.

The Peloponnesians had a head start, but the superior strength and skill of Phormio's crews soon began to tell. There came a moment when the leading Athenian trireme pulled level with the enemy vanguard and then began to draw ahead. It now appeared that the Athenians might win the race and save the city. But the Spartan commanders had never actually intended to assault Naupactus. The harbor was fortified, and their triremes carried no equipment for storming walls. The move to the north had been merely a feint to lure Phormio into fighting on their terms, and the feint had succeeded. It was time to spring the trap.

On signal the seventy-seven Peloponnesian ships executed a sharp left turn. On this new heading their rams pointed directly toward the Athenians. Four ranks deep they attacked. Phormio's ships were caught broadside to the charge. But the Spartans had been too slow. Thanks to their miscalculation, it was clear that that the foremost Athenians were going to escape. As the fleets collided, the nine trailing ships of Phormio's squadron were pushed onto the pebbly shore. The main body of the Peloponnesian fleet crowded after them, eager to take part in this historic victory over Athenians at sea. In the crush the men on some of the trapped ships remained at their posts, desperately fending off enemy grappling irons and boarding parties. When resistance became hopeless, the crews leaped down into the shallows and scrambled to land.

Eleven Athenian triremes had eluded the turning maneuver. These ships were still thrashing along toward Naupactus. To make the victory complete, Timocrates ordered the flying squadron on the Peloponnesian right wing to follow them. At the Spartan's command the twenty triremes swung around into the wake of the last free Athenian ship—the *Paralos*—and set off in pursuit.

The long race had brought the Athenians close to their goal. One after the other the leading Athenian triremes reached Naupactus and wheeled around to face the oncoming enemy. Their rams formed a barrier of bronze across the approach to the harbor. Close by stood a temple of Apollo, built on sacred ground near the water's edge. While they stood at bay, there came wafting to them the sound of distant music. The men in the Peloponnesian triremes were already chanting the paean to Apollo, the ancient hymn of victory. Their singing rolled across the water and echoed off the city walls.

Timocrates' flagship had pulled clear of the pack. Closely followed by another trireme, the ship from Leucas flew along in the wake of the *Paralos*. As they neared the harbor Phormio received a report from the lookout at the prow. Directly ahead a broad-beamed merchant vessel was riding at anchor off Naupactus. The first ten Athenians had already rowed past it, but its unexpected presence sparked an idea in Phormio's mind. Despite the disastrous events of the morning he had not given up hope of striking a blow before the end, whatever the risk. While the Peloponnesians sang, he quickly worked out a plan of action. The command would have to be given immediately, while the anchored freighter still lay ahead. Its bulky wooden hull held out a last chance, if not to win the battle, then to take one enemy ship down with him.

In Greece accidents sometimes happened during chariot races in open country. A leading charioteer had been known to misjudge his course around the turning point at the far end of the track. If he brought his team too far around the post, it would smash headlong into the chariot coming up behind. During the race of the ships toward Naupactus the *Paralos* had been unable to turn on its pursuer. Any change of course would have exposed it to the enemy's ram. Now opportunity had put in Phormio's path an obstacle that might screen his ship while it wheeled around on its pursuer. The freighter would be his turning post, the *Paralos* his chariot. The maneuver was reckless, even suicidal, but there was no time to consider. The Spartan's flagship was only a few lengths astern. Safety lay with the phalanx of ten Athenian triremes lined up across the harbor mouth, but Phormio ignored them. Instead he ordered the steersman to execute a racing turn around the anchored freighter.

The crew at the oars could see nothing outside their ship. The thick screens of hide concealed the stone walls of Naupactus, the merchant vessel, and the enemy fleet astern. With blind faith they answered the shrilling of the pipes and the yells of the coxswain. As the *Paralos* came abreast of the anchored merchantman, the steersman worked the big steering oars so as to turn the trireme as sharply as possible. The rowers, exhausted but still game, worked at pulling their ship around the turn. Halfway through the tight circle, at the crucial moment when the *Paralos* lay broadside to the pursuer's ram, the floating bulwark hid them from view, just as Phormio had foreseen. The moment of vulnerability passed. Bursting out of the turn, the *Paralos* was now aimed like an arrow at the foe. The roles of the two ships were abruptly reversed: the hunter had become the prey.

Phormio's unlikely action left Timocrates no means of saving his ship. To stop, to turn, or to retreat would be equally fatal. In the end the Leucadian trireme continued on course, perhaps hoping to outrun the ramming strike of the *Paralos*. It was not to be. The Athenian rowers took a final stroke and lifted their blades clear of the water. Like wings, gleaming and wet with spray, the outstretched banks of oars hovered motionless as the ship shot forward. Just before impact each man on board the *Paralos* grabbed the nearest timber and braced himself for the shock. Then bronze hit wood, and the Athenian ram plowed deep into the enemy's hull. In an instant both ships were struck motionless. The thunder of the oars gave way to the cries of the enemy wounded and the gurgle of water pouring into the shattered stern of the trireme from Leucas.

As the sea swirled into the breach, Timocrates lost his head. He could still have rallied his band of marines and led them up the towering prow of the Athenian ship. On other occasions fighting men had left their sinking ship, boarded their attacker, and claimed it as a prize. But for the Spartan commander the shock and shame were too great. True to his country's code of choosing death before dishonor, Timocrates drew his sword, braced it against the deck with its point toward his heart, and fell forward. A moment later his lifeless body toppled over the railing and pitched into the sea.

That moment could have been Phormio's last as well. The *Paralos* now lay immobilized before the entire enemy vanguard. His own end, and that of his ship and men, was surely imminent. Incredibly, no attack came. With their flagship destroyed and their commander quite spectacularly dead, the Peloponnesians stopped singing, stopped rowing, stopped steering. Leaderless, they panicked. Some ran aground on the muddy shoals; others lost their way and drifted. Whether aground or afloat, all nineteen were suddenly, fatally vulnerable.

The Athenian trierarchs in the ten triremes near the harbor had witnessed the unbelievable exploit of the *Paralos*. Now they seized the moment.

Someone gave the command to charge; the crews answered with a shout. All ten ships broke from their defensive formation and steered for the hapless Peloponnesians. Phormio's oarsmen backed their ship free from the sinking Leucadian and joined the attack. There was a brief struggle as the Peloponnesians tried to regroup and resist, but it was too late. Momentum now lay with the Athenians. All the Peloponnesians still afloat set off southward as fast as they could row. In their wake came the resurgent Athenians. Quickly they overtook and captured six of the laggards.

As the pursuit swept into the open water of the gulf, an amazing spectacle came into view. Around the nine Athenian triremes earlier driven ashore a battle was raging. The Messenian hoplites had reached the grounded ships as they were running toward Naupactus and turned aside to help. Splashing into the sea, the Messenians hoisted themselves aboard the empty warships and, hand to hand with Spartans at last, fought back from the decks. Already they had recaptured several ships. Pushed onto the defensive, the beleaguered Spartans were startled to see the remnant of Timocrates' squadron streaming toward them with the Athenians in pursuit. At once they gave up the fight and joined their comrades in flight. Those Peloponnesians who had managed to tow away captured triremes had to cut their prizes adrift to save themselves. In the course of the rout the Athenians regained eight of the ships they had believed lost.

At last Phormio called a halt. Most of the Peloponnesians had escaped, taking with them one Athenian trireme with its crew. Even with this loss Phormio and his small force had won an epic victory. The Athenians now sang the paean in their turn, then rowed back to Naupactus. Someone fished the body of Timocrates out of the harbor, where it had been washed up by the currents. The Athenians set up their trophy by the temple of Apollo, overlooking the place where the *Paralos* had turned the fortunes of war. Later they learned that the Spartans considered that there had really been two battles that day, and that the Peloponnesian fleet had won the fight on the shore. So the Spartans too set up a trophy—on their own safe shore at Panormus, well out of reach of vengeful Athenians.

The next morning the southern shore of the gulf, lately so crowded with ships and troops, was empty. Fearing the arrival of reinforcements from Athens, the Peloponnesians had slipped away in the night, too broken in spirit to face Phormio again, though they still outnumbered his little fleet more than three to one. A few days later as autumn ended, the twenty triremes from Athens finally appeared. The newly arrived trierarchs explained that contrary winds and various setbacks on Crete had delayed them. Their absence from the battle of Naupactus merely underscored the dazzling supremacy of Athenian seamanship and the genius of the navy's supreme tactician.

When spring came, Phormio bade farewell to his Messenian allies and took his fleet and his prizes back to the Piraeus. Now sixty, he had fought his last battle. He had also revived the Athenians' flagging efforts and will to fight. After Phormio's victories at Patras and Naupactus there was no more talk of suing the Spartans for peace. To commemorate his triumphs the Athenians dedicated an offering to Apollo in his sanctuary at Delphi. Shields and prows that Phormio had taken from enemy warships were set up in a stoa near the oracular shrine, and an inscribed stele listed the names of the eight members of the Peloponnesian League that Phormio had defeated. The man himself took on a numinous heroic aura. The next time that the Acarnanians sent to Athens for aid, they specified that a son or other kinsman of Phormio should be sent to help them.

The western adventure had begun when Phormio dedicated a lead tripod to Dionysus, and it was in the theater of Dionysus that he underwent his ultimate apotheosis. To honor the victor of Patras and Naupactus, a young Athenian playwright named Eupolis wrote a comedy called *Taxiarchs* after its chorus of regimental officers. The plot brought Dionysus down from Olympus to learn the art of war from Phormio, who put the soft and pleasure-loving god of wine through hard training in rowing and combat skills. At one point the actor playing Dionysus actually rowed a little boat across the playing area, while the actor who played Phormio stood in the bow, giving instructions and complaining when he was splashed by a misplaced stroke. Phormio also introduced Dionysus to the celebrated reed mat on which he slept when in the field. Eupolis' popular comedy was the first to exploit the humorous potential of a tenderfoot's transformation into a soldier. Along with accounts of Phormio's victories in histories and tactical manuals, it carried the great general's fame down to remote generations.

Phormio had been only a boy when Themistocles proclaimed that the

Delphic Oracle's Wooden Wall was in truth the Athenian navy, a god-given defense that would not fail the Athenians in their hour of need. Serving the navy had been his life, and at the end of his career he crowned the beloved Wooden Wall with a pair of unsurpassable victories. His stratagems would long be remembered and imitated by other naval commanders. All those gifts of mind and spirit that set Athenians apart shone at their brightest in Phormio: optimism, energy, inventiveness, and daring; a determination to seize every chance and defy all odds; and the iron will to continue the fight even when all seemed lost—even when the enemy had already begun to celebrate their victory. For Phormio, it was never too late to win.

After his death, a statue of Phormio was raised on the Acropolis near the west front of the Parthenon, where both Athena and Poseidon could look down upon this most favored son from their perches on the pediment. The people interred Phormio's ashes in a tomb beside the Sacred Way. Pericles had already been given the place of honor just outside the city gates, but next to him the Athenians made a monument to Phormio, the greatest naval hero of them all.

CHAPTER 12

Masks of Comedy, Masks of Command

[428–421 B.C.]

Anyone who commands a ship and keeps the sheet too taut, never slackening, is sure to capsize and go the rest of the cruise with his rowers' benches upside down.

—Sophocles

PERICLES WAS DEAD, AND NO ONE IN ATHENS COULD TAKE his place. Had Zeus himself disappeared from Mount Olympus, he could not have left behind a greater void. For over four decades Pericles had been at the forefront of Athenian politics, naval affairs, dramatic productions, the battle between science and religion, diplomacy, city planning, and temple building. The navy had been the cornerstone of his activity as leader. It provided power and prestige for the democratic element in the Assembly, funds for the building programs, and a seemingly invincible safeguard against the city's enemies. Pericles laid down a plan for winning the war against the Peloponnesians but died before he could bring it to a successful end. His overwhelming presence had cast a shadow over rivals and successors alike. The plague had carried off Pericles' sons, and his brilliant but unpredictable ward Alcibiades was still too young to hold a generalship or other elected office. For the first time in a century Athens seemed lacking in leaders.

During the prosperous years of the maritime empire, ordinary working Athenians with no connections to the old landed families had acquired immense fortunes through industry. Manufacturers of everything from bronze shields to musical instruments, these men represented a new elite class in Athens. With the departure of Pericles they promptly took the stage. The first was a rich sheep dealer named Lysicles, who married Pericles' consort Aspasia but was killed soon thereafter while leading a naval expedition to collect tribute in Asia Minor. Another was a fabulously wealthy silver-mining magnate named Nicias, who made up for his lack of noble ancestors with a great show of piety, genteel behavior, sponsorship of festivals—and naval successes at Megara and Cythera. It did not hurt Nicias' public image that his name meant "Man of Victory."

Nicias' chief rival was Cleon, a rich manufacturer of leather. This energetic citizen in his early forties wielded enormous influence in the Assembly, not through feats of arms but through oratorical prowess and a genius for politicking. Like Pericles he was a demagogue or "leader of the people," but a more un-Periclean figure would be hard to imagine. Cleon was passionate, blustering, and verbose. Casting aside statuesque reserve, he bestrode the speaker's platform as if it were the stage at the theater, stamping and gesturing to drive his points home. As watchdog of the empire, Cleon was completely Periclean in his conviction that imperial rule required an iron fist. He was also expert at squeezing ever-larger amounts of tribute from the allies. Athens needed the money to continue the war, and Cleon's brutal treatment led one important city, Mytilene on the island of Lesbos, to rebel. To pay for the siege of Mytilene, the citizens of Athens raised two hundred talents from a war tax on their own property—the first such tax in the history of the Athenian democracy.

Where Pericles and Nicias had been too honorable, or perhaps merely too rich, to take bribes, Cleon harked back to that first naval demagogue, Themistocles. Without shame he used his influence to feather his own nest. The common people supported him loyally, but most of the wealthy citizens who served as trierarchs and horsemen loathed him. Cleon returned their hostility with interest. When motions in the Assembly failed, the ever-litigious Cleon would drag his opponents into the courts.

Pericles' strategy for winning the war posed a serious stumbling block for all of his successors. Despite its ineluctable logic, nobody could pretend that it was succeeding. After years of fighting the Peloponnesians, the Athenians had no prospect of outright victory, nor even of a negotiated peace. And the Spartans were proving to be surprisingly troublesome opponents. Instead of seeing reason and realizing the hopelessness of continuing the war, they doggedly continued to march against the territories of Athens or its allies every campaigning season. Pericles had predicted that the Spartans would take a long time to learn seamanship, but they certainly seemed ready to make the effort. While the Spartans, of all people, were experimenting, the Athenians stuck doggedly to Pericles' plan and in so doing were losing momentum and control of the war.

Nevertheless they rose energetically to meet the many challenges related to the war and the pursuit of Periclean policy. Plague had depleted the ranks of citizens, so when hoplites were sent to Mytilene, they rowed themselves, as did the horsemen sent with their mounts to Corinth. In the war's fourth year the Assembly actually manned and launched 250 ships for the war effort—as many as at any time in the city's history. Athens seemed unsinkable still.

As the conflict between the Spartan and Athenian alliances continued, its alarms and excursions took on some of the theatricality of the dramatic festivals. A few days after their defeat at Phormio's hands, the Peloponnesian crews crossed the Isthmus in secret, each oarsman carrying his oar and oar loop and rowing pad. Arriving at Nisaea, they waited for darkness and then manned a fleet of Megarian triremes to undertake a sneak attack on the Piraeus itself. But the ships had spent so long in dry dock that their seams had opened. The more the triremes leaked, the slower became the Peloponnesian advance. In the end they gave up their grand plan and settled for a nighttime raid on Salamis Island. The alarm beacons touched off a citywide panic in Athens, though the feckless enemy got nowhere near the port.

An even greater sensation occurred two years later, when Cleon browbeat the Assembly into passing a sentence of death on all the citizens of Mytilene on Lesbos, as punishment for the rebellion that a few of the Mytilenean oligarchs had started. A trireme was dispatched that very day with the order for the mass execution. By the next morning the Athenians had come to their senses. They ordered a second trireme to carry the reprieve, but no one knew if it would be able to overtake the first.

In a rush the second crew dragged the trireme from its shed, loaded it with provisions, and set off to catch the first ship before it reached Mytilene, 185 miles away. From the moment the second trireme was launched, its oars were in constant motion. The rowers worked all day, into the evening, and through the night, eating barley mixed with olive oil and wine as they rowed. They took breaks for sleep in rotation. As they approached Mytilene, the lookouts could see the first ship already in the harbor. The Athenian general Paches had opened the original decree and was about to start the executions. The heroic efforts and breathless arrival of the second ship saved the day, as well as several thousand lives. But the episode marched inexorably on to a tragic climax. When Paches returned to Athens, he was brought to trial for his conduct as general. Beleaguered by relentless prosecution, he pulled out his sword and killed himself in the court.

In this fourth year of the war, the stage on which the Athenians were contending began to widen dramatically. Wherever the navy ventured in those years, natural disasters seemed to follow. In Sicily the Athenians saw fiery streams of lava pouring down the slopes of Mount Etna, a volcano that had not erupted in many years. In the Black Sea, while collecting tribute, the Athenian general Lamachus beached ten triremes at a river mouth in rainy weather and lost them all when a rising torrent lifted the empty hulls and swept them out to sea. And in the Euboean Gulf a tidal wave struck the Athenian guard station on the islet of Atalante, lifting a trireme over the wall and tossing it among the buildings inside. The tsunami had been triggered by an earthquake that split Atalante itself in two, opening a channel so wide that a trireme could pass through.

The deadlock in the fighting finally broke in Athens' favor during the war's seventh year. The turning point was a dramatic amphibious action masterminded by a tough and battle-hardened commander named Demosthenes (a distinguished soldier, not the orator of a later generation). This general had been following up on Phormio's victories in the west and had earned the respect of the Messenians and other western allies. The setting for his novel stratagem was to be the vast and lonely bay of Pylos in the southwestern corner of the Peloponnese. Demosthenes dared not air his plans in the open Assembly. Success would depend upon secrecy and surprise.

Early in a summer that was notable for its bad weather, Demosthenes landed at Pylos with a small expeditionary force and began to fortify a hilltop that overlooked the north end of the bay. The men collected rough fieldstones for the walls and carried clay for mortar on their own backs, stooping forward and clasping their hands behind them to form improvised hods. The Athenians also fortified a strip of beach to serve as a landing place for receiving supplies or reinforcements. Demosthenes manned his new base with the crews of five Athenian triremes and a boatload of Messenian troops from Naupactus. He intended for the Messenians to fight as insurgents, blending in with the helots in the countryside and spreading terror among the Spartans.

Word quickly reached Sparta, fifty miles away. The Spartans at home called their army back from Attica and also sent for the Peloponnesian fleet from Corcyra. Army and navy would meet at Pylos to deal with these squatters at Sparta's back door. After establishing camp on the coasts of the bay, the Spartans ferried 420 of their best officers and fighting men across to a ridge-backed island, three miles long, that closed off the bay from the open sea. The island bore the ominous name Sphacteria ("Place of Sacrifice"). The Spartan hoplites proceeded to bivouac in its dense scrub and rocky fastnesses, determined to deny any landing place to the Athenian fleet. Just so had Xerxes landed his best troops on Psyttaleia island before the battle of Salamis. Demosthenes sent messengers to summon the main Athenian fleet. Before it could reach Pylos, however, the enemy attacked.

Demosthenes and sixty Athenian marines took up positions on their landing place at the north end of Pylos Bay, while the rest of his force prepared to defend the newly fortified citadel. A landing by all forty-three Peloponnesian ships at once would have overwhelmed the Athenians, but submerged rocks prevented a mass assault. In the face of this natural barricade the Spartans had to divide their fleet into small detachments. While the main fleet waited beyond the line of surf, cheering them on, a few triremes at a time tried to thread their way through the reefs and force a landing. No maneuver could have been more hazardous than this attempt to reverse ships through shoals toward a hostile coast.

Among the impatient Spartans in the Peloponnesian fleet was Brasidas, now serving as a trierarch and still smarting from his encounter with Phormio four years earlier. Shouting that it was shameful to think more of saving ships' timbers than destroying Athenians, he ordered his own steersman to drive the trireme ashore with all speed. As the keel touched land, Brasidas set his foot on the boarding step beside the steersman's seat. Before he could jump, an Athenian arrow struck him. Wounded, he collapsed backward into

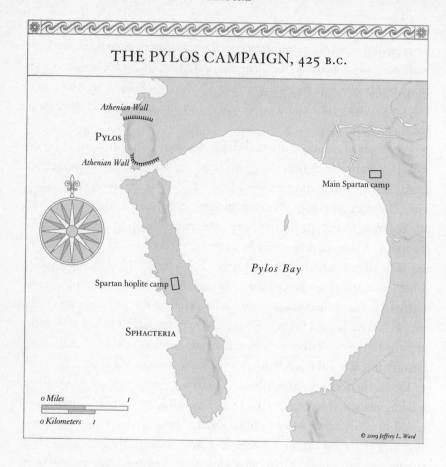

THE PYLOS CAMPAIGN, 425 B.C.

Athenian Wall

PYLOS

Athenian Wall

Main Spartan camp

Pylos Bay

Spartan hoplite camp

SPHACTERIA

0 Miles   1

0 Kilometers   1

© 2009 Jeffrey L. Ward

the rowing frame among the oars of the thranite rowers, and his big round hoplite shield fell into the sea. At once the Peloponnesian oarsmen pulled away from the beach and rejoined the rest of the fleet. Brasidas would live to fight another day, but the Spartan attack had lost its momentum.

All that day Demosthenes and his small force held off the enemy, a few dozen men keeping eight thousand at bay. The world had turned upside down. A Spartan fleet at sea was fighting an Athenian army on land, and even more paradoxically, the Athenians were winning. At evening the Peloponnesians gave up the attempt on Pylos. A wave washed Brasidas' shield onto the beach, and the Athenians set it up as a victory trophy. After two more days of futile Spartan assaults, the main Athenian fleet of fifty triremes finally arrived. When the Peloponnesian fleet declined to come out and fight in open water, the Athenians charged into the bay through the channels at either end of Sphacteria island. Once inside the bay they launched an impetuous attack on the Peloponnesian ships, capturing five and driving the rest onto the mainland shore.

The Athenians were now masters of the bay. One result of their victory hit the Spartans hard: more than four hundred of their best troops were now marooned on Sphacteria with almost no fresh water or provisions. The Athenians quickly grasped the plum that fortune had dropped in their laps. To prevent any escape to the mainland, a pair of Athenian triremes kept up a constant patrol by day, rowing around the island in opposite directions. By night, when the darkness made rowing dangerous, the entire Athenian fleet anchored in a great circle around Sphacteria. True Spartans were a dwindling breed, increasingly outnumbered by helots. The loss of any single Spartan citizen was a threat to all, and the news that the Athenians had trapped more than four hundred struck Sparta like a thunderbolt. Officials were sent at once to Pylos to negotiate an armistice. From Pylos an Athenian trireme conveyed the envoys to Athens.

At Athens the Spartan representatives offered the Assembly an immediate end to the war and even a treaty of alliance in exchange for the men on the island. The warmongering demagogue Cleon, however, demanded a more tangible ransom. He proposed that the Spartans hand over four strategic towns or territories that had been stripped of their Athenian garrisons twenty-two years earlier, at the end of the First Peloponnesian War, when the Athenians gave up their newly won land empire in exchange for a group of Athenian hostages. The enemy was now caught in a similar predicament, and Cleon's solution might be seen as no more than poetic justice.

The Spartans avoided any open discussion of exchanges or ransoms. They asked instead that the Athenians appoint a small committee to negotiate the terms one by one in a calm and orderly atmosphere. Cleon denounced them for preferring secret negotiations to plain talk in the Assembly, and the Spartans went back to Pylos without a settlement.

So the Athenian blockade resumed, while the Spartans sent away for more troops and looked for ways to provision the men on Sphacteria. In the end they recruited divers to swim across the bay with skins packed with honey, poppyseed, and linseed. On stormy days, when the Athenian triremes stayed in the bay, seafaring helots risked their lives—and hoped to win their freedom—by landing boatloads of flour, cheese, and wine on the island's seaward side. The Spartans on the island survived in this way for over a month, till the Athenians at home began to doubt the success of the entire enterprise. Their dissatisfaction boiled over at a session of the Assembly, when the people voted to send the general Nicias to Pylos with archers and javelin throwers. These light-armed troops could fight effectively on the rough terrain of Sphacteria, where it was difficult for a hoplite phalanx to operate.

Cleon could not resist issuing a few verbal barbs, for he hated Nicias almost as much as he hated the Spartans. During his speech he blamed the current board of generals for the long delay in capturing the stranded Spartans; he also insulted the mild-mannered Nicias, questioned his manhood, and claimed that he himself could do a better job if only given the chance. Acting with uncharacteristic decision, Nicias promptly offered to surrender his generalship to Cleon. At first Cleon jokingly proclaimed himself ready. When Nicias made it clear that his offer was serious, Cleon in dismay tried to wriggle out of his rash challenge.

By this time the Assembly had taken up the idea and greeted the proposal to substitute Cleon for Nicias with acclaim. Now that Cleon was cornered, his spirits rallied. He accepted command of the mission to Pylos and boasted extravagantly that he would return inside twenty days, bearing either Spartan hostages or news of their destruction. Many Athenians watched the fleet depart with amusement, sure that Cleon would return either dead or permanently discredited. But to the stupefaction of friends and foes alike, Cleon proved as good as his word. Before the twentieth day had passed, he and his ships were back in Athens, along with 292 Spartan prisoners. The rest had been killed in fierce fighting when Cleon's light-armed troops combined with Demosthenes' hoplites for a dawn attack on Sphacteria.

Exultation exploded in Athens. A new set of desperate Spartan envoys came to sue for peace and the return of their men. The Athenians followed Cleon's lead. They told the Spartans that they would immediately execute the hostages if the Peloponnesian army invaded Attica again. Having tied the hands of their enemies, the Athenians proceeded to celebrate. The most prized trophies from Pylos were the hundreds of round bronze shields taken from the dead and defeated Spartans. They offered them as dedications to the gods, to be hung up in sanctuaries and other public places, each shield displaying the proud inscription THE ATHENIANS FROM THE LACEDAEMONIANS ON PYLOS.

For the first time since the beginning of the war, the people pushed forward with new buildings on the Acropolis. Pylos was a victory that outshone any military success of Pericles. To celebrate it, the Athenians raised a new temple to Athena Nike, goddess of victory. It was set on a bastion that jutted forward pugnaciously beside the main entrance, elbowing aside Pericles' stately Propylaea. Thus the builders managed to capture in stone the brashness of Cleon and the pride that Athens took in his astounding victory. Cleon had indeed made himself, almost overnight, the first man in Athens.

Another monument to the victory at Pylos, just as enduring as the marble temple of Athena Nike, was a comedy called *Horsemen* by the young playwright Aristophanes. Before writing comedies himself, Aristophanes had passed through a varied apprenticeship in the theater. He likened his own career to a series of promotions on board a trireme.

Before handling the steering oars, one should first know how to row,
Then keep watch at the prow, then master the winds,
And only then be steersman oneself.

Though still in his teens, Aristophanes was Cleon's harshest critic. In an earlier play, *Acharnians,* he had ridiculed the atmosphere of paranoia that Cleon stirred up with his alarmist speeches and denunciations of harmless foreigners.

Informer: That lamp wick will set fire to the Navy Yard!
Citizen: The Navy Yard and a lamp wick? Oh my! How?
Informer: If this Boeotian sticks the wick in a beetle, then sends it, lighted,
     down the drain to the Navy Yard, when a stiff north wind is blowing,
     one trireme will catch fire, and in an instant all will be ablaze.
Citizen: You scoundrel—a blaze forsooth, with a wick and a beetle!

The same rich citizens who sponsored the dramatic productions also served as trierarchs for the navy. Most were loyal patriots who loved their city, yet many deplored the current war. In the Assembly they were out-numbered by the masses and drowned out by the demagogues. But in the theater these citizens could get their messages across without interruption. Aristophanes composed plays that popularized the views of his sponsors, the trierarchic class. Behind the raw jokes about sex and other bodily functions, his comedies routinely satirized demagogues like Cleon and urged an end to the war.

A few months after the astounding victory at Pylos, Cleon went to the theater. The occasion was the Lenaea, a late winter festival honoring Dionysus, god of wine. The festival's chief object of veneration—an erect wooden phallus as big as a man—set the tone. At this festival comedy, not tragedy, dominated the stage. The principal actors sported clownish potbellies, while the men in the chorus waggled giant phalluses, sometimes referred to as their "oars." Thanks to his recent appointment as general, Cleon for the first time had a seat of honor on the front row. To his left and right stretched the long curving line of priests, public benefactors, and generals, including his rivals and colleagues Nicias and Demosthenes. At his back crowded thousands of Athenians who had come to see and judge the contest.

It had been known for months that Aristophanes would be presenting a new comedy. Two years earlier, after the rebellion of Mytilene and the famous trireme race to Lesbos, Aristophanes had lampooned Cleon mercilessly in his *Babylonians*. Cleon counterattacked with an accusation of slander. Aristophanes was convicted and fined by the jury. Now, hedged about by the heroic aura of Pylos, Cleon could surely expect immunity from the bawdy humor of Aristophanes and his ilk. But Aristophanes had other ideas.

Backstage, officials marshaled the actors, choristers, pipers, costumers, and stagehands for three new plays: Cratinus' *Satyrs,* Aristomenes' *Scabbard Bearers,* and Aristophanes' *Horsemen.* Out front the three wealthy sponsors took their seats in the audience. Vendors were selling nuts and raisins. Then the statue of Dionysus was carried in so that the god could watch the plays. A torchbearer entered the theater and cried, "Call on the god!" The audience shouted, "Son of Semele! Iacchos! Giver of Wealth!" And the competition began.

Once *Horsemen* started, it quickly became evident that Aristophanes had written the play as his revenge on Cleon. Pylos figured prominently in the dialogue, and references to the Athenian navy peppered the play throughout. In the first scene, two actors dressed as kitchen slaves ran or limped onto the stage, howling. The first tilted his masked face up to the audience—a startled moment, then laughter—to reveal a portrait of the general Demosthenes. The second slave joined in the miserable wailing. More laughter: he was masked as Nicias. Both slaves, it was plain, had just been whipped.

Demosthenes explained to the audience that he and his fellow slave served a crusty old master named Demos (that is, the Athenian people), short-tempered and hard of hearing. Demos resided on the Pnyx. At the last new moon Demos had bought another slave, a tanner. The naming of the new slave's occupation stirred a ripple in the audience, for leather was of course the source of Cleon's wealth. The interloper had been scheming to make Demosthenes and Nicias look bad; hence the beatings and bruises. Any doubts about the identity of this third slave were laid to rest when Demosthenes complained, "The other day when I cooked up a Spartan cake at Pylos, he slipped by me, grabbed the dish, and brought it to the master as his own!"

To supplant their rival, Demosthenes and Nicias decided to recruit a passing sausage seller whom they saw trundling his stand toward the Agora, a true Athenian "man in the street." Finding the sausage seller reluctant to fall in with their plans, Demosthenes told him that tomorrow he would be ruler of all these rows of people (gesturing at the audience), not to mention the Agora, the harbors, the Assembly, the Council, and the generals.

Having assured himself of the sausage seller's qualifications (disreputable career, low birth, little education), Demosthenes proclaimed him the perfect demagogue and coached him on how best to confront the terrifying tanner. If the audience hoped for the sensation of seeing a mask that caricatured Cleon's familiar face, they were disappointed. Before the new slave made his entry onto the stage, Demosthenes explained in another aside that the mask makers had been too frightened to carve a true likeness, but that the audience would be bright enough to identify the man anyway. On this cue "Cleon" at last burst onto the scene, roaring with fury. Rumor said that Aristophanes himself was behind the mask, to spare any actor the danger of playing the hero of Pylos.

As the comedy continued the players decried Cleon as a cheat, a liar, and an embezzler. He was also a thief who had stolen the credit for Pylos from

Demosthenes, the true maker of the winning strategy. In answer to their taunts, Cleon stirred up big winds with his tirades, and the other characters "reef[ed] their sails" so as not to be blown offstage. The tanner (Cleon) then threatened to punish his enemies by assigning them old hulls and rotten sails whenever they served as trierarchs.

Old man Demos, disturbed by the uproar, came out of his house. Learning of the quarrel between the sausage seller and the tanner, Demos declared that he himself would sit in judgment. His buttocks were still sore (after fifty-six years!) from his hard rowing at Salamis, and he was touchingly grateful when the sausage seller offered him a cushion to sit on. In the *agon* or contest that ensued, Cleon claimed that he had done more for the city than the great Themistocles himself, and even quoted the famous Wooden Wall oracle about Athens' navy. The sausage seller countered that the appropriate wooden wall to enclose Cleon would be the public stocks. Each then tried to outdo the other in conveying tasty dishes to Demos.

Throughout the action the chorus of aristocratic horsemen joined in the verbal and physical attacks on Cleon, just as in the Assembly the real Cleon was opposed, though ineffectually, by the Athenian upper classes. Between charges, however, Aristophanes' chorus of horsemen offered the audience a more inspiring message—an appeal for reconciliation between masses and elite, between democratic navy and aristocratic cavalry. The chorus reminded the citizens that they had recently joined the naval effort themselves in the new horse carriers (an expedition commanded by Nicias). In a flight of fantasy, they told how their own horses had manned the oars and rowed all the way to Corinth to attack the enemy. Being horses, the equine crews naturally mixed cavalry commands with nautical orders and substituted a chant of *"Hippapai!"* for the proper Athenian rowing chant of *"Rhyppapai!"*

For the lyric high point of his play, Aristophanes composed an invocation to Poseidon, god both of horses and of the sea, patron of riders and seafarers alike.

> *Horse-lord Poseidon, O!*
> *You who hold dear the cymbal-clashing hoofbeats of horses,*
> *   And their neighing,*
> *And the speeding triremes, dark-beaked and mercenary,*

And the race of lads in chariots, lighthearted or unlucky,
  Come down to our dance.
O gold-tridented, O guardian of dolphins, adored at Sunium,
  O Geraestian son of Cronus:
Best beloved of Phormio, above all other gods,
  Stand by Athenians now!

Eventually Demos showed that his heart was in the right place. He cast off Cleon, promising in future to spend more of his funds on trireme building than on lawsuit hearings. Further, he resolved that when the navy came home, the rowers should immediately receive their back pay in full. ("Many well-worn rumps will rejoice at that!") Then Demos slipped off to his farm, arm in arm with two beautiful women identified as "Thirty-Year Peace Treaties." Cleon himself was condemned to trade places with the lowly sausage seller. In the final moments of the play the chorus carried the tanner offstage in the direction of the city gate, there to bawl his wretched merchandise among the bathhouses and brothels.

After all three comedies had been presented, the competing choruses trooped across the orchestra in turn so that the ten judges could determine which one received the loudest applause. Rarely did Aristophanes prove a favorite with the audience. So it was a bitter moment for Cleon, sitting in the full glare of ten thousand citizens, when the herald announced that *Horsemen* had won first prize.

Cleon's dramatic humiliation did not shake his hold over Athenian policy. For three more years the Athenians continued their attacks on the Peloponnesian coasts, their attempts to win back their old land empire, and their meddling in Sicily. None of these campaigns prospered, but one of them launched the literary career of yet another gifted young Athenian: the historian Thucydides. It happened after Brasidas had made a dash to the north and captured the rich Athenian colony of Amphipolis during a snowstorm. In an attempt to oust Brasidas and retake the city, Thucydides as general took a squadron of seven Athenian triremes up the Strymon River. When his mission failed, the angry Assembly sent him into exile. Their action deprived the city of a genius who might have become a statesman in the mold of Pericles. Withdrawing to his family's gold mines in Thrace (he was a kinsman of

Miltiades and Cimon), Thucydides began to compile and commit to writing every detail of the current war. If he could not make history, he would write it.

Finally the warmongering Cleon was killed while fighting at Amphipolis, and the same battle claimed the life of the Spartan hero Brasidas. With these two hawks out of the way, Nicias soon succeeded in negotiating a peace settlement, later called the Peace of Nicias. By its terms the Spartans formally recognized the rule of the Athenians over their maritime empire and even granted them Nisaea, the port of Megara. Otherwise both sides pledged to give back the places that they had captured during the war and agreed to open panhellenic sanctuaries such as Olympia and Delphi to all Greeks. They swore to keep the peace for fifty years. The terms were a triumph for Athens and would have gratified Pericles, had he been alive to hail this new accord.

The war had lasted almost exactly ten years. Important members of the Peloponnesian League—the Corinthians, Thebans, and Megarians—were bitter and blamed the Spartans for abandoning the war on such easy terms. To protect themselves against their irate allies, the Spartans went beyond the peace accords and concluded an independent fifty-year alliance with the Athenians. In fulfillment of Cimon's dream, Athens and Sparta seemed securely yoked as joint leaders of the Greeks. But already some viewed the Peace of Nicias as little more than an uneasy cessation of hostilities rather than a true peace.

At the next dramatic festival Aristophanes presented a new comedy called *Peace*. The play's hero, an Athenian grape farmer, flew up to Mount Olympus on a gigantic dung beetle to ask Zeus why he had allowed the Greeks to destroy one another. Did the gods not understand that the Persians might still conquer them all, once both sides were exhausted? Back on earth, a chorus of Greek farmers rescued the goddess Peace from a deep pit where the war god Ares had buried her. As they hauled Peace back to the light with ropes, the god Hermes rebuked those Athenians who still lusted after an empire on land. "If you want Peace to be saved, you must draw back and stick to the sea!"

Pericles began the war, Cleon prolonged it, and Nicias brought it to an end. But Aristophanes and comedy had the last word.

CHAPTER 13

The Sicilian Expedition

[415–413 B.C.]

Where there is hubris and self-will, know this:
The city, after a fair voyage, in time will plunge to the bottom.

—Sophocles

PEACE CAME TOO SOON FOR ONE AMBITIOUS YOUNG ATHENIAN.
Alcibiades had just turned thirty, old enough at last to take his rightful place among Athens' generals and civic leaders. Peacetime robbed him of his chances to shine in battle, exploit a great crisis, or pose as the savior of Athens. Happily for him, the Spartans were unwilling or unable to abide by the terms of the Peace of Nicias. So Alcibiades set out to stir up trouble among the Greeks, like a boy shoving a long stick into a hornet's nest.

Even without his incendiary policies, Alcibiades' flamboyant behavior and mannerisms kept him always in the public eye. The comic poets of Athens ruthlessly mimicked Alcibiades' idiosyncratic lisp and hesitant speech. He enjoyed the glory of seeing his four-horse chariots take first, second, and fourth place at the Olympic games. Even more than his sporting victories, Alcibiades' sexual adventures fascinated the Athenians. Far from hiding his erotic obsessions, Alcibiades went so far as to replace the traditional family crest on his shield with an image of the god Eros standing on a field of gold, wielding a thunderbolt. His marriage to the richest heiress in Athens did nothing to stop his scandalous escapades. When she sought a divorce, he seized her from the court and carried her home again through the crowds in the Agora.

Like all rich Athenians he had served the city as a trierarch, and his outrageous behavior carried over to the decks of his triremes. Alcibiades ordered the ship's carpenters to cut away sections of the stern decks so that his bed could be slung on ropes in the gap. No hard pallets for Alcibiades. He slept as if rocking in a cradle, the first recorded swinging of a hammock on a ship at sea. His steersman, a citizen named Antiochus, was befriended on the strength of nothing more than a prank in the Assembly. One day a pet quail escaped from under Alcibiades' cloak when he lifted his hands to applaud a speech. Antiochus happened to be standing nearby. He won Alcibiades' eternal regard by recapturing the bird following a noisy chase through the ranks of laughing citizens.

The fragile Peace of Nicias needed constant nurture if it was to survive, but the Athenians instead gave Alcibiades free rein in his provocative ventures abroad. So long as he did not violate the letter of the peace with a direct attack on Spartan territory, they supported all his schemes. Summer after summer this ambitious and charismatic young general set out with Athenian fleets to aid anybody opposed to the Spartans.

Alcibiades was good at impulsive beginnings, but all his projects had a way of fizzling out in the end. His character lacked the steadiness to push any enterprise through to completion. Even so, the trouble that he caused was enough to win congratulations from the famous misanthrope Timon of Athens. This eccentric hater of his fellow citizens seized Alcibiades' hand after one Assembly session and told him, "Well done! Keep this up and you will ruin them all!"

Five years after the signing of the Peace of Nicias, envoys from Segesta in Sicily arrived in Athens. The Segestan envoys asked that Athens send its navy to settle a squabble that involved the powerful Sicilian city of Syracuse. As a makeweight argument they threw in a fresh appeal from the Sicilians of Leontini, old allies of the Athenians, who had been expelled from their city by the Syracusans. Athens had already made one unsuccessful attempt to help the people of Leontini, and at least one veteran of that first Sicilian expedition, the general Eurymedon, could attest to the uselessness of another. Nevertheless the Assembly sent a delegation to find out the facts about Segesta. They returned with reports of a wealthy city along with sixty silver talents as a gift from the Segestans. It was enough money to pay the crews of sixty triremes for a month.

The veterans of the recent war with the Peloponnesians opposed new military undertakings, but younger Athenians took a different view. Their city and navy had emerged from the ten years' war unscathed. The treasury was filling up again. They longed for great enterprises worthy of Athens' power and glory. Even the dreary turn of events in Greece played its part. After they conquered Sicily, might they not finally subdue the Peloponnesians and make themselves masters of the entire Greek world?

In response to the appeal of the Segestan envoys, the Assembly voted to send a fleet of sixty triremes to Sicily, led by a team of generals that would include Alcibiades. A second debate was convened when Nicias urged the Athenians to change their minds while there was still time. When Alcibiades made a fervent plea that the Assembly stick to its resolve, Nicias tried to scare the citizens into abandoning the scheme. With a great show of concern he deliberately exaggerated the numbers and costs needed to win such a war. But his ploy backfired. The Athenians reaffirmed the decision to send out the expedition but also vastly increased its scope. Nicias himself, no more in control of this meeting than he had been at the debate with Cleon over Pylos, was cornered into specifying the excessive numbers that he deemed would guarantee safety and success.

The Athenians threw themselves into the preparation of the armada with feverish enthusiasm. Anyone not employed in fitting out the fleet congregated in the wrestling schools or stood on street corners in eager conversation. Those who knew Sicily used the tips of their walking sticks and drew maps of the island on the ground for their more ignorant friends. Sicily was three-cornered, and it was easy to pinpoint Syracuse on the side of the triangle closest to Athens. There was Italy! And there was Africa! Down in the sand at their feet it all looked so close, so small, so possible.

An outburst of religious piety thickened the atmosphere of runaway patriotism. Athenian oracle-mongers retailed prophecies that foreshadowed the destiny of Athens to conquer Sicily. During these days of preparation the sacred trireme *Ammonias* returned to the Piraeus from Africa bearing a favorable prophecy from the oracle at Siwa in the Egyptian desert. Zeus Ammon assured Alcibiades that the Athenians would capture all the Syracusans. Even the gods seemed to be urging the people forward.

Committed now to the expedition as one of its generals, Nicias worked with Alcibiades to arrange for a departure ceremony that would beggar description. As showy in his sanctimonious way as Alcibiades himself,

Nicias had once paid builders to contrive an extraordinary pontoon bridge of gilded and tapestried ships for a festival. The occasion was the great musical competition of choirs that drew Athenians and other Ionians across the sea to the sanctuary of Apollo on Delos. Normally the choirboys, pipers, and chorus masters disembarked on the island in an undignified scramble. On the occasion when Nicias was sponsor, the chorus of young Athenians caused a sensation when they paraded in stately array across the bridge of boats, singing as they came. His love of lavish spectacle now guided the plans to give the great armada a spectacular send-off.

Some citizens did oppose the venture. In the open Assembly they knew the majority would call them unpatriotic if they raised their hands and voted no, so they remained silent in public. The astronomer Meton, famous for devising the nineteen-year cycle of the official Athenian calendar, secretly set a fire that destroyed his own house. Through this domestic disaster he hoped to render his son exempt from service as a trierarch.

When the launching of the fleet was only a few days off, the city was shaken by the most terrible act of sacrilege in its history. One morning the Athenians awoke to find that parties unknown had mutilated the stone herms that stood outside every house and temple. These phallic statues represented the god Hermes, guardian of travelers and promoter of prosperous journeys. Apparently a well-organized gang of men had passed through the city streets by night, knocking off stone noses and genitals. The perpetrators, whoever they might be, failed to stop the armada from setting out, but their vandalism spread a cloud over the entire expedition.

The mutilation of the herms threw the city into an uproar. An investigation was launched to find the desecrators. Alcibiades' escapades now came back to haunt him as, with sublime illogic, many Athenians made him their chief target of suspicion. Alcibiades, eager to depart, indignantly proclaimed his innocence, but the Assembly reserved the right to call him back to Athens should evidence of his guilt appear. This burden of suspicion would inevitably weaken his prestige in dealing with his two colleagues, Nicias and Lamachus. The latter general was well known for having led two Athenian squadrons into the Black Sea. The people had assigned him to the Sicilian expedition in the hope of curbing Alcibiades' wilder impulses, while providing Nicias with some much-needed backbone.

The great armada finally set out on a midsummer morning. Before dawn the population of Athens was on the move, pouring down to the Piraeus to watch the departure of the ships. Families clustered around husbands and sons who were departing into the unknown. From docks and housetops the Athenians gazed out at a floating city, an entire community packed on board ships. The trierarchs had vied with one another in paint and gilding. Now the triremes shone resplendent in the sunlight, seeming more ready for a parade than for combat.

The dazzling hulls made it easy to overlook the hollowness within. The crews and fighting men were inexperienced in combat. So great was the city's maritime supremacy that its navy cruised the seas unchallenged. During the recent war with the Peloponnesians only small squadrons had been called on to fight the enemy. And as leaders from Themistocles to Sophocles had observed, the strength of a navy lay not in its ships but in its men.

When all were on board, the ships rowed out to their appointed places on the harbor's oval of blue water. Then the trumpeter sounded a signal. Immediately the multitude fell silent. A herald began to cry out the hymns and prayers for the launching of ships. To each line of the herald's chant, all the people responded in chorus. The generals and trierarchs then poured their libations into the sea from goblets of silver and gold. The leading trireme moved toward the mouth of the harbor, and in a majestic procession the ships fell into line behind it. Once clear of the Cantharus the triremes spurted off at high speed, racing toward Aegina as if the expedition were no more than a regatta. The people watched the hulls disappear over the southern horizon, then returned to their homes to wait for news of victory.

Over the next few days the fleet circumnavigated the Peloponnese without incident. Not until they joined the advance contingent at Corcyra did the Athenians realize that a gigantic force can be its own worst enemy. The same logistical difficulties that had once beset Xerxes now confronted the imperial navy of Athens. Their numbers were so vast that they might, like the Persian host of old, "drink the rivers dry." Nowhere on the voyage ahead would the Athenians find ports big enough to hold all their ships or supply their hordes of men. The great fleet had to be divided into three squadrons, with a general at the head of each.

In successive waves they crossed over to Italy. Many western Greek cities, alarmed by the number of ships, refused to let them land at all. Even places supposedly friendly to Athens kept their gates barred and their markets shut, providing no more than permission to land and take on water. Too late the Athenians realized that their expedition should have been preceded by a serious effort to build up a league of allies pledged to join the attack on Syracuse.

Their frustrations reached a climax at Rhegium on the Strait of Messina, an ancient ally that also refused to support the invasion. There the Athenians met the envoys with the three triremes that had been sent ahead to collect the promised money from Segesta, the money that was to cover the immense costs of the expedition. The envoys had their own tale of woe, and it was a most embarrassing one for the Athenians. The actual sum possessed by the Segestans was only thirty talents of silver, barely enough to pay the crews for seven or eight days. How had the first mission been so deceived?

The truth was soon revealed. The wretched Segestans, knowing that the Athenians would help them only if they appeared to be rich, tricked the members of the first mission with lavish dinners and seemingly limitless displays of gold and silver vessels. In fact, the Segestans had only a single set of expensive cups, bowls, and plates. Even this set had been pieced together by borrowing from neighboring Greek and Phoenician cities, who were certainly in on the joke. The glittering table service was secretly passed from house to house, always arriving at the kitchen door before the Athenians arrived for their next diplomatic dinner. The ruse had convinced the visiting envoys that even ordinary Segestans had huge fortunes.

This disastrous news led to a split among the three Athenian generals. Nicias recommended that they fulfill their original mission and leave the sixty fast triremes to aid Segesta against its enemies. The rest of the armada could then parade ceremonially around the shores of Sicily in a show of naval power before going home. Alcibiades dismissed this proposal as disgraceful. He advocated a campaign of diplomacy from city to city. When they had won over enough allies, the Athenians could attack and subdue Syracuse. The third and least prestigious general, Lamachus, had the soundest instincts. He urged an immediate assault on Syracuse before the city could organize its defenses. As this seasoned veteran knew, it was not only in Aesop's fables that familiarity bred contempt.

Finding that neither of his colleagues would listen to him, Lamachus broke the deadlock by favoring Alcibiades' plan of winning new allies through diplomacy. First, however, the Athenians planned a visit to Syracuse itself. In the Great Harbor they would deliver a warning to the city and justify Athens' actions to the world.

Syracuse had of course never attacked Athens. On the contrary, the Syracusans took Athens as their model for democratic government, freedom of thought, grand public works, and inventiveness. Their city resembled Athens as it had been in the time before the Persian Wars: a place of great but as yet unrealized potential. Syracuse even had its own Themistocles in the person of a visionary and patriotic citizen named Hermocrates.

While the bulk of the Athenian fleet remained at Rhegium, Alcibiades led the sixty fast triremes down the coast in single file, an intimidating array spread out against the skyline. When they reached Syracuse, the ten leading triremes rowed straight into the Great Harbor and took up a position within hailing distance of the city walls. The herald proclaimed that the Athenians had come to restore freedom to their Sicilian allies. All those in Syracuse who favored this cause should leave the city and join the Athenians.

No one from the city answered the Athenian herald. An eerie silence prevailed. As far as the Athenians could see, the Syracusans had no navy and were not prepared to withstand a siege. Nonetheless the sheer scale of the place was overwhelming. The Great Harbor was an irregular oval more than two miles long and a mile broad, big enough to swallow all three of the Piraeus harbors. On the western shore lay reedy wetlands; elsewhere rocky flats shelved into the water. The only good mooring facilities for triremes were the city's well-protected dockyards, one facing into the Great Harbor and the other facing the open sea.

Having surveyed the enemy's stronghold, Alcibiades led the Athenian fleet northward and set up a new base at Catana, near the forbidding cone of Mount Etna. The rest of the armada joined them there for the winter. As long as the fair weather lasted, Alcibiades led squadrons up and down the coast on raids to secure new funds or new friends. Returning to Catana after one of these excursions, Alcibiades found that the sacred trireme *Salaminia* had arrived with orders recalling him to Athens. The investigation

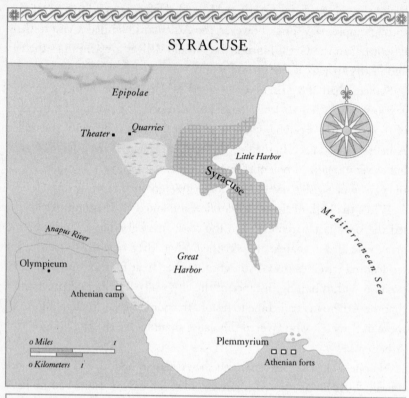

SYRACUSE

Epipolae

Theater ∎ ▪ Quarries

Little Harbor

Syracuse

Mediterranean Sea

Anapus River

Olympieum ∎

Great
Harbor

Athenian camp ▫

o Miles   I
o Kilometers   I

Plemmyrium   ▫ ▫ ▫
Athenian forts

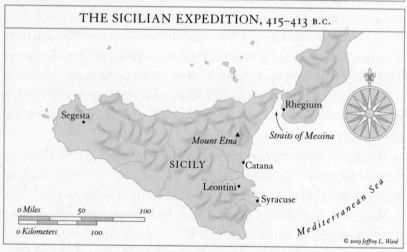

THE SICILIAN EXPEDITION, 415–413 B.C.

Segesta ∎

Rhegium ∎

Mount Etna ▲

Straits of Messina

SICILY

∎ Catana

Leontini ∎

∎ Syracuse

Mediterranean Sea

o Miles   50   100
o Kilometers   100

© 2009 Jeffrey L. Ward

into the mutilation of the herms had exploded into a welter of related and unrelated inquiries, and the Assembly wanted Alcibiades for questioning.

He went peacefully, leaving Nicias and Lamachus in charge of the expedition. At one of the landing places on the Italian coast, however, Alcibiades eluded the crew of the *Salaminia* and disappeared. Convinced now of his guilt, the Athenians at home condemned their scandalous general to death. When word of the sentence reached him, Alcibiades said only, "I shall show them that I am still alive." He soon sought refuge in Sparta, one of the few safe places for an Athenian outlaw, and offered the Spartans advice on how they might defeat his native city.

With Alcibiades no longer sharing command of the fleet in Sicily, Lamachus was able to bring Nicias briefly to life. Luring the Syracusan army overland to Catana by means of a false report, Nicias and Lamachus loaded their own troops onto the triremes and raced down the coast to the Great Harbor, where they landed unopposed. Before the Syracusans discovered the ruse and returned, Athenian carpenters and shipwrights had chopped down trees and built a stockade to protect the triremes. The next day, amid crashing thunder, lightning, and rain, the Athenians defeated the Syracusan army in a battle near the city walls. But the appearance of the enemy cavalry prevented the Athenian hoplites from gaining a decisive victory. They had no choice but to return to Catana. More optimistic now, Nicias and Lamachus sent a letter to the Assembly with a report on the expedition's first campaigning season and an appeal for more horsemen and money.

The workmen in the camp at Catana spent the winter making bricks and implements of iron. The Athenians were preparing to surround Syracuse with a siege wall on land and a blockade of ships at sea. Meanwhile Nicias entered into secret communication with pro-Athenian Syracusans who seemed ready to open the gates, once they convinced the other citizens that resistance was futile. With more battles like the one just fought in the Great Harbor, and more help from Syracusan turncoats, the generals hoped for a speedy end to their mission.

One year later the quick victory had failed to materialize. Nicias sent a second annual report from a new camp on land that the Athenians had seized within the Great Harbor itself. Far from being over, the war was dragging on with diminishing prospects for success. Nicias now commanded alone—Lamachus had died in the fighting when they brought the fleet to Syracuse and established a permanent base there. As would happen many times during the Sicilian expedition, an Athenian victory had lost more than it gained. The untimely death of the plain-speaking veteran extinguished the spark of Athenian initiative. Never known for forcefulness, Nicias' energy was sapped further by a debilitating condition of the kidneys. To justify his poor performance, he described the troubles that confronted the Athenian force.

"Our fleet was originally in first-class condition; the timbers were sound and the crews were in good shape. Now, however, the ships have been at sea so long that the timbers have rotted, and the crews are not what they were. We cannot drag our ships on shore to dry and clean them, because the enemy has as many or more ships than we have, and keeps us in the constant expectation of having to face an attack. We can see them at their maneuvers, and the initiative is in their hands. Moreover, it is easier for them to dry their ships, since they are not maintaining a blockade."

He also had to report that the diplomatic initiative had proved an utter failure. The arrival of the Athenian armada had united Sicily as nothing else could have done, just as Xerxes' invasion had once united the city-states of Greece. Faced with ever-growing numbers on the enemy side, Nicias begged the Assembly to recall the fleet or at least to recall *him,* in view of his illness. Trying to shock those at home into giving up their dreams of conquering Sicily, he warned that victory could be won at Syracuse only by reinforcing the original expedition with a new armada, a force of ships and men and money as great as the first.

Like his cautionary speech against Alcibiades at the original debate in the Assembly, Nicias' letter had the opposite effect to the one intended. The Athenians ordered him to remain in command and promised to send reinforcements the following spring. Athens could not abandon an enterprise in which it had already invested so much material and prestige. To command the new fleet, the Assembly appointed Demosthenes, one of the heroes of Pylos, and Eurymedon, a veteran of the first Athenian expedition to Sicily more than ten years before.

While Nicias was corresponding with the Assembly at the end of the war's second year, the Syracusans sent envoys to Sparta. Alcibiades supported their appeal for help. To ensure that the Spartans understood the full extent of Athens' imperialistic ambitions, Alcibiades revealed the master plan that lay behind the Athenian attack on Syracuse. The Athenians intended first to conquer Sicily and Italy, then cross to the African coast and take Carthage and its empire. The forests of Italy would yield timber for a new and even larger fleet, manned in part by warlike Iberian tribesmen. With this fleet Athens intended to blockade the Peloponnese, defeat the Spartans, and extend their rule throughout the Mediterranean. To prevent these calamities, Alcibiades said, the Spartans should send the Syracusans a general.

The man chosen for the mission was named Gylippus, a tough disciplinarian with a gift for strategy. He won the trust and respect of the Syracusans by scoring victories on land as soon as he arrived. When Gylippus learned that the Athenians were sending a new fleet, he decided to make a preemptive strike before the reinforcements arrived. During the first two years of the war the Syracusans had not dared to challenge the Athenian navy. Nicias had positioned the fleet on the opposite side of the Great Harbor from the main Athenian military base, at a rocky promontory called Plemmyrium ("Flowing of the Sea"). From there the Athenian ships kept up a blockade of the harbor mouth, protected by a row of three forts against attacks by land. Gylippus was determined to expel the enemy fleet from this advantageous site. He would use the untried Syracusan navy as bait to distract them during his assault.

Early one morning the Athenians at Plemmyrium were startled to see eighty Syracusan ships rowing boldly toward them from the city's two harbors. Two years after launching the great armada, the Athenians were facing a naval battle at last. At once they divided their fast triremes so that twenty-five confronted the Syracusan squadron inside the Great Harbor, while thirty-five blocked the entry of the fleet from the Little Harbor on the seaward side. A double battle began, with the outnumbered Athenians fighting on two fronts. Many Athenian soldiers from the forts came down to lend support in case any ships ran aground.

After the lines clashed, the triremes of the two sides fought each other to a standstill. Little by little the Athenians fell back. Then Syracusan inexperience began to tell. With clear water ahead of them, their ships straggled forward into the gap. Seeing the confusion, the Athenians launched a counterattack and chased the enemy back to the city walls, destroying eleven ships and losing only three of their own. After setting up a trophy on an islet, the Athenian commanders and crews attempted to return to Plemmyrium. They were too late. While they were busy fighting the Syracusan navy, Gylippus and his troops had appeared from the hinterland and taken all three forts.

Bewildered and disheartened, the victors had no choice but to join the Athenian army in the camp on the western shore. Their casualties had been heavy, and along with the three forts, Gylippus had captured the cruising masts and sails of the fast triremes and most of their naval stores. Money chests had been kept in the forts to pay for supplies, and they too joined the enemy's windfall. At once the Syracusans sent out squadrons to seek support abroad. In southern Italy they found boats filled with provisions for the Athenian forces and stockpiles of timber on shore that Nicias had been counting on to repair his rotting triremes. The Syracusans destroyed the boats and burned the wood. No naval supplies would reach the Athenians by sea.

Meanwhile the Great Harbor was becoming the scene of naval battles almost daily. Spurred to new stratagems by the constant warfare, both sides applied all their ingenuity and engineering skills to the naval effort. At Nicias' orders, Athenian engineers transformed the exposed shore of the main camp into an artificial harbor by driving long wooden stakes into the mud. When this offshore stockade proved insufficient, empty freighters were anchored in a widely spaced line with torpedolike "dolphins" of iron or lead suspended above the gaps. If a Syracusan trireme tried to break through, the heavy metal dolphins would plummet downward, punch holes through their hulls, and sink them.

The Athenians also converted one of their largest grain freighters into a floating fortress with wooden towers and screens. This behemoth, loaded with archers and dart throwers, was towed across to the city. In a dangerous operation, the Athenians kept up a running fire of missiles in order to cover the work of hired divers, who plunged into the water from small boats. Once under the surface these professionals pulled up or sawed through the wooden stakes that the Syracusans had hoped would protect their own naval station.

The Syracusans were not idle. Recognizing their inferior seamanship, they borrowed an innovation from the Corinthians and modified the design of their triremes. To counter Athenian maneuverability, they reinforced the forward sections of their rowing frames with long wooden beams. The Syracusan shipwrights also cut off the slender beaks of the ships' rams to leave blunt snub noses of solid wood. With these new prows, the Syracusan ships were able to attack the Athenians head on, smashing the vulnerable Athenian rowing frames and putting the upper ranks of oarsmen out of commission. Once an enemy trireme was immobilized, daring Syracusans in small boats dashed in under the oar banks and shot darts upward to wound or kill the defenseless rowers.

Throughout these operations the tide of victory ran steadily against Nicias and the Athenians. At last the long-awaited reinforcements from Athens arrived, seventy-three triremes packed with men and commanded by Demosthenes and Eurymedon. Still they could not regain the upper hand. Within a few days Demosthenes had managed to lose a nocturnal land battle on the heights northwest of the city. After this failure he abruptly declared that the long and costly expedition should be given up before it ruined Athens altogether. His colleague Eurymedon agreed. The military and naval defeats were serious enough, but now fever was spreading from the nearby marshes through the hot and crowded camp.

Nicias continued to hint at intelligence reports that a party inside Syracuse would soon open the gates. After wasting many days he finally agreed to the withdrawal, provided that no one held him responsible. As inconspicuously as possible, the crews prepared the ships while the troops loaded gear and supplies on board. The time chosen for the retreat was a night in the middle of the month when the full moon would allow the Athenian steersmen to make their way out of the Great Harbor in safety.

After sundown on the appointed evening, the Athenians watched the moon rise from the eastern horizon into the sky above the harbor mouth. Two hours before midnight the lunar disk was blotted out by a total eclipse. As darkness covered the Great Harbor, the Athenian troops and rowers saw the event as a warning sent by the gods. Terrified, they refused to embark on their voyage. Unfortunately there was no Pericles among the Athenian commanders to explain the celestial mechanics behind eclipses. Nicias, as devout as any of the men, consulted his diviners. They told him that no action should be taken until the time of the next full moon, thrice nine days away. Full of religious fervor, Nicias postponed the evacuation.

Long before the month passed, the Syracusan fleet attacked again. In yet another disastrous engagement the Athenians lost many ships, and the general Eurymedon was killed. The Syracusans attempted to destroy the entire Athenian fleet by bringing up an old freighter, packing it with dry brush and resinous pinewood, and setting it alight. Breezes wafted the fire ship toward the huddle of triremes, but with a desperate effort the Athenians fended it off.

The Syracusans could now cruise at will around the Great Harbor for the first time since the war began. Soon the Athenians observed signs of unusual activity. A mass of old triremes, freighters, and small craft were assembling at the mouth of the harbor. The Syracusans anchored some of these ships and lashed or chained others to their neighbors on either side. Gradually a barrier of ships began to form. The Athenians and their fleet were trapped. In obedience to instructions sent out before the eclipse and never rescinded, Athenian allies had stopped sending provisions to the camp at Syracuse. Even the healthy would soon go hungry. Nicias and Demosthenes now thought only of escape. They must break through the barrier.

In the end the Athenians resolved to launch every ship that could still float for a final battle. If victorious, they would force their way to freedom and the open sea. If defeated, they planned to burn their triremes and retreat overland. There were still enough healthy rowers and fighting men to fill 110 triremes. The last task of the Athenian ironworkers was to forge clawlike grappling irons that could snag an enemy ship and prevent it from backing away after ramming. The archers and javelin throwers could then shoot straight into the opposing throng, while Athenian hoplites leaped across for hand-to-hand combat. In these primitive tactics the generals now saw their only hope.

Nicias would remain on shore with a fighting force to defend the camp. As for the thousands of sick and wounded, nothing could save them now. Whether the escape went by sea or by land, they would be abandoned. After speeches, prayers, and sacrifices, Demosthenes launched all that was left of the armada and rowed straight for the barrier. The triremes had not reached it before a hundred Syracusan ships descended on them from all corners of the Great Harbor. As the enemy swarmed in, the Athenians saw that hides had been stretched over the prows and forward sections of their ships. Spies had carried word of the Athenian grappling irons to the Syracusan commanders, who had devised this method of shielding the woodwork of their vessels. Any "iron hands" cast from an Athenian ship would bounce harmlessly off the hides.

The leading Athenian triremes managed to smash their way through the Syracusans and reach the barrier. Desperately the men attempted to cut the cables that secured the moored ships. Before they could hack through, the full force of the enemy took them from the rear. To save themselves, the Athenians had no choice but to turn and fight. In a hail of missiles the Syracusans pushed the Athenians away from the barrier. When thirty Athenian triremes had been lost, the remainder broke away from the enemy and fled for their own shore. So broken were the Athenians that they did not even send a herald to ask permission to pick up their dead and dying.

Only the two generals still clung to the idea of a naval victory. Determining that even with their losses the Athenians outnumbered the enemy, Demosthenes and Nicias ordered their exhausted and demoralized men back on board to renew the battle. At this the crews mutinied. Powerless to oppose the rebellious mob, the generals yielded. The evacuation overland would start after sundown, under cover of darkness.

At that crucial hour, cause for hope unexpectedly reached the camp. From the city came the sounds of wild revelry. Songs and shouting echoed across the water. The Syracusans, almost to the last man, were celebrating their victory. With the enemy distracted or drunk, the Athenians could expect to make their escape unopposed and march overland to friendly territory. Unfortunately, one Syracusan remained sober. He was Hermocrates, the patriot who had led the resistance from the start. He was well aware that the Athenians might slip from their grasp that night and tried but failed to put an end to the drinking and dancing. A man of *mêtis,* Hermocrates hit upon a stratagem to keep the Athenians from escaping. Themistocles had once used a false report to lure the Persian fleet into the strait at Salamis. Perhaps the Athenians themselves could be tricked in the same way.

Extricating a few Syracusan horsemen from the riotous party, Hermocrates instructed them to carry a message to the Athenian camp masquerading as Nicias' covert sympathizers from the city. When these horsemen drew within hailing distance of the Athenian sentries, they called out a warning from the darkness. The Syracusan victory feast, they said, was only a sham. The main Syracusan force had in fact slipped out of the city and was wait-ing in ambush along the road. They would attack as soon as the Athenians left the safety of their palisade. Having delivered Hermocrates' message, the horsemen turned and vanished into the night.

Too exhausted to think clearly, Nicias and Demosthenes made the fatal mistake of postponing the retreat yet again. Their credulity sealed their doom. When the Athenians finally broke camp two days later, the Syra-cusans had sobered up and were waiting for them in deadly earnest. The long line of retreating Athenians met enemies at every pass and ford. They had little food or water, and the thousands of rowers did not even have weapons. The Syracusans, mounted or on foot, harried and hounded them along like a pack of wolves around a herd. Many Athenians had already been slaughtered by the time the generals surrendered to save the lives of the rest.

A few Athenians got away into the countryside to become bandits. Most were marched back to the city as prisoners. The democratic Syracusans convened an assembly to decide their fate. Shouting down the objections of Hermocrates, Gylippus, and the other leaders, the vengeful Syracusans demanded the blood of the two Athenian generals. Nicias and Demosthenes were butchered, and their bodies were dumped outside the city gates. The seven thousand remaining captives were penned up in the city's famous limestone quarries. These vast pits had been excavated in a hillside next to the theater of Syracuse. The theater had been inaugurated fifty years earlier by Aeschylus himself with a performance of *Persians*. It was a bitter irony that a place that once celebrated Athenian liberty and naval victory should have adjoined a prison for the defeated remnant of Athens' imperial navy.

The prisoners' daily rations were a pint of meal and half a pint of water. As the months passed they died of exposure, hunger, and sickness. Conta-gion spread from the rotting corpses, which were soon heaped up on all sides. By midwinter the Syracusans began to remove some prisoners. A few who knew by heart the latest songs of Euripides came to the notice of young

Syracusans, who released these lucky ones to sing at drinking parties. Most of the Athenians were kept in the quarries for eight months. After that any who survived were taken out, branded, and sold as slaves.

No one escaped to carry word home. Athens knew nothing of the disaster until one day a stranger from overseas arrived at the Piraeus and sought out a barbershop. Once in the barber's chair and engaged in the inevitable chatter, the traveler began to speak about the catastrophe in Sicily as if it were already well known everywhere. The barber, horror struck, abandoned his customer and darted out into the street. He ran all the way from the Piraeus to Athens. There he found the archons sitting in the Agora and told them what he had heard.

The officials violently denied the possibility of such a disaster, until more messengers arrived bearing the same tale. Unbelievably, the magnificent fleet launched with such fanfare from the Piraeus, as well as all the ships and men sent afterward as reinforcements, had perished to the last dispatch boat. In their fury and grief the Athenians looked for scapegoats. At first they laid the blame on Alcibiades or Nicias or the oracle-mongers. But in the final reckoning they could blame only themselves. Those whom the Assembly sent to conquer Syracuse had paid with their lives for the folly and hubris of Athens.

Part Four

CATASTROPHE

What I should wish is that you should fix your eyes every day on the greatness of Athens as she really is, and should fall in love with her. When you realize her greatness, then reflect that what made her great was men with a spirit of adventure, men who knew their duty, men who were ashamed to fall below a certain standard. If they ever failed in an enterprise, they made up their minds that at any rate the city should not find their courage lacking to her, and they gave to her the best contribution that they could. They gave their lives.

—Pericles to the Athenians

CHAPTER 14

The Rogue's Return

Let him come! Let him come! Do not stop the ship of many oars that carries him, until he makes his way home to the city.

—Sophocles

AFTER THE DISASTER AT SYRACUSE MOST GREEKS EXPECTED universal rebellion among Athens' allies and the fall of Athens itself soon afterward. Pleasant anticipations warmed the Spartans through the winter months as they waited for the start of the next campaigning season. But nothing turned out as they had imagined. The troublesome Athenian democracy declined to accept the destiny that seemed so inevitable to everybody else. And by a strange twist of fate, the leading role in Athens' recovery was to be played by that traitorous and evil genius of the Sicilian expedition, Alcibiades.

For two years he had lived among the Spartans, doing his best to wreak vengeance on the Athenians. Alcibiades knew Athens well, and he used his knowledge to hurt his native city more deeply than any stranger could have done. The Spartans were mere tools in his campaign for revenge. Thanks to the success of his counsels, Alcibiades stood high in their regard, but what had really won their respect was his total adaptation to Spartan ways: a regimen of black broth, daily exercise, and hard living. He had embraced the simple life of a Spartan warrior as if born to it. So complete was the transformation that his contemporaries likened him to a chameleon. Biding his time, Alcibiades awaited the overthrow of his political enemies and his triumphant return to Athens. As the playwright Aeschylus put it in one of his tragedies, "Men in exile feed on dreams."

The prestige of Athenian democracy suffered with the failure of the

Sicilian expedition, but Alcibiades and the rest of the Greeks overestimated the disaster's impact. In this supreme crisis the Assembly rallied swiftly. Timber was found and new ships built. To retrench, the Athenians called in the triremes and troops from distant outposts. Messengers were sent to Athenian garrisons in allied cities, warning them that the Spartans could back oligarchic coups. All these steps were taken over the winter. When the historian Thucydides recorded the people's energetic response, he observed that democracies are always at their best when things seem at their worst.

Even before the Sicilian expedition ended, the Athenians had begun to seek a more just relationship with their maritime allies. On their own initiative they ended the annual demand for tribute, the most hated practice of their imperial rule. Instead they collected a five percent tax on all maritime commerce. The new system was more directly tied to the benefits conferred by Athenian rule of the sea, and it actually brought in more money than the annual tribute payments. Above all, the Assembly tacitly renounced the terrible practice of enforcing imperial rule through the wholesale killing of defeated populations. Athens was rewarded for its reforms by the loyal adherence of most cities in the empire.

Alarms and excursions might come and go, but at Athens the theater was eternal. The eighty-year-old Sophocles had been appointed to a new board of councilors, so his younger colleague Euripides came to the fore. Retreating to an isolated cave on the island of Salamis, Euripides undertook to write tragedies for a people whose lives were now steeped in real tragedy. Thousands of citizens had lost loved ones in Sicily. The entire city was still in a state of trauma from the horrors of the disaster. At this time of deep grief, any tale of bloodshed or divine punishment would have seemed unendurable. In the past, Euripides had produced plays like *The Trojan Women* that savagely rebuked Athenian arrogance and inhumanity, but he was now a changed man. His new plays were meant not to cut but to heal.

Instead of harping on death, sorrow, and retribution, Euripides invented a different type of tragedy: the romance. His themes were deliverance, redemption, and reunion. The new plays featured the stock mythological characters and situations of Attic tragedy, but they ended happily. Gods and heroes rescued the innocent from great perils, and loved ones believed dead were discovered alive and well. In his romances Euripides fashioned a theater of escape, but on a higher plane than mere physical escapism and diversion. The new plays were metaphors for renewal, purification, and fresh beginnings.

The sea dominated Euripides' romantic tragedies, both as a setting and as a force of nature. His protagonists now always faced dangers at sea, but their trials concluded with daring and joyful rescues. In *Iphigenia Among the Taurians* the young Orestes, son of King Agamemnon, crossed the Black Sea and rescued his long-lost sister Iphigenia from savage local tribesmen. At the end the actor playing Athena was hoisted up by the crane and hovered over the stage as a deus ex machina. The goddess assured the audience that Poseidon would smooth the waves, while fair winds wafted the wanderers safely to the shores of Attica. Wish fulfillment could go no further. Euripides put his most hopeful and consoling line into the mouth of Iphigenia, a woman stranded upon a foreign shore who had given up hope of rescue: "The sea can wash away all human ills."

Soon after the festival of Dionysus, the sea became the theater for an epic conflict that most ancient chroniclers called the Ionian War, though Thucydides regarded it as the final eight-year phase of his great Peloponnesian War. Continuous naval actions and amphibious assaults raged up and down the coasts of Asia Minor from Halicarnassus to Byzantium and embroiled the islands of Rhodes, Samos, Chios, and Lesbos as well. For the Athenians, survival depended upon holding on to Ionia and the Hellespont. For the Spartans, these eastern seaways held the key to defeating a city that was still impregnable at home, thanks to its Long Walls. The Athenians established their principal naval base on the loyal island of Samos, while the Spartan fleet used the harbor at Ephesus on the Asiatic mainland.

Among the first commanders to cross from Greece to Ionia was Alcibiades. He had pressing personal reasons for making a speedy exit from Sparta. Eros with his thunderbolt had struck again. As sexually irrepressible as ever, Alcibiades had taken advantage of King Agis' absence with the Spartan army in Attica to seduce his wife, Timonassa. Now he had every reason to believe that the child she was bearing was his own. It would be best for him to get away before the secret became known. After stirring up a revolt against Athens on the island of Chios, he continued eastward to Asia.

Since neither the Spartans nor the Athenians had enough money to pay their crews, the Great King and his satraps became once again an important force in Greek affairs. In exchange for Persian gold sufficient to engineer the defeat of the Athenian navy, the Spartans were even willing to restore the Greek cities of Asia to Persian rule—an extraordinary offer from men who claimed to be fighting for Greek liberty. Alcibiades took advantage of the negotiations between Spartans and Persians to ingratiate himself with Tissaphernes, the satrap at Sardis. The two men were rogues and opportunists of the same stamp. Amid the cushions and courtesies of the satrap's court, Alcibiades transformed himself into the luxury-loving companion of Tissaphernes' feasts and hunting parties.

Alcibiades gave Tissaphernes two pieces of advice. First, he should provide as little money as possible for the rowing crews, to keep them poor and tied to the Spartan fleet. Second, he should not favor the Spartans exclusively but should also give something to the Athenians so that the two sides would wear each other down. Alcibiades had in fact been distancing himself from the Spartan cause ever since an Athenian victory on a plain near Miletus (another Athenian ally that Alcibiades had persuaded to revolt). It had been a shock for Alcibiades to confront his fellow citizens on the battlefield and to witness their vigorous resistance to the Spartans. Now almost forty, he felt dissatisfied with his life. A great yearning grew in him to be accepted back by his own countrymen. Alcibiades had played the part of a Spartan, and more recently of a Persian. Now he meant to be an Athenian again.

To achieve this end, Alcibiades decided to instigate an oligarchic revolution among the Athenians. He envisioned himself returning home as leader of the revolutionary party. His complicated intrigues brought about in rapid succession a brutal oligarchic coup at Athens, the overthrow of the democracy, and the establishment of a new government under a group of oligarchs called the Four Hundred. The crew of the *Paralos* brought word of the revolution to the Athenian naval base on Samos. Defiantly, the mass of citizens serving with the fleet repudiated the tyrannical oligarchs, set up a democratic assembly on the island, and declared themselves to be the true, legitimate Athens. Democracy now resided not in the Agora or on the Pnyx but in the triremes of the navy. Themistocles' vision of a city in ships had unexpectedly become a reality.

After their declaration of independence the Athenians with the fleet realized that well-trained crews and good intentions would not win the war with the Spartans. Victory required a master strategist. In this crisis they were driven to offer command of the fleet to the one man who had done more than any other to injure both the democracy and the navy: Alcibiades. He was again with Tissaphernes at Sardis, since the oligarchs in Athens, having happily accepted his hints about a revolution, wanted nothing more to do with him. Now the seemingly impossible had come to pass. As Aristophanes said, puzzling over the mysterious obsession of his fellow citizens for Alcibiades, "They love him and they hate him. They cannot live with him and they cannot live without him."

The man sent to fetch Alcibiades was Thrasybulus, a former trierarch who was now the most popular general of the "democracy in exile." He returned from Sardis with Alcibiades in tow, a legendary figure of larger-than-life vices and powers, a demon who might yet prove to be a savior. Exerting all his charismatic appeal, Alcibiades spoke to the men about his star-crossed life and of the dangers that still faced them. Most of all he spoke of his conviction that he could bring the Persians over to their side. Once he deprived the enemy of Persian gold, the Spartan naval effort would soon wither away. It was a moving and optimistic speech. The men elected him general on the spot. Alcibiades soon showed his value as a leader by deterring a rash plan to launch the fleet and fight a civil war against Athens itself. He pointed out that as soon as the democratic navy left for Athens, the Spartans would quickly seize all the cities of Ionia and the Hellespont.

In the end, no action on the part of the fleet was needed to terminate the oligarchic regime in the city. Shortly after Alcibiades' return a naval setback sealed the fate of the Four Hundred. An enemy fleet was menacing Athenian strongholds on the island of Euboea. Under the command of the oligarchs a hastily assembled Athenian fleet suffered a shameful defeat outside the harbor of Eretria. (The inexplicable failure of the Spartans to attack Athens immediately after this battle led Thucydides to dub them "quite the most convenient enemies that the Athenians could possibly have had.") The disaster at Eretria exposed the impotence of the oligarchs at sea. And if they could not rule the sea, they were unfit to govern Athens. Spontaneously the citizens assembled on the Pnyx and voted to depose the Four Hundred. The revolution was over.

Alcibiades now turned his attention to the Persians. The Great King was sending a large fleet of Phoenician triremes to aid the Spartan war effort. Tissaphernes had been ordered to oversee the union of the Spartan and Persian fleets at the Eurymedon River, and Alcibiades boldly voyaged there himself with a few Athenian triremes in order to frustrate the plan. No one will ever know what wiles or promises Alcibiades employed with his bosom friend, but against all odds they succeeded. To the incredulous rage of the Spartans, Tissaphernes dismissed the newly arrived armada and sent it back to its home ports of Tyre and Sidon.

Alcibiades took full credit for saving Athens, but when he arrived back at Samos, he found no one to congratulate him. During his absence the theater of war had abruptly shifted to the Hellespont. The new Spartan admiral Mindarus, angered by Tissaphernes' broken promises, had accepted the invitation of the more trustworthy satrap Pharnabazus to make war in northern waters. Together the Spartan and the Persian hoped to win control of the grain route from the Black Sea and starve Athens into submission. The entire Athenian fleet had followed the Spartans north. Their new base was at Sestos, facing the Spartans at Abydos, on the Hellespont's southern shore. Thrasybulus and his colleagues had already won a naval victory near a headland called Cynossema ("Bitch's Tomb"). Expecting another naval battle, the generals in both the Spartan and the Athenian fleets were appealing far and wide for more ships. Alcibiades quickly manned eighteen triremes and set off for the north.

The seaways were strangely empty, every available galley having been drawn off to the Hellespont. At their overnight stops on shore the Athenians learned that they were following in the wake of a fleet of Spartan reinforcements from Rhodes, now less than a day's row ahead of them. Should Mindarus launch his attack as soon as those ships reached him, Alcibiades might miss the battle altogether. It was late afternoon when the Athenian squadron finally turned into the mouth of the Hellespont. No ships were in sight, but the stream carried the wreckage of a great battle: oars, timbers, corpses. Beyond a turn in the channel the struggle came into view: two fleets locked in midstream, clashing and colliding as victory still hung in the balance. Alcibiades had arrived in time.

Both sides took heart when they saw the eighteen triremes coming up the channel with the sun behind them. Each believed the new arrivals to be ships of their own. Not until Alcibiades ran up his purple flag was he recognized. The hard-pressed Athenians cheered; the Spartans and their allies braced for a flank attack. Mindarus had posted an allied contingent from Syracuse on his left wing, at the downstream end of the line. With grim satisfaction Alcibiades bore down on these Sicilian ships, smashing through their ranks and driving them back toward their own shore. The rest of the enemy line went the way of the Syracusans. Unable to reach their harbor at Abydos, they formed a barrier of ships along a stretch of coast where their army could hold off the Athenian attack.

The Persian cavalry rode up in support as well, led by the satrap Pharnabazus, a conspicuous figure wearing the high-peaked tiara of a Persian lord. He was witnessing at first hand the fruit of his dubious investment in the Spartan naval enterprise. Pharnabazus was not a man to hang back, however, even in a rout. With heroic zeal he urged his stallion far out in the waves, calling on Persians and Spartans alike to join him in driving back the Athenians. His efforts, along with the rising wind, balked the Athenians in their efforts to destroy all of Mindarus' ships. Even so, they were able to tow back to Sestos not only thirty enemy triremes as prizes but also Athenian ships that had been captured by the Spartans in the early hours of fighting. Alcibiades joined the other generals in erecting a second trophy, this time for victory in the battle of Abydos.

Alcibiades and his colleagues spent the winter combing the Aegean Sea and Ionia for money and ships. By early spring they had managed to assemble a fleet of eighty-six triremes near the mouth of the Hellespont. At last, thanks to the winds that had destroyed Spartan reinforcements and to their own successes in battle, they outnumbered the enemy. Along with Alcibiades the Athenian naval command was shared by Thrasybulus and Theramenes, a young general recently sent out by the Assembly at Athens. While the three considered their next move, news came that Mindarus and the Spartans had seized Cyzicus, on the southern shore of the Sea of Marmara.

The Athenians knew Cyzicus well. This prosperous city was a longtime Athenian ally. It lay on a narrow isthmus joining the mainland of Asia Minor to a large rugged landmass that projected far out into the sea. The

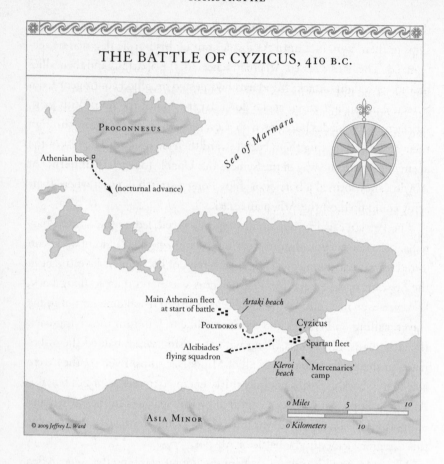

THE BATTLE OF CYZICUS, 410 B.C.

PROCONNESUS

Sea of Marmara

Athenian base

(nocturnal advance)

Main Athenian fleet
at start of battle

Artaki beach

POLYDOROS

Cyzicus

Alcibiades'
flying squadron

Spartan fleet

*Kleroi
beach*

Mercenaries'
camp

0 Miles   5   10

0 Kilometers   10

© 2009 Jeffrey L. Ward

ASIA MINOR

Spartan fleet was lying in Cyzicus harbor, a sheltered embayment in the sand flats of the isthmus. Alcibiades and his colleagues decided first to recapture the city and then, having robbed the Spartans of their base, destroy them in a sea battle at a time and place favorable to the Athenians. With Spartan sea power broken, they might go on to recover Byzantium, the Bosporus, and control of the grain traffic from the Black Sea.

Secrecy was now essential. Should Mindarus get wind of their actual numbers, they might never lure him out into the open. So the Athenian fleet became a nocturnal animal, sleeping by day and moving forward only under cover of darkness. On the first night they rowed up the Hellespont, unseen by the Spartan watchmen on the walls of Abydos. On the second they left the Hellespont behind and crossed the open Sea of Marmara to an island that lay north of Cyzicus. No word of their coming was allowed to reach the enemy—the Athenians adopted Alcibiades' effective policy of arresting any traveler unlucky enough to cross their path, and at their final landfall on the island of Proconnesus they impounded all local shipping and held it in the port. Alcibiades even had the herald proclaim the death penalty for anyone who tried to cross over to the Asiatic mainland.

As the third night drew on, Alcibiades assembled the men and fired their spirits for what lay ahead. The troops and rowers would face the challenge that had confronted the Persian forces at Salamis: sleepless hours of ceaseless activity, followed by an attack on an enemy that had enjoyed a full night's rest. Alcibiades reminded his men that the Athenian fleet now had no money at all, while the Spartans enjoyed the unlimited bounty of the Great King. If they wanted to remedy that situation, they must be prepared to tackle every kind of obstacle: enemy fleets, armies, and fortified cities and camps. "You must be ready to face fighting at sea, fighting on land, fighting on walls," he told the men. A different general might have appealed to patriotism and noble causes. Alcibiades somehow hit the right note with a speech that could have been made by a pirate chief.

In darkness the thousands of men boarded the ships and pushed off. Ahead lay the rough promontory and desolate range of hills that guarded the northern approaches to Cyzicus. During the night it began to rain. The spring shower thickened to a heavy downpour, drenching the soldiers and officers on the decks. The men might curse, but to the generals the bad weather was a blessing. Rain and mist would wrap the fleet in a cloak of invisibility and drive watchers on the coast to take shelter indoors. The drumming and hissing of the rain on the sea would help them by drowning out the sound of the oars, which could travel far on a still night.

Guided by reports from the lookouts in the prows, the steersmen felt their way along the coast until they reached the wide curving beach at Artaki. Here the generals set most of the troops ashore. With Chaireas of the *Paralos* in the lead, the hoplites were ordered to march over the shoulder of the hills to the northern side of Cyzicus. It would be their mission to create a diversion when the fleet launched the main attack on the harbor. By gray dawn light the army company filed inland and vanished into the gloom of the wet, wooded slopes.

Riding lighter now, the triremes resumed their slow advance until a rocky islet loomed up ahead of them. This landmark was the island of Polydoros, broad at its base but tapering to a conical summit. Here the Athenians divided. Thrasybulus and Theramenes stayed behind, concealing the main fleet behind the islet, just as Homer's Greeks had once hidden their ships behind the isle of Tenedos near Troy. Alcibiades forged ahead with the force that would serve as the Athenians' "Trojan Horse," a vanguard of twenty fast ships. His mission was to lure the unsuspecting Spartan fleet away from Cyzicus. Thrasybulus and Theramenes would then move forward to attack the harbor, while Chaireas and the Athenian troops assaulted the city's landward side. Alcibiades might even be able to sprint back in time to assist in recapturing Cyzicus, leaving the outnumbered and disconcerted Spartans bereft of their naval station. That, at any rate, seems to have been the modest and workmanlike plan for the day. Given the involvement of Alcibiades, however, something was bound to go wrong.

The rain had stopped, and the sky was brightening as Alcibiades led his flying squadron through the channel that ran between Polydoros and the neighboring coast. As the Athenian triremes burst into the sunshine, Alcibiades saw that by a stroke of luck Mindarus had already accomplished half his task for him. The full Spartan naval force was already clear of the harbor, though unaware of the Athenian approach. Their admiral had brought them out for morning exercises. Back and forth in front of Cyzicus they were practicing their maneuvers. There were famous men in the Spartan ranks: the general Hermocrates, nemesis of Nicias and the Athenian expedition to Sicily, led the Syracusans; an Olympic athlete named Dorieus commanded a squadron from Thurii in southern Italy. Pharnabazus and his cavalry were still in winter quarters well inland, on the far side of a range of hills, but the satrap's mercenary army occupied a fort on the heights above the bay. To Alcibiades' left lay Cyzicus itself, the prize for which all these forces would soon contend.

The stratagem that would lure the Spartans away from Cyzicus followed the precepts of Alcibiades' old commander Phormio: "Feign weakness to make your enemy overconfident. Draw a disorderly charge by making your own force appear small." Alcibiades moved forward until the enemy lookouts saw him, and enemy ships broke away from the drill to challenge the newcomers. Then he ordered his steersmen to veer west toward the open sea, drawing the Spartans after him in an exuberant chase. Mindarus' entire fleet was soon racing along in the Athenians' wake, losing order as the faster triremes outdistanced the rest. Once the chase had pulled west of Polydoros island, Thrasybulus and Theramenes moved into the open. A short row brought them far enough into the bay to cut off Mindarus' retreat. On seeing his colleagues take up their new position, Alcibiades hoisted the signal for his own squadron to attack its pursuers. At once the twenty ships swung into a hard turn that brought them back around until their rams pointed at the enemy fleet. Then each trireme picked a target and charged.

Alcibiades' sudden turn and the appearance of the main Athenian fleet took the hapless Spartans completely by surprise. Mindarus could tell that he had lost Cyzicus, but he still hoped to save his fleet. With the way to the harbor blocked, he turned toward the only stretch of level shore in the area, a beach below the mercenary encampment. If his fleet could reach land, the conflict would no doubt degenerate into a standoff between Spartans entrenched on the beach and Athenians fearful of leaving their ships. The sea, not the land, was the Athenians' element. In the battles of Cynossema and Abydos, back in the autumn, the Spartans had been beaten on the water but survived the struggle on shore without much difficulty.

As the Spartan forces fled back toward the southeastern corner of the bay, Alcibiades' triremes were close behind, smashing into the rear guard. Despite the Athenians' best efforts, most of the enemy fleet managed to reach land at a place called Kleroi. It was time now for Alcibiades to abandon the naval battle and return to the main fleet. Thrasybulus and Theramenes were waiting for him in the middle of the bay, ready for the assault on Cyzicus.

For Alcibiades, however, the prospect of one more inconclusive victory seemed suddenly intolerable. His marines were casting grappling irons on enemy hulls at the water's edge, hoping to tow them off as prizes. The Spartans and their allies, led by Mindarus, were fighting back from the decks of their own ships. Away to the Athenians' right, beyond the chaotic mass of triremes in the shallows, lay a strip of open beach. Ignoring his colleagues, Alcibiades rallied his fastest ships and made a dash for the shore west of the grounded Spartan fleet. Despite his many failings, he possessed a lionlike physical courage, and it did not desert him now. As soon as the steersman brought his ship close enough, Alcibiades jumped to shore fully armed, like Achilles leaping onto the sands at Troy.

The marines and archers followed him. The fighting force from all twenty triremes amounted to fewer than three hundred men. As soon as Mindarus got his own troops off the ships and onto shore, the Athenians would be outnumbered by about three to one. But at their head was a general in the grip of full battle fury, behaving like a man possessed. The mania quickly spread through the ranks behind him. Their position was hemmed in on the left by the hulls of the beached ships, and on the right by the hillside. Surprised once again, Mindarus called his troops together to crush this mad charge on his flank.

Watching from the deck of his flagship, Thrasybulus realized that the naval battle was melting into a fight on land. He could also see Pharnabazus' mercenaries as they came streaming out of their fort to join the struggle on the beach. Unless he acted quickly, Alcibiades and his men would soon be overwhelmed by sheer force of numbers. Plan or no plan, the assault on Cyzicus would have to wait. Thrasybulus was well known for his stentorian voice. Shouting across the water, he told Theramenes to fetch Chaireas and the Athenian land forces, now stranded on the northern side of Cyzicus. If they were to join the battle by the ships, Theramenes would have to ferry them across the bay.

As his colleague hurried away with half the remaining Athenian ships, Thrasybulus headed for the beach. The crisis gave him only moments to consider how to save Alcibiades. Deciding that his best hope lay in dividing their opponents, Thrasybulus steered for a point east of the beached fleets, at the opposite end from the place where Mindarus and Alcibiades were now locked in combat. The main enemy force was too busy with Alcibiades to prevent Thrasybulus' triremes from setting his men ashore. When word reached Mindarus of yet another Athenian landing, he sent some of the allied Greeks along with the freshly arrived Persian mercenaries to dispose of Thrasybulus. This horde quickly closed in around their prey. Though successful at the start, Thrasybulus and his company of marines and archers were soon thrown on the defensive. Still they resisted, and the losses were heavy on both sides.

The Athenians were close to exhaustion when Theramenes' squadron finally arrived, the ships crowded with Chaireas' troop of hoplites. As these reinforcements disembarked on the short length of beach still held by Thrasybulus, the tide of battle began to turn. The Persian mercenaries gave way first, then the Peloponnesians. Theramenes' men were still full of fire, and he led them west along the beach to relieve the sorely beleaguered Alcibiades. To meet this new threat from his rear, Mindarus was compelled to divide his forces a second time. Shortly after Theramenes' arrival the Spartan admiral was killed, and once he had fallen even the Spartan hoplites broke ranks and ran. The Athenians chased them inland, until the thunder of hooves on the road from the hills warned them that Pharnabazus and his Persian cavalry were approaching.

As they turned back to the sea, the Athenians saw flames spouting from the row of triremes that the Syracusans had abandoned. These Sicilians had voyaged all the way across the Greek world to lend a hand in the destruction of the Athenian navy. Now the crews from Syracuse had chosen to burn their ships rather than see them fall into Athenian hands. So the day that began in rain ended in fire. All the other ships of Mindarus' fleet were captured intact. Alcibiades' wanton disregard for plans and prudence had transformed what would have been a modest gain at Cyzicus into the greatest Athenian naval victory since the Peloponnesian War began.

The triumphant Athenians put up two trophies: one on the islet of Polydoros for Alcibiades' victory at sea; the other on the mainland for the battle by the ships. That night the Peloponnesian garrison slipped out of Cyzicus, and the next day the Athenians marched in and took the city, unopposed by Pharnabazus and the Persians. Soon afterward the Athenians intercepted a secret message sent back to Sparta by the officer who had taken Mindarus' place. Written in the true laconic style favored by Spartans, the text was short, but very sweet to Athenian eyes: SHIPS LOST MINDARUS DEAD MEN STARVING DON'T KNOW WHAT TO DO.

One casualty of the naval battles in the Hellespont was the playwright Eupolis. He had taken advantage of the license granted to comic poets in Athens to criticize the conduct of the war. As he wrote in one play, "Men whom once you would have deemed unfit to be wine inspectors you now elect to be generals. O Athens! Athens! You are more lucky than wise."

Eupolis had lampooned Alcibiades in a play called *Baptai* or "The Dippers." To the poet's misfortune, he had been posted aboard one of Alcibiades' ships. Eupolis soon discovered that the general had neither forgotten nor forgiven his witty insults. Alcibiades had him dunked in the sea, calling the dip in the brine a return for the dipping that Eupolis had given him in the theater. When Eupolis was killed in action, the Athenians were so distraught at the loss of this shining comic light that they passed a law exempting poets from military service.

As for Alcibiades himself, his exploits at Cyzicus were immortalized in histories, biographies, and tactical manuals. It was the great battle that he had been restlessly seeking all his life, and it improved his reputation in Athens more than anything else could have done. Ever since the democratic restoration in Athens the previous year, an active faction in the city had been working to bring Alcibiades back from exile. He seemed a talisman of victory. The fortunes of Athens had prospered until his condemnation and exile. The Spartans' star had been in the ascendant during the years when Alcibiades advised them. And the goddess Nike had started to smile on the Athenian navy as soon as the democratic assembly on Samos elected him general.

Even the venerable poet Sophocles lent his support to the "Return of the Exile" movement with his *Philoctetes,* first performed in the dramatic contests that followed the great victory at Cyzicus. The play, which was Sophocles' contribution to the new genre of romances, featured the rescue of the marooned hero Philoctetes from an island, and a happy ending as he rejoined his old companions (who had themselves banished and marooned him) to help them win a war. There were still dissenters who blamed Athens' troubles on Alcibiades and pointed out that it was really Thrasybulus who had won the battle of Cyzicus, but they were increasingly in the minority.

In the campaigning seasons that followed the victory at Cyzicus, Alcibiades and his colleagues went on a rampage. Sometimes they worked together; often they undertook separate expeditions. Thrasybulus recovered Thrace and the mining district, Theramenes fought against Pharnabazus on the Asiatic side of the Bosporus, and Alcibiades used stratagems and night attacks to recover the greatest prize of all, Byzantium. From a fort that they named Chrysopolis ("Golden City"), the Athenians levied a ten percent tax on all cargoes passing through the Bosporus from the Black Sea. Enriched by tolls and by booty from Cyzicus, Alcibiades and the other Athenian generals extended their campaigns to Ionia. The Spartans, stripped of naval power, were unable to prevent their opponents from rolling back many of the gains made since the war resumed.

Part of the money from the Bosporus tolls was shipped back to Athens, and from that moment the city's finances began to recover. Up on the Acropolis, architects and stone carvers resumed work on a wondrous new temple called the Erechtheum, for the naval victories and the flow of wealth from overseas gave a buoyant impulse both to the public works projects and to offerings of gratitude to the gods. Now the treasury could pay artisans to complete the Erechtheum's marble statues and fluted columns. As delicate and mysterious as the Parthenon was massive and orderly, the new temple was graced by a high porch where six marble maidens, in place of columns, held up the roof. These strong young women gazed across the ruins of the old temple that Xerxes had destroyed toward the Parthenon and were silent observers at each summer's Panathenaic procession. The Erechtheum provided a spectacular setting for Athena's sacred olive tree, but it celebrated Poseidon as well as Athena. Here stood an altar to the sea god, here was the ancient mark where Poseidon's trident had struck the bedrock of the Acropolis, and here too lay Poseidon's deep saltwater well or "Sea." Athenians who hung their heads over the well believed that they could hear the surf when the wind blew in from the coast.

After three years of fighting on Athens' behalf, Alcibiades finally felt that it might be safe to return to the city. The final mark of civic forgiveness was his election in absentia to the post of general, not by the men in the fleet this time but by the entire Athenian Assembly voting on the Pnyx. By now he was back on Samos, so it was from the island that had witnessed the turn of his fortunes that Alcibiades began his long voyage home.

Most of the men and ships had been away from Athens for years, and Alcibiades wanted their return to be a triumphal procession. He loaded the holds of his twenty triremes with figureheads from captured Spartan warships, and he hung Spartan shields and other trophies from the railings. A purple sail billowed on his flagship's mast, a famous virtuoso played the pipes for his crew, and an equally famous singer chanted the rowing cadence. Alcibiades and his friends decked themselves with garlands of leaves and flowers. In his splendid progress he visited the island of Paros and even took a detour to the Spartan harbor at Gythium. There Alcibiades looked alertly for signs of shipbuilding even as he brazenly flaunted his trophies to the Spartans on shore. He was reminding them, as he had reminded the Athenians during the Sicilian campaign, that he was indeed still alive.

At the Piraeus, Alcibiades' bravado deserted him. The crowd was immense, the shouting incoherent. Not sure whether they were hailing or cursing him, Alcibiades hesitated on the deck of his flagship until he spotted his cousin Euryptolemus and other family members waving a welcome. Then at last he climbed down from his ship and set foot on shore. Well-wishers mobbed him, laughing, cheering, weeping. Someone put a crown on his head, as if he were a victorious athlete, a divine hero—or a king. Through a cordon of friends Alcibiades made his way up the road between the Long Walls.

As soon as possible he presented himself to the Council and then spoke before the Assembly. The people revoked the death sentence, restored his citizenship and property, and even voted him *strategos autokrator,* commander supreme on land and sea. Priests and priestesses lifted their ritual curses from his head. The marble slabs inscribed with the record of Alcibiades' condemnation were pulled down and thrown into the sea, from which they have not yet risen. The beautiful line that Euripides gave to his heroine Iphigenia had proved to be prophetic: "The sea can wash away all human ills."

CHAPTER 15

Of Heroes and Hemlock

[407–406 B.C.]

There I lie, one moment on the shore, another in the sea's swell, carried along by the constant ebb and flow of the waves, with no one to weep for me or give me burial.

—Euripides

NOW THAT THE ANNUAL INFLUX OF TRIBUTE MONEY HAD ENDED, the Assembly was perennially strapped for cash. Rather than sending their generals to sea with an adequate war chest from the public treasury, the Athenians had fallen into the bad habit of expecting them to raise the money for their crews while on the move. This was no way to run a war, let alone to win one, and it led to many abuses. These ranged from extorting money from neutral coastal cities, to committing acts of piracy on the high seas, to taking mercenary service in local wars outside the realm of official Athenian influence. Some desperate generals even resorted to hiring out their crews as migrant workers. The rowers would leave their oars and rowing pads to pick fruit at harvesttime.

After a halcyon summer at home, capped by a spectacular celebration of the Eleusinian Mysteries (the rites that he had once been accused of desecrating), Alcibiades was sent out as general in command of a fleet. The Assembly was counting on him to bring the war in Ionia to a speedy conclusion. As usual in those years, his war chest was empty. Alcibiades should have protested at once and used his charisma and popularity to squeeze funds out of the treasury. Unfortunately he had sold himself to the adoring people as a superman, a demigod. It was too late now to confess that he was a mere mortal like themselves.

Alcibiades' dreams of leadership at Athens ended in disgrace at Notium, near Ephesus. Unable to pay his men, he set off on a round of money-raising and left his steersman, Antiochus, in charge of the fleet. The triremes were moored in the sheltered cove at Notium. This Antiochus was the very man who had long ago caught Alcibiades' notice by capturing the runaway quail during the Assembly meeting. The wealthy Athenian trierarchs could not have been pleased with the prospect of taking orders from their general's steersman and drinking partner. To ensure that nothing went wrong in his absence, Alcibiades left Antiochus with strict orders not to engage the enemy fleet, which lay a few miles east of Notium at Ephesus.

Alas, Antiochus seems to have picked up rashness and opportunism from Alcibiades himself. Soon after the general left Notium, the misguided steersman foolishly precipitated a naval battle in which he himself was killed and twenty-two Athenian triremes were lost. When Alcibiades returned, he led the fleet to Ephesus and challenged the enemy to a fair fight, but the Spartan admiral Lysander would not come out. In these circumstances Alcibiades, though guilty of little more than bad judgment and worse luck, dared not return to Athens to face the wrath of the Assembly. Instead he departed northward with one trireme and went to ground at his private fortress on the northern shore of the Sea of Marmara. This stronghold at Pactye was a bolt-hole that Alcibiades had created for just such an emergency. There he played the role of local warlord in conflicts between Greek settlers and Thracian tribesmen, much as the great Miltiades had done a century before. An evil destiny seemed to hound him still.

After the fiasco at Notium the Athenians urgently needed a reliable general in Ionia. Their choice fell on Conon, a commander with experience at Naupactus. At Samos Conon found a dispirited and depleted fleet. Conon manned seventy triremes with the best crews that he could muster and boldly headed north to confront the Peloponnesian fleet. As he rowed up the broad seaway between Lesbos and the Asiatic shore, messengers brought him word that the enemy had captured the city of Methymna on Lesbos. The Athenian garrison had been sold into slavery. Conon also learned that the Spartan admiral had sent him a warning and a challenge: "I shall stop your fornicating with the sea. She belongs to me."

These bold words came from the new Spartan *navarchos,* a brash young man named Callicratidas. He had succeeded Lysander as admiral and commanded a Peloponnesian fleet of 140 triremes, twice the size of Conon's force. The unequal opponents skirmished the next day. Callicratidas managed to capture 30 of Conon's triremes and chased the rest into the harbor at Mytilene. A pitched battle was fought along the breakwater at Mytilene. The Athenians anchored inside the barrier and used their ships' yardarms as catapults to hurl large stones at the enemy. Hopelessly outnumbered, Conon finally ordered a retreat to the city's inner harbor. Here for the moment he was safe. But Callicratidas did not depart. Almost half of Conon's ships, the cream of the Athenian navy, were already in his hands, and the Spartan admiral was determined not to leave Lesbos till he had taken the rest. The Spartans settled down to a blockade. Two Athenian triremes broke through and made a dash for freedom. The Spartans captured one, but the other reached Athens with news of the disastrous defeat and blockade.

The unexpected news from Mytilene shook Athens to its foundations. All of the city's gains since the Sicilian expedition stood suddenly in jeopardy. Should the Spartans capture Conon and his men, the Athenians would be forced to beg for terms, just as the Spartans had done after the Pylos affair. No effort was spared to avoid that fate. Sacred images and other treasures from the Acropolis were melted down to mint new coins. The rich citizens serving as trierarchs, short on cash themselves, agreed to share the financial burden by serving in pairs. The Assembly had luckily approved Alcibiades' proposal to build new triremes in Macedon, and young Pericles, the son of Pericles and Aspasia, had conveyed them on completion to Athens. To aid the Athenian cause, the Macedonian king had made a gift of shipbuilding timber and oars. Pericles, newly elected to the generalship, handled the finances and fitting out of the new fleet.

Temple treasures and Macedonian forests could provide the material for war but not the tens of thousands of men needed at the oars and on the decks. Even if only the oldest and youngest age-groups stayed in Athens to guard the walls, a full conscription of the remaining male population—horsemen, hoplites, thetes, and resident aliens—would fall short. Fortunately Athens possessed one currency even more precious than silver: citizenship. To be a citizen of Athens was to partake of the world's most liberal commonwealth. The citizenship rolls were jealously protected, and only rarely did the Assembly approve new grants. By law, only the child of an Athenian father and an Athenian mother could claim citizenship. Young Pericles himself was a citizen only by special vote of the people, since his mother, Aspasia, had been a woman of Miletus. Now the Assembly voted to offer Athenian citizenship to foreigners residing in Athens in return for service with the navy.

When that move failed to provide sufficient numbers, wealthy Athenians offered to free their slaves so that they too could man the oars. In ancient Greece slavery was a misfortune that had nothing to do with any stigma related to race or class. It had always been possible for individual slaves to earn their freedom. The liberal attitudes of Athenian naval democracy exerted a positive effect on the lot of slaves, as one oligarch complained, observing that at Athens one could not strike another man's slave, or even expect a slave to step aside for a free man in the street. The same writer noted that in serving their hoplite masters on troop carriers, some Athenian slaves had already become seasoned rowers.

When they heard the offer of the wealthy citizens, the people were fired by a spirit of emulation. After a hasty vote the Assembly proclaimed that any slaves who were willing to risk their lives at sea would receive not only freedom but citizenship as well. The revolutionary decision was carried through in a rush. Thousands of slaves came forward, willing to give up the exemption from military service that was one of the few benefits of slavery. A river of liberated humanity poured down the Long Walls to the Piraeus. There was no time to train the crews. Shortly after midsummer the anxious Athenians on shore watched the launching of the relief fleet, knowing that they had just taken part in a miracle. Only thirty days had elapsed since the arrival of the trireme from Mytilene that carried Conon's appeal for a rescue.

At their naval base in Samos the Athenians managed to assemble more than 150 ships. The fleet was led by no fewer than eight generals. Thrasybulus and Theramenes, former generals who had covered themselves with glory at Cyzicus, were present with the fleet but only serving on individual ships as trierarchs for this rescue mission. The fleet's size was impressive, but speed and seamanship were lacking. The short voyage north to

Lesbos showed that the raw crews, however willing, could hardly hope to be *synkrotoi*—beating and beaten together—by the time they faced the enemy fleet.

Rather than risk a landing near the Spartan forces blockading Mytilene, the Athenians avoided Lesbos and instead camped across the channel on the Arginusae ("White Islands"). A sheltered lagoon lay between the largest two islands in the little archipelago. Along its shores the crews disembarked and lit their cooking fires and watch fires. The Arginusae Islands, ordinarily home to a few Aeolian Greeks, now had a population of some thirty thousand men, the majority of the Athenian citizen body.

The camp extended up a slope to a high ridge overlooking the channel. Standing on the heights, Thrasyllus, Pericles, and the other generals took stock of their position. Southward, to their left, stretched the open sea. In the other direction, half a mile from the island where they had camped, the third and smallest of the Arginusae formed a lonely outpost to the north. And at their feet the chalky white cliffs plunged into the water, bordered in places by treacherous reefs. As night fell, the Athenians saw twinkling lights appear on the opposite shore. The Spartans, aware of their arrival, had moved south along the coast of Lesbos to confront them. Certain of a battle in the morning, the generals ordered their crews to strip the triremes of cruising masts and sails to ready them for action. For most of the crew members it would be the first combat they had ever known. For some it would be the last. About midnight a storm blew up, with wind and heavy rain.

Among the eight generals, supreme command rested with Thrasyllus. He had held a place of honor in Athenian affairs ever since the historic day on Samos five years earlier when he stepped forward from the hoplite ranks to support the cause of democracy. That night at Arginusae Thrasyllus had a dream, one that could have come only to an Athenian. He dreamed that he was at home in the theater of Dionysus, acting a play. Six other generals from the fleet sang and danced with him in the chorus. The play was Euripides' *Phoenician Women,* and their opponents were performing Euripides' *Suppliants.* Both plays had the same tragic themes: the defeat of the Seven Against Thebes; the fate of unburied and dishonored corpses. Thrasyllus

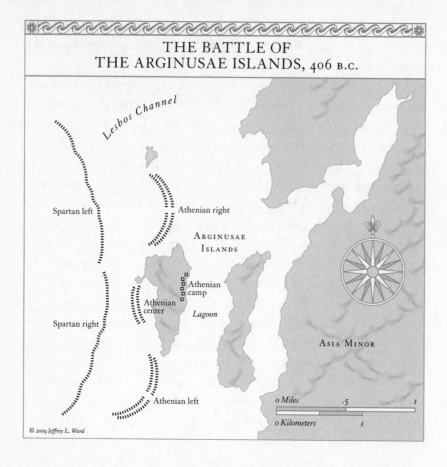

THE BATTLE OF
THE ARGINUSAE ISLANDS, 406 B.C.

Lesbos Channel

Spartan left

Athenian right

ARGINUSAE
ISLANDS

Athenian
camp

Athenian
center

Lagoon

Spartan right

ASIA MINOR

Athenian left

0 Miles   .5   1

0 Kilometers   1

© 2009 Jeffrey L. Ward

and his team won the prize. But it was a Cadmean victory, for they all lost their lives. When he awoke, Thrasyllus immediately told his dream to the prophets.

By dawn the sky had cleared and the sea was calm. The prophets declared that the signs at the morning sacrifices were favorable for victory. Zeus, Apollo, and the Furies would preside over the coming battle. These lucky predictions were announced to the men, though at Thrasyllus' request his dream was not. Ignoring omens, Thrasyllus had worked out a plan that would keep his inexperienced crews close to the protection of the islands. In fact, Thrasyllus would incorporate the islands themselves into the Athenian battle line—a stroke of genius that would render the Athenians unbeatable so long as they held their station. There had been no time for advance planning: the idea had come to him only the previous evening, as he stood on the cliff surveying the channel, the islands, and the reefs.

Thrasyllus divided his fleet into powerful right and left wings bracketing a much less formidable center. The right wing would extend from the northern end of the large island where they had camped across half a mile of water to the lonely islet at the northern end of the little archipelago. Sixty ships arrayed in a double line would compose the right wing, with Thrasyllus himself among the four generals in command. The islet would screen the outermost ships and prevent a flank attack or a *periplous.* Thrasyllus posted his own flagship on the right wing.

Meanwhile the sixty ships of the left wing, also arrayed in a double line, took up a position with one end backed against the southern point of the island and the other reaching into the open sea. Pericles was among the four generals posted on the left wing. The ships of the hopelessly weak center—ten sacred triremes of the Athenian tribes, traditionally rowed by cadets; three ships commanded by the navarchs; ten ships from Samos and a handful from other allies—were strung out along the ragged seaward edge of the island, protected from enemy attack by the treacherous reefs and sheer cliffs behind them.

When all were in position, the Athenian ships formed a wall some two miles long, bristling with bronze beaks and wooden oars. The battle of the Arginusae Islands would be a contest between the best rowers that Persian money could buy and untested crews of Athenian horsemen, commoners, resident aliens, and former slaves. Callicratidas had advanced more than halfway across the channel before his lookouts could take in the amazing Athenian formation sitting immobile on the calm morning sea. Callicratidas' fleet numbered only 120, since he had left 50 triremes at Mytilene to prevent Conon from escaping. In any case, he had never expected the Athenians to produce so many ships. His own fleet was strung out in a single line abreast.

The steersman on the Spartan flagship recognized the danger and told the admiral that he should abandon any idea of attacking. It would be folly to tackle the Athenians in their well-entrenched position, and there was no need to do so. To rescue Conon, the new arrivals would eventually have no choice but to cross to Mytilene. Whenever that happened, they could easily be encircled and defeated in the open channel. But Callicratidas was a Spartan of the old school. Manhood, not *mêtis,* won battles. Retreat was unthinkable.

Ignoring the weak Athenian center, Callicratidas divided his line in two so as to match at least the length of each Athenian wing. Then the trumpeter sounded the charge, and the Peloponnesians swept forward. Callicratidas with his ten triremes from Sparta held the right wing, facing Pericles and his colleagues on the Athenian left. Crowds of camp followers, noncombatants, and local folk lined the top of the cliffs. These spectators had the unique experience of watching four separate fleets engage in combat.

As the Athenians neither advanced nor retreated, the naval action took on the character of a land battle, as if one hoplite phalanx were shoving and heaving against another. The turning point in the long struggle came with the death of the Spartan admiral. His flagship broke through the Athenian front line and then rammed Pericles' trireme with such force that its beak stuck fast in the Athenian hull. Pericles and his marines leaped across and fought their way along the deck of the enemy flagship. Either the shock of the ramming impact or a blow from an Athenian soldier knocked Callicratidas off his feet. He fell into the sea, and the weight of his armor carried him to the bottom. With the disappearance of their admiral, the rest of the Peloponnesian right wing fled. The Athenians surged after them, catching and destroying nine of the ten Spartan ships. The Spartan allies at the northern end of the line held out longer, but eventually they too had to row for their lives. In the ensuing rout the Athenians overtook and rammed a grand total of seventy-seven ships before the end. Athens' new citizens had prevailed.

Thrasyllus summoned his colleagues to a council on shore. Back on the beach, in the azure tranquillity of the island's leeward side, the generals debated their next move. One proposed that the fleet form a line and row through the field of battle, picking up corpses and rescuing shipwrecked Athenians and their allies. Another argued that they should set out immediately for Mytilene to liberate Conon. Thrasyllus proposed a compromise. All eight generals would join in an immediate attack on the Spartan fleet at Mytilene. The former generals Thrasybulus and Theramenes, along with the lower-ranking officers known as taxiarchs, would stay at Arginusae with forty-seven triremes and comb through the floating wreckage for survivors and the bodies of the dead.

While they were making their plans, a north wind had been rising to gale force in the channel. As the Athenian camp afforded no view of the open sea, the generals were unaware of the change in the weather. By the time they voted to adopt Thrasyllus' proposal, the wind had caught the scattered debris of battle. The vast expanse of broken hulls and shipwrecked humanity was suddenly on the move, shifting southward with the storm. The sea was by this time too rough for either part of Thrasyllus' plan to be carried out. Athenian insistence on democratic deliberations, however praiseworthy in principle, now cost the generals their chance. Triremes were not built to survive in heavy seas: even the Athenian marines spoke out against risking more lives in a rescue effort. The generals had no choice but to halt. On the beach they raised a victory trophy, then settled down to wait out the storm.

By morning the wind dropped, but the sea was empty. Wrecks, corpses, and survivors had passed out of sight and out of reach, swept away to beaches far to the south. Grieving for those lost, the Athenians launched their ships and rowed toward Mytilene. Almost immediately they spotted an approaching fleet. It was Conon at the head of his forty ships. The previous evening the Spartan blockaders, learning of Callicratidas' death and the defeat of their comrades, had set fire to their camp and disappeared into the night. Unable to track down the remnant of the Peloponnesian fleet, the Athenians returned to their base at Samos.

The Assembly at home was overjoyed by news of the victory but dissatisfied with the generals for failing to collect the bodies of the dead. To save themselves from prosecution, Theramenes and Thrasybulus (the trierarchs who had been charged with the task of picking up the corpses) joined the accusers of the generals. After debating the issue, the Assembly recalled all of the generals except Conon to stand trial. This summons was a serious setback for the war effort at a moment when Athens had again seized the upper hand. The accused generals brought many ships back to the Piraeus with them: they wanted the support of their crews when the crisis came.

Two of the eight slipped away into self-imposed exile rather than face the Assembly. Their flight seemed to confirm the guilt of the rest. As the affair wound its tortuous way through inquiry boards, Council sessions, and emotional Assembly meetings, the claims and counterclaims mounted. At length the people voted to imprison, pending a hearing, the six generals who had returned to the city: Thrasyllus, Pericles, Diomedon, Lysias, Aristocrates, and Erasinides. When they were led before the Assembly, the generals insisted that no one could have succeeded in collecting the dead once the storm began. Steersmen who had served at Arginusae testified to the violence of the wind. The mood began to swing in favor of acquittal, but the fading daylight brought a premature end to the debate. Before darkness fell, a final vote charged the Council of Five Hundred with the task of deciding upon the correct charge, if any, and the appropriate form of trial.

When the Assembly reconvened, the citizen of the tribe Antiochis who presided over that day's meeting was the philosopher Socrates. Presidents were chosen by lot and served for just one day; it was only a coincidence that such a prominent citizen's name had been drawn. After completing the ritual of sacrifices and prayers, Socrates opened the meeting by asking the secretary to read the Council's proposal. It called for the six generals to be tried not separately but together, and not in a jury court but by the Assembly itself that very day. Each of the ten tribes would set up two urns, one marked "guilty" and the other "not guilty." The citizens would then file past the urns and cast their ballots.

Athenians had at times imprisoned, tried, fined, or banished generals, but they had never yet put a general to death for decisions made during battle. Equally unprecedented was the proposal to try the six accused men as a group. To distract the Assembly from questions of military consequences or judicial procedure, a survivor of Arginusae came forward with a sensational story. When his trireme had been rammed, he saved himself by clinging to a wooden flour tub amid the flotsam. He told the Assembly that he had heard all around him the cries of drowning men. Unable to save themselves, they called on him to tell the Athenians at home how the generals had abandoned them. To the crowd on the Pnyx the tragedy was now palpable, the flour tub unforgettable.

This testimony touched off an uproar that overwhelmed any speaker who came forward to support the generals. Strident voices demanded that nothing must thwart the people's will, and that the president should put the

Council's proposal to an immediate vote. To Socrates the issue was personal as well as legal. One of the accused generals, young Pericles, was a close friend and disciple. Socrates had often talked over the city's affairs with him and had personally encouraged Pericles to seek the generalship. Now Socrates told the angry mob that Athenian law required individual trials for citizens accused of crimes. He then declared the Council's proposal to be illegal and refused to put it to the vote. The chief accusers launched another vociferous attack, but Socrates was used to opposition and stood his ground.

In this breathing space a kinsman of Pericles and Alcibiades came forward. He was the same Euryptolemus who had greeted Alcibiades on his return the previous year. He pointed out that at least one of the generals was entirely blameless, since he had been swimming to shore from his sinking flagship at the time of the fatal council. Of what could he be guilty, except bad luck? "Men of Athens," said Euryptolemus, "you have won a great and fortunate victory. Do not act as though you were smarting under the ignominy of defeat. Do not be so unreasonable as not to recognize that some things are in the hand of heaven. These men are helpless; do not condemn them for treachery. They were unable because of the storm to do what they had been ordered to do. Indeed it would be fairer to crown them with garlands than to punish them with death at the instigation of rogues."

Euryptolemus moved that each of the six generals be given a separate trial by jury. Socrates willingly consented to put his motion before the Assembly. A majority were raising their hands in favor when an objection was suddenly lodged, possibly by an enemy of the generals, possibly by a stickler for the rules of order. The original proposal of the Council for a trial of all six generals was still tabled. It must be decided before any other motion could be approved. Confident of a rational outcome, Socrates put it to the vote. But he had misjudged the crowd. With insane fickleness the majority unexpectedly voted for an immediate trial of all the generals. Hopeful still of a "not guilty" verdict, Socrates ordered the urns to be set up. Tribe by tribe the citizens filed past and cast their pebbles. A count showed that the generals had been condemned to death.

From the Pnyx the officials known as the Eleven conducted the condemned men back down to the prison. Athenians customarily carried out death sentences at once, though families and friends might visit the jail to take leave of loved ones. The method of death varied according to the nature of the crime and the status of the condemned. Pirates were crucified on wooden boards set up along the road to the Piraeus. Enemies of the state and polluted persons were thrown into a pit called the Barathron. Respectable citizens such as the generals, however, were allowed to drink hemlock.

The poisonous draft of hemlock was extracted from a branchy weed that grew wild throughout Attica. In fields and scrublands the hemlock plants raised their umbels of white flowers to a towering height. When gathered, brought to an apothecary, and pressed in a mortar, the hemlock's ferny leaves and small fruits yielded a bitter juice, clear and oily. A cupful was enough to kill a man. The jailer recommended walking about to help the poison spread quickly throughout the body. Drowsiness led slowly to paralysis of the limbs, followed by loss of speech. Consciousness remained clear to the end. Once the poison reached the lungs, the victim lost the ability to breathe and died as if drowning on dry land. One after another the heroes of Arginusae drank their vials of hemlock juice and departed this life.

The Athenians soon cooled off and repented. They blamed not themselves but the political leaders who had conspired to lead them astray. But no recriminations could bring the generals back to life, or repair the rupture of trust between the people and their elected military leaders. Democracy unchecked by reason proved as violent and unjust as any tyranny. In the cramped rooms of the prison, Thrasyllus had seen his ominous dream fulfilled, and the career of young Pericles was cut short almost before it had begun.

CHAPTER 16

Rowing to Hades

[405–399 B.C.]

The power of fate is a wonder; dark, terrible wonder.
Neither wealth nor armies, towered walls nor ships,
Black hulls lashed by the salt, can save us from that force.

—Sophocles

THREE MONTHS AFTER THE TRIAL OF THE GENERALS THE Athenians celebrated the Lenaea or festival of wine vats. Revels and comic plays honored Dionysus as the grape juice bubbled and fermented under the lids of the vats, making its magical transformation into wine. The city was mourning the passing of two dramatic geniuses. Death had claimed Euripides in Macedon, where he was visiting the royal court. Sophocles too had died, at the age of ninety—no living Athenian could remember a world without him.

At this time of loss Aristophanes produced a new comedy, *Frogs*. His themes were reconciliation, unity, and commitment to the navy. There was also a salute to the slaves who had earned their citizenship at Arginusae. Many of these new Athenians were taking their places in the theater for the first time, freed from bondage by their own heroism.

The action of *Frogs* started with the entrance of Dionysus, the god of the theater, setting out for Hades to bring Euripides back to life. Dionysus sought out the grim boatman Charon and rowed across the River Styx in his boat. A chorus of frogs helped the god keep time with an amphibian rowing chant: *"Brekekekex ko-ax, ko-ax! Brekekekex ko-ax, ko-ax!"* On the far side of the river Dionysus located Euripides and his much older predecessor Aeschylus, author of *Persians,* both residing in the poets' corner of Hades. Dionysus promptly announced a competition, appointed himself judge, and proclaimed that he would take the winner back with him to Athens. After many trials failed to decide the contest on the basis of poetry alone, Dionysus asked a final question: "How can Athens be saved?" Aeschylus won the day with blunt Themistoclean advice: commit everything to the war at sea and look after the navy. At the play's end Euripides remained in Hades, but Aeschylus ascended to the upper world. There he would share his patriotic wisdom with the current generation of Athenians.

Frogs won first prize. The public even demanded that the play be performed again—a rare honor. After the second performance the Athenians crowned Aristophanes not with Dionysus' ivy but with leaves from Athena's sacred olive, an award reserved for the city's greatest benefactors.

The Peloponnesian War was entering its twenty-seventh year. Had Aeschylus actually been able to return to Athens that spring, he could have found no fault with the people as far as the navy was concerned. The ship-building program that they had pursued ever since the Sicilian disaster had equipped Athens with almost two hundred triremes ready for active service. Thanks to the revolutionary enfranchisement of slaves and resident aliens, the whole fleet could be manned with the city's own population. Since the Persians continued to pay the cost of the Spartans' efforts at sea, it was crucial that the Athenian navy be self-sustaining.

Ships and crews were plentiful; leaders were scarce. The generals who had commanded the fleet during its recent victories were now either dead, passed over by the voters, or unwilling (understandably) to serve. Alcibiades was in exile at his fortress on the Sea of Marmara. Conon had been either navarch or general for many campaigning seasons, but he had done no more than stay out of trouble and win half a naval battle—unfortunately the first half. (It happened off Lesbos as he was being chased into Mytilene harbor by Callicratidas the previous summer.)

Seven years had passed since the disaster in the Great Harbor at Syracuse—a defeat that the Greeks had expected would finish Athens' rule of the sea. With a Spartan army besieging the city from a base in Attica and repeated naval actions in Ionia and Hellespont, ceaseless war was producing a world both inured to and traumatized by violence. Rumors of atrocities floated about the Aegean like a miasma. One of the new Athenian generals, a warmonger named Philocles, was reported to have captured two enemy triremes on the high seas and thrown their entire crews overboard, leaving them to drown. He was also notorious for proposing that the Athenians should cut off the right hands (or some said, right thumbs) of all prisoners of war, so that when ransomed or released they could never again pull an oar or wield a weapon against Athens. On the Spartan side, the popular commander Lysander was accused of wantonly butchering noncombatants in coastal towns.

Lysander was the most brilliant strategist and tactician that Sparta had ever produced. He was also a man of infinite *mêtis* or cunning. He had been the admiral at Ephesus who avoided direct confrontation with Alcibiades but then struck like lightning as soon as the foolish steersman Antiochus gave him an opening. Far more than any of Athens' own generals, Lysander was the true heir of Themistocles, Cimon, and Phormio. Like them, he knew that a winning general had no use for scruples. "Deceive boys with knucklebones," said Lysander, "and men with oaths." He was immensely popular with Greek allies and Persian princes alike. Lysander had been sent out this year on their insistence as an "adviser" with full authority to command at sea, since Spartan law prevented any man from holding the post of admiral more than once.

As summer began, Lysander's big Peloponnesian fleet seemed to be here, there, and everywhere in the Aegean. The Athenian navy, based once more on Samos, could neither pin him down to a battle nor prevent his strikes against their few remaining allies. Reports reached the frustrated Athenians that he had raided Rhodes, the coast of Asia Minor, even Attica itself. Sometime after midsummer Conon and his colleagues finally determined that Lysander was heading north to the Hellespont. The Athenians set off in pursuit with all their available forces, including six generals, 180 triremes, the state ship *Paralos,* and more than thirty-five thousand men. At all costs they must prevent Lysander from closing the grain route. Within a month the heavily laden freighters would begin their annual descent through the Bosporus and Hellespont. Clearly the Spartans meant to capture the flotilla or at least block its passage to the Piraeus, as they had previously done when Mindarus was admiral. The Athenian generals knew that a strong and undefeated navy would count for nothing if the city lacked bread.

By the time the Athenians reached the Hellespont, Lysander had already struck his first blow. After a short siege he captured Lampsacus, allowing the hoplites of the resident Athenian garrison to evacuate the city in return for their prompt surrender. Lampsacus guarded the upper entrance to the Hellespont, which at that point was some three miles wide. The loss of Lampsacus was a serious blow, but the Athenians could still hope to blockade Lysander there till the grain fleet had passed safely downstream, or even entice him out into the open for a proper naval battle. The Athenian triremes took on provisions at Sestos and then rowed upstream to Lampsacus. Lysander's ships lay safe within the curving bay that served the city as a harbor, while a large Spartan field army kept the Athenians from making a landing anywhere on the Asiatic shore. So the generals turned north to search for a base on the opposite shore.

In those days there was no city on the European side of the Hellespont's upper entrance. Many years later some Greeks would build Kallipolis ("Beautiful City") directly across from Lampsacus. Over the passage of centuries the city's name would be worn down to Gallipoli. As modern Gelibolu, the city boasts a fine enclosed harbor. But no such secure base was available to the Athenians as they confronted Lysander and his forces.

Lacking a port city, the Athenians required an open beach for their ships and a campsite for the crews. The swift current prevented sandy beaches from forming along the straight coastline within the Hellespont itself, but just outside the channel's mouth stretched a fine sandy beach more than a mile and a half long. Lapped by the waters of the Sea of Marmara, the beach faced east toward Byzantium. From this stretch of pale shelly sand the Athenians would be able to see the grain fleet as it approached, or intercept Lysander's naval force should it make a move toward the Bosporus. The distance from the beach to Lampsacus was about six miles, and a lofty cape at the beach's southern end screened the position from Lysander's lookouts. Inland, a wide plain afforded room for the vast horde of men, and a pair of little watercourses running down from the hilly hinterland supplied drinking water. The two streams gave the spot its name: Aegospotami ("Goat Rivers"). It was fortunate that the fleet had picked up provisions at Sestos, for there were none to be had at Aegospotami.

With confidence born of their recent victories at Cyzicus and the Arginusae Islands, the Athenians launched their ships at dawn the next day: outside Lampsacus harbor they arrayed the fleet in line of battle. But Lysander would not come out and fight. The Athenian lookouts could not even tell if he had manned his ships. After hours of desultory rowing against the stream to keep their station in front of Lampsacus, the Athenians gave up hope of a battle and rowed back to Aegospotami for their midday meal. The next day the challenge was repeated and again declined. A third day passed in this way and a fourth, with no sign that Lysander intended to leave Lampsacus while the huge Athenian fleet was in the vicinity. In the face of what appeared to be Spartan cowardice, the spirits of the Athenians rose even as their food supplies dwindled.

One frustrated Athenian observer was a helpless witness to these daily maneuvers. From the battlements of his fortress at Pactye, on the neck of the Gallipoli peninsula, Alcibiades had a view of the entire panorama from Aegospotami to Lampsacus. After spending little more than a year as warlord, he was now a force to be reckoned with in the region. It was a poor exchange for the Athenian generalship that he had forfeited, but Alcibiades believed that his local power could provide some much-needed leverage. With it he meant to insinuate his way into command of the fleet that had unexpectedly planted itself at his doorstep.

From his stronghold he rode on horseback along the shore to Aegospotami. Conon and the other generals gave him permission to speak. The Athenians were in a perilous position on their open beach and would never prevail over their enemies without a strong force to fight on land. Two neighboring kings had promised Alcibiades an army of Thracian warriors. Ferried across the Hellespont in Athenian triremes, they could attack Lampsacus by land. Alcibiades promised either to defeat the Peloponnesian army or to force Lysander to face the Athenian fleet at sea. He asked only one thing in return: a share of the command.

The generals were not interested. They knew Alcibiades too well. If his plan failed, the Assembly would blame the officially appointed generals. If it succeeded, he would get all the credit. Brusquely the generals ordered their uninvited guest to leave the camp and never come back. He offered one piece of advice before he departed: they should withdraw from Aegospotami to

Sestos with its proper harbor, walls, and granaries. The generals were neither grateful nor impressed. "We are in charge now," they told Alcibiades.
"Not you."

Alcibiades was silenced. The Athenians seemed bent on self-destruction.
Mounting his horse, he made his way through the camp, past the trierarchs'
field tents, the long row of ships' sterns, and the bivouacs of the crews. From
this familiar universe of Athenian men and ships Alcibiades was now forever barred. He could only return to his fortress and gaze from a distance
at the unfolding drama.

In true democratic fashion, the generals were rotating the command
among themselves on a daily basis. Having taken the initiative to offer battle at sea, they now seemed incapable of changing or adjusting their plan.
The challenge to Lysander had become a morning ritual. Discipline continued to slacken as the chances of battle seemed to grow more remote. Each
afternoon the careless crews relaxed or even slept on shore, or scattered farther and farther from the ships in search of food. In time the overconfident
generals even stopped posting lookouts on shore.

Unfortunately for the Athenians, Alcibiades was not their only observer.
Each day, unregarded by the rearmost ships in the fleet, two or three enemy
spy ships were trailing the Athenians from Lampsacus back toward Aegospotami. As the Athenians disembarked on shore for their midday meal,
scouts were watching them from the leading trireme, positioned well out
in the Sea of Marmara. Lysander was waiting for a signal from his little
chain of spy ships—a signal that the Athenians had dispersed too far inland
to get back to their ships in case he attacked.

The scouts carried polished bronze shields so that they could flash messages between ships and ultimately back to Lampsacus. When on the afternoon of the fifth day Lysander saw a gleam of reflected sunlight from the
nearest spy ship, he knew that the crews had deserted the triremes of the
Athenian fleet and that the camp was unguarded. Immediately Lysander
eased his entire fleet away from Lampsacus harbor and advanced to a low-
lying promontory called Abarnis, also on the Asiatic shore. There the Peloponnesian crews unloaded the big masts and cruising sails of the triremes
and deposited them on shore, to be collected if the day's battle went against

them and they needed to escape. Lysander knew that if he were defeated, there would be no returning to Lampsacus.

With the crews back on board and his triremes stripped for action, Lysander gave the command to the trumpeter. The brazen call rang out over the water, and the long line surged away from shore. With powerful strokes the rowers overcame the inertia of wooden hulls and crowded decks. Younger Spartans in the fleet had been waiting all their lives for this moment. Their hopes rested on reaching Aegospotami before the Athenians became aware of the attack and gathered their forces. Speed was all.

On Lysander's orders the steersmen headed first for an unguarded sandy cove south of the Athenian camp. Their initial landing would be screened from Aegospotami by a high cape. As the ships reached land, the Spartan troops instantly leaped ashore and sprinted to seize the headland. Once entrenched on the high ground, they could either attack the Athenian camp or (in case the Athenians repelled their assault) at least establish a Peloponnesian base on European soil. As soon as the soldiers were safely ashore, Lysander ordered the triremes back to sea.

As the fleet swung around the cape, Lysander's leading ships took by surprise an Athenian squadron cruising directly toward them. This small detachment was commanded by the fire-breathing general Philocles. The trierarchs and steersmen of his squadron immediately saw that they had blundered into the entire enemy fleet. In headlong flight they turned back toward Aegospotami. Beyond them stretched the long line of Athenian ships drawn up along the beach, deserted by their crews.

Hot on the sterns of the fleeing Athenians, Lysander's triremes bore down on their targets. They hit the southernmost end of the line first, then swept up the beach like a wildfire in the hope of trapping them all. Lysander had stationed men armed with grappling irons at the prows of his ships. As the steersmen brought the triremes ram-first into the shallows, these men cast their hooks onto the empty hulls in front of them. Once the irons held fast in Athenian timber, the Peloponnesian crews backed their oars hard and towed their prizes out to sea.

In the Athenian camp, chaos reigned. Amid the confusion some tried to pull their triremes back to shore, while others clambered on board to resist.

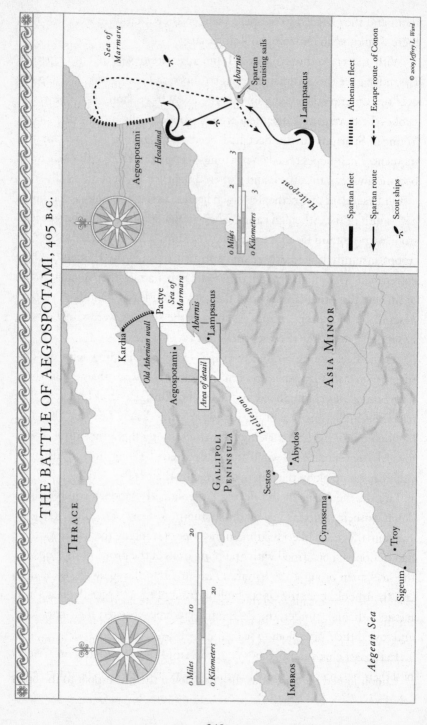

THE BATTLE OF AEGOSPOTAMI, 405 B.C.

THRACE

Sea of Marmara

Kardia

Old Athenian wall

Pactye

Aegospotami

Abarnis

Lampsacus

Area of detail

GALLIPOLI PENINSULA

Hellespont

Sestos

Abydos

ASIA MINOR

Cynossema

Troy

Sigeum

Aegean Sea

IMBROS

0 Miles   10   20
0 Kilometers   20

Sea of Marmara

Abarnis

Spartan cruising sails

Aegospotami Headland

Lampsacus

Hellespont

0 Miles   1   2   3
0 Kilometers   3

Athenian fleet

Escape route of Conon

Spartan fleet

Spartan route

Scout ships

© 2009 Jeffrey L. Ward

240

Here and there Peloponnesians were ramming the bows of Athenian ships even as their crews were climbing up the ladders at the stern. Frantic Athenian commanders launched ships with only one or two oar banks manned, only to have them quickly snapped up by the enemy. Some hulls floated off almost empty. Lysander and his marines landed and advanced on the camp through gaps in the Wooden Wall of ships. They joined the Spartan soldiers who had been set ashore near the cape, stamping out the small pockets of resistance and rounding up thousands of fleeing Athenians. The army moved so efficiently that only a few escaped into the countryside. Tens of thousands of Athenians were taken prisoner; three thousand would be executed the next day, starting with Philocles and the other generals. Thanks to Lysander's carefully worked out plan, the so-called battle of Aegospotami was in fact a rout almost from the first moment. A war that had lasted for a generation had ended in a single hour on a summer afternoon, with almost no casualties on the Spartan side.

Only one Athenian general and a handful of crews kept their heads. Conon had stayed near his ships that afternoon and was among the first to see the enemy fleet. He managed to man eight triremes and row out to sea before the Peloponnesians reached his section of the beach. There he was joined by the *Paralos*. Like Conon's crews, the Paraloi had managed to get on board and run out their oars in time to escape. It was impossible for Conon to aid the thousands of his fellow countrymen caught on the beach, where Lysander and his forces were rapidly completing the capture of the Athenian navy. He could only hope to save his own life and the lives of his men.

Putting as much distance as possible between themselves and the slaughter, the escaping Athenians came in sight of the promontory at Abarnis where Lysander had left his cruising gear. Here was a heaven-sent sliver of luck. The Athenians had had no time to fit out their ships for sailing before they made their escape, and they were in desperate need of masts and sails for the long voyage ahead. Landing on the flat shore, Conon's men quickly took what they needed from the equipment the Spartans had fortuitously left in their path.

Conon joined the *Paralos* as they fled down the Hellespont to the open sea. Lysander's dispatch vessel, a Milesian pirate ship bearing news of the tremendous victory to Sparta, would soon be on their heels. When word of the catastrophe at Goat Rivers spread, no port would be safe for an Athenian ship. From the mouth of the Hellespont, Conon led his little squadron away into southern waters, seeking refuge beyond the reach of Spartan power and Athenian retribution. He had no intention of ending his days with a draft of hemlock. The Paraloi, however, had a sacred duty to carry word back to the Assembly. Having parted from Conon near Troy, the *Paralos* made its solitary way homeward through the Aegean.

Young Xenophon, a disciple of Socrates, recollected years later how the report reached the city. "It was at night that the *Paralos* arrived at Athens. As the news of the disaster was told, one man passed it on to another, and a sound of wailing arose and extended first from the Piraeus, then along the Long Walls, until it reached the city. That night no one slept. They mourned for the lost, but more still for their own fate. They thought that they themselves would now be dealt with as they had dealt with others." The navy was gone, and hope seemed to have gone with it.

Next morning the people rallied. At an emergency meeting of the Assembly they voted to barricade the entrance to the two military harbors of Zea and Munychia—now empty and useless—and keep only the Cantharus Harbor open to receive shipments of food. Rather than surrender, they intended to withstand a siege. The city braced itself for the arrival of Lysander's triumphant fleet from the Hellespont.

Instead, more survivors of Aegospotami arrived, followed by ships loaded with Athenian soldiers from the garrisons at Byzantium and Chalcedon. The men explained that they had surrendered to the overwhelming forces of the Spartans, and, to their surprise, had been released on condition that they return home. More and more ships continued to pour in, filling Athens with soldiers, settlers, and traders who had been similarly expelled from former allied cities. It was Lysander's plan to fill Athens with as many hungry mouths as possible, then starve the multitude into submission. By his orders, anyone carrying food to Athens was to be executed.

Among Athens' allies, only the democratic islanders of Samos held out for a time against the Spartans. In a burst of gratitude, the Assembly voted to extend Athenian citizenship to the loyal Samians. Had they seen fit to offer citizenship to all the allies in their days of power, the fate of their maritime empire might have been very different. Lysander installed Spartan governors and garrisons in "liberated" Greek cities from the Bosporus to Ionia. The old Athenian Empire was thus transformed into a vast new Spartan domain. Then the victor of Aegospotami brought his fleet to the island of Aegina and settled down to the blockade of Athens.

The city held out over the winter, but hunger and hopelessness eventually drove the people to surrender. In the spring the Athenians opened the mouth of the great harbor, and Lysander's fleet rowed in to take possession. The long struggle was over. Athens had been at war with the Peloponnesians off and on for fifty-five years, and it was twenty-seven years almost to the day since the outbreak of the conflict that Thucydides (and posterity) would call the Peloponnesian War.

Among Sparta's allies, the Corinthians and Thebans were quick to demand that Athens be destroyed and its people enslaved. At a banquet held during the congress of victorious allies, however, a man from Phocis happened to sing a well-known chorus from Euripides' tragedy *Electra*. The great works of Athens' Golden Age were now the common property of all Greeks. The song moved the delegates to tears, and the vengeful plan to raze the city was given up. Athens had been made rich and powerful by its navy, but it was saved by its poets.

In the end, the Spartans spared the city and its people but destroyed anything and everything that had contributed to Athenian rule of the sea. The democracy was terminated. Athens would be ruled by an oligarchy of thirty rich citizens handpicked by Lysander. The Long Walls and the fortifications of the Piraeus must be torn down. The navy itself, the heart of Athenian power and glory, would be reduced to just twelve triremes—probably the sacred ships *Paralos* and *Salaminia,* and the ships dedicated to the ten Attic tribes. Athens would no longer have any overseas policies of its own but would follow Sparta's lead on land and sea alike.

On the day that the Long Walls began to come down, Lysander decided to make a holiday of the historic event. He had pipers brought out from the city—not the men who kept time for the rowers but girls who performed at parties. So it was to the music of drinking songs that the Spartans dismantled the towering ramparts. Once those symbols of democracy and maritime empire had toppled, the umbilical cord that had linked Athens to the sea for half a century was cut.

The new government of thirty oligarchs shared Lysander's ruthlessness. Soon to be known as the Thirty Tyrants, they moved swiftly to eliminate every trace of the navy. The shipsheds of the Piraeus, built at a cost of a thousand talents and among the architectural wonders of the Greek world, were sold off to salvagers for three talents and demolished. On the Pnyx, where the speaker's platform for Assembly meetings had always faced out to sea, the Thirty ordered that it should be reversed to look inland, away from the dangerous element that had fostered the Athenian maritime empire.

Within a short time the tyranny of the Thirty became so violent and lawless that a leader came forward to oppose it. Thrasybulus was a veteran of naval victories at Cynossema, Abydos, Cyzicus, and Arginusae. In the same spirit of defiance to tyrants, this former trierarch had stepped from the ranks on Samos, seven years before, to lead the navy's own counterrevolution against the oligarchs. Now he led a resistance movement that took as its headquarters the old democratic stronghold of the Piraeus. Even with the fortifications in disarray, thousands of Athenians rallied around Thrasybulus and defied the forces of the Thirty. The Spartans themselves bowed to the voice of the people after their oligarchic puppets had ruled for little more than a year. Democratic government was restored. Whether Athenian democracy could survive without ships or walls remained to be seen.

Two momentous deaths marked the demise of the old order: Socrates and Thucydides. Five years after the city's surrender Socrates was accused of heresy and of corrupting the minds of the young. At his trial Socrates denied the charges and reminded the 501 jurors of his war record under Phormio and Lamachus. "When the generals whom you chose to command me assigned me my positions at Potidaea and Amphipolis and Delium, I remained at my post like anyone else and faced death. Afterward, when god appointed me, as I believed, to the duty of leading a philosophic life, examining myself and others, how inconsistent I should have been to desert my post then, through fear of death or any other danger!" He also spoke of the role he played in the trial of the generals after Arginusae, when he had upheld the law rather than give in to the crowd.

The jury sentenced Socrates to death, but his execution was unexpectedly delayed because of a ship. One day before the trial began, the sacred galley *Delias* had embarked on its annual spring voyage to Delos for the festival of Apollo. Until the triakontor returned, the city could put no man to death. So Socrates lived on in prison, passing his time by creating poetical versions of Aesop's fables, comforting his family, enjoying long talks with the jailer, and holding philosophical conversations with a few faithful disciples. His life was preserved for many days by the strong winds that blew over the Aegean, holding back the sacred ship.

In his last days Socrates reminisced about his career as a philosopher. His early scientific interest in the workings of the cosmos had given way in midlife to an obsessive questioning about human nature and the pursuit of virtue. Borrowing a proverbial phrase from Athenian seafarers, he called his change of course a *deuteros plous* or second voyaging. When mariners cruising under sail met with a dead calm, they would run out the oars and venture on by rowing. In the same way Socrates had turned away from the natural world and studied mankind instead. When word came that the *Delias* had landed near Cape Sunium, his reprieve was over. Like so many others who had incurred the anger of the Athenians, Socrates drank the hemlock, walked about for a little while, and then lay down to die. He had written down nothing of his philosophy, asserting that the only thing he knew was that he knew nothing.

The historian Thucydides had returned to Athens after his twenty-year exile in Thrace. He settled down to finish writing his history of the Peloponnesian War but died (or, according to one account, was assassinated) before he could finish. In view of the war's outcome, Thucydides believed that in the final analysis the decisive factors had been ships, money, and sea power. The sea had been the true battleground, and all the major turning points in his history were naval actions. The Athenians had largely adhered to Pericles' policy of avoiding land battles; the Spartans had surprised everyone by patiently mastering the nautical skills that Pericles had claimed they would never learn.

Thucydides died believing that the war between Athens and Sparta had ended with the surrender of Athens, and that it had lasted twenty-seven years. He was wrong. The contest was not over, and Athens was not yet beaten. It was not enough to pull down its walls and destroy its beloved triremes. Thucydides had reckoned without the unsinkable spirit of the Athenian people. Athens itself was about to embark on a *deuteros plous*. Soon the battered ship of state would again be afloat, lifted from its resting place and swept one final time into the surge.

Part Five

REBIRTH

It is right to endure with resignation what the gods send, and to face one's enemies with courage. This was the old Athenian way. Do not let any act of yours prevent it from still being so. Remember, too, that the reason why Athens has the greatest name in all the world is because she has never surrendered to adversity, but has spent more life and labor in warfare than any other state. Thus the city has won the greatest power that has ever existed in history, a power that will be remembered forever by posterity, even if now (since all things are born to decay) there should come a time when we were forced to yield.

—Pericles to the Athenians

CHAPTER 17

Passing the Torch

[397–371 B.C.]

*Brave men are made bolder by ordeals, but cowards achieve nothing.
We have not come this long way by oar only to turn back now from
our goal.*

—Euripides

AFTER THE SURRENDER OF ATHENS AND ITS NAVY TO THE
Spartans, eight Athenian triremes under Conon's command still remained
at large. The runaways had found shelter on Cyprus, far beyond the reach
of the Spartans. There they landed at an ancient city called, auspiciously
enough, Salamis. Its Greek ruler, King Evagoras, was a vassal of King
Artaxerxes but nursed secret hopes of liberating all Cyprus from Persian
rule. Evagoras welcomed this windfall of an Athenian squadron. He encouraged Conon and his sixteen hundred men to stay as his guests. A remnant
of the Athenian navy would live on in Cyprus, homeless but still free. And
where there was life, there was hope.

Now in his forties, Conon could look back on a decade's experience as a
naval commander. His record was dubious. It was not only at Aegospotami
that he had dodged actions where other generals had lost their reputations
or even their lives. At the time of the Sicilian expedition, Conon had led a
squadron to guard duty at Naupactus instead of to death and destruction
at Syracuse. Two years later he missed the fleet's democratic revolution on
Samos, being otherwise engaged on Corcyra. After Alcibiades' steersman
lost the battle of Notium, it was Conon who took charge of the demoralized
fleet, but he had been well out of range during the debacle itself. And Conon
had watched the distant battle of Arginusae from the walls of Mytilene,
where he lay blockaded by the Spartan fleet. Glory eluded Conon, but no

one could deny that he had a knack for survival. Now a rapid current of events in the distant Aegean was about to sweep Conon back into the very eye of the maelstrom.

If there had been any harmony among Spartan leaders or any honor in Spartan treatment of the other Greeks, Athenian democracy and naval power might have sunk without a trace. "Freedom for the Greeks" had been the Spartans' rallying cry against Athens. Yet within months of winning the war, the Spartans betrayed the trust of the very allies who had made their victory possible. They handed the Greek cities of Asia back to the Great King of Persia in return for the gold that he had poured into their naval effort. In the islands Lysander's brutal military governors took control of the cities. Shattered pieces of the old Athenian maritime empire were quickly reforged into an even more oppressive Spartan maritime empire.

To pay the costs of their new navy, the Spartans demanded tribute at more than double the rate once assessed by Aristides the Just. Under Athenian rule the allies had complained when they had to go all the way to Athens for legal redress of official abuses. Under the new regime these same allies found that they had no legal redress anywhere. Spartan officials, even private Spartan citizens, operated outside the law, with nothing to curb their greed, their lust, and their congenital Spartan urge to give orders.

The Spartans' hubris touched off an ominous reaction. Foolishly they antagonized their old partners the Persians with attacks on the satrapies of Asia Minor. Chief among the injured parties was Pharnabazus, satrap of the lands along the Hellespont. This impetuous leader once rode his horse into the sea to help Spartans keep Athenian triremes off a beach. It was a dark day for Sparta when the embittered Pharnabazus sent a messenger up the Royal Road to Susa, urging that some action be launched against them. A war at sea, Pharnabazus suggested, might curb Spartan aggression on land.

In response to this appeal, King Artaxerxes II, great-grandson of Xerxes, named as his admiral the only experienced naval commander within the realm: Conon. The Great King also ordered Cyprus, Cilicia, and Phoenicia to contribute triremes for an expedition against the Spartans. Only seven years had passed since a Persian prince provided the pay for Lysander's crews at Aegospotami. Overnight Conon the Athenian was catapulted from his obscure exile into the forefront of a new campaign.

Within the Persian Empire the cities were slow to answer the king's call for ships. Once news of Conon's royal appointment reached Athens, however, the effect was electric. Hundreds of Athenians rallied to his distant banner. Triremes began to slip away from the Piraeus to join Conon on Cyprus. Even the Assembly dispatched a few ships, then blandly disowned them (on Thrasybulus' recommendation) when the Spartans protested. Renegade Athenians manned other triremes on their own initiative and at their own expense. Ship by ship an Athenian "navy in exile" began to congregate in the harbor of Cyprian Salamis.

Conon was still waiting for the full Persian levy of triremes. The delays and false starts stretched into years, until Conon at last took his grievances directly to the Great King at Babylon. The negotiations were strained. Go-betweens had to carry messages back and forth from Artaxerxes to Conon, who refused to kowtow in the groveling obeisance that would have admitted him into the royal presence. Nevertheless the king attended to every one of Conon's complaints. He confirmed Conon's position as supreme admiral, ordered all Persian officials to follow his lead, and provided more money to pay the crews. Artaxerxes also offered Conon the privilege of choosing a Persian colleague to command with him. Conon asked for Pharnabazus.

Midsummer was well past when Conon and Pharnabazus led their fleet of almost one hundred triremes west to the Aegean. They established a base near Cnidus, in the southwestern corner of Asia Minor. The city was famous for its temple of Aphrodite, a goddess whose birth from the foam of the sea had made her a patron of mariners. In happier days Cnidus had been an Athenian ally. Now it served as the base for the Spartan fleet. Conon's antagonist was the Spartan admiral Peisander, who owed his command not to experience but to nepotism. (King Agesilaus of Sparta was his brother-in-law.) Possessing eighty-five triremes, Peisander was slightly outnumbered. To draw Peisander into battle before reinforcements arrived, Conon decided to employ the same ruse that had helped Alcibiades bring on the battle at Cyzicus.

Conon began by leading a small vanguard of Athenian triremes across the bay in full view of the Spartans. As he intended, Peisander impulsively manned his ships and put out to sea. In the ensuing clash all seemed to go well for the Spartans at first. Then the allies on the left wing of Peisander's fleet saw Pharnabazus bearing down on them with the main body of Persian triremes, a move that threatened to envelop them. Abandoning their foolish admiral to his fate, they turned and began to row back toward Cnidus. Their flight exposed Peisander to a flanking attack. Athenian triremes surrounded the Spartan flagship and forced it toward shore, where the ship was rammed and Peisander killed. Conon ordered a chase of the fleeing Spartan allies, snapping up fifty triremes and five hundred prisoners. Most of the crews ignominiously abandoned their vessels, jumping overboard and swimming to shore.

The victory at Cnidus really belonged to the Great King, but the Athenians celebrated as if it were their own. As for Conon, he had redeemed a lifetime of near misses in one glorious action. When a solar eclipse darkened the sky a few days after his triumph, it seemed to signify the passing of Spartan thalassocracy. The maritime empire created by Lysander had lasted only eleven years.

Conon and Pharnabazus immediately set out on a cruise through the eastern Aegean, liberating the Greeks from their despised Spartan governors. Cities and islands as far north as Lesbos joined the revolution. At Samos and Ephesus, citizens erected bronze statues of Conon and his son Timotheus, honoring these saviors as if they were divine heroes. On Conon's advice, Pharnabazus assured the Greeks that if they left the Spartan alliance of their own free will, he would respect their traditional forms of government and install no Persian garrisons. Such honorable treatment prompted even more defections from Sparta.

The Persian-Athenian fleet now enjoyed the freedom of the seas. Conon and Pharnabazus used that freedom to take their ships to the Isthmus of Corinth. There in the sanctuary of Poseidon the two victorious admirals found the estranged allies of Sparta sitting in council. Less than a century earlier the Spartans had summoned their allies to the Isthmus to plan the resistance to Xerxes. Now the world was turned upside down. The satrap Pharnabazus urged the Corinthians and Thebans to push forward with their war against the Spartans, and he provided Persian cash to back up his words. He then prepared for the voyage back to Asia, confident that he had caused Sparta enough trouble.

Conon had other ideas. He asked that he might keep the Great King's fleet in Greek waters to continue hostilities. No money would be required: loot and contributions from the islands would cover the costs. Conon also suggested that the fleet relocate to Athens. If refortified, the Piraeus would provide a secure naval base. Pharnabazus approved and gave Conon both the fleet and the princely sum of fifty talents to pay for work on Athens' fortifications. The satrap felt no friendship for Athens—he meant simply to punish Sparta. As Conon had said, "I can think of no action that would hurt the Spartans more. By doing this you will not only have given the Athenians something for which they will be grateful, but will really have made the Spartans suffer. You will make null and void that achievement of theirs which cost them more toil and trouble than anything else." As Pharnabazus' flagship rowed away from the Isthmus into the blue of the Aegean, Conon launched the rest of the fleet, now his and his alone, and steered for home.

Even before Conon's return, the Athenians had tried to rebuild the Long Walls. But the work might never have been completed had Conon not arrived with Persian money to pay for stone and timber, and for skilled masons and carpenters to complete the work. Conon's crews—thousands of Athenian citizens who had not seen their city for over a decade—came ashore to help raise those mighty ramparts. With his own money Conon built a temple for Aphrodite in the Piraeus. As goddess of Cnidus, she was dear to his heart, and it was as Aphrodite Euploia ("Aphrodite of the Fair Voyage") that he and his fellow Athenians now worshipped her.

One hundred years had passed since the archonship of Themistocles, and work on the new Piraeus foundations laid bare the foundations of his original walls. Themistocles' descendants had long ago brought the great man's ashes back from Asia, where he had died in exile. To celebrate the restoration of the Piraeus, the Assembly honored the hero of Salamis with a tomb, an altar, and a pillar on a point of land just outside the Cantharus Harbor. An Athenian poet wrote commemorative verses.

> *Fair is the point where your tomb is raised,*
> *A welcome sight to greet all traders.*
> *It gazes on them, outward or homeward bound,*
> *And views the long ships racing past.*

With the raising of this monument to the founder of the navy and the hero of Salamis, the Athenians formally rededicated themselves to the quest for victory at sea.

Not all Athenians were happy about the resurrection of Athenian naval power. The philosopher Plato told his students that the walls "should continue to slumber in the bosom of the earth." And in Aristophanes' new comedy *Ecclesiazusae* ("The Assembly Women") a chorus of Athenian matrons noted the difficulty of dealing with a public opinion divided against itself. They observed that the mass of citizens voted for new ships, but the farmers and the rich opposed them. In the real-life Assembly, Conon warned the Athenians to be satisfied with getting back their freedom and their walls. The imperialistic plans advocated by Thrasybulus, as Conon reminded them, came from a man whose very name meant "Rash Adviser."

Sent out to the Hellespont with a fleet, Thrasybulus had once again defeated Spartans and won Byzantium and other cities back to friendship with Athens. The time of the older generation, however, was drawing to a close. Aristophanes had written his last play. Conon and Thrasybulus, architects of Athenian reconstruction, died within four years of each other, Conon in the course of a diplomatic mission to the Persians, Thrasybulus while campaigning on the Eurymedon River. Their ashes were brought back to Athens and buried in the public cemetery along the Sacred Way.

Now the mission to restore Athenian sea power was taken up by a younger generation of Athenian generals. So successfully did they assert Athens' claims to the Hellespont, the Aegean, and points east that the Spartans appealed for help to their former paymaster, the Great King of Persia. Vexed by endless wars on his western frontier, Artaxerxes handed down a peace and commanded the Greeks to swear obedience to its terms:

"I, King Artaxerxes, regard the following arrangements as just. The cities in Asia and, among the islands, Clazomenae and Cyprus should belong to me. The other Greek cities, big and small, should be left to govern themselves, except for Lemnos, Imbros, and Scyros, which should belong to Athens, as in the past. And if either of the two parties refuses to accept peace on these terms, I, together with those who accept this peace, will make war on that party both by land and by sea, with ships and with money."

No sooner had the Spartans secured the oaths of the Athenians and other

Greeks than they began to violate the King's Peace themselves, attacking small cities and installing pro-Spartan regimes or even Spartan garrisons. Finally a Spartan commander led an army of ten thousand in a night raid against the Piraeus. Even though unsuccessful (dawn had found the slow-moving Spartans still on the march, miles away from the port), this outrage led the Athenians to declare that the Spartans themselves had now violated the King's Peace. At once they hung the massive gates back on the portals of the Piraeus, which had been open since they swore their oaths at Sardis, and prepared for war.

Athens was not alone. Twenty-six years had passed since Spartans stripped Athens of its allies and claimed them as their own. Now fear and loathing of Sparta had driven a number of cities to seek alliances with Athens. One year after the abortive attack against the Piraeus, these and many other Greek states united with Athens in a formal confederation. This was in fact nothing less than a Second Maritime League, which resurrected the Delian League of a century before. (Like the so-called Delian League, the Second Maritime League was known in its own day simply as "the Athenians and their allies.") This time, however, there would be no assessment and no tribute. In every way possible the Athenians purged the new league of all the evils and abuses that had bedeviled its predecessor.

The Delian League had united its members in a perpetual fight against the menace of Persia. The new alliance just as explicitly named Sparta as the common enemy. The charter stated that it was formed "so that the Spartans shall leave the Greeks free and autonomous, to enjoy peace, holding their own lands in safety." So appealing was the charter of this Second Maritime League that some seventy cities and peoples eventually became members. The upsurge of goodwill toward Athens seemed a redemption, a wiping away of past guilt. Athens had stumbled only to rise again.

While the Second Maritime League offered its members protection from the Spartans, the charter also safeguarded them from their own hegemon, Athens. Any Athenian who owned or claimed land in the territory of an allied city now had to give it up. The much-resented practice of sending out Athenian colonists or cleruchs was explicitly forbidden on lands belonging to league members. To finance the enterprises of the league, Athens would collect not tribute but a tax, one-fortieth of the value of cargoes that passed through the Piraeus. Every clause of the charter breathed a new air of liberalism. The Athenians seemed determined to avoid the path of oppression and empire that had ruined them before. They were in truth a changed and chastened people and had learned as much from the misfortunes they inflicted on others as from their own.

The league charter called for a fleet of 200 triremes. At present the Athenians had 106—a motley collection that included some ships brought to Athens by Conon, others captured in naval engagements with the Spartans and their allies, and still others recently built in the Piraeus. So the Athenians tackled the challenge of rebuilding their navy. They meant not just to match the old navy of Periclean Athens but to surpass it, drawing more Athenian citizens than ever before into the navy's funding, organization, and operation. The Assembly counted on the new navy to protect the allies, secure the grain route, and raise money but also to provide employment for the mass of the Athenian population. Sea power and democracy would again work hand in hand.

The waterfront of Zea Harbor was limited, the dreams of the Assembly vast. Shipbuilding was now the responsibility of the Council, who would annually appoint ten *trieropoioi* or trireme builders. This board was assisted by a treasurer of naval funds and five naval architects who supervised the design and refitting of triremes by the city's shipwrights. The tasks were so arduous that the members of the Council routinely received gold crowns for successful completion of a year's work.

The shipbuilding campaign called for timber. By now the Athenians had stripped Attica of its forests. The philosopher Plato, looking up at the bare hillsides around the city, noted that the trees that had provided mighty roofbeams in the days of his forefathers were long gone. The forests had been replaced by heather, the loggers by beekeepers. And as Plato foresaw, the process was irreversible. Without trees, rain eroded the soil from the hills and carried it away to the sea. The barren rocky hills that remained (and that still remain) were "like the skeleton of a body wasted by disease." Athenian deforestation had prompted the first awareness that the resources of the earth were not inexhaustible.

The big new navy would have to be constructed entirely from imported timber. To accommodate more triremes, the shipsheds at Zea were rebuilt

SHIPSHEDS AT ZEA HARBOR, Fourth Century B.C.

with slipways double the length of the original ones. Two triremes could now be fitted end to end between each row of columns. The roofs of the new shipsheds were made with whitened tiles, so that they gleamed in the sunlight like marble.

The might of the resurrected navy was soon to be tested. Conon's victory at Cnidus had been only a beginning: the war against the Spartans at sea had still to be won. The adversities of the last quarter century had bred an extraordinary new generation of naval commanders, led by Chabrias, Phocion, Timotheus the son of Conon, and Iphicrates. Relay races were popular events in Athens: instead of a baton, a lighted torch was passed from hand to hand through the team of runners. Never before had the navy enjoyed the services of such a team as was about to take up the torch in the cause of Athens' new maritime league. Their efforts would determine, once and for all, the outcome of the long struggle between Greece's two warring alliances.

Chabrias, the son of an affluent Athenian trierarch and horse breeder, took an interest in the technical side of naval operations. He invented new foul-weather fittings that improved his triremes' performance on rough seas, including extra steering oars and an extension of thick screens that completely enclosed the rowing frames. To train inexperienced oarsmen, Chabrias built wooden rowing frames on shore where beginners could learn technique and timing before they went on board ship. On one occasion he lashed his triremes together in pairs to create double-hulled catamarans, a ploy that fooled Spartan scouts into believing the Athenian fleet to be only half its actual size.

One year after founding the Second Maritime League, the Athenians sent Chabrias to protect the incoming flotilla of grain ships from a Spartan fleet that was hovering, piratelike, in the vicinity of Cape Sunium. At the approach of Chabrias and his squadron the Spartans melted away, and the grain arrived safely at the Piraeus. To lure the Spartans to a decisive battle, Chabrias cruised south to the green and hilly island of Naxos, rich in vineyards, almond trees, and fine white marble. The oligarchs of Naxos were still loyal Spartan allies, and Chabrias rightly guessed that an attack on their walls would bring the enemy fleet to him at once. Shortly after he unloaded his siege machinery, the Spartan fleet appeared over the horizon.

Over and above his orders, Chabrias had a personal score to settle with the Spartan admiral, Pollis. The Athenian philosopher Plato happened to be a close friend of Chabrias. A dozen years earlier, when Plato voyaged to Sicily for a view of Mount Etna, Pollis took him captive and sent him to be sold at the slave market on Aegina. Plato's friends were able to buy his freedom, but the degrading insult had yet to be avenged.

The battle at Naxos would be the first actual sea fight between Athenian and Spartan fleets since the battle of the Arginusae Islands, thirty years before. Unlike Chabrias' force, the Spartan fleet was an amalgam of various contingents, each bearing its own heraldic emblems. Before launching his ships, Chabrias ordered his trierarchs to remove the golden images of Athena that identified all Athenian warships in order to disguise, if only briefly,

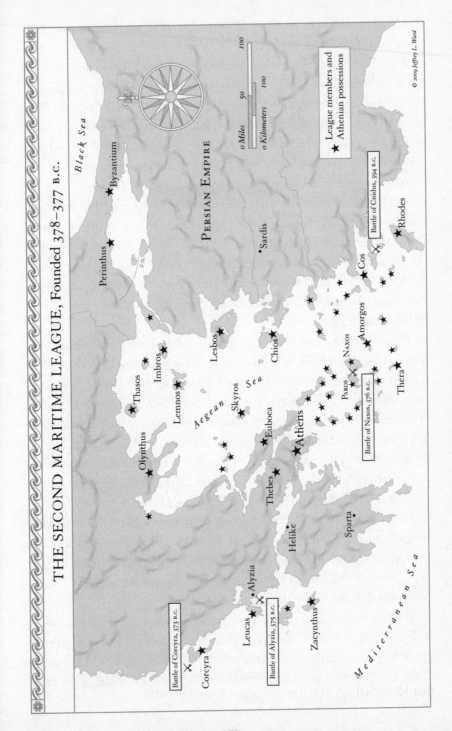

THE SECOND MARITIME LEAGUE, Founded 378–377 B.C.

Black Sea

PERSIAN EMPIRE

Byzantium

Perinthus

Sardis

★ League members and Athenian possessions

0 Miles 50 100
0 Kilometers 100

Battle of Cnidus, 394 B.C.

Rhodes

Cos

Amorgos

Thasos

Imbros

Lennos

Olynthus

Lesbos

Chios

Naxos

Skyros

Paros

Thera

Aegean Sea

Battle of Naxos, 376 B.C.

Euboea

Athens

Thebes

Helike

Sparta

Battle of Corcyra, 373 B.C.

Corcyra

Leucas

Alyzia

Battle of Alyzia, 375 B.C.

Zacynthus

Mediterranean Sea

© 2009 Jeffrey L. Ward

259

their identity. His crews were still untried, and he intended to give them every possible edge.

The antagonists met at dawn in the wide channel between Naxos and the neighboring island of Paros. The Spartan admiral Pollis scythed through the Athenian left wing, killing the commander Cedon in the process. Chabrias had his hands full with the ships attacking his center and right, so he ordered a young trierarch named Phocion to take a contingent and save whatever might remain of the now-leaderless Athenian left.

As the two original lines disintegrated into a mass of dueling ships, the enemy lookouts and steersmen began to hesitate in ordering their ramming strikes. Without the familiar golden figureheads of Athena to guide them, they could not quickly distinguish Athenian ships from their own allies. The removal of the ensigns bought precious moments for the Athenians as the Spartans held off. Though the Spartans rammed and destroyed eighteen Athenian triremes, the Athenian tally was twenty-four, more than a third of the Spartan fleet.

Young Phocion's dash to the left wing turned the battle. With defeat looming, Pollis signaled his ships to break off the engagement and save themselves. Chabrias could easily have taken prizes during the rout. Instead he ordered a rescue mission on the watery battlefield, now littered with wrecks, to save Athenian survivors who were clinging to timbers or swimming for shore. Even after three decades, the Arginusae Islands cast a long shadow.

So Pollis and the Spartan navy survived, though with diminished force and prestige. Athens had no funds to follow up the victory at Naxos. In this hour of need Chabrias turned again to Phocion. He put the twenty-six-year-old hero in command of twenty triremes and assigned him the formidable task of collecting contributions from Athenian allies in the Aegean. Phocion, clear-sighted and blunt-spoken, told his general that twenty was the wrong number: too many for a friendly visit, too few for a fight. Chabrias gave in and let him go in a single trireme.

Phocion made such a good impression on his cruise that the league members not only provided money but assembled a fleet to carry it to Athens. Thus began a remarkable career. The grateful Athenians would in years to come elect Phocion general a record-breaking forty-five times, more often even than they had elected Pericles.

Chabrias won his great victory on the sixteenth of Boedromion, the second day of the Eleusinian Mysteries. As the navy fought at Naxos, the Athenians at home were answering the herald's cry of "Seaward, Initiates!" and wading into the sea to purify themselves. For the rest of his life Chabrias provided a celebratory bumper of wine to every Athenian household on that date. With the recurring commemorations of Naxos and Salamis, the latter falling on the nineteenth of Boedromion, the victory celebrations for the Athenian navy became intertwined with the city's annual rites of mystical rebirth.

The Aegean was secure, but Sparta still ruled the western seas. The following spring the Assembly sent sixty triremes around the Peloponnese. The torch of command now passed to Timotheus. His expedition was intended to forestall Spartan attacks on league members and win over new allies. Timotheus had spent his youth in Cyprus, sharing the exile of his father, Conon. Growing up far from Athens, he tended throughout his life to be more at ease with foreigners than with Athenians. His fellow citizens saw in Timotheus a small and unprepossessing fellow who could not exhibit the strong physique expected of a war hero. But his lack of brawn was offset by an excess of intelligence, energy, and honor.

Timotheus' unmatched record of bringing twenty-four cities over to the Athenian alliance with apparently little trouble made him the good-humored target of the world's first known political cartoon. The anonymous artist depicted Timotheus as a fisherman dozing beside his lobster pot, as city after city crawled up to the trap and fell in. Above the scene floated the goddess Tyche ("Fortune"). She was directing the procession of lobsters while Timotheus enjoyed his nap.

The western campaign was Timotheus' first independent naval command. He quickly succeeded in bringing Zacynthus, Cephallenia, Corcyra, and even some mainland cities back to the Athenian alliance. This string of diplomatic victories posed a starker threat to Sparta than any number of successful raids. When Timotheus learned that the Spartan fleet had landed on the island of Leucas, he bivouacked on the mainland opposite at an isolated place called Alyzia. This curving beach near a sanctuary of Heracles occupied a place in his family lore. Thirty-eight years earlier, at the time of the Sicilian expedition, Timotheus' father, Conon, had been cruising the western seaways to protect Athenian allies from attack by the Peloponnesians.

At Alyzia Conon bade farewell to Demosthenes and Eurymedon as those two ill-fated generals voyaged west to their meeting with destiny at Syracuse.

A high ridge hid Timotheus' camp at Alyzia from Spartan scouts, but from its crest the Athenians had a clear view of the Spartans. With fifty-five triremes the enemy fleet was already almost a match for the Athenians, and Timotheus knew that reinforcements were on their way to the Spartans: ten triremes convoying a fleet of Italian grain freighters, and half a dozen more from the Ambracians in the Gulf of Arta. These western Greeks had been bitter enemies of the Athenians since the early campaigns of Phormio. Timotheus decided to attack while he still held the advantage in numbers.

The battle coincided with the Athenian religious holiday known as the Skira, held on the twelfth of the early-summer month of Skirophorion. Garlands for the Skira were traditionally woven of myrtle branches. Mindful of his crews' morale, Timotheus let them cut myrtle from the surrounding countryside and decorate the triremes with green wreaths. In this way the ships were consecrated to the gods being honored that day in far-off Athens: Athena, Poseidon, and the sun god Helios.

As the crew boarded Timotheus' flagship, a man happened to sneeze while coming up the ladder. At the omen, the steersman called a halt to the boarding process. But Timotheus was no Nicias, to let a portent interfere with his plan of campaign. Myrtle wreaths were one thing; calling off a battle because of a sneeze was quite another. "Do you think it a miracle," he demanded of his superstitious steersman, "that out of so many thousands one man has caught a cold?" The men laughed at the rebuke, and the process of boarding resumed.

Timotheus first launched only twenty of his triremes, leaving the others behind on shore. As soon as this ridiculously small Athenian squadron rowed into view around the southern tip of the promontory, the entire Spartan fleet eagerly advanced to meet it. The Athenian vanguard had plenty of sea room, but Timotheus did not intend to use it at present for the classic maneuvers of *diekplous* or *periplous*. Instead, he instructed his trierarchs and steersmen to break formation and execute any maneuvers they pleased, provided that they kept the Spartans on the attack and stayed out of range of enemy rams and missiles. So the scattered Athenian ships led the Spartans in a lively chase, turning, twisting, or feigning flight, transforming the sea west of Alyzia into a watery dancing floor.

The sun rose high; the enemy's oar beats grew sluggish and weak. Seeing that he had worn them out, Timotheus told his trumpeter to sound the retreat. The Athenians raced back toward Alyzia, and the Spartan fleet trailed behind: hot, weary, and thoroughly annoyed. At that moment Timotheus' forty reserve triremes emerged into view from around the promontory, fresh and ready for anything.

The result was a foregone conclusion. The Athenians took full advantage of their superior energy and their general's tactics, and the ramming attack continued until the appearance of the long-awaited Spartan reinforcements. Faced with this fresh threat, Timotheus ordered some of his trierarchs to lasso the hulls of disabled ships and take them in tow. He then arrayed all the others in a vast crescent around them. The convex curve of this half-moon shielded the prizes, and its backward-reaching horns prevented attacks from the flanks. As soon as the tow ships were under way, the rest retreated with their rams continually pointed toward the frustrated Spartans, backing water all the way to their haven at Alyzia. Though the Spartans now held the advantage in numbers, Timotheus' novel mode of retreat prevented them from renewing the battle or claiming any prizes.

It would be left to another Athenian general, Iphicrates, to aim the final blow at Spartan naval power. Unlike his colleagues, Iphicrates grew up in poverty, the son of a shoemaker. At the age of only twenty his remarkable qualities as a soldier earned him a command under Conon at Cnidus. Like Chabrias, Iphicrates introduced innovations into Athenian warfare. He championed the use of lightly armored, mobile troops known as peltasts (so called for the small rimless leather shields or *peltai* that they carried) rather than the hoplites who had served Athens with such mixed results during the century since the battle of Marathon.

He was also a pioneer in coordinating fleets and armies in joint attacks and stratagems. During his first expedition to the Hellespont he devised a "Trojan Horse" ploy. First, Iphicrates' triremes departed ostentatiously from their station, luring overconfident Spartan hoplites into an unguarded position; then Iphicrates' peltasts, who had been lying concealed on high ground, ambushed the enemy with deadly effect.

On another occasion Iphicrates borrowed not from Homer's epic but from Aesop's fable of the wolf in sheep's clothing. Faced with the problem of telling friends from foes among the islanders of Chios, Iphicrates secretly put some of his Athenian troops on shore. He then sent his triremes into the harbor decorated with Spartan insignia, and with the trierarchs disguised as Spartan officers. The sight of these supposed allies brought all the local Spartan sympathizers running down to the docks. Now that they had obligingly revealed their true loyalties and assembled without arms, Iphicrates had them rounded up and arrested.

Athens scarcely provided a wide enough stage for this brilliant and daring tactician. At times Iphicrates could be found, not on the deck of an Athenian flagship, but serving as a soldier of fortune in Asia or the northern Aegean. His personal services to the royal house of Macedon led to Iphicrates' being formally adopted as a son by the Macedonian king. Farther east in Thrace, Iphicrates' victories carried him to such dizzying heights that he was able to marry the sister of a Thracian king, thus following in the footsteps of the legendary Miltiades.

Iphicrates named his son Menestheus after an ancient king of Athens, celebrated in Homer's *Iliad* as the monarch who led fifty Athenian ships to Troy. The original Menestheus was singled out in Homer's epic verses as the Greek leader most skilled at ordering and marshaling troops in battle— a skill that Iphicrates valued highly. A born leader himself, Iphicrates held the commander to be the most important element in warfare. "When other parts are lost," he reminded his listeners, "the army may be lame and disabled. But when the general is lost, the entire army is useless." Every poor citizen could see in Iphicrates the fulfillment of the Athenian democratic dream, a cobbler's son who rose through his own efforts to fame and fortune. Iphicrates never let the world forget his humble origins. "Consider what I was," he would say, "and what I now am."

Now one of the city's most honored generals, Iphicrates decided that the fleet allocated to his upcoming western cruise was inadequate. He demanded more ships, as if he ruled the Assembly rather than the other way around. Meekly the Assembly complied. Timotheus in the same position had been too proud or too principled to beg for sufficient forces. Iphicrates ultimately assembled a fleet of seventy that included the state triremes *Paralos* and

Salaminia and even guard ships from the coastal patrols. He also cracked down on his trierarchs, making them take responsibility for recruiting their own crews.

His destination was Corcyra, where a Spartan fleet and army were besieging the democratic islanders. Iphicrates was determined to reach Corcyra in record time, and he meant to bring his crews to a perfect pitch of discipline and fitness while doing so. He left all the mainsails behind in the Piraeus, as if he intended to meet the enemy in battle on the first day of the expedition and every day thereafter. Without cruising sails, the twelve thousand oarsmen in the fleet were compelled to row throughout the voyage, with only occasional help from the small boat sails when the winds were favorable.

As they rowed, Iphicrates drilled the helmsmen and crews in recognizing signals and in executing battle maneuvers, turning from line ahead formation to line abreast, without ever ceasing the relentless forward motion. He also made the daily landings for meals into occasions for rowing races, starting far out at sea and ending on the beach, where the winners were first in line for food and drink. While the fleet was on shore, the small masts were stepped so sentries could climb to their tops and watch for approaching enemies. On some fine afternoons Iphicrates put to sea again after dinner. The crews then rowed in shifts, each taking turns to sleep through the hours of evening.

Word of this extraordinary cruise reached the Athenian exile Xenophon, now living on a farm near Olympia and collecting material for a history that would continue the unfinished work of Thucydides. Xenophon gave high praise to Iphicrates for this tactical use of a cruise into the battle zone. "I know, of course, that when people are expecting to fight a naval action, all these tactical exercises and all this training are quite usual. But what I admire in the conduct of Iphicrates is this: when he had to arrive quickly in an area where he expected to engage the enemy, he found a way by which his men would be none the worse trained tactically because of having to make the voyage, and the voyage would be none the slower because of the training given to the men."

Inevitably the rumor of Iphicrates' approach reached Corcyra. The Spartans on the island were so alarmed that they broke off the siege and slipped away to a safe harbor nearer home. With them went their sixty triremes. Thanks to Iphicrates' show of strength and readiness, the Athenians won their victory without fighting a battle. A politician named Peitholaus had once called the state trireme *Paralos* "the People's Big Stick." Thanks to Iphicrates, the epithet could be applied with justice to the entire Athenian fleet.

Only one mopping-up operation remained. Ten Syracusan triremes were on their way to Corcyra from Sicily. Iphicrates learned that the latecomers expected to finish their long crossing at night. The Syracusans would light a beacon on an offshore islet as they approached their destination. If they saw an answering signal fire on the northern cape of Corcyra, the Syracusans would know that the Spartans still controlled the island and would press forward the next morning to reinforce their old allies.

Iphicrates led twenty triremes to the northern tip of the island and waited through the night. Out at sea in the black night a beacon flared. Lighting a blaze in answer, Iphicrates steered his squadron across the dark water toward the beacon of the ignorant enemy. At first light he reached the islet—and swooped down on the unsuspecting Sicilians, capturing ships and crews together. In his mortification, the Syracusan commander committed suicide. Although neither Iphicrates nor anyone else could know it at the time, this remote and minor exploit was to be the last naval action in the long, long war. But one last disaster still awaited the Spartan fleet.

A year after Iphicrates made his cruise to Corcyra, ten Spartan triremes lay at Helike, a city on the southern coast of the Corinthian Gulf. Their commander was the same Pollis whom Chabrias and Phocion had defeated at Naxos three years before. While the Spartan ships were in the harbor at Helike, a strange phenomenon was observed. For days, an exodus of snakes, mice, and other small animals—even beetles—streamed out of the city, making for higher ground.

On the fifth night a violent earthquake shook the gulf. Some hours later, as the survivors were trying to save themselves and their families, the sea rose in an immense wave and swept over the site, destroying everything. By morning Helike had disappeared, along with Pollis and the ten Spartan ships. Only a shallow lagoon remained. Local ferrymen claimed that for years afterward they had to steer clear of a submerged bronze statue of Poseidon. The Earthshaker still stood erect in his ancient sanctuary, menacing watercraft with his trident at the place where he had blotted out the last vestige of the Spartan navy.

The string of naval defeats and the great wave that swallowed up the triremes at Helike left the Spartans bewildered and demoralized. The following summer Athenian envoys arrived in Sparta with a proposal of peace. A popular leader named Callistratus accompanied the embassy. Callistratus had been so worn out during his recent trierarchy on board the *Lampra* ("Radiant") that he had made an unprecedented deal with the general in command of the fleet. If Iphicrates would only let him go home, Callistratus swore either to raise new funds for the navy or to negotiate a peace. He kept his word.

From Callistratus, the Spartans heard the kind of straight talk that they could respect. "All the cities of Greece are divided among those who are on our side and those who are on yours, and in each individual city there is a pro-Spartan party and a pro-Athenian party. Now if you and we became friends, would there be any quarter from which either of us could reasonably expect trouble? Certainly, if you were with us, no one would be powerful enough to do us any harm on land; and with us on your side, no one could hurt you by sea."

The Spartans agreed to the terms, which were in reality nothing more than a reaffirmation of the King's Peace of fifteen years before, minus the threats of Artaxerxes. The events of the following days, however, linked this peace to one of the great turning points of Greek history. Spartan supremacy on land was about to be shattered. In his speech Callistratus had failed to mention the one power that could now challenge the Spartan hoplite phalanx: Thebes. The peace accord with Athens could not help Sparta against this new rival. When the two great armies met near the town of Leuctra, the Theban general Epaminondas launched an attack that resembled, in Xenophon's words, "the ram of a trireme."

By the end of the battle, the myth of Spartan invincibility was exploded. Already stripped of its thalassocracy, Sparta lost at Leuctra its ancient claim to be the supreme moral and military leader of Greece. To ensure that Sparta would never revive, the Thebans liberated the Spartan fiefdom of Messenia, the rich land of the southwestern Peloponnese, and called its people home. For the first time in centuries Messenia was again an independent state; the exile of the Messenians at Naupactus was finally over.

The Peloponnesian War had lasted twenty-seven years and settled nothing. The Spartan War, fought by generals from Conon to Iphicrates, had also lasted for a full generation, and it changed Greece forever. Taking the long view, Athenians could now see that they had ultimately triumphed over the Spartans in a contest that began with the battle of Tanagra in the days of the Delian League and lasted more than eighty-five years. The struggle had weakened both cities, but in the end Athenian democracy, leadership, and naval tradition had prevailed.

The return of Athenian sea power breathed new life into the city's Golden Age. Chabrias and Phocion regularly attended Plato's lectures at the Academy; Timotheus could be found on the other side of the city studying rhetoric with Isocrates at the Lyceum. Phocion's brother-in-law, a sculptor named Cephisodotus, created a monument in the Agora to honor the goddess Eirene ("Peace"), whom he depicted as a happy mother holding a baby named Plutus ("Wealth"). A sculptor named Praxiteles was the brightest light in Athens' artistic renaissance. Praxiteles raised Athenian sculpture to new heights with his nude Aphrodite. From her temple at Cnidus in Asia Minor, Praxiteles' famous marble goddess looked out over the bay where Conon had struck the first blow against Spartan hegemony at sea.

The rebirth of Athens reached a high point eight years after the peace with Sparta, on a night enlivened by torchlit processions and the music of pipes and lyres. Timotheus' daughter was marrying Menestheus, the son of Iphicrates. An ornate wedding wagon carried the young couple from the door of the bride's house, which Timotheus had decked with laurel and olive branches. Friends sang the marriage hymn as the wagon rolled through the streets. Iphicrates, crowned with myrtle, met them at his door. Beside him stood his wife, the northern princess whose own wedding had taken place in a Thracian royal hall. Now she held aloft a flaming torch to welcome the bride. In a shower of nuts and dried fruit Timotheus' daughter descended from the wagon, ate the ceremonial quince, and entered the home of her new family. Her children would unite the bloodlines of Conon and Timotheus with Iphicrates, three of the city's greatest naval heroes. Their victories had brought to pass the seemingly impossible: Athens was alight again with a final flaring up of its ancient glory.

CHAPTER 18

Triremes of Atlantis

[370–354 B.C.]

In one day and night of terror all your fighting men were swallowed up
by the earth, just as the island of Atlantis was swallowed up by the sea
and disappeared.

—Plato

WHEN PEOPLE OF LATER AGES LOOKED BACK AT THE REVIVAL
of Athens' Golden Age, the figure of Plato dominated the scene. The philosopher possessed the most towering intellect that the city, or perhaps any
city, ever produced. Like Thucydides before him, Plato saw the quest for
sea rule as the defining issue of Athenian politics and history. In time he
became the navy's most articulate and vehement opponent, though only in
his writings, not in the Assembly.

Plato liked to trace things back to their beginnings, but his revisionist
view of Athenian history differed widely from the version recited by the
jingoistic demagogues. Theseus' heroic action in ending the tribute payments to Minos took a darker turn in Plato's vision: "It would have been
better for them to lose seven youths over and over again rather than get into
bad habits by forming themselves into a navy." He also disputed the popular belief that Themistocles, Cimon, and Pericles had been benefactors of
the people. "Yes, they say these men made our city great. They never realize
that it is now swollen and infected because of these statesmen of former
days, who paid no heed to discipline and justice. Instead, they filled our city
with harbors and navy yards and walls and tribute and such-like trash."

Part of Plato's hostility to the navy was inherited, part was personal. His
uncle Critias had been the powerful arch-oligarch who led the government
of the Thirty Tyrants, so Plato grew up among men opposed to democracy

and the "naval mob." In his teens he became a disciple of Socrates, most of whose disciples came from aristocratic and oligarchic families. Antagonism to the popular majority was natural in a young man whose uncle had been killed during the restoration of democracy led by Thrasybulus, and whose beloved teacher had been condemned to death by a jury of his fellow citizens. After these two tragedies, Plato left Athens to study the lore and customs of distant cities, voyaging southeast to Egypt and west to Sicily. It was on one of these voyages that he had suffered the insult at the hands of a Spartan commander that his friend Chabrias avenged at the battle of Naxos. On his return to Athens, Plato established a school at a grove of the hero Akademos on the Sacred Way, the world's original "Academy."

Despite his abhorrence of the navy, Plato's famous Socratic dialogues were full of ships and the sea. To Plato, a man's will was the steering oar of his soul; a quick-tempered man was like an unballasted ship, easily swept away; and the passing of a human life was like a boat slipping from its moorings and drifting from shore. He even described his vision of the cosmos in nautical terms: "This light is the girdle of the heavens, like the girding cables of a trireme, and in the same way it holds together the entire revolving vault."

How, according to Plato, did the gods govern the first humans? "They did not use blows or bodily force, as shepherds do, but governed us like steersmen from the stern of the ship, holding our souls by the steering oars of persuasion." What is his mission as a philosopher? "To frame the shapes of lives according to the modes of their souls. Thus figuratively laying down their keels, I try rightly to consider by what manner of living we shall best navigate our vessel of life through this voyage of existence." Why will a philosopher never become the head of state in a democracy? "The true steersman must give his attention to the time of the year, the seasons, the sky, the winds, the stars, and all that pertains to his art if he is to be a true ruler of the ship. He does not believe that there is any art or science of seizing the steering oars, with or without the consent of the others." Plato used the venerable metaphor of the ship of state to demonstrate the folly of democratic rule. How could it be right or even safe for inexperienced passengers to share equal votes with the captain? These were not academic questions. When

Plato was in his seventies, Athens was confronted with a crisis at sea that threatened to revive all the city's most dangerous imperialistic instincts.

The demise of Spartan power had abruptly knocked away the cornerstone on which the Second Maritime League had been founded. The charter of the alliance proclaimed the league's purpose: to protect the allies from Spartan aggression. Why then should it continue to exist after the fall of Sparta? Pericles had managed to keep the Delian League together even after concluding peace with the Great King. Now the Athenians of a later generation decided to hold on to their naval hegemony with or without a Spartan menace to justify it. Fortunately for them, marauding fleets of pirates or Thessalians or Thebans almost annually stirred up trouble in the Aegean. The raids endangered trade and shipments of grain and thus obligingly provided Athens with a pretext for maintaining the league. As so often happens in empire building, an apparent enemy proved a valuable friend.

The allies were still haunted by the specter of the old oppressive Athenian Empire, with its imperial tribute and bloody massacres. Despite the Assembly's original pledge to promote liberty and justice, it was drifting in the direction of empire once more. Ignoring the league's charter, the Athenians installed governors and garrisons in certain cities and islands, just as in the bad old days. Because the Assembly continued to send expeditions to sea with insufficient funds to pay the crews, Athenian generals had to raid the territories of neutrals and even allies. Blatantly Athenians interfered in the internal politics of other states and increasingly employed the navy on missions that had nothing to do with the league.

This rising tide of abuses almost washed out the benefits that the league still provided to its members and to the Greeks at large. The Athenian navy policed the seas, kept down piracy, and protected small allies against aggression from powerful neighbors. Athenian maritime courts offered fair and speedy judgments to all. And the Athenians were carrying out all these duties and services without the steady income from tribute that had sustained them in the days of the empire.

To ensure that Athens would be able to finance its fleet without recourse to tribute, a citizen named Periander proposed a major financial and administrative reform of the trierarchy. Periander himself knew the burden of outfitting and maintaining a trireme: at the time when he made his proposal, he was serving as joint trierarch on a ship with the appropriate name of *Hegeso* ("Leadership"). His reform called for enrolling no fewer than twelve hundred Athenians as potential contributors for the trierarchic fund. Most would never command at sea. Periander's new list was based solely on wealth and even included heiresses. The twelve hundred were to be grouped into sixty boards called *symmoriai* ("joint contributors"). The Assembly voted the proposal into law, and from then on it sent out fleets of sixty ships, calling up one trireme from each of Periander's new symmories.

With all their failings, the Athenians had learned as much from the sufferings they inflicted on others as they had from their own. It was inconceivable that the Assembly in the time of Plato would have voted to kill or enslave entire populations as their forebears had done in the time of Socrates. The city had gone far to purge itself of hubris. Ironically, its own liberal spirit encouraged rebellions and enemy attacks. The allies did not love the Athenians, but neither did they fear them.

The storm broke fourteen years after the final peace with Sparta, when Byzantium joined the islands of Chios, Rhodes, and Cos in seceding from the league. Their mutiny provoked Athens to send out sixty triremes under Chabrias. Almost two decades had passed since he faced the Spartan fleet at Naxos, but the veteran had lost none of his fire. When the rebel fleet refused to come out of Chios Harbor and fight, he ordered his steersman to force an entrance. The Athenian trierarchs in the other ships hesitated, and as the enemy swarmed in around him, Chabrias was cut off. A rebel rammed his flagship. As water poured through the breach, the rowers scrambled overboard, followed by the archers and marines. All swam toward the main Athenian force that was hovering outside the harbor mouth. Chabrias stood on the foredeck in full armor, apparently unaware that only his ship had advanced and that his own men had abandoned him. He fought on while his trireme slowly sank: one old warrior—but an Athenian!—against an entire fleet. Once the enemy leaped across to the foredeck, Chabrias was quickly overwhelmed and killed. The Athenians conceded defeat, having lost exactly one ship and one man.

From this wretched beginning the War with the Allies or "Social War" went from bad to worse. As news spread of Athens' humiliation at Chios, the rebellion gained momentum. Naval squadrons of the former allies rampaged through the Aegean, raiding, destroying, and threatening islands along the grain route. The Assembly sent out another fleet of sixty triremes under a group of generals that included Timotheus, Iphicrates, Menestheus, and a former mercenary commander named Chares. They met the rebel fleet at a place called Embata. Chares attacked while the other generals stayed on shore. A storm had blown up with high winds and dangerous seas. On their return to Athens, Chares accused the other three generals of failure to do their duty. Timotheus was fined a staggering one hundred talents, the largest fine in Athenian history. After their trials the accused generals either withdrew from active service or left Athens never to return.

As if they were bent on self-destruction, the Athenians had let the greatest generals of the age slip through their fingers like water. Meanwhile the Byzantines were in a position to close the Bosporus, and the Great King threatened to send three hundred triremes into the Aegean to support the rebels. A crisis had been reached. Envoys arrived at Athens from Chios and the other mutinous cities to discuss the future. Some demagogues urged the Assembly to continue the struggle. Would the Athenians choose peace and renounce their imperial ambitions? Or would they battle on, as so many generations of their ancestors had done? The great thinkers of the Academy and the Lyceum were in complete accord: the quest for sea rule was threatening to destroy Athens.

The Assembly bowed to the inevitable. Considering the magnitude of the forces opposing them in the War with the Allies, as well as their own shortage of funds and commanders, it had little choice. Athens officially recognized the independence and autonomy of Chios, Byzantium, Rhodes, and Cos. In so doing it left the door open for other allies to secede from the Second Maritime League. The War with the Allies had lasted only two years and cost very few lives, but its outcome was bitter. Athenians had often experienced and recovered from failure; they were unaccustomed to shame.

During the alarm stirred up by the War with the Allies, Plato and other men of his generation were moved to put their fears and recommendations in writing. The peace movement found an advocate in Isocrates, teacher of rhetoric at the Lyceum. At twenty-one Isocrates had sat in the Assembly and listened to Alcibiades and Nicias debating the Sicilian expedition. He had turned thirty in the year of the battle of the Arginusae Islands and the trial of the generals. Now eighty-one, Isocrates offered his advice in an oration called "On the Peace."

"I say that we should make peace," he proclaimed, "not only with the citizens of Chios, Rhodes, Byzantium, and Cos, but with all mankind." Sea rule was a virulent sickness. As proof, Isocrates pointed to its devastating effect on the once-mighty Spartans. Their ancestral constitution had endured with rocklike solidity for more than seven centuries, only to be dashed to ruin by three decades of naval imperialism. Thalassocracy was a *hetaira* or whore of the highest class, equally attractive and equally deadly to all comers.

Xenophon, another luminary in the Athenian renaissance, sent a letter to the Athenians from his self-imposed exile in Corinth. It was published under the title "Poroi" ("Revenues"). During his half century away from Athens, Xenophon had written a completion of Thucydides' history, as well as an account of his march through the Persian Empire with the Greek army known as the Ten Thousand. His soldiers' cry of *Thalassa! Thalassa!* ("The sea! The sea!") rang in the imagination of every reader. Xenophon loved order and practical wisdom. To fill the city's coffers without preying on allies, he recommended the creation of a new kind of navy: a merchant marine. The Athenians should invest in a fleet of freighters that could be leased out like the mines and other public property. Shipowners whose business benefited the state would be encouraged to stay at Athens by such amenities as new hotels at the Piraeus and front-row seats at the theater. In the end the Athenians accepted Xenophon's advice to reopen the silver mines at Laurium, but the merchant marine remained no more than a gleam in the old campaigner's eye.

At about the same time that Isocrates and Xenophon were advocating an end to maritime empire, Plato embarked on a set of dialogues that would put the insatiable quest for sea rule in a cosmic context. In the dialogues *Timaeus* and *Critias* he recounted the story of a war between an imperial naval power and a small but valiant state that relied entirely on its army. The naval power had a capital city built on and around a hill that stood five miles from the sea. Its ships were served by three circular harbors of graduated size. The smaller harbors accommodated the immense fleet of triremes while the largest harbor was filled with merchant ships that brought the wealth of the world to the port. A long wall with towers and gates surrounded the harbors and the central citadel. There were cisterns for water, and the region was cut up in a rectangular grid.

The people who ruled this maritime empire had good land of their own, but in their greed and arrogance they set out to take over others, including neighboring islands and the continent beyond. In the end they controlled the waters and coasts of half the Mediterranean. So much good fortune eventually led to a fall from grace. As Plato put it, "They appeared glorious and blessed to those who could not recognize true happiness. Yet at the very same time they were in fact full of greed and unrighteous power."

The proud and wealthy city of the sea met its nemesis in the forces of a land power that lived in simplicity, virtue, and righteousness. The people of this other city had no use for seafaring or trade. The state was governed by an elite class of fighting men—and in fact the women of this class were as warlike as the men. They lived apart from the lower classes and did no work with their hands, constantly vigilant for the safety of the state. The fighting men held all possessions in common and even built communal dining halls for their meals. Their courage and virtue had made them leaders of other Greeks, who followed them willingly.

All appearances to the contrary, Plato was not rewriting the history of the Peloponnesian War. He did not name his maritime empire Athens; nor were the noble warriors who opposed it Spartans. On the contrary, he claimed that the land power was really primeval Athens as it had been "before the deluge," while the sea power was a lost continent or island called Atlantis. His account of the war between Atlantis and Athens combined myth and history into a gigantic allegory on the evils of sea power.

Plato presented his allegory in a Socratic dialogue. Socrates has joined three friends for conversation on the day of the Panathenaic festival. Among them are Plato's uncle Critias and, of all people, the Syracusan patriot Hermocrates, who masterminded his city's resistance to the armada from Athens. The one thing that these two historical figures had in common was their opposition to the Athenian navy. The subject of their conversation with Socrates is the ideal city, which was also the subject of Plato's earlier dialogue the *Republic*. Socrates says that a static description is not enough: he wants to see their ideal state in action, struggling for survival. At this Hermocrates chimes in with a happy thought. Critias should repeat a story that he told on the previous day when Socrates was absent: the tale of early Athens, a truly ideal state, and its daring resistance to the power of Atlantis.

Critias explains that this story, unknown to other Greeks, was told to him by his grandfather, who heard it from the lawgiver Solon, who in turn learned it from Egyptian priests at a temple in the Nile delta. These Egyptians knew more than Solon himself about Athens' origins. "Many great and wonderful deeds are recorded of your city in our histories. But one exceeds all the rest in greatness and valor. For these histories tell of a mighty power which unprovoked made an expedition against the whole of Europe and Asia, to which your city put an end."

Ten thousand years ago, according to Plato's story, a gigantic island called Atlantis lay in the ocean beyond the Pillars of Heracles, bigger than Asia and Africa put together. From Atlantis it was possible to cross westward to other islands and ultimately reach the mainland on the far side of the ocean. When the gods divided the world among themselves, Poseidon claimed Atlantis. On the island's southern side was a rectangular plain that stretched three hundred miles along the coast and two hundred miles inland. Encircling mountains protected the plain from the harsh north winds, making it an earthly paradise. Poseidon married a local girl named Cleito. To protect his bride, he surrounded a hill near the sea with three rings of water. The couple named the first of their ten sons Atlas, and the island was called Land of Atlas or Atlantis after him, just as the surrounding ocean was called the Atlantic. Poseidon allotted a portion of the island to each son, but Atlas ruled them all. The Atlanteans were great delvers in the earth, digging mines for clay and metal ores as well as quarries for building stone.

The people were also seafarers. Poseidon's three rings of water became circular harbors. Though Atlantis was rich, it imported goods and luxuries from abroad. The Atlantean navy boasted twelve hundred triremes, housed by pairs in double slipways cut into the rock. Nearby was storage space for the naval gear. The central plain of the island was divided into sixty thousand districts by a crisscrossing grid of canals. Each district was required to furnish four men for service in the Atlantean trireme fleet, along with two hoplites, two slingers of missiles, three slingers of stones, and three javelin throwers. Atlantis was first and foremost a state organized for war.

In the beginning the Atlanteans were noble and long-lived, but with time and affluence the race degenerated. Zeus decided to punish their hubris. With their great fleet the Atlanteans had already seized the neighboring islands. Now, goaded by Zeus, they launched an armada against the peoples of the Mediterranean. None could withstand them. The navy and army of Atlantis conquered the African coast as far as Egypt, and Europe as far as central Italy. At last their forces confronted the soldiers of Athens, leaders of a Greek alliance.

While Poseidon had taken possession of Atlantis, Athena and her brother Hephaestus had claimed the territory of Attica as their portion. Attica was small by comparison to Atlantis, but it had a perfect climate, good soil, and abundant natural resources. Faced with the Atlantean armada, the Greek allies abandoned the Athenians, who fought on alone. Thanks to their strength, valor, and military prowess, the Athenians finally defeated the Atlanteans in battle. They liberated all the countries that had been enslaved, and the world's first maritime empire came to an end. But the story told by the Egyptian priests did not end here. Violent earthquakes and floods engulfed the fighting men of primeval Athens; the same disaster swallowed up Atlantis, which vanished from sight.

No trace of the Atlantis story has been found in other ancient writings, Greek or Egyptian. In creating his lost continent of Atlantis, Plato included details that linked this archetypal maritime power to the thalassocracies known to contemporary Greeks. From the Crete of the first sea ruler, King Minos, Plato borrowed an elaborate cult of bull sacrifice. The number 1,200 given for the island's trireme fleet recalled not only Periander's recent creation of 1,200 new trierarchs at Athens, but also the catalog of Agamemnon's 1,184 ships for the Trojan War and Xerxes' grand armada of 1,207 for the invasion of Greece. The circular harbor surrounding a circular island conjured up the image of Carthage, and the Atlanteans' obsession with luxuries, Corinth. Again like Atlantis, both Athens and Syracuse used double shipsheds to house their triremes. As for the earthquake and tidal wave that

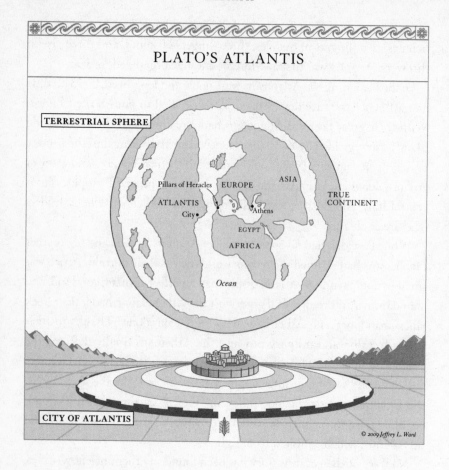

PLATO'S ATLANTIS

TERRESTRIAL SPHERE

Pillars of Heracles EUROPE ASIA
ATLANTIS
City Athens TRUE
CONTINENT
EGYPT
AFRICA

Ocean

CITY OF ATLANTIS

© 2009 Jeffrey L. Ward

submerged Atlantis, they recalled the recent disaster at Helike, when a great wave engulfed the Spartan triremes commanded by Pollis and destroyed the last vestige of Sparta's naval power.

A similar historical disaster may have suggested the name that Plato gave to his island-continent. He had been born at the time when an earthquake in the Euboean Gulf split the little island of Atalante in two; the resulting tsunami picked up an Athenian trireme moored on the shore and threw it far into the town. From "Atalante" it was a short step to a description of a North African tribe called "Atlantes" that was recorded in the history of Herodotus, as well as the Atlas Mountains and Atlantic Ocean (all of which had been given their names long before Plato invented Atlantis). So using details from myth, history, geography, and his own fertile imagination, Plato fashioned an ancient thalassocracy to stand as the forerunner of all later naval powers, and devised for it a tragic fate as a warning to all its successors. Naval power breeds hubris, and the gods punish hubris with destruction.

More than anything else, however, the story of Atlantis was an allegory of Athens. With wishful thinking, Plato pulled apart the city of his own day, disentangling the realm of Poseidon and triremes from the "true Athens" of Athena, Hephaestus, and traditional virtues. In setting his true Athens in opposition to Atlantis, the philosopher expressed his dream that Athens' better self might overcome the seductive temptations of maritime wealth and power. Atlantis embodied everything that was wrong with Athens, and its destruction was a warning to the Athenians of Plato's own time.

Later Greeks forgot Plato's moral purpose and plunged into a hunt for Atlantis on maps or in ancient history. Could Atlantis really have been Troy? Or perhaps the island of Scheria, home of the seafaring Phaeacians in Homer's *Odyssey*? Eventually the myth of Atlantis floated free of Plato altogether and became world famous. The location of Atlantis became a topic of intense interest and debate for enthusiasts who had never read a word of the *Timaeus* or *Critias*. The lost continent was identified with the volcanic island of Thera, with Minoan Crete, with Helgoland in the North Sea, even with Bimini in the Bahamas. Plato's pupil Aristotle, however, seems to have classified Atlantis, not among places of real history or geography, but among poetic creations. Aristotle's pronouncement on such works of the imagination may have applied specifically to Atlantis: "He who created it, destroyed it."

But Aristotle was mistaken. Atlantis was real and clearly visible from the Acropolis. To visit it, one had only to follow the line of the Long Walls down to the sea and enter the Piraeus, noisy hub of shipping and maritime enterprise. After climbing around the shoulder of Munychia Hill and descending through Hippodamus' grid of streets, one reached the edge of Zea Harbor and the double shipsheds, the home of the Athenian navy. Centuries later the remains of the Navy Yard would glimmer through the water of the harbor, submerged by the rising sea and subsidence of the land. Here lay the heart of Plato's dark vision. This was Atlantis.

CHAPTER 19

The Voice of the Navy

[354–339 B.C.]

When mariners are swept along by rushing winds, in the matter of steering, two points of view, or a whole body of experts, are no match for one man of average ability exercising his independent judgment.

—Euripides

WHILE PLATO WAS DOING HIS BEST TO TURN ATHENS AWAY FROM the sea, one obscure citizen embarked on a campaign to resurrect the city's pride and naval dominance. Demosthenes of Paiania had only one gift that qualified him as a champion of the Athenian navy: a genius for writing and delivering speeches. But his patriotic fervor was strong, and during his lifetime Athens had to contend with one of the most dangerous enemies it would ever know. The threat came from northern Greece, where King Philip of Macedon was rapidly building an empire on land. Inevitably Philip's conquests began to impinge on Athens' maritime realm. In speech after speech Demosthenes warned his fellow citizens of their peril. His zeal for naval reform and his opposition to Philip inspired orations of such power that they were hailed as classics even in Demosthenes' own lifetime—even by his antagonists.

A tortuous path had led Demosthenes to the speaker's platform. His boyhood had been lonely. A weakling with a chronic stutter, he made no friends at wrestling practice or hunting parties. His father died when Demosthenes was only seven, and from then on Demosthenes lived at home with his mother and sister. To an outside observer the boy must have appeared starved for companionship. But he had one constant friend, a familiar spirit from the past: Thucydides. The historian had been dead for some three decades, but his stirring voice lived on. Thucydides' account of the Peloponnesian War fired Demosthenes' imagination with tales of perilous adventures and epic battles. Unrolling his copy, he was transported back to an age when Athens blazed with glory, its navy seemingly indomitable and its leaders larger than life. Demosthenes read the whole book eight times and knew parts of it by heart.

Demosthenes' father had left him an inheritance worth fourteen talents, some of it tied up in a factory that manufactured swords. He therefore expected to be financially independent when he turned eighteen, an event that took place five years after Athens made its final peace with Sparta. But it proved a painful coming of age. The three guardians appointed in his father's will had stolen or squandered most of his inheritance. Of the fourteen talents in money and property left to Demosthenes, only a little over one talent remained. To rub salt in the wound, the embezzlers had concealed their depletion of the estate by enrolling young Demosthenes in the highest bracket for taxes and liturgies. At the age of seventeen he was already listed among the trierarchs and had made partial payment for the outfitting of a trireme. Two of the guardians were his own cousins, but Demosthenes filed a lawsuit against them, family or no.

Two years passed before the case came to trial, and during that time Demosthenes prepared tirelessly for his day in court. Athenian juries expected citizens to speak for themselves, even if professional speechwriters had been hired to compose the speeches. Demosthenes, intensely self-critical, knew that he made a poor impression. He could do nothing about his wretched physique or habitual scowl, but he learned by listening to actors and orators that he could at least train and strengthen his voice. He began to make solitary excursions to a deserted beach and strained to make himself heard through the whistling wind and crashing waves. To overcome his speech impediment, Demosthenes would put a pebble in his mouth and work his tongue around the stone while still trying to pronounce words clearly. Away from the beach, he declaimed speeches while walking or running up steep hillsides. Skinny legs working, narrow chest heaving, his delivery eventually became smooth even as he almost gasped for breath. Demosthenes had inherited a true Athenian's competitive nature, but he turned it not toward wrestling or running but toward public speaking.

Demosthenes decided to write his own speeches for the trial. The best speechwriters commanded fees higher than he could afford to pay. In any case, over the years he had mastered the principles of rhetoric from a superlative teacher. His absorption with Thucydides had immersed him in a great school of oratory: Pericles delivering a funeral oration; Phormio rallying his mutinous men; Alcibiades urging the Athenians onward to Sicily; Nicias exhorting the doomed men at Syracuse before the last battle. Demosthenes found in Thucydides a style that was concentrated, analytical, lively, and passionate—a balance of clear ideas and vividly reported facts.

It must have been a shock to the guardians—rich men with established reputations and influence—when the jury voted in favor of their untried and unknown accuser, just twenty years old. It was Demosthenes' first victory, but like many of his later ones, it proved hollow. His guardians dodged the court's ruling with a barrage of ploys both legal and illegal. Demosthenes was left with nothing.

And yet, not quite nothing. He had acquired in his legal battle a skill that could provide a steady income. As a speechwriter for hire, he began to make his way in the world. Athens being Athens, this new endeavor inevitably brought him into intimate and constant contact with the maritime world. Trierarchs were continually embroiled in legal battles over the performance of their duties and the equipping of their triremes. Seafaring merchants and shipowners had special courts in the Piraeus to resolve disputes concerning freighters, investments, and loans on ships and cargoes. Demosthenes familiarized himself with a daunting mass of laws, decrees, and historical precedents, as well as such arcana as the cost of a set of oars and the change in interest rates after the rising of the star Arcturus. He worked far into the night, a young man whose little household consumed more lamp oil than wine.

As Demosthenes' income grew, so did his ambitions. He dreamed of using his gifts of argument and persuasion on behalf of his city. In those days Timotheus was capturing outposts in the Aegean and along the Hellespont: adventurism and imperialism were on the upsurge in Athens. Once Demosthenes reached the age of thirty, he could address these momentous issues in speeches before the Assembly. But why would anyone listen to him? The famous leaders of the past had first proved themselves as men of action before they achieved leadership in the Assembly.

At the age of twenty-four, already a rich and self-made man, Demosthenes put his name forward for a trierarchy. This would be no paper appointment, however, such as the joint trierarchy forced on him when he was seventeen. Now he intended to equip the trireme himself and command it at sea. An old friend of Demosthenes' father had been elected as general, a man named Cephisodotus. He received orders from the Assembly to lead a squadron of ten triremes on a mission that promised to be both difficult and dangerous, and Demosthenes volunteered to serve under him.

Trierarchs were thrown into daily contact with every element of Athenian society: generals, treasurers, and bankers; the Assembly, the Council, the boards of finance and inspection; merchants, porters, scribes; and then the crew, from the highly skilled steersman who directed the trireme's course to the lowly piper who kept the rowers in time. The city provided the trierarch with an empty hull and with oars and gear in a condition that depended on the honesty of the previous trierarch. The trierarch also received a modicum of money to hire a crew. The rest was up to him.

Demosthenes threw himself into the task with naïve fervor. While other trierarchs farmed out the burdensome duty to contractors, Demosthenes went himself to the shadowy shed where "his" trireme rested and undertook to bring the ship into first-rate condition. By offering bonuses, he attracted the best rowers in the Piraeus to his crew. His zeal was contagious, and before any of the other nine ships were on the water, Demosthenes' trireme had been fitted with its girding cables, dragged down the slipway, and launched on the harbor. His crew rowed around to the jetty in the Cantharus harbor, where the inspectors waited to assess the presence and working condition of all sails, rigging, oars, and anchors.

All was in order. Demosthenes eagerly applied for the golden crown or wreath that was awarded to the first ship to reach the jetty. Then came the exhilarating experience of taking the fully manned trireme into open water for its sea trials. As was the custom at the Piraeus, a crowd of interested citizens lined the shore to criticize the performance. The steersman and crew executed the maneuvers, and the young trierarch—the least experienced man on board—stood proudly on the afterdeck. So impressive was the crew's performance that Cephisodotus chose Demosthenes' trireme for his flagship. At the launching Demosthenes had the honor of standing beside the general in the sacrifices and libations.

Their destination was the historic seaway that ran through the Hellespont, the Sea of Marmara, and the Bosporus to the Black Sea. Thanks to the recent campaigns of Timotheus, Athens had secured the mouth of the Hellespont and was now attempting to regain control of the rest of the route by concluding treaties with a Thracian king. Demosthenes estimated that the harbor duties collected along the waterway amounted to two hundred talents per year. But he also had a family interest in the route to the Black Sea: his grandfather on his mother's side had commanded an Athenian garrison in the Crimea during the waning days of the Peloponnesian War.

Demosthenes had undertaken the trierarchy in search of experience. He was not disappointed. During his time at sea he saw the mighty Hellespont with its river of shipping, legendary coasts and islands, great walled towns, amphibious assaults, ambushes at dawn (in fact, in the middle of breakfast), mercenary armies, and piratical bands. The expedition also laid bare to the young idealist the true state of Athens' naval forces: ill prepared, overconfident, and easily outmaneuvered in both combat and diplomacy.

After many adventures Cephisodotus set out for Athens with a covenant signed by the Thracian king. This document proved so unsatisfactory to the Assembly that the people fined the general five talents. Demosthenes himself was taken to court by some of his envious fellow trierarchs, who challenged his right to the golden crown. Thus the expedition ended in legal charges and countercharges, the leaders suffering more harm from their fellow citizens at home than they had from their enemies overseas.

Demosthenes was realistic enough to absorb this dose of bitter medicine, but he did not abandon the hope that the Athenians could mend their ways. He believed that he knew how to make his city great again, and, like Themistocles before him, he meant to make himself great in the process. Six years had to pass before he would be old enough to present his ideas to the Assembly. He continued to write speeches and to volunteer for trierarchic service, most notably under Timotheus for an expedition to Euboea. Shortly after this exhilarating campaign Demosthenes put his name forward to address an Assembly meeting on a day when naval matters were up for debate.

In the six years since his first overseas campaign, Demosthenes had seen conditions deteriorate. Athens had been defeated at sea by rebellious allies. Triremes sat in the shipsheds at the Piraeus, unfit for service. A treasurer of the shipbuilding fund had absconded with public money that should have paid for new triremes. And when King Philip of Macedon attacked coastal cities in the northern Aegean, the Athenian fleet always arrived too late to intervene.

In one of Aesop's fables, passengers from a sinking ship suddenly find themselves in the sea. An Athenian among the survivors calls on the gods for help. A man swimming for shore hears the prayer. He turns to the Athenian and says, "Pray by all means! But also move your arms!" Demosthenes intended to be just such a wise counselor to Athenians who seemed to have forgotten that the gods help those who help themselves.

The morning came when Demosthenes walked up to the Pnyx to make his maiden speech to the Assembly. In due course the herald called upon Demosthenes of Paiania, from the tribe of Pandion, to come forward. As Demosthenes mounted the bema, his head was full of a speech into which he had poured his all. It called for nothing less than a complete reorganization of the Athenian navy. Plans for reform and new beginnings were afloat everywhere that year. Isocrates had just written "On the Peace," Xenophon had cast his advice into the essay "Revenues," and Plato was busy at the Academy envisioning lost continents and ideal commonwealths. None of those older Athenians, however, had been bold enough to face the Assembly, the body that Plato had once called "the great beast." Standing for the first time in the place where Themistocles and Cimon and Pericles had made history, Demosthenes launched into the opening of his speech: "Those who praise your forefathers, O men of Athens, seem to me . . ."

As he would do throughout his career, Demosthenes plunged quickly into his main theme: how could Athens best prepare for war? In his view the most obvious threat was Persia. Yet he was urging the city not to embark on a new war but rather to prevent future wars by strengthening the navy: "The first requirements for every war must be, in my view, ships and money and strong positions, and I find that the Great King is more fully supplied with these than we are." In order to surpass the Persians, Demosthenes advocated an elaborate plan for overhauling and restructuring Periander's *symmoriai,* the groups of propertied citizens who contributed naval funds. (The speech later became known as "On the Symmories" or "On the Navy-Boards.") He proposed raising the number of citizens who directly financed the naval effort from Periander's twelve hundred to two thousand, all of them potential trierarchs. It would be a people's navy with a vengeance.

An enlarged fleet of three hundred triremes would be divided into twenty squadrons of fifteen triremes, each assigned to one of Demosthenes' new navy boards. He went on to talk about equipment and crews and proposed that specific areas of the Navy Yard be assigned to the tribal divisions so that each citizen would know exactly where to muster in case of an emergency. To round out his speech, Demosthenes again invoked the Persians: "The Great King knows that with two hundred triremes our ancestors destroyed a thousand of his ships. Now he will hear that we have three hundred ships of our own ready to launch. Even if he were mad, he would not lightly provoke the hostility of Athens." Finally he appealed to the Athenians to prove themselves worthy of their fathers not through speeches but through actions.

There was no outburst of approval, no spontaneous vote to adopt the plan over which he had labored. As Demosthenes returned to his place, the machinery of the Assembly rolled on, and the attention of the people passed to other matters. The speech had perhaps been too Thucydidean in its analysis of data and statistics, too Periclean in its dispassionate recommendation that Athens keep quiet but take care of its fleet. And surely he could have found a more compelling incentive than the remote menace of King Artaxerxes III. For the moment, as he must have been gloomily aware, he had failed.

Three years later Demosthenes was back on the bema. This time he ignored due order and usurped first place among the speakers. His urgency was brought on by new threats to the Athenian ships and even the coast of Attica, all emanating from a single source: Philip. The Macedonian king was responsible for kidnapping Athenian citizens on the islands of Lemnos and Imbros, launching piratical raids on Athenian shipping, and attacking Piraeus-bound freighters off the southern cape of Euboea. One of his roving squadrons had actually landed on the beach at Marathon and brazenly towed off one of Athens' sacred ships. Demosthenes had found the cause he had been seeking.

Demosthenes' speech against Philip was the first in a bitter and angry series that came to be known as *Philippics*. The King of Macedon was only thirty-one, two years younger than the orator himself. Philip's boyhood had been as difficult and uncertain as Demosthenes' own. His father, King Amyntas, was so unsure of his power that he adopted the Athenian general Iphicrates as a son, hoping that this strong man would protect young Philip, his older brother, and the rest of the royal family. As a youth Philip had been handed over as a hostage to the Thebans, who had recently beaten the Spartan phalanx at the battle of Leuctra. Like Demosthenes, Philip turned his predicaments to his own advantage. He studied phalanx warfare carefully in Thebes, and when he returned to his mountain homeland, he first usurped the throne and then created a formidable Macedonian phalanx armed with eighteen-foot pikes. Constant drill transformed brawling warriors into professional soldiers who ignored distance and time of year in service to their master, Philip.

No Macedonian was physically tougher than the king himself. Philip put himself at risk in all his battles, suffering a broken shoulder, maimed limbs, and the loss of an eye in the process. Warlike and robust, he would nevertheless use diplomacy, intrigue, and deception whenever they served his purpose. And his purpose was to rule a Macedonian empire that would stretch from the Danube River southward into the heart of Greece. The only important obstacle to his ambitions was the Athenian navy.

Macedon's rise had been fueled in part by Athens itself, for the navy required constant supplies of timber. Plato had already described the deforestation of Attica and its devastating effects on the Athenian countryside. With the trees cleared from the hillsides, the soil had eroded to the sea. Athens' loss had been Macedon's gain. Over many years Athenian silver had been enriching the northern kingdom through purchases of oak, fir, and pine for ships and oars. Philip could now cut off this resource at will. Up to now Athenians had paid little heed to Macedon's growing power or to the remarkable abilities of Philip. In his first *Philippic,* Demosthenes set out to open their eyes.

The Macedonian king had grown powerful, he told the Assembly, not because he was strong but because they were negligent and weak. State festivals and religious processions at Athens were always lavishly funded and well rehearsed, while everything to do with war was disorganized and uncertain. To check Philip's advance, Demosthenes called on the people to man and launch two emergency fleets.

One fleet would be a small amphibious force of troop and horse carriers convoyed by ten fast triremes. It would operate year-round in northern waters: "If we are unwilling to fight Philip there, we may be forced to fight him here." Citizens would serve in relays during this running war. In summer Demosthenes' proposed northern fleet would avoid pitched battles with the Macedonian phalanx, waging guerrilla warfare instead. In winter they would station themselves on three islands. From Skiathos they would watch the approaches to Attica, from Lemnos the route to the Hellespont, and from Thasos the mining regions of the north. Demosthenes estimated the annual cost of maintaining this force at ninety talents—scant wages, which the men would be eager to increase by plundering enemy territory and ships. "If this proves not to be the case," he said, "then I am ready to voyage with the fleet as a volunteer and to suffer the worst myself."

His second fleet would consist of fifty triremes, permanently equipped and on call at the Piraeus: "We must get it into our heads that if necessary we citizens will go on board and man them ourselves." The triremes would be augmented with carriers for horses and troops, so that a land army could be rapidly transported to strategic points such as Thermopylae. "My proposal is bold, but it will soon be tested in action, and you will be its judges." It was a touching article of faith with Demosthenes throughout his life that evils would melt away as soon as one took action against them.

It was not to be. Only a few years had passed since Athens' renascent imperialism had been punished in the war with Byzantium, Chios, Cos, and Rhodes. Isocrates, a fervent advocate of peace, denounced Demosthenes as a warmonger and alarmist. Many influential citizens felt a natural aversion to overseas campaigns and to policing the entire Aegean with little or no allied support. Others were actually in Philip's pay and ready to pour oil on any waters that Demosthenes might trouble with his speeches. A handsome actor named Aeschines was the leader of these apologists for Philip. Other Athenians were just as Demosthenes described them: self-absorbed. To them, the remedy that Demosthenes proposed looked worse than the illness he sought to cure.

So Athens took no effective action against the Macedonian king. Demosthenes once compared the Athenians to unskilled boxers, always one move behind Philip. Foolishly they grasped the spot where his last punch had fallen instead of looking to prevent the next. For the next ten years Athens kept up its flailing attempts to parry both Philip's military advances and his diplomatic maneuvers. The Assembly was so bewildered by Philip that it did not take strong action even when his plot to burn the Navy Yard was exposed. The man sent to start the fire had actually reached the Piraeus when he was apprehended, yet still Demosthenes' speeches could not unite the city in resistance to the threat.

With nine other Athenian ambassadors Demosthenes traveled north to Philip's court and at last came face-to-face with his larger-than-life antagonist. Both men were at this time in their late thirties, and both were famous for their eloquence. But in all other respects the sociable, hard-drinking monarch, wreathed in battle scars and unexpected charm, appeared the complete antithesis of the scrawny, nervous Athenian. As the youngest envoy, Demosthenes spoke last. It was the only occasion on record when he fumbled over his speech. On Philip's home ground, surrounded by Philip's vibrant aura, he was unmanned.

From the beginning Demosthenes had said that the most serious threats to Athens' survival would come not from Philip but from the Athenians themselves. At the age of ninety Isocrates wrote an open letter to Philip, urging him to unite the cities of Greece under his leadership. After that the king should muster the forces of the Athenians and the other Greeks for a great war in the east. There he might reasonably hope to conquer the entire Persian Empire and liberate the Greeks of Ionia. It was the same dream of a panhellenic campaign that Isocrates had long ago proposed for the Athenian navy and the Spartan army. Unlike his previous addressees, however, Philip seems actually to have read the letter and taken the advice seriously.

Soon Philip's army was marching eastward through Thrace. It first brought the remainder of the northern Aegean seaboard under Macedonian control and then threatened Athenian settlements on the Gallipoli peninsula beside the Hellespont. Philip had already made alliances with the cities of Perinthus and Byzantium. It seemed inevitable that he would go on to seize control of the grain route.

As he had done so often over the previous decade, Demosthenes addressed the Assembly. With Philip about to grasp the entire seaway from the Hellespont to the Bosporus, Demosthenes was filled with the spirit and almost

THE RISE OF MACEDON
UNDER PHILIP II, 359–336 B.C.

PAEONIA

THRACE

Black Sea

MACEDON

Amphipolis

Perinthus

Byzantium

Bosporus

Pella

CHALCIDICE

Sea of Marmara

Olynthus

EPIRUS

PERSIAN EMPIRE

THESSALY

Aegean

EUBOEA

Chaeronea

CHIOS

Sardis

Thebes

Athens

Sea

Argos

0 Miles   50   100

0 Kilometers   100

Messene

Cos

Olynthus   Philip's conquests and alliances

RHODES   © 2009 Jeffrey L. Ward

the very words of Themistocles: "Do not court disaster by fixing on the naïve strategy of your former war against the Spartans. Instead, order your policies and your armament so that your line of defense may lie as far as possible from Athens. Give Philip no opportunity to move forward from his base, and never let him close in on you." Athens was still strong; it must attack Philip while its strength was undiminished: "While the ship is still safe and sound—*that* is when the mariner and steersman and the rest must show their zealous care for it, so that it may not be overturned by sabotage or by accident. Once the sea overwhelms the ship, care comes too late." In this third *Philippic* Demosthenes proposed that the Assembly send out ambassadors to seek allies against Philip. But with or without allies, Athens should prepare to fight.

For years Demosthenes had been asking and urging this course of resistance in his *Philippics* and *Olynthiacs* and other harangues, with no result. But now his persistence and Philip's threat to the grain route had finally brought popular opinion in Athens to the tipping point. Even so he must have been astounded when the vote was taken, and the count of raised hands showed that his proposal had passed. The Assembly would dispatch envoys throughout Greece and the Aegean, even to the Persians. Athens was roused at last.

To Demosthenes himself fell the most difficult assignment: Byzantium. The city was already allied to Philip, whose army was close while Athens was distant. The Assembly sent Demosthenes in a trireme to persuade the Byzantines to abandon the Macedonian alliance and join Athens. He had to overcome deep resentment over the tolls on shipping that the Athenians had for years exacted on all commerce passing through the Bosporus. But in the end, Demosthenes registered one of the most important victories of his career when the Byzantines swore allegiance to the Athenians.

Philip regarded this alliance as a hostile act. He demanded that the Byzantines and Perinthians support him in a war against the Athenians. They refused. Loading siege equipment on board his ships, Philip moved through the straits to bring these allies to heel. Even with siege towers more than one hundred feet tall, however, he could not capture Perinthus. The rows of houses were built up a theaterlike slope so that each row formed its own defensive wall. When he saw Byzantine vessels slipping into Perinthus Harbor to aid the resistance, Philip abruptly took his army east and assaulted Byzantium itself. Messengers set out at once to appeal for help from the Athenians.

Summer was ending; the annual fleet of some two hundred grain freighters from the Black Sea was assembling in a bay on the Asiatic side of the Bosporus. Riding at anchor, they awaited their convoy, a fleet of forty Athenian triremes under the general Chares. Such a prize was too tempting for Philip to ignore. When his fleet failed to capture the freighters, Philip sent part of his army to attack them from the landward side. He succeeded, and the sale of the cargoes brought in seven hundred talents.

Meanwhile the news of his sieges spread throughout the Aegean. In Athens Demosthenes was the first to call for war and the launching of a fleet.

The ardor of the Assembly was now equal to his own. It voted that the inscribed marble slab that bore the terms of the peace treaty with Macedon be taken down and destroyed. More important, it voted the immediate preparation of a fleet of triremes and appointed the veteran general Phocion, hero of the battle of Naxos, to command it. As Phocion led the Athenian force to the scene of action, he found that they were not alone. Athenian diplomacy and Macedonian aggression had raised fears among the islanders. Ships from Chios, Rhodes, and Cos joined the fleet that now swept up the Hellespont to save Byzantium. The former antagonists from the War with the Allies were reunited.

Their arrival staggered Philip. He had supposed that once he seized the grain fleet, the Athenians would come to terms. All the world knew that they had surrendered to Lysander and the Peloponnesians once the supply was cut off, and some years later Athens had accepted the King's Peace when Artaxerxes II threatened to hold up the grain. Yet here they were in force, with allies beside them as in the old days.

Philip had no intention of risking a battle with this armada from Athens. Like all master tacticians, he believed in attacking weak points, not strengths. He decided to give up the siege of Byzantium and return home. Unfortunately for him the oncoming Athenian fleet was blocking his route back to Macedon. He could not risk a naval battle with Phocion. Casting about for a way to elude the enemy, Philip repeated Phormio's ruse of a mock summons. He sent a letter in his own handwriting to one of his generals, a Macedonian named Antipater, naming a rendezvous point to which he was moving his forces. Deliberately Philip arranged for both messenger and letter to fall into Athenian hands. The upright and unsuspecting Phocion never considered the possibility of a trick. While the Athenians and allies dashed off in the wrong direction, Philip launched his ships and escaped.

Though Philip eluded them, the Athenians were elated at the success of their naval expedition and gave full credit to Demosthenes. For ten years he had been telling the Athenians that the best way to check their enemy was through decisive action. The events at Byzantium proved his wisdom. The Athenians had put their navy to sea, and the Macedonian threat had disappeared before it like snow before the summer sun. Byzantium was saved. For the first time in Demosthenes' life, he found himself popular.

There was no resting on laurels, however. He immediately used his credit with the Assembly to ram through the long-needed reform of the navy boards and other financial arrangements for building and equipping the ships. Demosthenes' measures relieved Athenians with middling incomes of a monetary burden that they had been unable to sustain and placed a proportionately heavier share on the rich. The Assembly gave him everything, in spite of the open protests and undercover bribes of the wealthy citizens. Political enemies took him to court over his reorganization of the *symmoriai,* but he was triumphantly acquitted of wrongdoing by the jury. His reforms were divisive, but the abuses involving trierarchs that had once endangered the very existence of Athenian sea power now became a thing of the past.

The struggle had been hard, and Demosthenes did not hesitate to point out the difficulties faced by a democratic leader compared to a despot like Philip: "First, he had absolute rule over his followers, which is the greatest single advantage in war. Second, his followers were armed for war all the time. Third, he was well equipped with money, and did whatever he decided, not publishing his decisions in decrees, not being constantly brought to court by malicious accusers, not defending himself against charges of illegality, not accountable to anyone, but simply ruler, leader, master of all. When I took my position against him (for it is fair to examine this), of what was I master? Of nothing. For even the opportunity to speak on policy, the only privilege I had—and a shared one, at that—you extended equally to Philip's hirelings and to me."

Demosthenes, the man whose advice the Assembly had rejected for so many years, was now first citizen in Athens, more clearly in control of policy than any leader since Pericles. The lonely young man on the beach had climbed to a pitch of fame and influence that seemed to rival Philip's. With his immortal speeches he had inspired his fellow citizens to believe once more in the destiny of Athens and the vital importance of naval power. For the moment, with Philip in retreat from Byzantium and Athens surrounded by admiring allies, Demosthenes seemed poised to preside over the Athenian ship of state in a new age of peace and prestige. The navy's experienced steersmen could have warned him: smooth and smiling seas sometimes conceal the deadliest reefs.

CHAPTER 20

In the Shadow of Macedon

[339–324 B.C.]

Reversals of fortune are frequent, for sovereign rule never remains in the same hands for long.

—Isocrates

THE JOY OF THE ATHENIANS AFTER PHOCION'S EXPEDITION to Byzantium lasted less than a year. Philip had temporarily abandoned his designs on the grain route, but the war was not over yet. He accepted the fact that his Macedonian fleet was no match for the Athenian navy. Further operations against the Greeks would be carried out on land. Thanks to Demosthenes the navy was once again a formidable force, but there had been no Demosthenes to work a similar transformation on the Athenian army. Worst of all was the dearth of talented commanders. The best Athenian tacticians and strategists now served as mercenaries abroad.

Philip's opportunity came when a minuscule squabble erupted about the plowing of sacred fields near Delphi. Invited to help protect the Delphic Oracle, Philip marched south with his army through the pass at Thermopylae. The Sacred War, however, was only a pretext. Now that Philip had entered Greece, he intended to stay. His well-drilled army would subdue or eliminate his opponents on their own ground. Only Thebes stood between the Macedonians and the frontiers of Attica, and Thebes was by long tradition hostile to Athens. Demosthenes carried out a mission even more difficult than his embassy to Byzantium when he persuaded the Thebans to ally themselves with Athens in resistance to Philip.

Preparations for a decisive land battle engaged both sides for months. Late in summer the two armies met on a plain near the town of Chaeronea. Philip's forces destroyed the power of Thebes and inflicted heavy losses on the Athenian hoplite phalanx as well. His young son Alexander took part in the historic victory as commander of the Macedonian cavalry. Rumors from the battlefield quickly reached Athens, seemingly on the wind—terrifying reports that Philip was now marching toward the city. Always energetic and decisive when prospects were at their worst, the Athenians immediately prepared to resist a siege. They appointed Demosthenes to secure the grain supply and sent him by ship to seek support in other cities. The older men marched down to the Piraeus to man the harbor fortifications; others strengthened the city's defenses. To replace the thousands of citizens killed or taken prisoner at Chaeronea, the Assembly voted to enfranchise slaves and metics, as their forefathers had done before the battle of Arginusae.

In the midst of this frenetic activity envoys arrived from the Macedonian headquarters in Boeotia. Unexpectedly, Philip was in a conciliatory mood. The two thousand Athenian prisoners were to be returned to the city without a ransom. The Macedonians would also burn the bodies of the fallen, and a guard of honor would convey their ashes to Athens. What could account for this unexpected show of kindness to a beaten enemy?

Athens had been saved by its ships, though no battle had been fought at sea. Ever since the naval action at Byzantium, Philip felt a renewed respect for the Athenian navy. In its own element it was still invincible, and the Piraeus was still a well-nigh impregnable base. He would no longer attempt to defeat Athens at sea. Instead, even as he extended a conciliatory hand toward Athens, Philip was devising plans that would harness Athenian naval power to his own purposes, along with other military forces of Greece.

Philip followed up his victory at Chaeronea not with an assault on Athens but with a summons to a peace conference at the Isthmus. At Corinth, surrounded by anxious envoys from Athens and the other cities, Philip created a new Hellenic League with an ancient goal: a holy war on the Persian Empire. The rhetoric was religious: Xerxes' burning of the Greek temples was at last to be avenged. Philip told the cities that he expected them to contribute troops and ships. Isocrates would have been happy to see his dream fulfilled, but he did not live to see it. He had died at the age of ninety-eight, just as the news of Philip's victory at Chaeronea was brought to Athens.

One casualty of the new alliance against Persia was Athens' Second

Maritime League, founded almost forty years before. Philip could brook no hegemony alongside his own, so Athens must free its remaining maritime allies from their oaths of allegiance. Even here he was willing to make concessions. In view of Athens' vital role in patrolling the seas, Philip recognized the city's right to retain its essential territories abroad: the island of Samos with its Athenian cleruchs; the holy isle of Delos; and Skyros, Lemnos, and Imbros on the route to the Hellespont. So along with the other allied delegates at the Isthmus, the Athenians swore to follow Philip in making war on Persia and on all those who broke the peace that Philip had established. With Greece now brought to heel, Philip returned north. Before attacking the territory of the Great King, he planned to preside at his daughter's wedding.

At Athens the citizens awaited the royal order that would levy ships and men for the war in Asia. Long accustomed not to follow but to lead, the prospect of obeying Philip as commander in chief was galling. Yet it was technically no worse than the subordination of their ancestors to Spartan leadership in the alliance against Xerxes, and infinitely better than their subjection to Sparta after the Peloponnesian War. Looking back over the years of struggle against Philip, Demosthenes pondered the wisdom of the course he had pursued.

"If the lightning that struck us was too great not only for us but for the rest of Greece, what were we to do? One might as well put the blame for a shipwreck on the ship's captain, even after he has taken all precautions and fitted his vessel with everything he believes will guarantee its safety. Then the ship encounters a storm, and its rig is damaged or utterly destroyed. But I was not captain of a ship, nor was I in command as general, nor could I rule fate. No, it was fate that ruled all."

Instead of mobilization orders, earthshaking news arrived from Macedon. King Philip was dead, struck down during a public procession by a lone assassin. The killer, one of Philip's own household officers, brought a concealed dagger to the royal wedding celebration and stabbed the king as he rode by. On hearing the news, the Athenians voted public ceremonies of thanksgiving. A jubilant Demosthenes almost convinced the Assembly that Philip's death meant the end of Macedonian power. He proved a poor prophet.

Within months a Macedonian army marched once again into Greece. At its head, astride the legendary stallion named Bucephalas, rode Alexander, the son of Philip. Though just twenty years old, the new king had already eliminated threats to his succession at home. He was now moving at high speed to reassert his control over Greece. Alexander aspired to be not another Philip, but rather a second Achilles. Hoping to absorb the fiery spirit of his hero, he slept with a copy of Homer's *Iliad* under his pillow. In imitation of the eternally youthful Achilles, he even declined to grow that indispensable symbol of Greek manhood: a beard. The royal moods, too, were Achillean, swinging unpredictably from warmhearted enthusiasm to murderous wrath.

Athens had the good luck to be one of Alexander's enthusiasms. The new king revered the city as the central hearth of Hellenic culture. He especially loved Athenian tragedies and took scrolls of Aeschylus, Sophocles, and Euripides to read while on campaign. Not only did he respect Athens, he sincerely courted the city's friendship and approval. Athenians had been slow to acknowledge him as their overlord. But Alexander gave a friendly welcome to the envoys that brought him the Assembly's apology. The message was carried not by Demosthenes, who prudently stayed at home, but by a bluff and hearty citizen named Demades, a shipwright and ferryman who had lately taken up a career as an orator.

For all his boyish looks and ways, Alexander made it clear from the start that he would not loosen his father's iron grip on Greece. He summoned the Greeks back to the Isthmus, where they renewed their oaths of loyalty to the Hellenic League, and to Alexander himself as hegemon, commander supreme on land and sea. Alexander in turn pledged himself to the league's goals: peace in Greece and war in Asia. He had inherited Philip's dreams of eastern conquest along with Philip's army. After two years of campaigning, Alexander had secured his frontiers in Europe all the way to the Danube River in the far north. The time was ripe for his invasion of the Persian Empire.

Alexander needed ships to transport his army across the Hellespont, and he ordered his Greek allies to provide the ferry service. Athens' share of the burden was light: only twenty triremes, leaving the main fleet untouched at the Piraeus. Alexander considered Athens most valuable to him as a free and self-sustaining maritime ally. The famous navy would assist his impe-rial ambitions by policing the seas and suppressing piracy—at Athenian expense, not his. To keep a watchful eye on Greece in his absence, Alexander left his father's old general Antipater behind him as regent in Macedonia.

As the third year of Alexander's reign began, the 20 Athenian triremes voyaged to the Hellespont to join an allied Greek fleet of 160. Alexander's forces crowded the northern shore in tens of thousands: foot soldiers, cav-alry, engineers, armorers, bakers, doctors, prophets, heralds, day runners, grooms, camp followers, and slaves. No Persians troops appeared on the Asiatic shore. No Persian ships blocked the channel. Alexander would cross the Hellespont unopposed.

After sacrificing to the gods, Alexander performed the symbolic actions of steering the first trireme across and casting a spear into the soil of Asia from the deck of his ship. Then he leaped ashore, Achilles incarnate. Once the commander in chief had enjoyed his theatrical moment, the army could follow. The main crossing route ran from Sestos to Abydos, like Xerxes' bridges of long ago, where the channel between the two continents narrows to about a mile. In these familiar waters the Athenians plied back and forth across the swiftly rushing stream, carrying Alexander's army on the first stage of its immense journey into the heart of the Great King's empire. Freighters were also pressed into service, their holds packed full of men and provisions. It was impossible to employ sails in the narrow Hellespont, so the triremes took the freighters in tow.

When all had crossed, Alexander sent his fleet south under the command of a Macedonian admiral named Nicanor. Unlike Xerxes, Alexander made no effort to coordinate the movements of his army and navy. The land forces struck inland, bearing the entire brunt of Alexander's mission of conquest. Meanwhile the fleet cruised independently along the coast of Asia Minor to a rendezvous at the port city of Ephesus. By the time Alexander rejoined his ships, he had already triumphed over the Persian cavalry at the Granicus River, accepted the surrender of Sardis, and enrolled newly liberated Greek cities in the Hellenic League. With his customary flamboyance, Alexander sent Persian shields from Granicus as trophies to Athens, where they were hung in a long row on the east front of the Parthenon.

On a darker note, the victory at the Granicus also netted hundreds of

Athenian prisoners. These men had fought as mercenaries in the Persian ranks. Furious with the "traitors," Alexander shipped them off to do hard labor in the mines of Thrace. Along his march Alexander would encounter many more Athenian soldiers of fortune, including a younger son of the great Iphicrates.

Had Athens possessed the funds to keep them at home, these men could have restored the fortunes of the Athenian navy. The eastward trickle that began with Themistocles, however, had become a torrent after the Peloponnesian War, and the loss of so many potential commanders was an irreparable tragedy. But it was not only Persian gold that lured ambitious young Athenians across the Aegean. Given the Assembly's relentless attacks on its democratically elected generals, and the punitive record of Athenian juries and review boards, service to the Great King had become less hazardous than service to their own fellow citizens. Alexander's experiences proved that Athenian families were still producing tactical geniuses and valiant warriors. If they were absent from the city in the crises that lay ahead, the blame lay with Athens itself.

After the Ephesians opened their gates, Alexander advanced to his next target: the ancient metropolis of Miletus. Scouts reported that a Persian armada was in the offing, some four hundred ships from Phoenicia and Cyprus. At all costs they must be kept out of Miletus Harbor and prevented from reinforcing the Great King's garrison of Greek mercenaries. The veteran Macedonian general Parmenio urged the king to challenge the new arrivals in a naval battle. He said that he had seen an eagle near the Greek ships beached on the island of Lade, outside Miletus Harbor, and claimed it as a portent of victory. Parmenio was the father of the young admiral Nicanor and may have hoped to give his son a moment of glory. Alexander rejected the idea outright. Like Philip before him, he would use actions on land to defeat enemies at sea. Despite his appointment of Nicanor as admiral, all Alexander's trust still rested on his phalanx, his cavalry, and his engineers.

Alexander merely commanded the Athenians and other naval allies to crowd their ships together and block the harbor mouth at Miletus. He himself had already neutralized the enemy fleet by the simple expedient of occupying all landing places anywhere near Miletus. Unable to beach their

EARLY CAMPAIGNS OF
ALEXANDER THE GREAT, 336–331 B.C.

Black Sea

THRACE

MACEDON

• Pella

Hellespont

Granicus R.

• Troy

PERSIAN EMPIRE

Aegean Sea

GREECE

• Chaeronea
• Thebes

• Athens

Isthmus

• Sardis

Ephesus •
Meander R.
• Tralles

• Miletus

CARIA

Halicarnassus •

CRETE

Mediterranean Sea

© 2009 Jeffrey L. Ward

0 Miles _____ 100

0 Kilometers _____ 100

ships, the stymied Persians cruised away in search of fresh water, food, and campsites. Once they had left the scene of action, Alexander struck.

The Macedonian siege engines rolled forward to batter the walls and towers, followed by an irresistible rush of Macedonian troops. As the defense of Miletus collapsed, desperate Greek soldiers attempted to escape across the water using their hollow shields as skiffs and their hands as paddles. Most were killed. The survivors surrendered from a rocky islet, the site of their last stand. The Persian armada, outmaneuvered and impotent, vanished away to the south. Alexander soon learned that it had gone to ground within the circular harbor of Halicarnassus. In that historic city of Artemisia and Herodotus, the naval forces of King Darius would again try to halt Alexander's headlong advance.

With Miletus in hand and the Persian fleet in retreat, Alexander saw no reason to go on paying hard-won money to his Greek crews. At two hundred men per trireme, he had almost as many mariners as soldiers. So the king dismissed the levy of ships from the Hellenic League, except for the Athenians. They would perform one final service. As Alexander and his army marched through the rough terrain of Caria toward their next target, the city of Halicarnassus, Macedonian engineers loaded the wooden siege machinery onto the decks of the twenty Athenian triremes. It took no more than a day for the crews to row south to their rendezvous point near Halicarnassus, where they set the heavy equipment ashore.

Alexander ignored the Persian fleet in the harbor at Halicarnassus, making all his assaults from the landward side. The commander of the city's garrison was an Athenian mercenary named Ephialtes, perhaps a descendant of the famous democratic reformer. Though he fought with daring, Alexander prevailed. When the fall of Halicarnassus seemed inevitable, the Persian fleet slipped out of the harbor under cover of darkness and fled to distant havens. Next morning Alexander marched into the city. With winter coming on, he sent the Athenian triremes with the siege equipment north to Tralles on the Meander River. From Tralles the Athenians turned their backs on the historic Macedonian adventure and voyaged home, their duty done.

Over the next three years reports of Alexander's amazing progress reached Athens. The conqueror cut the famous knot at Gordium, defeated King Darius and his field army at Issus in Syria, and took the Phoenician cities of Tyre and Gaza by siege. Egypt welcomed Alexander as liberator and pharaoh; the oracle of Zeus Ammon in the desert hailed him as son of the god. Amid these triumphs Alexander began to show a new and ominous interest in the sea. He assembled a fleet of Phoenician and other ships to give his Macedonian commanders some much-needed naval experience. West of the Nile delta he laid out the new city of Alexandria, a future cosmopolitan capital, port, and center of learning that would one day surpass both Athens and the Piraeus in grandeur and power.

When the Athenians heard that Alexander had returned from Egypt to Tyre to prepare an expedition into the heart of the Persian Empire, they sent envoys on board the *Paralos* to seek the release of the Athenian prisoners taken at Granicus. The king had already turned down one appeal: he was keeping these Athenians as hostages for the good behavior of Athens itself. Knowing Alexander's obsessions, this time the Assembly actually found a citizen named Achilles to deliver the petition. The *Paralos* arrived as the Macedonian army was about to start its long march to Susa. In a mellow mood Alexander unbent and granted the Athenian prisoners their freedom.

As the crew of the *Paralos* rowed homeward, happy with their success, Alexander left the Mediterranean behind. He met and crushed the army of Darius III at Gaugamela near the Tigris River, a victory that made Alexander, in effect, the new Great King. At Susa the Macedonians discovered long-lost Athenian marble statues, ancient loot from the Acropolis carried off by Xerxes. During the Macedonian victory banquet at Persepolis, a beautiful Athenian camp follower named Thaïs incited Alexander to put the great palace of the Persian kings to the torch. Thus an Athenian—and a woman—exacted final payment for Xerxes' burning of Athens.

But the conqueror could not rest from conquest. Beyond Persia, far beyond, the insatiable Alexander pursued roads and tracks into Afghanistan and the Hindu Kush. Like a storm blowing away over the rim of the world, he and his army passed eastward toward India. With their disappearance, a deep peace settled down over the Aegean Sea. The shadows departed, the sun shone, and Athens began to bud and grow again.

Taking full advantage of this halcyon spell, the Athenians step by step restored the fabric of their navy. As long as Alexander's charmed life continued, they could scarcely hope to change the balance of power. But Athenians were as patient as they were energetic. Whenever an opportunity

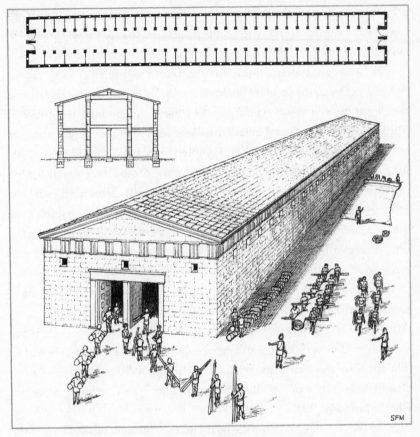

PHILO'S ARSENAL

presented itself, they meant to be ready. New ships, new naval installations, and new training programs would ultimately help restore Athens to its traditional place as ruler of the sea.

During these years the most influential man in Athens was neither an orator nor a general but a financial minister named Lycurgus. His severe and incorruptible character commanded universal respect, as did his position as hereditary priest of Poseidon. Carefully husbanding the city's revenues, mainly from maritime trade, Lycurgus first filled the depleted treasury and then embarked on a truly Periclean campaign to renew, strengthen, and beautify Athens. The gods received their due: for Athena, a new Panathenaic stadium; for Apollo, a temple in the Agora; for Dionysus, a theater

rebuilt in shining marble; and for the goddesses at Eleusis, a vast new pil-
lared hall of initiation. Yet with so much attention paid to the spiritual well-
being of the city, Lycurgus was equally mindful of its naval sinews.

The Lycurgan program directed money toward the military training of the
Athenian *epheboi,* the cadets of hoplite class. Under Lycurgus' efficient regime
they spent their first year on duty in the Piraeus—manning the fortress on
Munychia Hill, guarding the naval base, and learning to row in the triremes
of their tribes. The second year was devoted to garrison duty in the frontier
fortresses. The ceremonies and processions of these fine young men delighted
the Athenians. So too did the annual regattas. Crews of cadets from each tribe
raced in triremes around the perimeter of the Piraeus promontory, from the
start in Cantharus Harbor, past the tomb of Themistocles, to the finish at the
little harbor of Munychia. Spectators who watched the start could then run
across town to witness the end of the race and hail the winning trireme.

In these years the Athenians also made a thorough review of their ships.
Ever since the end of the Peloponnesian War, more than sixty years before,
Athens had been losing ground to other naval powers in the area of innova-
tive design. The fast trireme still ruled supreme at Athens, just as it had in
Themistocles' day. But while the naval architects of Athens held aloof from
change, new types of warships began to appear in Carthage, Syracuse,
Rhodes, and Phoenicia.

Now the Assembly ordered the board of naval architects to modernize the
navy with new ship types, larger and heavier than the trireme. The sweeping
campaign led to the introduction of the quadrireme and quinquereme. Their
Greek names *tetreres* ("rowed by four") and *penteres* ("rowed by five") derived
from the novel system of manning the oars. In the trireme each man pulled
his own oar, and three oarsmen in echelon formed the basic unit of the rowing crew. Within the quadrireme the unit was reduced to two oars, but the
length of the oar increased and two men rowed on each oar. In the quinquereme five rowers were fitted into the unit by multiple manning of oars.
More men could thus row in a given space, and the ship could be built more
heavily yet maintain a speed comparable to that of a trireme.

In these new ships, only half the rowers needed any experience or skill.
While one rower maneuvered the oar handle, his partner simply provided
brute force to drive the oar through the water. The oars were worked

through an enclosed oar box instead of the trireme's open and vulnerable rowing frame. The crews grew in size: a quinquereme employed 300 rowers compared to the trireme's 170. The building of these superships bore witness to Athens' determination to retain the rule of the sea. Thanks to Lycurgus, Athens eventually boasted a navy of 360 triremes, 50 quadriremes, and 2 quinqueremes, plus troop carriers, horse carriers, and triakontors.

All these activities brought renewed life to the Piraeus. In the years after Lycurgus instituted his new financial regime, the naval base once again provided steady employment for thousands of citizens who found work as administrators, inspectors, guards, scribes, craftsmen, and crew members. The resident aliens who had established themselves at the Piraeus as merchants or manufacturers also prospered. Some gave generous contributions every year to support the finances of their adopted city. Others beautified the Piraeus with temples of their own gods.

To house the growing fleet of warships, Lycurgus and his successors at the public treasury provided funds for the building of yet more shipsheds. At the same time they repaired the Long Walls and the other fortifications. The greatest single achievement of the Lycurgan program, however, was the completion of a gargantuan building to house the sails and rigging from the warships. Later known as "Philo's Arsenal," its proper name was the Skeuotheke ("Storehouse for the Hanging Gear"). Never had canvas and cordage received such a palatial home. Like the Parthenon, Philo's Arsenal was built in the Doric style, but it surpassed in size any temple in Greece. Seventeen years in the building, the Arsenal extended from the gate at the west corner of Hippodamus' Agora to the shipsheds of Zea Harbor. Philo himself, who had also designed the new hall of initiation for the Eleusinian Mysteries, felt so proud of his naval arsenal that he wrote a book about it. No such sign of respect or public interest had been accorded the more prestigious Parthenon on the Acropolis.

The Arsenal was plain; the walls of soft yellowish Piraeus limestone were ornamented only by gray marble frames for the doors and windows. The corners were given a touch of additional grandeur and strength by ashlar blocks that projected beyond the surface of the walls. Down each long side ran a row of thirty-four small windows, set high up under the eaves of the low-pitched roof. The roof itself was covered with tens of thousands of Corinthian tiles.

On entering through double doors sheathed in gleaming bronze, one passed immediately from the glare and uproar of Hippodamus' Agora to a vast quiet space, cool and dimly lit. Thirty feet overhead the wooden rafters almost vanished in the shadows. To the left and right were bays, like stalls in a barn, enclosed by wooden railings and filled with equipment. Within the bays were wooden shelves, chests, and cabinets to hold the sails and rigging for 134 warships. Despite its immense size, Philo's Arsenal could meet less than half of the navy's storage requirements. The cabinets had openwork sides, so stored items could dry quickly if brought in wet. Space was also found for various odds and ends—anchors, chains, and the thin oval-shaped plaques of painted marble that served as eyes for the ships. Except at noon when the sun stood overhead, the windows high up in the walls admitted shafts of light, along with ventilation to prevent rot or mildew.

Finally, stretching from end to end was the longest covered walk in the Greek world, a spacious aisle twenty feet wide and four hundred feet long. Through this central aisle Athenian citizens could stroll as on a promenade, conversing, gazing, and marveling at the magnificent array of naval gear. Their pride in the Arsenal, like the Arsenal itself, was the mark of a people who valued their past but whose eyes were fixed firmly on the future.

Among Lycurgus' other building projects was a new gymnasium at the Lyceum. In the year after Alexander became king, the philosopher Aristotle arrived in Athens and made the Lyceum his headquarters. His school of scientific, political, and ethical studies formed the brightest light in Athens' constellation of new undertakings. Aristotle was a northern Greek whose father had served as doctor to Philip of Macedon. He first came to Athens at the age of seventeen to study with Plato, in the days when Chabrias and Timotheus also frequented the Academy. Master and pupil did not see eye to eye. Plato nicknamed Aristotle "The Colt" and criticized his sardonic expression, incessant talking, and objectionable haircut. Aristotle eventually left Athens and for several years investigated marine life around a lagoon on Lesbos, laying the groundwork for his unprecedented scientific works of description and classification. In time he was called away from his octopi and barnacles to fill the most prestigious academic post on earth: tutor to the young prince Alexander of Macedon.

Now that his royal charge had grown up and left the nest, Aristotle was free to return to Athens. Morning and evening he walked through the groves and colonnades of the Lyceum, surrounded by young disciples. Occasionally a shipment of exotic zoological specimens arrived, gifts of Alexander to his old teacher. Unlike Plato's Academy, the Lyceum gave pride of place to practical and applied knowledge. Thus it happened that in the final years of the Athenian navy, ships and maritime matters (along with most other things under the sun) were subjected to a more searching formal study than ever before.

One of Aristotle's followers compiled a book called *Problems*. Some of the mysterious problems were maritime. "Why do ships seem to be more heavily loaded in harbor than out at sea?" And "Why is it that if anything (for example, an anchor) is thrown into the sea when it is rough, a calm ensues?" And again, "Why is it that sometimes vessels that are journeying over the sea in fine weather are swallowed up and disappear so completely that no wreckage even is washed up?"

For Aristotle, the prime example of energy overcoming inertia, and of living things imparting motion to inanimate ones, was the image of a crew dragging a ship down to the sea. One of his followers included a number of nautical questions in a book called *Mechanics*. "Why is it that those rowers who are in the middle of the ship move the ship most? Is it because the oar acts as a lever? The fulcrum then is the tholepin (for it remains in the same place); and the weight is the sea that the oar displaces; and the power that moves the lever is the rower." This particular observation related particularly to the new quadriremes and quinqueremes, where the oars were double-manned and the rower seated inboard did indeed have more leverage. "Why is it that the rudder, being small and at the extreme end of the ship, has such power that vessels of great burden can be moved by a small steering oar and the strength of one man only gently exerted? Is it because the rudder, too, is a lever and the steersman works it?" And again, "Why is it that the higher the yardarm is raised, the quicker does a vessel travel with the same sail and in the same breeze? Is it because the mast is a lever, and the socket in which it is fixed, the fulcrum, and the weight which it has to move is the boat, and the motive power is the wind in the sail?"

Aristotle's favorite student was Theophrastus, his faithful companion from the years of wading and waterside research on Lesbos. In his monumental *Enquiry into Plants* Theophrastus collected the lore of shipwrights concerning the trees traditionally used in shipbuilding and listed the species most appropriate for the various parts of a trireme. His researches even included the folk wisdom of woodsmen concerning the best seasons of the year for cutting different types of timber, and the direction of slope—north-facing and shady, or south-facing and exposed to the sun—that would produce the best wood. In his treatise Theophrastus reported a miracle. An oar carved from olive wood was left propped up with its handle resting in a pot. The pot contained some damp earth, and after a few days the oar suddenly came back to life and sprouted green leaves.

Yet another follower of Aristotle, a disciple whose name is now forgotten, wrote about weather and atmospheric phenomena in a work called *Meteorology*. He noted that rainbows occurred at sea when sunlight struck the spray kicked up by a trireme's oars. "The rainbow that is seen when oars are raised out of the sea involves the same relative positions as a rainbow in the sky, but its color is more like that around lamps, being purple rather than red." In terms of scientific study the Athenian navy was inspiring more focused inquiry than at any other time in its existence.

During these years Aristotle himself was working on his *Politics* and *Nicomachean Ethics*. At the end of the latter work he wrote, "From the collection of constitutions we must examine what sort of thing preserves and what sort of thing destroys cities." In Aristotle's view, one of the destructive things was sea power. He identified four species of maritime people—those involved with triremes, like the Athenians; ferrymen, like the islanders of Tenedos; traders, as at Aegina and Chios; and fishermen, like those at Byzantium and Tarentum. Some harm to the city might arise even from seaborne trade, with the influx of foreigners and exotic merchandise that it promoted. The real enemies of a well-ordered state, however, were not merchantmen but triremes. Aristotle agreed with Plato on very few things, but the danger of thalassocracy was certainly among them.

Among the eleven stages or revolutions in the life of the Athenian constitution, Aristotle called the seventh "the constitution to which Aristides pointed and which Ephialtes accomplished by overthrowing the Areopagus. In this the city made its greatest mistakes, because of the demagogues and its rule of the sea." Geography played a role in national character. "At Athens there is a difference between the dwellers in the city itself and those in Piraeus; the latter are more emphatically democratic in outlook."

At the end of his *Politics* Aristotle considered the importance of the sea for a well-ordered state. A city seeking greatness, or simply security, might be compelled to build up a navy. In that case Aristotle concluded that the only safe course was to exclude rowers and other mariners from participation in the city's political affairs. "The large population associated with a mob of seamen need not swell the citizenship of the state, of which they should form no part. The troops that are carried on board are free men belonging to the hoplite infantry. They are in sovereign authority and have control over the crews. A plentiful supply of rowers is sure to exist wherever the outlying dwellers and agricultural laborers are numerous."

Aristotle here passed from a condemnation of maritime empire—no novelty in Athens, even among patriots like Isocrates and Demosthenes—to a more dangerous claim. Naval power was compatible with good government only if the nautical, democratic element could be suppressed. Walking under the trees of the Lyceum, Aristotle planted in the minds of wealthy young Athenians the conviction that a "trireme democracy" was inevitably an evil to itself and others. With or without Aristotle, such treasonous ideas were swiftly gaining ground among the city's upper classes.

While Aristotle's students were collecting the constitutions of existing city-states, the Athenians were preparing an expedition to found a new city of their own—a colony in the Adriatic. In recent years Athens and the rest of Greece had suffered bad harvests and food shortages. The Hellespont and Egypt lay under the thumb of the Macedonians, who might at any time cut off the vital shipments of grain. As war clouds gathered in the east, Athens felt once again the lure of the golden west. This time they aimed not at Sicily but at the great Adriatic Sea, running wide and free from the heel of Italy northward to within sight of the Alps. With this bold and (for Athens) unusual plan to found a colony, the city's great rejuvenation reached its high-water mark.

The colony's purpose was to secure Athens' grain supply "for all time to come." Its harbor would offer a safe emporium for Greeks and non-Greeks alike and provide a base for operations against marauding Etruscan pirates.

The Athenian colonists would keep the expedition's fourteen ships to form the nucleus of their own fleet: eight triremes and quadriremes, two horse transports, and four triakontors.

The Assembly appointed a citizen named Miltiades to lead the mission. The choice of this man symbolized the return of the old heroic days. Seven generations earlier his ancestor Miltiades had led the Athenians to victory at Marathon. An even earlier Miltiades had founded the famous colony among the Thracians on the north side of the Hellespont. Because of the high priority set on the Adriatic mission, the Assembly ordered the Council to go down to the Piraeus and hold their sessions on the jetty itself every day until the fleet departed. Anyone who impeded the expedition was to be fined ten thousand drachmas, payable to the goddess Athena herself.

One member of the expedition was Lysicrates, trierarch of the *Stephanophoria* ("Bearer of the Crown"). He had recently made his mark on Athens by erecting one of the loveliest monuments in the city: a victory trophy for a boys' chorus that he had sponsored at one of the annual festivals. The song that his winning team had performed took as its theme the mythical triumph of the young god Dionysus over a shipload of Etruscan pirates. Lysicrates' monument stood in the shadow of the Acropolis, and its ring of slender Corinthian columns provided a delicate counterpoint to the massive Doric order of the Parthenon on the high rock above it. Atop the columns ran a circular frieze carved with the figures of the pirates who had kidnapped Dionysus and as a punishment were transformed into dolphins. The grotesque metamorphosis was shown through strange creatures with human legs and dolphin heads, plunging into the sea. With his service in the colonizing mission, Lysicrates would have an opportunity to deal with the contemporary descendants of those legendary Etruscan pirates in a much more practical way.

The expedition to the Adriatic had only a little time to create an Athenian stronghold overseas. As Miltiades and his fellow emigrants were pursuing their way west, momentous events in the east overshadowed their venture. The Macedonian army, after six years of wars and wanderings in lands almost unknown to the Greeks, had suddenly reappeared in Persia. Alexander was back, convinced now of his own divinity and determined that the Greeks should do his bidding. Athens would need all its newfound strength to resist him.

CHAPTER 21

The Last Battle

[324–322 B.C.]

Walls and ships are nothing without men living together inside them.

—Sophocles

ALEXANDER LOST NO TIME IN MAKING HIS PRESENCE FELT. At Olympia that summer an emissary from the king made a most unwelcome proclamation to the Greeks who had gathered for games of the 114th Olympiad. It was the will of the king that all Greek cities should take back their exiles, restore them to citizenship, and then give them back their lands. The Exiles Decree was intended to dissipate the hordes of mercenaries adrift in Alexander's new dominions. But the decree violated the autonomy of the Greeks. Alexander had forgotten by now that they were nominally his allies; viewed from his imperial capitals at Susa and Babylon, they looked like nothing more than distant subjects. To provide a sort of legal basis for his autocratic act, the new Great King also told the Greeks that they could now worship him as a god.

Demosthenes brought the bad news back to Athens from Olympia. Quite apart from the horde of undesirables—traitors, criminals, and troublemakers—that would be forced on the Athenians, the decree threatened to rob them of Samos. The rich island had been liberated from Persian control by Timotheus more than forty years before (the biggest of all the lobsters that fell into his famous pot) and held tenaciously by Athens ever since. So even at the risk of triggering a war with the divine Alexander, the Athenians ordered to sea that bulwark of democracy, the *Paralos.* The flagship of the navy reached Samos before the exiles returned. And as the elated Samian oligarchs sailed back to Samos to reclaim their estates under the terms of the decree, an Athenian general took them prisoner as they landed and sent them to Athens. Samos was almost the only remnant of maritime empire left to the Athenians, and they would defy the world and the gods to keep it.

If Alexander had his way, the Athenian navy would soon be overshadowed by new Macedonian fleets. Ever since his trek back from India, the king's head had been full of ships. In his early campaigns Alexander had given scant attention to the sea. Now he launched ships to explore the Caspian Sea and the Arabian Gulf, started an immense new harbor at Babylon, and contemplated a circumnavigation of Africa. Alexander even dreamed of building one thousand new warships, all bigger than triremes, for an expedition against Carthage and the lands of the western Mediterranean. There were, after all, many worlds, and he had not yet completely conquered even one.

Early the next summer, one year after promulgating the Exiles Decree, Alexander held a conference with his new admiral Nearchus to discuss these naval initiatives. It was to be his last act as king. Already feverish following a heavy bout of drinking, further sickened by the steamy summer heat of Babylon, and perhaps the victim of poison poured into his cup by someone near the throne, Alexander fell mortally ill. He died at the age of thirty-six without naming an heir.

The news of his death at first provoked incredulity in Athens. Demades exclaimed, "Alexander dead? Impossible! The whole world would smell of his corpse!" Once the report from Babylon was confirmed, the majority of citizens swiftly voted that Athens should lead a war of liberation against Alexander's successors. The landowners and other rich Athenians opposed the war but were outnumbered. Messengers departed at once to seek the support of other Greek cities. The Assembly's resolution rang with the same idealistic fervor that had motivated Themistocles in the face of Xerxes' invasion: "The Athenian people recognize it as their duty to risk their lives and treasure and ships in the cause of the common freedom of Greece." Cities throughout central Greece and the Peloponnese rallied to the call.

At first all went well. The Macedonian regent Antipater attempted to crush the uprising, but he was no Alexander, nor even a Xerxes. Under Athenian leadership, the Greeks successfully held the pass at Thermopylae against the invaders. Helpless to deal with the rebels alone, Antipater appealed to the Macedonian generals in Asia for reinforcements and a fleet. The ultimate test of the new Greek alliance, and of Athenian sea power, would come in the following spring.

Pressing forward with the war effort, the Athenians resolved to equip themselves with two hundred new quadriremes and forty new triremes. That winter every Athenian citizen under the age of forty was conscripted for service. Three tribal regiments would defend the frontiers of Attica. The other seven prepared for campaigns abroad. As the warm weather returned, armies of Macedonians began to cross the Hellespont into Europe, preparing to reinforce Antipater's troops and crush the rebellion in Greece. In an effort to stop these troops, the Athenians launched a fleet of triremes and quadriremes and sent it northeast across the Aegean. Of that year's board of generals, Phocion alone could claim experience of a naval battle, and that had been at Naxos, more than half a century before. As he was now almost eighty, it seemed best to send a younger man. Euetion from the *deme* or township of Cephisia, an aristocrat and a former cavalry commander, was given charge of the war at sea.

If the Athenians had hoped for the same happy outcome that had met Phocion's expedition to Byzantium eighteen years before, when he faced down Alexander's father Philip, they were deluding themselves. The days of Macedonian timidity at sea were long gone. Arriving in the Hellespont, Euetion and his fleet encountered a force commanded by a Macedonian general named Cleitus. A battle was fought in the familiar waters off Abydos, and the Macedonians were victorious. Euetion managed to escape with the bulk of the fleet, but he left many Athenians behind, stranded or captured. Loyal friends of Athens in the city of Abydos rescued as many of these men as they could, gave them money for the voyage back to Athens, and sent them home.

Cleitus then gathered a fleet of 240 ships and with this immense force left the Hellespont to seek the remnant of the Athenian navy. Despite the hundreds of empty hulls resting in the shipsheds at the Piraeus and the grandiose shipbuilding proposal of the previous year, the Athenians in this moment of supreme crisis were able to provide crews for only 170 ships.

ATHENS VERSUS
THE SUCCESSORS OF ALEXANDER, 323–322 B.C.

Black Sea

MACEDON

Pella •

Hellespont

Crannon ✕

Aegean Sea

ALEXANDER'S
EMPIRE

ECHINADES
ISLANDS

• Athens

SAMOS

OLYMPIA

CALAURIA

AMORGOS ✕

Mediterranean Sea

0 Miles 100

0 Kilometers 200

© 2009 Jeffrey L. Ward

Preference was given to the quadriremes, virtually all of which were manned
and launched. The two quinqueremes were dispatched also. The rest of
Euetion's force was made up of triremes.

Their course took them to the waters off Amorgos, a narrow rugged
island on the farthest eastern edge of the Cyclades. Amorgos was no match
in size, wealth, or fame to Naxos, its neighbor to the west. However, it possessed on its western coast the finest natural harbor in the archipelago,
ringed by fine beaches. Perched on a hill overlooking the harbor, the fortified settlement of Minoa was a reminder of ancient Cretan sea kings and
their vanished thalassocracy. Amorgos had been tributary to Athens in
imperial days and loyal through the years of the Second Maritime League,
yet up to now it had scarcely figured in Athenian naval history.

When the Macedonian fleet loomed up over the horizon, Euetion arrayed his own fleet for battle—the greatest number of ships to fight for Athens since the debacle at Aegospotami. Even so the Macedonian superiority in numbers was overwhelming. Equally daunting was the reputation of the soldiers on their decks, members of the most ruthlessly effective fighting force on earth. There was a brief clash, and some of Cleitus' ships managed to overturn three or four Athenian triremes. Before the Macedonians broke through the Athenian line or surrounded their fleet, and before the hopeless contest could turn into a slaughter, Euetion signaled from his flagship to Cleitus' that the Athenians were ready to surrender.

Over the last century and a half Athenian fleets had been ambushed in Egypt, annihilated at Syracuse, chased back to their base at Notium, and captured on shore at Aegospotami. The surrender at Amorgos marked the first time in history that an Athenian general had voluntarily yielded to an enemy fleet. Themistocles or Phormio or Chabrias would never have conceded victory without doing his best for Athens in a mighty struggle first. What had changed?

Athenians of the upper classes had opposed the war of liberation from the first. And there was at least one wealthy citizen on board every ship: the trierarch. The long odds that the Athenians faced at Amorgos would not have intimidated the men who held command during the Persian and Peloponnesian wars, but the generals and trierarchs at Amorgos had approached the battle with no will to win or even to fight. Somehow in the aftermath of surrender Euetion managed to convince Cleitus that the Athenians not only conceded the victory but would never again challenge the Macedonians at sea. Nothing short of such a promise could have justified Cleitus' action after the battle: instead of claiming prizes, he allowed his enemies to take their damaged ships in tow and depart.

Without Macedonian harassment or escort, the Athenians left the scene of their defeat in full force. Ahead was the voyage back to the Piraeus. It was a long row home with heavy hearts among the majority who had voted for the war. Did they comfort themselves with hopes that Alexander's successors would treat Athens as Alexander himself had done? Or that the navy would rise again in months or years to come?

A false report preceded them across the Aegean—a report of victory. The

Athenian triremes had been seen after the battle with their damaged ships in tow, which was ordinarily a sign of the winning fleet. The first man at Athens to hear the rumor put a victory wreath on his head and rode through the city, shouting the glad tidings to his fellow citizens. In an ecstasy of joy, the Assembly ordered sacrifices to the gods and ceremonies of thanksgiving. The euphoria lasted two or three days, until the great fleet arrived at the Piraeus to tell the true story.

The confrontation with the Macedonian forces on land mirrored the failure at sea. The armies met at Crannon in Thessaly, where a narrow victory for the Macedonians precipitated a complete surrender by the Greeks. Shortly after this debacle Cleitus' fleet, fresh from its victories in the Hellespont and at Amorgos, caught the squadron of Athenian warships operating in western waters and destroyed them near the Echinades Islands. Even without Philip or Alexander, the Macedonians had been able to master the ancient city-states of Greece.

The Assembly sent Phocion and Demades and Xenocrates, the head of the Academy, to ask Antipater about terms: a war hero, an orator, and a philosopher to negotiate the fate of a once-great city. Antipater demanded payment of an indemnity equal to the full cost of the war, the handing over of Demosthenes and other enemies of Macedon, and the evacuation of Samos. The thetes of the *demos,* defined as all citizens with a net worth less than two thousand drachmas, were to be expelled from Athens. The wealthier citizens who remained must surrender the fort on Munychia Hill in the Piraeus to a Macedonian garrison.

The three envoys had expected very different terms. They accepted the exile of the thetes, but protested desperately against the loss of Samos and the presence of a Macedonian garrison on Attic soil. Antipater backed off to the extent of referring the case of Samos to the new king, Alexander's half brother Philip Arrhidaeus. As for the occupation of the Piraeus, the Athenian protest met with laughter. The headquarters of the legendary Athenian navy was a far more strategic stronghold for the Macedonian conquerors than the Acropolis or even the entire city of Athens. Antipater had no need to destroy the naval base or burn the ships. The exile of the troublesome thetes would guarantee the end of Athenian sea power, and its material remains could be useful to the successors of Alexander.

So the envoys returned to Athens with terms of surrender that gave up Athenian independence and, for all practical purposes, Athenian identity. The incredible had happened. Almost three-fifths of the citizens—12,000 out of 21,000—failed to pass Antipater's test of wealth. They were the rabble, the mob, the radical democrats who were everywhere blamed for all the crimes of a restless, ambitious, and expansionist Athens. They were now to be banished for the good of all, not merely from Athens but for the most part from Greece itself.

Only now could the Athenians understand what had happened at Amorgos. They had saved their lives and most of their ships; they had experienced no defeat to match the horror of Syracuse or the totality of Aegospotami. Yet in the waters off Amorgos they had suffered a loss more costly and decisive than any other in their history. With good reason the Macedonians honored Cleitus as a god, a Poseidon, for overturning those few Athenian triremes. He had accomplished what neither Xerxes nor Lysander nor Philip had been able to achieve: the final defeat of the Athenian navy. In reality, however, Athens had been its own worst enemy. The judgment that Thucydides passed on the Athenians at the end of the Peloponnesian War applied in full force to their final collapse: "It was only because they destroyed themselves with their own internal strife that they were forced to surrender."

Land was to be provided for the exiles in Thrace, that harsh northern country that so many Athenians of previous generations had died trying to win. Helpless, the citizens packed up their households and made their way down to the Piraeus for the embarkation. All around hundreds of triremes and other warships still rested in the shipsheds, but their time was over. Without the harmony that had drawn all Athenians together for a common purpose, the ships were so many lifeless hulks of timber and pitch. At the harbor the exiled citizens and their families embarked for the long voyage to Thrace and their new homes. Many would never see Athens again.

As autumn came the depleted city celebrated the Mysteries at Eleusis, but the rites were marred by a terrible portent. One of the initiates who had waded into the sea to make a sacrifice was attacked and killed by a shark. On the nineteenth of Boedromion the city observed the anniversary of Salamis and the birthday of Athenian maritime supremacy. The triumphant Macedonians, either mocking, ignorant, or indifferent, chose to send a garrison to the Piraeus the following day. Armed with their long pikes, men who had followed Alexander the Great across the Persian Empire now established themselves as an army of occupation in the fort on Munychia Hill.

Macedonian troops hunted down Demosthenes, who had taken refuge in the sanctuary of Poseidon at Calauria. As the soldiers approached, Demosthenes stepped outside the precinct so as not to desecrate holy soil, then quickly drank poison that he had hidden in his pen. His suicide deprived the Macedonians of their chance to take revenge for his many speeches against Philip and Alexander. In the same year Aristotle died of natural causes. An age was ending.

When they surrendered to the Macedonians, the Athenians had more ships and a better-equipped naval base than ever before. Philo's Arsenal was still brand-new. Some mysterious spiritual essence, however, had vanished. As Nicias once reminded the Assembly, a trireme's crew could remain at the peak of performance for only a short time. For the Athenian ship of state, thanks to the unremitting effort and self-sacrifice of its people, the peak had been prolonged for over a century and a half. Now rule of the sea would pass to other city-states and empires: Rhodes, Carthage, Alexandria, Rome. As for the creative explosion called the Golden Age, it ended with the naval power on which it had been built. With the Athenian people divided and the Piraeus in foreign hands, the reign of Themistocles' navy reached its final day.

The gleaming city of marble and bronze still enshrines the memory of many heroes whose ashes lie buried in tombs along the Sacred Way. Thucydides set down a Funeral Oration delivered by Pericles for citizens who died in the Peloponnesian War. Near the end of his speech Pericles issued a challenge: "Famous men have the whole world as their memorial. It is not only the inscriptions on their graves in their own country that mark them out. No, in foreign lands also, not in any visible form but in people's hearts, their memory abides and grows. It is for you to try to be like them." Many have tried, chasing the same goals of democracy, liberty, and happiness that generations of Athenians pursued in their ships. Few can claim to have equaled their achievements; fewer still to have surpassed them.

CHRONOLOGY

All dates are B.C.

ca. 524 Birth of Themistocles. Athens is ruled by the tyrant Hippias and his brother Hipparchus, sons of the original tyrant Peisistratus.

ca. 521 Darius becomes Great King of Persia.

ca. 510 With Spartan aid the Athenians expel the tyrant Hippias and his family, who seek refuge in lands controlled by the Persians. Athens joins the alliance of Greek city-states led by Sparta.

508–507 Athenian lawgiver Cleisthenes initiates democratic reforms.

ca. 506 Hostilities flare up between Athenians and the islanders of Aegina.

THE PERSIAN WARS [499–449 B.C.]

ca. 499 Aristagoras of Miletus seeks aid among the Greeks for the revolt of Ionian cities from Persian rule. The Spartans decline, but the Athenians agree to send help.

ca. 498 Twenty Athenian warships, along with six triremes from Eretria, cross the Aegean and join the rebellious Ionians in an attack on the Persian provincial capital at Sardis. They burn the city but are beaten by a Persian force as they return to their ships. According to Greek tradition, King Darius swears to remember the Athenians.

ca. 494 The Persians suppress the Ionian revolt with a naval victory at Lade, followed by the capture of Miletus.

493–492 As eponymous archon of Athens, Themistocles persuades his fellow citizens to turn to the sea and fortify the promontory of the Piraeus in case the Persians invade Attica. During this initial phase the walls are built up to half the height that Themistocles intended.

ca. 492   Darius' first expedition against Greece ends in disaster when the Persian fleet is wrecked by violent winds off Mount Athos in the northern Aegean. Nonetheless the Persians add parts of Thrace and the kingdom of Macedon to their realm.

490   Wary of the northern approaches to Greece, Darius sends a second expedition directly across the Aegean Sea, including cavalry in horse carriers. The Persians capture Eretria, but their hopes of punishing Athens for its part in the burning of Sardis are dashed when Miltiades leads the Athenian hoplite army to victory on the plain at Marathon.

486   Darius prepares a third invasion of Greece but dies before it can be launched. He is succeeded by his son Xerxes, who is diverted from the plan to attack Athens by a series of revolts in the empire.

483–482   Themistocles takes advantage of a silver strike in the Athenian mines at Laurium and persuades the Assembly to devote the windfall to the building of a fleet. At his urging, one hundred new triremes are built. Within three years the Athenians have a fleet of two hundred triremes, the largest in the Greek world.

482   The Athenian statesman Aristides, who opposed Themistocles' shipbuilding proposal, is ostracized by vote of the citizens. He leaves Athens for a ten-year period of banishment, but is recalled in 480 B.C.

481   Xerxes leads an immense army westward from his capital at Susa to the city of Sardis. His engineers prepare bridges across the Hellespont and cut a canal through the peninsula at Mount Athos. The Spartans summon those Greeks who are willing to resist the Persians to a council at the Isthmus of Corinth. Themistocles attends as the delegate from Athens.

480   In early spring the Greeks take Themistocles' advice and transport an army north to the vale of Tempe, in the hope of blocking Xerxes as far forward as possible. When that line is given up, Themistocles uses the words of the Delphic Oracle to persuade the Athenians to evacuate Attica and put their entire trust in the navy or "Wooden Wall." Later in the

summer the Athenian fleet forms the backbone of Greek resistance at sea, defeating the Persians at Artemisium and Salamis.

479 While the Greek army deals with the Persian army that Xerxes left behind, the allied fleet carries war across the sea to Persian territory and destroys the Persian triremes at Mycale. The newly liberated Ionians are admitted to the Greek alliance. The Athenian general Xanthippus leads them in the capture of Sestos on the Hellespont.

478 Thanks to Themistocles, the Athenians rebuild their city walls despite Spartan recommendations to the contrary. The Athenian general Aristides follows the Spartan regent Pausanias with an Athenian squadron to Cyprus and then Byzantium, where the Ionians beg the Athenians to become their hegemon.

477 The Athenians and their allies establish the so-called Delian League. Athens will lead punitive campaigns against the Persian Empire, and the allies will contribute either ships or money. Aristides assesses the contributions. The Athenian general Cimon leads the first annual campaign, capturing the city of Eion on the Strymon River in Thrace.

476 Themistocles sponsors a performance of Phrynichus' *Phoenician Women* to remind the Athenians of his own contribution to the victory over the Persians.

ca. 475 Cimon makes a naval pilgrimage to Skyros, brings the island into the alliance, and returns to Athens with the bones of the mythical hero Theseus.

472 Though still in his twenties, Pericles, the son of Xanthippus, sponsors the first performance of Aeschylus' *Persians*.

ca. 466 After many successful campaigns, Cimon leads the allied fleet east to the Eurymedon River in southern Asia Minor and wins a victory over Persian forces on sea and land.

465 Xerxes dies. He is succeeded as Great King by his son Artaxerxes.

ca. 464 Ephialtes and Pericles lead Athenian naval expeditions to the eastern Mediterranean.

462–461   Ephialtes leads a democratic revolution in Athens, stripping powers away from the aristocratic council of the Areopagus.

461   Cimon, who opposed Ephialtes' reforms, is ostracized.

ca. 460   The Athenians lead an allied fleet first to Cyprus and then to Egypt, where they aid the native ruler Inarus in his revolt against the Persians.

THE FIRST PELOPONNESIAN WAR [459–446 B.C.]

459   While leading the Delian League in continued strikes against the Persian Empire, the Athenians embroil themselves in a new war with the Peloponnesian League and ultimately the Spartans themselves. This war in Greece is touched off when Megara withdraws from the Peloponnesian League and allies itself with Athens, thus providing the Athenian navy with new ports on both the Saronic and Corinthian gulfs.

458   Athenian fleets fight Corinthians and other enemies in the Saronic Gulf and take the island of Aegina, ending its autonomy.

457   Athenians build the Long Walls to the sea to secure the city's link to the port at the Piraeus. Athenian oligarchs intrigue with the Spartans to stop the construction, and the patriotic Athenian hoplites oppose the Spartan army at Tanagra in Boeotia to ensure that Athens shall remain free of outside interference.

456   As a reprisal for Spartan willingness to aid oligarchic traitors, Tolmides leads an expedition around the Peloponnese, striking many targets in a series of amphibious raids.

455   In the wake of Tolmides' successful expedition, the Athenians send a fleet west under the command of Pericles. At about this time the sculptor Phidias raises a gigantic bronze statue of Athena on the Acropolis

454   Pericles' second campaign in the west is cut short by news of defeat in Egypt, after six years of lucrative collaboration with Inarus. Athenians begin to inscribe "tribute lists" on the Acropolis; by this time the treasury of the alliance has been shifted from Delos to Athens.

ca. 450 Cimon, returned from ostracism, leads a campaign to Cyprus and also sends ships to Egypt. He dies during the expedition, but the Athenians go on to win major victories over Persian forces.

449 At the invitation of Artaxerxes, the Athenian envoy Callias travels to Susa and negotiates a peace treaty between Athens and the Great King, thus ending the Persian Wars.

447 Tolmides rashly leads an Athenian army to Coronea in Boeotia, where a decisive defeat terminates Athenian visions of a land empire. Work begins on building the Parthenon.

446 Athenians conclude a Thirty Years' Peace with the Spartans and their alliance.

ca. 443 Athenians divide their maritime empire into five districts, to regularize the collection and recording of tribute.

THE SAMIAN WAR [440 B.C.]

440 Samos rebels against Athenian rule. Pericles, Sophocles, Phormio, and other generals lead Athenian fleets in a war to recover the island.

436 Athenians establish a colony at Amphipolis on the Strymon River to secure control of the Thracian mining region.

435 War breaks out between Corinth and Corcyra.

433 Ten Athenian ships aid the Corcyraeans at the battle of Sybota. Over the winter Corinthians, Megarians, and others urge Spartans to declare war on Athens.

432 Athenians send a series of expeditions to Potidaea, a rebellious subject city in the northern Aegean. One expedition is led by Phormio and includes among the soldiers Socrates and the eighteen-year-old Alcibiades.

THE PELOPONNESIAN WAR [431–404 B.C.]

431 First year of the Peloponnesian War, by computation of Thucydides. Athenians evacuate the countryside and take refuge within the Long Walls. Spartans lead the army of the Peloponnesian League on a rampage of destruction through Attica. Pericles responds with an amphibious expedition around the Peloponnese.

430 Second year of war. Peloponnesians again invade Attica; the Athenian navy again raids the Peloponnese. Athenian horse carriers make their debut with the fleet. The plague breaks out in Athens, killing up to one-third of the population.

429 Third year of war. Phormio with twenty ships defends Athenian allies in the west and beats large Peloponnesian fleets in battles at Patras and Naupactus. The Peloponnesian fleet attempts a surprise night raid on the Piraeus. Pericles dies.

428 Fourth year of war. Mytilene on Lesbos revolts. Recovered from effects of the plague, Athenians put 250 ships to sea in campaigns all around Greece and the Aegean.

427 Fifth year of war. Peloponnesians challenge Athens at sea with fleets in western waters and (for the first time in decades) in the Aegean. Mytilene finally surrenders. Cleon urges the harshest treatment of the rebels, but the Assembly ultimately relents. Athenians send a naval expedition to Sicily and aids allies at Rhegium, in southern Italy.

426 Sixth year of war. The annual Peloponnesian invasion of Attica is deterred by an earthquake at the Isthmus of Corinth. The Athenian navy pursues the war in the Aegean, western Greece, southern Italy, and Sicily.

425 Seventh year of war. The Athenian general Demosthenes masterminds the establishment of an Athenian beachhead at Pylos in the southwestern Peloponnese. When Cleon joins him with reinforcements, they capture Spartan hoplites on the island of Sphacteria. The Spartans sue for peace, but at Cleon's urging the Assembly rejects the offer.

424 Eighth year of war. Aristophanes satirizes the generals Cleon, Nicias, and Demosthenes in the comedy *Horsemen*. Nicias achieves successes

with the navy at Cythera and Megara. The Athenians abandon the war in Sicily with nothing to show for their efforts.

423 Ninth year of war. After the Spartan general Brasidas captures the important northern city of Amphipolis, the Athenians and Spartans agree to a one-year truce. The Athenian general Thucydides fails to save Amphipolis with his small naval force and is subsequently exiled. He takes advantage of his enforced leisure to write the history of the Peloponnesian War.

422 Tenth year of war. After truce expires, Cleon and Brasidas die in battle at Amphipolis.

421 Eleventh year of war, which Thucydides considers to continue despite a cessation of major hostilities. In early spring Nicias negotiates a peace between the Athenians and Spartans. The event is celebrated in Aristophanes' comedy *Peace*. Attempts to resolve residual issues from the ten years of war spark new conflicts.

420 Twelfth year of war. Alcibiades launches himself in Athenian politics and diplomacy, tricking Spartan envoys and forging an Athenian alliance with several cities in the Peloponnese.

419 Thirteenth year of war. Alcibiades continues to stir up trouble in the Peloponnese.

418 Fourteenth year of war. Spartans defeat disaffected Peloponnesians at Mantinea.

417 Fifteenth year of war. At Alcibiades' instigation, the democratic faction at Argos allies with Athens. The Athenian fleet blockades Macedonian ports.

416 Sixteenth year of war. The Athenian fleet seizes the island of Melos in the southern Aegean and executes Melians for refusing to join the Athenian alliance.

415 Seventeenth year of war. The Athenians send a major naval expedition against Syracuse in Sicily, led by Alcibiades, Nicias, and Lamachus.

Alcibiades is called home for questioning about matters of sacrilege but escapes and joins the Spartans.

414 Eighteenth year of war. The Athenian fleet establishes a base within the Great Harbor at Syracuse, but Lamachus dies in the fighting. Nicias sends a letter to the Assembly appealing for relief. The Athenians reform their finances, replacing the "imperial" tribute from the allies with a tax on maritime trade.

413 Nineteenth year of war. The Athenians send reinforcements to Syracuse under the generals Demosthenes and Eurymedon, but the entire expeditionary force is destroyed in a series of disastrous naval battles and a final pursuit on land. Survivors are penned in local quarries.

412 Twentieth year of war. The Persian satraps Pharnabazus and Tissaphernes offer to pay for Spartan campaigns against Athenian allies in Asia Minor. After Alcibiades instigates a rebellion on Chios, the Athenians resolutely build more ships and set up a naval base on Samos to save their empire. Despite losses in Sicily, the navy holds its own against a Spartan force established at Ephesus.

411 Twenty-first year of war. In Athens, oligarchs seize control of the government and establish the rule of the Four Hundred. On Samos, Athenians serving with the fleet set up their own democratic government and invite Alcibiades to come from Sardis and take command. Thrasybulus and Thrasyllus play prominent roles. Alcibiades prevents the fleet from attacking oligarchic Athens and thus averts civil war. While he voyages to Aspendus to divert a Phoenician fleet sent to reinforce the Spartan naval effort, the theater of war shifts to the Hellespont, where Thrasybulus and Thrasyllus (eventually joined by Alcibiades) win naval battles at Cynossema and Abydos.

410 Twenty-second year of war. The Athenian fleet wins a great victory at Cyzicus over the combined forces of the Spartan admiral Mindarus and the Persian satrap Pharnabazus. Democracy is restored at Athens following the defeat of the oligarchic forces by Spartans in a naval battle at Eretria. The Athenians turn down a Spartan peace offer.

409 Twenty-third year of war. The Athenian fleet overseas pursues a semi-independent course under Alcibiades, Thrasybulus, and other commanders, with campaigns in the Hellespontine district and Ionia. Sophocles

presents his tragedy *Philoctetes,* perhaps as part of a campaign to recall Alcibiades to Athens.

408 Twenty-fourth year of war. Alcibiades and his colleagues recapture Byzantium, taking control of the Bosporus with its lucrative toll station on Black Sea commerce. Funds sent home to Athens allow the completion of the Erechtheum on the Acropolis.

407 Twenty-fifth year of war. Alcibiades returns to Athens and is elected general by the Assembly. In the autumn he is sent to Ionia with a fleet but without adequate funds to pay the crews. Prince Cyrus of Persia meanwhile is bankrolling the Spartan naval effort through gifts to the admiral Lysander. Alcibiades' steersman Antiochus is responsible for a naval defeat at Notium near Ephesus. Alcibiades returns to his perennial exile.

406 Twenty-sixth year of war. The Spartans blockade Athens' best ships in Mytilene harbor, but the Athenian general Conon gets an appeal for help through to the Assembly. In order to man a relief fleet, the Athenians enfranchise metics and slaves. Thrasyllus, young Pericles, and other generals lead a large fleet to the Arginusae Islands opposite Mytilene and win a victory over the Spartan fleet. Afterward the generals are tried and condemned to death for their failure to pick up Athenian corpses and survivors from the sea.

405 Twenty-seventh year of war. Aristophanes comments on Athens' desperate plight and the importance of the naval effort in his comedy *Frogs.* An Athenian fleet tracks the Spartans under Lysander to the Hellespont, where the Athenians are defeated at Aegospotami in the final battle of the war.

404 The Peloponnesian War ends in early spring with the surrender of Athens to Lysander's forces. The Long Walls are torn down, the navy is reduced to twelve triremes, and an oligarchy of Thirty Tyrants is imposed on Athens. Alcibiades dies in Asia Minor. Thrasybulus initiates a democratic resurgence.

403 Democracy is restored at Athens. Lysander falls from power.

401 Xenophon of Athens embarks on his expedition with the Ten Thousand, a Greek mercenary army hired by Prince Cyrus of Persia. Their defeat

at Cunaxa near Babylon confirms the rule of Artaxerxes II as Great King.

399 Trial and execution of Socrates.

THE SPARTAN WARS [397–371 B.C.]

397 Conon the Athenian, living in self-imposed exile on Cyprus, is appointed admiral of the Persian fleet, with orders to end Spartan rule of the sea and Spartan attacks on Persian territory.

395 Resurgent Athenians join Thebans and Corinthians in war on Sparta and begin to rebuild the Long Walls. Meanwhile Athenian men and ships are crossing the sea to join Conon.

394 After years of delays Conon leads a combined Persian and Athenian naval force against the Spartans and wins a victory at Cnidus in southwestern Asia Minor.

393 Conon wins permission from his colleague in command, the satrap Pharnabazus, to return to Athens with his triremes and money. He restores the naval base at the Piraeus and helps finish the rebuilding of the Long Walls.

392 Conon dies in Asia Minor.

389 Thrasybulus tries with some success to reestablish Athenian rule in the Hellespont.

388 Thrasybulus is killed while campaigning near the Eurymedon River. The Athenian general Iphicrates continues the policy of aggressive war.

386 In answer to a Spartan appeal Artaxerxes II calls representatives of the Greek cities to Sardis, where his ministers hand down the King's Peace. Athens retains a few islands in the Aegean but must swear to give up the naval and military effort to re-create an Athenian alliance.

380 Isocrates of Athens writes his *Panegyricus,* urging a panhellenic crusade against Persia under joint leadership of Athens and Sparta.

377 After years of Spartan provocations the Athenians establish a Second Maritime League, in which Greek cities band together against the Spartan threat.

376 Chabrias and Phocion lead the Athenian fleet to victory over the Spartans at Naxos.

375 Timotheus leads an Athenian fleet to victory at Alyzia, thus challenging Spartan supremacy in western Greece.

373 Iphicrates leads an Athenian expedition around the Peloponnese and ambushes a fleet from Syracuse on an islet north of Corcyra.

ca. 372 Spartan naval power in the west is symbolically destroyed when a tsunami at Helike in the Corinthian Gulf overwhelms a Spartan squadron of triremes.

371 Peace is concluded between Athens and Sparta. Within less than a month the once-invincible Spartan army is beaten by the Thebans at Leuctra. As Sparta is eclipsed, Athens embarks on a second Golden Age in the fields of sculpture (Praxiteles), rhetoric (Isocrates and Demosthenes), and above all philosophy (Plato and Aristotle).

360 Though only twenty-four-years old, Demosthenes volunteers to serve as trierarch under the command of Cephisodotus in an expedition to the Hellespont and the Gallipoli peninsula.

THE WAR WITH THE ALLIES [357–355 B.C.]

357 Demosthenes volunteers again to serve as trierarch under the command of Timotheus in an Athenian expedition to recover Euboea from Theban domination. As the specter of Athenian naval imperialism rises once more, major allies such as Chios, Rhodes, Byzantium, and Cos are persuaded by Mausolus of Halicarnassus (a leader who will one day be buried in the original "Mausoleum") to rebel against Athens, thus launching the so-called Social War or War with the Allies. Chabrias leads a fleet to Chios but is killed fighting in the harbor.

355 The War with the Allies ends when Athens recognizes the right of states to secede from the Second Maritime League. Many small allies remain loyal, but the navy is in poor condition, suffering from a leadership crisis at the levels of both generals and trierarchs, as well as severe financial shortfalls. The Athenian statesman Periander creates trierarchic organizations called symmories to deal with the crisis.

354 Demosthenes makes his maiden speech in the Assembly, calling for naval reform in "On the Symmories."

351 Following encroachments into the Athenian sphere of influence by the Macedonian king Philip II, Demosthenes attempts unsuccessfully to stir the Athenians to aggressive naval action with his speech known as the *First Philippic.*

349 Demosthenes delivers speeches called the *Olynthiacs,* urging the Athenians to oppose Philip's conquest of the northern city of Olynthus.

THE MACEDONIAN WARS [340–322 B.C.]

340 After a decade of Macedonian expansion, Demosthenes finally persuades the Assembly to declare war.

339 At the approach of an Athenian and allied fleet led by the veteran Phocion, Philip abandons his expedition against Byzantium and Perinthus and gives up attempts to gain control of Greeks through sea power.

338 Philip II and his son Alexander lead a Macedonian army south into Greece and defeat the forces of Thebes and Athens at Chaeronea.

337 Declaring himself the hegemon of the Greeks, Philip convenes a council at the Isthmus and announces his plan of war against the Persian Empire.

336 While the Athenians are awaiting mobilization orders, a lone assassin strikes Philip dead in Macedon. Alexander ("the Great") succeeds to his father's throne and inherits the mission to attack the Persians.

335 Aristotle establishes his school at the Lyceum in Athens.

334 Twenty Athenian triremes help ferry Alexander's army across the Hellespont, then take part in successful campaigns to capture Miletus and Halicarnassus.

331 The Athenian ship *Paralos* is sent to petition Alexander for the release of Athenian citizens who fought as mercenaries on the Persian side. Alexander grants the request before marching into the interior of the Persian Empire.

330 Alexander establishes himself as new ruler of the Persian Empire. The Athenians complete Philo's Arsenal in the Piraeus.

327 Alexander invades India.

324 The Athenians send a colonizing expedition to the Adriatic under the leadership of Miltiades, to ensure the grain supply and suppress Etruscan piracy. Demosthenes brings back to Athens from Olympia the text of Alexander's Exiles Decree.

323 Athenians send the *Paralos* to secure their control over Samos. Alexander dies in Babylon and is succeeded by his half brother Philip Arrhidaeus. The Athenians call on the Greeks to wage a war of liberation against the Macedonians, known as the Hellenic War or Lamian War.

322 The Athenian fleet is defeated by the Macedonians in the Hellespont, then decisively at Amorgos, and finally in a mopping-up operation at the Echinades Islands. According to the terms of surrender, the Macedonians take control of the Piraeus, and most Athenians of the *demos* or thetic class are exiled from the city. This year sees the deaths of Aristotle and Demosthenes and the end of Athenian naval power.

GLOSSARY

admiral: Spartan naval commander annually appointed to lead the allied fleet; the office could not be held more than once. The Greek term was *navarchos*. Confusingly, at Athens the naval commands were the responsibility of the ten annually elected generals *(strategoi)*, and their term *navarchos*, which is rendered as "navarch" in this book, referred not to an admiral but to a naval officer in command of a small squadron and subordinate to the generals. Unlike Sparta, Athens had no unified command of its entire naval effort under a single individual.

Agora: An open space in Athens and other Greek cities that served as a civic, commercial, and ceremonial center.

archon: An Athenian official, one of nine, who held a leading position in the government each year. Archons were originally elected; the office lost much prestige when the people decided to select archons by lot. The eponymous archon gave his name to the year, presiding from one midsummer to the next.

Areopagus: A hill near the Acropolis where the aristocratic council of ex-archons held their meetings. The council of the Areopagus accumulated prestige and power after the invasion of Xerxes, but it was stripped of most prerogatives during Ephialtes' democratic revolution of 462–461.

Assembly: Greek *ekklesia;* the gathering of citizens who debated and voted on policies and affairs of state. In Athenian democracy the Assembly held supreme power.

Athenian Empire: A modern term for the territory controlled by Athens at the height of its power in the fifth century B.C., when more than 150 islands and maritime cities paid annual tribute to Athens. According to Thucydides, Pericles did once tell the Athenians that they governed an *archê* or empire, but in its own day it was never called anything other than "the Athenians and their allies."

333

bema: The speaker's platform for Assembly meetings on the Pnyx.

cleruch: An Athenian who was allotted a tract of farmland abroad and sometimes emigrated there but retained his Athenian citizenship. A colony of such expatriate Athenians is called a cleruchy and was often resented by the local population.

Council: Greek *boulê;* a group of citizens or delegates who acted in an advisory or executive capacity. At Athens the Council of Five Hundred was composed of fifty citizens from each of the ten tribes, each serving for a single year and holding the presidency of the Assembly in rotation. The Council was specifically charged by the Athenian Assembly with responsibility for administering the navy and ensuring that new triremes were built on schedule.

Delian League: The modern term for the organization of the Athenians and their allies formed in 478 or 477 B.C. after the invasion of Xerxes. The league maintained a naval force to preserve the freedom of Greek islands and cities and carry on perpetual war against the Persian Empire. The alliance originally held its meetings and kept its treasury on the holy island of Delos in the Aegean Sea.

democracy: Greek *dêmokratia,* from *demos* ("the people") and *kratis* ("power"); a form of government in which the majority rules, thus in theory giving power to the common citizens.

diekplous: A naval maneuver in which a warship or file of warships breaks through a gap in the opposing line, then attacks the enemy ships from the flank or rear. One could counter a *diekplous* by arraying one's own fleet in two lines or by backing one's line up against the shore.

drachma: A Greek measure of weight, but also a small silver coin. In classical Athens a skilled worker earned a drachma per day. One hundred drachmas made a mina (roughly a pound), and six thousand drachmas made a talent.

general: Greek *strategos,* or "army leader"; the term used by Athenians to designate their supreme commanders both on land and sea. Each of the ten tribes of Attica elected a general annually, so there was always a board of ten generals. These citizens were generals only during their annual term of office, though the post could be held repeatedly. No military or naval experience was required, nor was there a regular path of promotion from lower ranks to the generalship. The rank of general did not stick to a man after his term of office expired. In addition to the annual elections, the Assembly could also appoint citizens (or in the fourth century even non-Athenians) to the generalship for specific campaigns or initiatives. As some of the only officials chosen by vote rather than by lot, Athenian generals exercised political power at home as well, especially in the fifth century.

Great King: The Persian term for the monarchs who ruled the Persian Empire. Ancient Greek texts customarily refer to Darius, Xerxes, Artaxerxes, and the other rulers simply as "the King."

hippagogos: A ship serving as a horse carrier or cavalry transport.

hipparch: Athenian commander of the aristocratic cavalry. Two were chosen each year to command the city's horsemen.

holkas: A broad-beamed sailing ship or freighter with a large carrying capacity for cargo.

hoplite: A heavily armed foot soldier equipped with a panoply of large round shield, helmet, cuirass, greaves, spear, and sword. Hoplites fought in a tightly packed formation called a phalanx. In Athens, the ten thousand or so citizens of the third class were expected to serve as hoplites.

horseman: Attic Greek *hippes;* at Athens, a citizen of the second class (numbering about twelve hundred) who were wealthy enough to own a horse and serve in the city's cavalry. The horsemen were traditionally aristocratic and antidemocratic. The term is sometimes translated "knight," but Athenian horsemen were neither heavily armored nor part of a feudal system. (*Knight* derives from Old German *Knecht,* or "one who serves.") Nor did they adhere to any chivalric code. Aristophanes' play *Horsemen* is sometimes called *Knights.*

hubris: Arrogant and wanton violence; a much stronger term in Greek than in English.

hypozomata: Girding cables for a trireme, wrapped around the outside of the hull and kept taut with spindles or winches to reinforce the ship's light and slender design.

keleustes: A petty officer on a trireme who called out the beat to the rowers, among other duties; equivalent to a coxswain in a modern racing crew.

kubernetes: The steersman of a ship; on a trireme the second in command after the trierarch.

kyklos: A fleet formation, adopted by Greek triremes at Artemisium and by Peloponnesian triremes at Patras, in which the ships form a stationary circle with their rams pointing outward.

Long Walls: Athenian fortifications many miles in extent that connected the city to the sea. The original pair of Long Walls, built in the 450s, enclosed a wide triangle of land between Athens, the Piraeus, and the village of Phaleron. Later a Middle Wall was built close to and parallel with the wall to the Piraeus, thus forming a narrow but easily protected corridor between Athens and its principal port.

metic: A resident alien who had settled in Athens, enjoying certain civic and ceremonial rights and at times fighting for the city as well.

mêtis: Cunning intelligence, a quality highly prized by Greek strategists.

mina: A measure of weight (and when consisting of silver or gold, of wealth) equal to one hundred drachmas, or roughly a pound.

naumachia: Naval battle.

naupegos: Shipwright or ship's carpenter.

navarch: An Athenian naval commander in charge of a squadron. Navarchs appear in the latter part of the fifth century and play only a small role in the city's naval affairs. They are subordinate to the generals. The same Greek term, *navarchos,* was used at Sparta for the admiral in supreme command of the Spartan and allied naval force each year.

Navy Yard: Greek *neorion;* a protected place for ships, especially warships.

oligarchy: Rule by the few.

ostracism: An Athenian institution in which citizens who had committed no crime but were perceived as potentially disruptive could be exiled for ten years. Votes were cast by inscribing names on potsherds or *ostraka.*

pentekontor: A galley of fifty oars. Both Persians and Greeks were still using some pentekontors at the time of Xerxes' invasion in 480 B.C., but they were rapidly giving way to triremes and played no part in the classical Athenian navy.

peplos: Athena's robe, woven anew each year for her statue in the temple on the Acropolis and hung as a sail on a processional ship as it was wheeled through the streets of Athens during the Panathenaic festival.

periplous: A naval maneuver in which a warship or file of warships rows around the end of the opposing line to attack enemy ships from the flank or rear. A *periplous* could be countered by doubling one's line, backing one's line up against a shore, or arraying one's ships in a *kyklos* formation. The term *periplous* also refers to the circumnavigation of a landmass, as in Tolmides' expedition around the Peloponnese in 456 B.C.

Pnyx: The meeting place of the Assembly at Athens, a rocky hill in the southwestern part of the city.

quadrireme: Greek *tetreres,* or "rowed by four"; a larger warship than a trireme that was adopted by the Athenian navy in the latter part of the fourth century B.C.

quinquereme: Greek *penteres,* or "rowed by five"; an even larger warship than a quadrireme. Two were added to the Athenian navy in its final years before the surrender to the Macedonians. The design remains somewhat conjectural.

rowing frame: Greek *parexeiresia,* often referred to as the outrigger; an open wooden rectangular structure fixed atop the hull of a trireme. The tholepins for the thranite oars were fixed along its lower edges, while its upper timbers provided supports and places of attachment for the cloth and hide screens that protected the rowers from sun and enemy missiles. In quadriremes and quinqueremes the trireme's rowing frame was replaced by a completely enclosed rowing box or oar box.

satrap: Persian for "protector of the realm"; an official who governed a province (called a satrapy) on behalf of the Great King and was responsible for collecting the local tribute each year and also for mustering military and naval forces to participate in royal wars and expeditions. The most important satrap to the Athenians was the Persian who ruled from Sardis, in western Asia Minor.

Second Maritime League: The organization of city-states led by Athens in the mid-fourth century B.C., officially (as with the Delian League) known as "the Athenians and their allies," banded together against the common threat of Spartan aggression. The second league fueled Athens' naval and civic revival but strictly limited Athens' control over the allies and never reached the heights (or depths) of its fifth-century predecessor.

shipsheds: Greek *neosoikoi*, literally "ship houses"; long narrow colonnaded structures with sloping stone floors that served as slipways for triremes and other galleys, protecting them from the elements and the teredo. By the fourth century Athens had built so many ships that immense double shipsheds had to be constructed to accommodate them in pairs, end to end.

strategos: See general.

symmories: Athenian naval boards created by the statesman Periander and reformed by Demosthenes, each composed of a group of citizens who contributed jointly to the financing and outfitting of a trireme.

talent: A measure of weight and also (if consisting of silver or gold) of wealth. A talent of silver was equal to six thousand drachmas or sixty minas and therefore weighed about sixty pounds.

tamias: Treasurer, as in *Hellenotamias,* "treasurer of the Greeks," or *Tamias Paralou,* "treasurer of the *Paralos.*"

thalamian rower: An oarsman in the lowest of a trireme's three tiers, enclosed within the hold of the ship and working his oar through an oar port enclosed by a leather sleeve. There were twenty-seven thalamians on each side of the ship.

thalassocracy: Greek *thalassokratia,* or "sea rule," from *thalassa* ("sea") and *kratis* ("power").

thete: An Athenian citizen of the fourth and lowest class; a member of the democratic majority and generally a proponent of the navy and naval initiatives.

thranite rower: An oarsman in the uppermost of a trireme's three tiers, seated within the rowing frame. There were thirty-one thranites on each side of the ship. These rowers sometimes received higher pay than the zygians and thalamians.

triakontor: A galley of thirty oars; important in the Athenian navy as a support vessel. The sacred ship that made the annual mission to Delos each spring (probably called the *Delias*) was the Athenian triakontor par excellence.

trierarch: An Athenian citizen who served as the commander in charge of outfitting, financing, and supervising a trireme as part of his civic duty. The official term *trierarchos* was also used for those who performed their service by commanding triakontors as well. At Athens the "trierarchic class" was the first, wealthiest, and smallest class of citizens, probably numbering only three or four hundred citizens or households. In other Greek cities *trierarch* was the generic term for the commander of a trireme, even when the post carried no element of civic obligation.

trireme: Greek *trieres,* or "rowed by three"; a warship type that formed the backbone of the Athenian navy throughout its existence. The English term *trireme* comes from the Latin *triremis,* a designation that indicates that the ancient Romans thought the Greek name meant "rowed by three" and not "three-fitted" as has been claimed by some modern scholars since the nineteenth century.

zygian rower: An oarsman in the middle of the three tiers in a trireme; there were twenty-seven zygians on each side of the ship.

NOTE ON SOURCES

This book presents a reconstruction of Athenian naval history from 483 to 322 B.C. based on ancient historical sources, archaeological discoveries, and surveys of the islands, coasts, channels, and seas in which Athenian mariners operated and fought their battles. In sticking as closely as possible to the primary evidence, the narrative in *Lords of the Sea* departs at a number of points from the interpretations of many modern scholars. Notes on each chapter are listed below, followed by the principal ancient sources listed alphabetically and a bibliography of modern scholarly works. Major historical controversies are indicated in the chapter notes along with citations of the relevant sources. For modern works cited in the chapter notes below, publication data not found in the notes is provided in the bibliography, beginning on page 370.

CHAPTER NOTES

In the epigraphs, as elsewhere in this book, translations are by the author unless otherwise noted.

Epigraph for front matter, page ix: Pericles' speech to the Athenians in 430 B.C., recorded in Thucydides, *History of the Peloponnesian War,* 2.62.

Introduction

Spartan accuses Athenian navy of "fornicating with the sea": Xenophon, *Hellenica,* 1.6.15. Naval warfare in the Mediterranean: Alfred Thayer Mahan, *The Influence of Sea Power upon History* (Boston, 1890), page 33. "Everything is going with the beat": Jack Kerouac, *Desolation Angels* (New York, 1965), page 123.

Democracy based on sea power: Aristotle, *Politics,* 4.4 and 5.4, translation by T. A. Sinclair. Peitholaus and the "People's Big Stick": Aristotle, *Rhetoric,* 3.10, translation by G. C. Armstrong. The claim of Socrates to be a "citizen of the world": Plutarch, *On Exile,* 600F. "O Athens, queen of cities! How fair your Navy Yard!": anonymous fragment of a lost Athenian comedy, R. Kassel and C. Austin, *Poetae Comici Graeci* VIII, Berlin, 1995, fragment 155.

Delphic oracle predicting that Athens would ride the waves of the sea: Plutarch, *Life of Themistocles,* 24.

Chapter 1. One Man, One Vision [483 B.C.]

Epigraph, page 3: Aristophanes, *Wasps,* lines 28–30.

Themistocles proposes to use silver from Laurium to build a fleet: Herodotus, 7.144; Aristotle, *Constitution of Athens,* 22.7. Themistocles starts to fortify the Piraeus during his archonship of 493–492 B.C.: Thucydides, 1.93. Details of Themistocles' family, character, and career: Nepos, *Life of Themistocles;* Plutarch, *Life of Themistocles.* Plutarch is also the source for his father Neocles' observation about the abandoned triremes, and for Themistocles' own signature motto on "how to make a small city great." In his *Life of Cimon* Plutarch explains that the source of the latter quotation was Ion of Chios, who heard it at a symposium in Athens within the lifetime of Themistocles. Modern studies of Themistocles: Frank J. Frost, *Plutarch's Themistocles: A Historical Commentary;* Robert J. Lenardon, *The Saga of Themistocles.*

Poetical description of *mêtis:* Homer, *Iliad,* 23.358–62. Modern analysis of *mêtis:* Marcel Detienne and Jean-Pierre Vernant, *Cunning Intelligence in Greek Culture and Society.*

Athenian Assembly procedures: David Stockton, *The Classical Athenian Democracy.* Rules for speakers: Aeschines, *Against Timarchus,* 35. Archaeology of the Assembly's meeting place on the Pnyx: Björn Forsén and Greg Stanton, eds., *The Pnyx in the History of Athens.* The four classes of Athenian citizens: C. Hignett, *A History of the Athenian Constitution to the End of the Fifth Century B.C.* Aristides opposes Themistocles' navy bill and is subsequently ostracized: Nepos, *Life of Aristides;* Plutarch, *Life of Aristides.* The Athenian ten-drachma coins struck in the early fifth century, possibly for the annual dole of silver from Laurium, described and illustrated by C. Seltman in *Athens, Its History and Coinage Before the Persian Invasion.* On the question of what ten drachmas would buy in ancient Athens, see William T. Loomis, *Wages, Welfare Costs and Inflation in Classical Athens.*

Chapter 2. Building the Fleet [483–481 B.C.]

Epigraph, page 15: Homer, *Odyssey,* 8.34–35.

Fifty Athenian ships participate in the Trojan War: Homer, *Iliad,* 2.573–759 (the "Catalog of Ships"). Early naval history of Greece, the Aegean, and the eastern Mediterranean: Herodotus, books 1 and 3; Thucydides, 1.2–17. Both these ancient historians take it for granted that triremes were already in use during the age of Greek exploration and colonization starting in the eighth century B.C., though triremes were not used in naval battles until the late sixth century B.C.

Themistocles decides to build fast triremes without overall decks: Thucydides, 1.14. Wood for Athenian fleets and building projects: Russell Meiggs, *Trees and Timber in the Ancient Mediterranean World*. (An invaluable compendium of ancient evidence, but Meiggs's view that the Athenians in 483 B.C. procured wood from southern Italy rather than using their homegrown timber is hard to credit.) Ships sewn with linen: Rosalba Panvini, *The Archaic Greek Ship at Gela;* M. E. Polzer, "An Archaic Laced Hull in the Aegean: The 2003 Excavation and Study of the Pabuç Burnu Ship Remains." Manufacturing a ram for an ancient warship: Asaf Oron, "The Athlit Ram Bronze Casting Reconsidered." Construction of the ship *Olympias* in 1985–86: Frank Welsh, *Building the Trireme,* for comparisons.

Exactly how a Greek trireme was designed and rowed is one of the longest-standing controversies in the entire field of classical studies. For the author's interpretation of the evidence see the article by John R. Hale, "The Lost Technology of Ancient Greek Rowing."

Chapter 3. The Wooden Wall [481–480 B.C.]

Epigraph, page 29: Xenophanes, fragment 17.

Xerxes' expedition and the Greek resistance up to midsummer 480 B.C.: Herodotus, book 7, which includes the text of the "Wooden Wall" oracle; Diodorus Siculus, book II, chapters 1–5; Nepos, *Life of Themistocles;* Plutarch, *Life of Themistocles.* Young Cimon's example to his fellow horsemen in consenting to pull an oar: Plutarch, *Life of Cimon.* The Athenians resolve to face the Persian fleet, with or without the Spartans: Thucydides, 1.18 and 1.74.

The reconstruction of events in early summer 480 B.C. that is presented in this book is based on the inscription known as the "Themistocles Decree." The inscribed stone was found at Troezen and published by Michael Jameson of the University of Pennsylvania in 1960. Subjects covered by the decree match those that would have been raised by Themistocles during a debate on the interpretation of the "Wooden Wall" oracle as described by Herodotus (7.143), namely trusting in a wooden wall (i.e., the embarkation of all the citizens in the triremes), the oracle's command to flee from the Persians (hence the plan to evacuate noncombatants from Attica), and the oracle's naming of Salamis as a critical site in the coming conflict (thus leading to the transfer of the Athenian government to the island of Salamis). Many scholars consider the "Themistocles Decree" to be a literary patchwork created long after the Persian Wars; some dismiss it altogether as an ancient forgery. Its authenticity seems to be supported by the testimony of Thucydides cited above. Given the oblivion into which the Artemisium campaign sank among Athenian orators of the fourth century, it is unlikely that a forger of that period or later would have made Artemisium the focus of a forged "Themistocles Decree." Opposing views on the question of authenticity are collected in Donald Kagan, *Problems in Ancient History: The Ancient Near East and Greece.*

Recent scientific work conducted at the site of the Delphic Oracle: William J. Broad, *The Oracle: Ancient Delphi and the Science Behind Its Lost Secrets.* A modern study of Xerxes' expedition: C. Hignett, *Xerxes' Invasion of Greece.* Persian history and civilization: Lindsay Allen, *The Persian Empire.*

Chapter 4. Holding the Pass [Summer, 480 B.C.]

Epigraph, page 43: Plutarch, *Life of Themistocles,* 8, quoting the poet Pindar, fragment 93.

Battles between Persians and Greeks at Artemisium and Thermopylae: Herodotus, 8.1 to 8.39; Diodorus Siculus, 11.6–11.13; Nepos, *Life of Themistocles;* Plutarch, *Life of Themistocles.* Modern study of the campaigns of August 480 B.C.: Andrew Robert Burn, *The Persian Wars: The Greeks and the Defence of the West, c. 546–478 B.C.* An ancient inscription unearthed in 1883 on the northern coast of Euboea confirmed the identification of Artemisium with the splendid sandy beach at Pevki Bay. The inscription came from a nearby shrine of Artemis, the goddess whose shrine gave the beach its ancient name.

Chapter 5. Salamis [End of Summer, 480 B.C.]

Epigraph, page 55: Aeschylus, *Persians,* lines 402–5.

Principal ancient sources for the battle of Salamis in September, 480 B.C.: Aeschylus, *Persians;* Herodotus, book 8; Timotheus of Miletus, fragments of a poem on Salamis; Diodorus Siculus, 11.14–11.19; Nepos, *Life of Themistocles;* Plutarch, *Life of Themistocles* and *Life of Aristides;* Polyaenus, *Stratagems,* 1.30. The contribution of money from wealthy members of the Areopagus to support Athenian citizens: Aristotle, *Constitution of Athens,* 23.

The tactics and maneuvers that determined the outcome of the battle of Salamis have been a source of controversy since ancient times. The reconstruction presented in this book is based on the early accounts by Aeschylus and Herodotus. The former was a participant and eyewitness; the latter interviewed men who had fought on both the Greek and the Persian sides. The topography of the narrow Salamis channel, even allowing for a rise of two to three meters in sea level since antiquity, seems to support their versions of the battle.

Later writers added details unrecorded by Aeschylus and Herodotus and in some cases flatly contradicted the early accounts. The fragments of Timotheus' poem on Salamis, which was probably written at least eighty years after the battle, include a reference to burning ships. This use of fire in a naval battle appears to be an anachronism inspired by the Syracusan use of fire ships against the Athenian fleet in 413 B.C., much closer to Timotheus' own time.

The version of the battle presented by Diodorus Siculus probably derives from the fourth-century B.C. historian Ephorus of Cyme. This version makes Salamis mirror the battle of Thermopylae. The Salamis strait plays the role of the narrow pass that Leonidas defended, and two hundred Egyptian triremes (not mentioned by Aeschylus or Herodotus) repeat the encircling maneuver of Xerxes' Immortals at Thermopylae. The main Persian fleet then tries to punch its way through the Greek ships that block the narrows. This time, however, the Greeks have their revenge and win the day.

It seems preferable to stick with Herodotus' explicit testimony that the Persian right wing extended westward toward Eleusis and the left wing eastward toward Munychia at the Piraeus. In other words, Xerxes' commanders backed their long triple line of ships up against the mainland of Attica, where they could count on the support of Persian troops on shore. They then charged across the width of the channel to engage the Greeks along the rocky coast of Salamis.

Plutarch in his *Life of Themistocles* seems bent on introducing as many novelties and contradictions of Herodotus as possible. The order of events is shuffled, spectacular human sacrifices are added to the narrative, and the outcome of the battle is determined by the structural design of the opposing triremes: proud and towering on the Persian side, low and unostentatious on the Greek side. Plutarch claims that Themistocles held off his attack until the morning wind caught the high Persian hulls and rendered them unmanageable; the Greek ships remained unaffected. Even in antiquity one commentator observed that Plutarch had stolen this stratagem of "waiting for the wind" from Phormio in his victory over the Peloponnesian *kyklos* at Patras in 429 B.C. (See the *scholion* to Aelius Aristides, *On the Four,* 2.282, referring to Thucydides, 2.83.) Plutarch was certainly wrong to claim that Themistocles launched the Greek attack at Salamis: the admiral in command of the allied fleet was Eurybiades of Sparta. Plutarch's version appears to owe more to a sense of poetic justice than to genuine traditions that somehow eluded Aeschylus and Herodotus.

For reconstructions of the battle of Salamis that incorporate material from Diodorus and Plutarch, see John S. Morrison and R. T. Williams, *Greek Oared Ships, 900–322 B.C.,* and Barry Strauss, *The Battle of Salamis.*

Epigraph for Part Two, page 75: Pericles' Funeral Oration of 431 B.C., in Thucydides, 2.37, translation by Rex Warner.

Chapter 6. A League of Their Own [479–463 B.C.]

Epigraph, page 77: Thucydides, 1.142, translation by Rex Warner.

The naval battle of Mycale and the Greek assault on Sestos: Herodotus, book 9;

Diodorus Siculus, 11.27–11.37. The exact site of the battle at the foot of Mount Mycale is uncertain. Sediment from the Meander River has silted up an extensive area of former coastline, including the spot where the Persians drew their ships onto land. The most important monument to the Greek victory over Xerxes' forces is the Serpent Column of Plataea. It was originally set up at Delphi but later carried off at Constantine's orders to adorn his new hippodrome at Constantinople (ancient Byzantium, modern Istanbul). The bronze column can be seen today in the park near Hagia Sophia, and the thirty-one names of the cities and islands that resisted Xerxes are still visible on the lower coils. The island of Tenos was added to the list, to recognize the heroism of the Tenian crew who brought their trireme over to the Greek side on the night before the battle of Salamis.

Herodotus' account of the Persian Wars ends with the triumphal return of the Athenian fleet from Sestos in the autumn or early winter of 479 B.C. Thucydides began his account of Athens' acquisition of maritime supremacy so as to pick up the story where Herodotus left off.

Themistocles instigates the building of walls at Athens, and Aristides takes the lead in creating a new "Delian League" of the Athenians and their allies: Thucydides, 1.89–93 and 1.94–97; Nepos, *Life of Themistocles* and *Life of Aristides;* Plutarch, *Life of Themistocles* and *Life of Aristides;* Diodorus Siculus, 11.38–11.47; Aristotle, *Constitution of Athens,* 23–24.

Cimon leads the Athenian and allied fleet in over a dozen campaigning seasons, from the early 470s to the late 460s, including a great victory over the Persians at the Eurymedon River in about 466 B.C.: Thucydides, 1.97–101; Diodorus Siculus, 11.60–11.62; Nepos, *Life of Cimon;* Plutarch, *Life of Cimon;* Polyaenus, *Stratagems,* 1.34. Cimon's stratagem of turning the course of the Strymon River against the walls of Eion is recorded only in Pausanias, *Description of Greece,* 8.8.7. According to Plutarch, the south wall of the Acropolis was built with the proceeds from Cimon's victory at the Eurymedon River. It is still a spectacular Athenian landmark, best viewed from the esplanade that runs from the theater of Dionysus to the theater of Herodes Atticus.

Cimon recovers the bones of Theseus from Skyros: Plutarch, *Life of Theseus* and *Life of Cimon;* also, William Blake Tyrrell and Frieda S. Brown, *Athenian Myths and Institutions.* The artist Mikon paints a scene showing Theseus with the sea goddess Amphitrite on the wall of the new temple of Theseus: Pausanias, *Description of Greece,* 1.17.2–3. An Athenian red-figure *kylix,* now in the Louvre, is painted with the same scene: see Thomas H. Carpenter, *Art and Myth in Ancient Greece,* figure 244. The triakontor of Theseus in Athenian lore and ritual: Plutarch, *Life of Theseus;* Plato, *Phaedo.* The identification of the sacred triakontor with the ship *Delias* in an ancient lexicon was suggested by Borimir Jordan in *The Athenian Navy in the Classical Period.*

Themistocles flees to Persia and is welcomed by the Great King: Thucydides, 1.135–38; Diodorus Siculus, entry for the year 471–470 B.C.; Nepos, *Life of Themistocles;* Plutarch, *Life of Themistocles.* Praise of Themistocles' genius: Thucydides, 1.138.3, translation by Rex Warner.

Based on the testimony of Plutarch in his *Life of Cimon,* some modern scholars argue that the Peace of Callias negotiated in 449 B.C. between Athens and Persia was preceded by a similar, short-lived peace also negotiated by Callias immediately following Cimon's victory at the Eurymedon River in about 466 B.C. For a full review of the evidence see Ernst Badian, *From Plataea to Potidaea: Studies in the History and Historiography of the Pentecontaetia.*

Chapter 7. Boundless Ambition [462–446 B.C.]

Epigraph, page 95: Xenophon the Orator, *Constitution of the Athenians,* 1.2.

The radical democratic reforms of Ephialtes in 462–461 B.C. and the ostracism of Cimon: Aristotle, *Constitution of Athens,* 25–26; Diodorus Siculus, entry for the year 460–459 B.C. in 11.77 (as is often the case, Diodorus' chronology is unreliable); Plutarch, *Life of Cimon.* Early career of Pericles, including his sponsorship of Aeschylus' *Persians* in 472 B.C. and his association with Ephialtes: Plutarch, *Life of Pericles.* Quote from Aeschylus, *Persians,* lines 241–42.

The Athenian and allied expedition to Egypt: Thucydides, 1.104 and 1.109–111; Diodorus Siculus, entries for the years 463–462 to 460–459 B.C. in 11.71–11.77. (Diodorus' chronology is too early, but he provides more details about the Egyptian expedition than Thucydides. The correct dates should be about 460 or 459 to 454 B.C.) Ancient evidence for the short-lived Athenian control of Dor (or Dorus) on the coast of Palestine, south of Phoenicia, is discussed by Russell Meiggs in *The Athenian Empire,* at pages 102, 245, and 420–21.

War in the Saronic Gulf and on the Greek mainland, including the battle of Tanagra and the circumnavigations of the Peloponnese by Tolmides and Pericles (an extended period of conflict also known as the First Peloponnesian War) from about 459 to 446 B.C.: Thucydides, 1.103–8 and 1.111–15; Diodorus Siculus, 11.78–11.88. Inscription recording Athenian citizens of the Erectheid tribe who fell in a single year in Cyprus, Egypt, Phoenicia, Halieis, Aegina, and Megara: inscription of about 459 B.C. listed as IG II², 929. The Athenians build Long Walls to join Athens to the coast at Phaleron and the Piraeus: David H. Conwell, *Connecting a City to the Sea.*

The Peace of Callias that ended the wars between Athens and Persia: Diodorus Siculus, 12.4. Thucydides does not mention this Peace of Callias, and its existence was challenged even in antiquity. Scholars are still divided on its date, nature, and exact terms.

Chapter 8. Mariners of the Golden Age [Mid-fifth Century B.C.]

Epigraph, page 110: Strabo, *Geography,* 1.1.16.

Everyday life for Athenian mariners: Robert Flacelière, *Daily Life in Greece at the Time of Pericles.* A bone of fin whale found in the Athenian Agora: John K. Papadopoulos and Deborah Ruscillo, "A Ketos in Early Athens: An Archaeology of Whales and Sea Monsters in the Greek World," *American Journal of Archaeology.* Naval life at sea and ashore: M. Amit, *Athens and the Sea: A Study in Athenian Sea-Power.* The trireme *Paralos* and its crew, also the sacred trireme *Ammonias* and its missions to the oracle of Zeus Ammon in North Africa: Borimir Jordan, *The Athenian Navy in the Classical Period.* Hazards and ailments of rowers: *Hippocratic Corpus*—"Epidemics," 5.32 (the man who fell on the anchor) and "On Fistulas," 1.102 (cures for fistula of the anus in rowers). "As the Athenian goes into the harbor": Aristophanes, *Babylonians,* fragment 87.

The Piraeus: Robert Garland, *The Piraeus from the Fifth to the First Centuries B.C.;* an overview of the Piraeus with a focus on inscriptions and religious cults. Hippodamus of Miletus: biography reconstructed by Vanessa B. Gorman in *Miletus: The Ornament of Ionia.* Excavations that revealed Hippodamus' street grid and the typical Piraeus house: George A. Steinhauer, "Ancient Piraeus: The City of Themistocles and Hippodamus," in *Piraeus: Centre of Shipping and Culture.* The wit who asked for silence during his haircut was King Archelaus of Macedon. Lines describing cargo of Dionysus: Hermippus, *Porters,* fragment 63. The Phoenician tombstone with the ship-headed god is in the collections of the National Archaeological Museum, Athens.

Symposia and metaphorical seafaring: M. I. Davies, "Sailing, Rowing, and Sporting in One's Cups on the Wine-Dark Sea," in *Athens Comes of Age: From Solon to Salamis,* ed. William Childs. Seafarers and sex: Jeffrey Henderson, *The Maculate Muse: Obscene Language in Attic Comedy.*

Epigraph for Part Three, page 123: Pericles' speech to the Athenians in 430 B.C., in Thucydides, 2.64, translation by Rex Warner.

Chapter 9. The Imperial Navy [446–433 B.C.]

Epigraph, page 125: R. Kassel and C. Austin, *Poetae Comici Graeci,* vol. VIII, fragment 155.

The life and vision of Pericles: Plutarch, *Life of Pericles;* Thucydides, 2.35–46, "Pericles' Funeral Oration"; also Donald Kagan, *Pericles of Athens and the Birth of Democracy;* Philip A. Stadter, *A Commentary on Plutarch's Pericles;* and Loren J. Samons, ed., *The Cambridge Companion to the Age of Pericles.* The building program, including the Parthenon: Plutarch, *Life of Pericles;* Jeffrey M. Hurwit, *The Acropolis in the Age of Pericles.*

Pericles' eloquence compared to the work of bees: Eupolis, *Demes,* fragment 102. Pericles explains the nature of an eclipse to his steersman: Plutarch, *Life of Pericles,* 35. Pericles likens Athens to the "School of Greece" and gives his opinion of the citizen who does not participate in public affairs: Thucydides, 2.41 and 2.40. Herodotus on the poor performance of the rebellious Ionian fleets at Lade in 493 B.C.: Herodotus, 6.7–16 and 7.139, translations by Aubrey de Sélincourt. Sophocles on the cowardly commander during a storm at sea: Sophocles, *Ajax,* lines 1142–46, translated by E. F. Watling.

The maritime empire: Russell Meiggs, *The Athenian Empire,* a work that includes maps of each district, lists of subject cities and the tribute that they paid, a chronological overview of the empire, and numerous specialist studies. For the expansion into the Black Sea, see also Marianna Koromila, *The Greeks and the Black Sea.* The Samian War of 440 B.C.: Thucydides, 1.115–17, and Diodorus Siculus, 12.27–28. The Panathenaea festival: Jenifer Neils, et al., *Goddess and Polis: The Panathenaic Festival in Ancient Athens.*

Chapter 10. War and Pestilence [433–430 B.C.]

Epigraph, page 138: Aeschylus, *Suppliants,* lines 438–42, adapted from the translation by Philip Vellacott, Penguin Classics, 1961.

Athenian conflicts with Corinth and Megara escalate into a full-blown Peloponnesian War: Thucydides, books 1 and 2 (including all quotations attributed to Pericles); Diodorus Siculus, 12.30–45; Plutarch, *Life of Pericles.* The adventures of Socrates and Alcibiades at the siege of Potidaea: Plato, *Symposium.* Pericles on the difficulties faced by Spartans in trying to learn seamanship: Thucydides, 1.142, translation by Rex Warner. The fear felt by the people on seeing their steersman fail: Sophocles, *Oedipus Rex,* lines 922–23. Many attempts have been made to identify the great plague of Athens, but no known disease fits all the symptoms listed by Thucydides. Overview of the events leading up to the war, and the campaigns of the first two years: Donald Kagan, *The Outbreak of the Peloponnesian War.*

Chapter 11. Fortune Favors the Brave [430–428 B.C.]

Epigraph, page 154: Xenophon, *Memorabilia,* 3.1.6.

Life and character of Phormio: Eupolis' comedy *Taxiarchs* (fragments); Pausanias, *Description of Greece,* 1.23.12, with information on Phormio's background linked to mention of his statue on the Acropolis. Pausanias mentions Phormio's disgrace and the people's discharging of his debts so that he can accept the command in Acarnania in the winter of 430–429 B.C. For additional details see book 3, fragment 8 of Androtion's *Atthis,* or local chronicle of Attica, published with translation and commentary in Phillip Harding, *Androtion and the Atthis.* The lines from an Athenian comedy that describe Phormio setting up a lead tripod (instead of three silver ones) are fragment 957 in R. Kassel and C. Austin, *Poetae Comici Graeci,* vol. VIII.

Phormio's early campaigns: expedition to Acarnania to capture the city of Amphilochian Argos (in the 450s?) leading to an alliance between Acarnanians and Athenians, reported in Thucydides, 2.68. Phormio uses playacting to fool the citizens of Chalcis (probably the Chalcis in Aetolia, west of Naupactus) into opening their gates: Polyaenus, *Stratagems,* 3.4.1. With thirty Athenian ships Phormio uses cavalry-style maneuvers to gain a victory over an enemy fleet of fifty: Polyaenus, *Stratagems,* 3.4.2. Polyaenus is the only source for this major battle. For a discussion of Phormio's tactics see John R. Hale, "Phormio Crosses the T." Phormio and two other Athenian generals bring a relief fleet to join Pericles at Samos during the Samian War of 440 B.C.: Thucydides, 1.117.

The topography and history of Naupactus: Pausanias, *Description of Greece,* 10.38.5. Phormio sent with twenty ships to Naupactus in winter 430–429 B.C.: Thucydides, 2.69. The little walled harbor at Naupactus is artificial and just the right size for the twenty triremes that the Athenians habitually stationed there during the Peloponnesian War. Although the harbor fortifications visible today are Venetian (Naupactus is the ancient name for Lepanto, famous for the last great battle of galleys in A.D. 1471), it is possible that the walls rest on ancient Greek foundations laid down by Phormio in the winter of 430–429 B.C.

The battle of Patras in summer 429 B.C.: Thucydides, 2.83–84, and Diodorus Siculus, 12.48. Some scholars have asserted that the "dawn wind" that disrupts the Peloponnesian *kyklos* seems too convenient to be true, but it still blows almost daily in the eastern part of the Gulf of Patras and is mentioned in manuals for pilots in the Mediterranean.

Thucydides calls the cape where Phormio camped Rhium of Molycria. This was also the site of the sanctuary of Poseidon. Its modern name is Antirrio, while modern Cape Rhium or Rhio lies across the channel on the southern shore. Today a spectacular suspension bridge joins the two capes.

Phormio's speech to the mutinous crews and the battle of Naupactus: Thucydides, 2.88–92 (translation by Rex Warner), and Diodorus Siculus, 12.48 (where Phormio is called "puffed up with pride" for tackling an enemy so much more numerous than his own fleet). Some medieval manuscripts of Thucydides' text state that Phormio faced seventy-seven enemy ships in the battle at Naupactus; others give the figure as fifty-seven. The higher figure seems more likely in view of the Peloponnesian array in four lines of ships (their line would have been shorter than Phormio's if the

Spartans commanded only fifty-seven ships) and the statement that Timocrates' flying squadron of twenty triremes was added to the right wing, rather than being itself the right wing.

The racing turn around the anchored freighter is credited to Phormio and the *Paralos* in Polyaenus, *Stratagems,* 3.4.3. (Thucydides identifies neither the ship nor its commander.) Victory trophies from the battle set up in the stoa of the Athenians at Delphi, with an inscription also mentioning the dedication to Poseidon and Theseus at Rhium: Pausanias, *Description of Greece,* 10.11.5.

Phormio's tactical genius: Marcel Detienne and Jean-Pierre Vernant, *Cunning Intelligence in Greek Culture and Society,* where a comparison is drawn between Phormio's encircling maneuver against the Peloponnesian *kyklos* at Patras and a traditional Mediterranean tuna hunt or "mattanza." See also John R. Hale, "General Phormio's Art of War," in *Polis and Polemos,* ed. Charles D. Hamilton and Peter Krentz, in which Phormio's approach to tactics is compared to that of the slightly earlier Chinese military genius Sunzi or Sun-tzu.

Chapter 12. Masks of Comedy, Masks of Command [428–421 B.C.]

Epigraph, page 171: Sophocles, *Antigone,* lines 715–17.

Historical narrative: Thucydides, 2.93–5.25; Diodorus Siculus, 12.49–74; Plutarch, *Life of Nicias.* Modern works on this period include Donald Kagan, *The Archidamian War,* and John B. Wilson, *Pylos 425 B.C.: A Historical and Topographical Study of Thucydides' Account of the Campaign.* Remarkable archaeological evidence for Cleon's successful expedition is a crumpled bronze hoplite shield inscribed THE ATHENIANS FROM THE LACEDAEMONIANS ON PYLOS that was discovered in a cistern during the American excavations in the Agora: see John M. Camp, *The Athenian Agora: Excavations in the Heart of Classical Athens.*

The comedies of Aristophanes: *Acharnians* in 425 B.C. (source of the exchange about the beetle and lamp wick setting fire to the Navy Yard), *Horsemen,* or *Knights,* in 424 (source of his comparison of a playwright to a rower working his way up to the office of steersman, as well as the choral *Hymn to Poseidon*), and *Peace* in 421. For a reconstruction of the conditions under which Aristophanes wrote and produced his plays, see Kenneth McLeish, *The Theatre of Aristophanes.*

Chapter 13. The Sicilian Expedition [415–413 B.C.]

Epigraph, page 185: Sophocles, *Ajax,* lines 1081–83.

Historical narrative: Thucydides, books 6 and 7. (Nicias' letter sent to the Assembly in winter 414–413 is quoted from Thucydides, 7.11–15, translation by Rex Warner.) Additional historical material: Diodorus Siculus, 12.77–13.33; Nepos, *Life of*

Alcibiades; Plutarch, *Life of Alcibiades* and *Life of Nicias;* Polyaenus, *Stratagems,* 1.39 (Nicias), 1.40 (Alcibiades), 1.42 (Gylippus), and 1.43 (Hermocrates). Excavations at Athens have unearthed official inscriptions related to various phases of the Sicilian campaign, ranging from the vote of the Assembly that enlarged the original plan of the expedition to Syracuse, to the list of Alcibiades' personal property put up for public auction after his condemnation in absentia. Modern accounts of the Athenian campaign at Syracuse include Donald Kagan, *The Peace of Nicias and the Sicilian Expedition,* and Peter Green, *Armada from Athens.* Timon of Athens congratulates Alcibiades: *Life of Alcibiades,* 16. The promise to show the Athenians that he is "still alive": Plutarch, *Life of Alcibiades,* 22.

Archaeological surveys and excavations at Syracuse have revealed that in the fifth century B.C. the Little Harbor covered an extensive area that is now dry land. The theater and the nearby quarries where the Athenian prisoners were held after their surrender can still be visited today. The impressive fortifications that crown the heights of Epipolae postdate the Athenian campaign. On the other hand the inconvenient rocky coast at Plemmyrium where Nicias stationed his triremes is still exposed, as is the stretch of shore south of the marshy estuary of the Anapus River in the Great Harbor where the Athenians built their stockaded camp. The remains of ships and weapons that sank during the naval battles in the Great Harbor now lie sealed under a protective layer of mud from the Anapus River. In this zone underwater archaeologists may one day recover extensive physical evidence for the battles described by Thucydides, from javelin points to entire charred hulls of Syracusan fire ships.

Epigraph for Part Four, page 203: Pericles' Funeral Oration of 431 B.C., in Thucydides, 2.43, translation by Rex Warner.

Chapter 14. The Rogue's Return [412–407 B.C.]

Epigraph, page 205: Sophocles, *Women of Trachis,* lines 655–57.

Historical narrative of Athenian naval recovery after the Sicilian disaster, the split between oligarchic Athens and the democratic fleet on Samos, and naval victories up to the return of Alcibiades to Athens in 407 B.C.: Thucydides, book 8, which breaks off after the victory at Cynossema in autumn 411 B.C.; Xenophon, *Hellenica,* 1.1–5 (including text of the Spartan message home after the battle of Cyzicus); Aristotle, *Constitution of Athens,* 29–33 (on the oligarchic regime of the Four Hundred); Diodorus Siculus, 13.34–69; Nepos, *Life of Thrasybulus* and *Life of Alcibiades;* Plutarch, *Life of Alcibiades.* For this and the following two chapters, an authoritative account with references to modern scholarship can be found in Donald Kagan, *The Fall of the Athenian Empire.* "Men in exile feed on dreams": Aeschylus, Agamemnon, line 1668, translation by Gilbert Murray. The observation that democracies are at their best when things look worst: Thucydides, 8.1. "The sea can wash away all human ills": Euripides, *Iphigenia Among the Taurians,* line 1192. The Athenians both love and hate Alcibiades: Aristophanes, *Frogs,* lines 1425–26. The Spartans as "most convenient enemies": Thucydides, 8.99.

Despite the central role that the Hellespont played in Greek history, the waterway and its coasts have not been extensively explored by archaeologists. The exact location of many sites, including important cities like Sestos, remains to some extent conjectural. Part of the problem lies with the burial of ancient settlements under modern construction. In addition, the course of the stream may have altered over the last twenty-five hundred years, eroding away some classical sites altogether and leaving others well inland from the modern coastline. It is clear that the naval battles of Cynossema and Abydos (fought in late summer 411 B.C.) must have taken place in the lower reaches of the Hellespont, but it is difficult to be more precise at this time.

Cyzicus, a Greek city on the southern coast of the Sea of Marmara, or Propontis, presents a different set of problems. First, aerial photographs show that the ancient harbor of Cyzicus, held by the Spartans in the spring of 410 B.C., lay on the sandy isthmus that joins the peninsula to the Asiatic mainland, but is now completely silted up. Second, the accounts of Xenophon, Plutarch, and Diodorus (supplemented by Frontinus, a Roman writer on military tactics and stratagems) do not make it absolutely clear where the Athenians set their army ashore on the night before the battle. In 2006, in company with Muharrem Zeybek of Izmir, I conducted a survey of the mainland shore west of the isthmus. We found that the steep and rocky coasts would have prevented a landing anywhere except at the point where the isthmus joins the mainland. This spot was identified as Mindarus' emergency landing place (equivalent to the ancient site of Cleri, or Kleroi, "the allotments") by Kagan, *Fall of the Athenian Empire,* pages 242–43. I believe that in the darkness before dawn the Athenians set their army ashore on the long sandy beach of modern Erdek (ancient Artaki), close to the unwalled city of Cyzicus but hidden from Spartan lookouts by a high rocky spur of land. Alcibiades' speech to his men before the battle of Cyzicus: Xenophon, *Hellenica,* 1.1.14, adapted from translation by Rex Warner.

The little island called Polydoros, where Thrasybulus and Theramenes concealed their fleet and where the Athenians erected a trophy after the battle, lies just off the point of this rocky spur, and is separated from it by the channel through which Alcibiades led his flying squadron of twenty to lure Mindarus away from the safety of Cyzicus harbor. It rained heavily when I visited Erdek in 2006, with conditions like those Xenophon described on the night before the battle. As a result of the downpour some of the modern roads and streets were impassable due to runoff and mudslides. The Athenian troops would have found it hard going to work their way along the coast to the northern edge of Cyzicus, but they could certainly have counted on accomplishing their mission undetected by the Spartans who held the city. Spartans' message home after their defeat at Cyzicus: Xenophon, *Hellenica,* 1.1.23. The Athenians now elect as generals men who would formerly not have been chosen as wine inspectors: Eupolis, *Cities,* fragment 219.

Chapter 15. Of Heroes and Hemlock [407–406 B.C.]

Epigraph, page 221: Euripides, *Hecuba,* lines 28–30, translated by John Davie, Penguin Classics, 1998.

Historical narrative of the naval battles at Notium, Mytilene, and the Arginusae Islands, and the trial of the Athenian generals in 406 B.C.: Xenophon, *Hellenica,* 1.5–7 (including Euryptolemus' speech in defense of the generals, translation by Rex Warner); Oxyrhynchus historian or "P," fragment 4, mentioning a *naulochein,* or naval ambush, associated with the battle of Notium; Diodorus Siculus, 13.69–103 (including the episode of Thrasyllus' dream before the battle of the Arginusae Islands); Nepos, *Life of Conon;* Plutarch, *Life of Alcibiades.* Message of Callicratidas to Conon regarding Athenian fornication with the sea: Xenophon, *Hellenica,* 1.6.15.

Socrates as *epistates* or president of the Assembly at the trial of the generals: Xenophon, *Hellenica,* 1.7.15, and *Memorabilia,* 1.1.18 and 4.4.2; Plato, *Apology,* 32, and *Gorgias,* 473. Socrates is not mentioned in the account of the trial in Diodorus Siculus, 13.101–2, nor is his participation included in the anecdotes about Socrates presented in Diogenes Laertius' *Lives of Eminent Philosophers.* Because Socrates' heroic role at the trial is attested to only by his former students Xenophon and Plato, some modern historians doubt the truth of their account.

There are a number of important Athenian official inscriptions that survive from these years, including a marble slab that thanks king Archelaus of Macedon for allowing the Athenians to build new warships in his country. See Russell Meiggs, *Trees and Timber in the Ancient Mediterranean World,* page 128. The most important inscription is IG II² 1951 (now renumbered IG i³ 1032), which is spread over a number of fragments that were found in the area of the Erechtheum on the Acropolis and the slope below it. This is a list of complete crews for a fleet of triremes. At least eight ships are represented on the surviving fragments. Each ship was commanded by a pair of trierarchs, an innovation that links the inscription to the last decade of the fifth century B.C. or later. Each crew includes large numbers of non-Athenians and slaves (identified by place origin and name of master, who is in some cases a trierarch on board the same ship).

Any explanation of this inscription should take into account its provenance: the sanctuary atop the Acropolis, not the Agora or the Navy Yard at the Piraeus. (Most of the fragments came from the foundations of a small Christian church that was erected within the shell of the Erechtheum.) Lionel Casson supported the interpretation of earlier scholars that linked this inscription to the battle of the Arginusae Islands. See Casson's *Ships and Seamanship in the Ancient World,* page 323. The inscription may have been set up on the Acropolis as part of a victory monument. It is my belief that the placement on sacred ground would also ensure that slaves who fought in the battle could point to a permanent and ineradicable record of their emancipation. Similar inscriptions attesting to the emancipation of slaves cover the wall of the Athenian Stoa in Apollo's sanctuary at Delphi. The interpretation of events presented in this book places the emancipation of the slaves *before* the battle as an emergency measure to man the ships (like the offer of Athenian citizenship to metics or resident aliens), rather than bestowed in gratitude after the battle as is commonly thought.

An important ancient source on the question of slaves in the navy is Xenophon the Orator (Pseudo-Xenophon or the "Old Oligarch") whose *Constitution of the Athenians* has been quoted in this chapter to show Athenian attitudes toward and treatment of slaves. Xenophon the Orator noted that slaves learned to row when they accompanied their masters to sea, and that they earned bonus money for themselves when their masters hired them out to the navy. Whether they worked in the Navy Yard or on board the triremes is not specified. I follow Lionel Casson, John Morrison, and other scholars in holding that in Athens slaves did not row on warships except in exceptional cases such as the battle of the Arginusae Islands (and if these men were freed before the battle, then slaves did not row there either). Other scholars believe that slaves routinely rowed on Athenian warships and also served as petty officers: see Borimir Jordan, *The Athenian Navy in the Classical Period,* and Peter Hunt, *Slaves, Warfare, and Ideology in the Greek Historians.*

Topography helps explain the Athenian disaster at Notium and the Athenian victory at the Arginusae Islands, though uncertainties about the layout of ancient Mytilene on Lesbos still leave us in the dark about the exact location of its inner and outer harbors, and how Conon moved his triremes from one to the other. With regard to Notium, lying west of Ephesus with a view south to Mount Mycale and the island of Samos, the ancient town lay on a high promontory that blocked off the view toward Ephesus for anyone on the beach below. Thus the Athenian trierarchs could see nothing of Lysander's sudden attack on the squadron of the rash steersman Antiochus. The promontory would have continued to screen the approach of Lysander's fleet until the last minute, resulting in the scramble of Athenian launchings from the beach at Notium and the ultimate victory of the Spartans.

Visiting the Arginusae Islands in 2006, I told the fisherman who kindly ferried me out to the archipelago from the coastal village of Bademli that I only wanted to see the two big islands. He insisted that we visit a third island, one that is omitted from many modern maps. It lay north of the outer Arginusae, surmounted by a crumbling chapel and surrounded by reefs and flocks of cormorants. Clearly in antiquity this had been an island of considerable size. The half mile of sea between it and the northern tip of the outer Arginusae was great enough to accommodate the Athenian right wing, which would then have been protected on its south flank by the reefs of the big island, and on its north and most exposed flank by the islet. The presence of this islet also explains why Xenophon described the opposite or south wing of the Athenian formation as being "out to sea," since there was no islet in that direction to protect the outermost triremes (Xenophon, *Hellenica,* 1.6.29). It also gives more point to Diodorus' statement that Thrasyllus "embraced" or *symperiélabe* the Arginusae Islands in his formation (Diodorus Siculus, 13.98.4). The eastern island lies too far away to have been incorporated in the Athenian battle line; it must be the northern islet that justified Diodorus in referring to islands in the plural.

Chapter 16. Rowing to Hades [405–399 B.C.]

Epigraph, page 233: Sophocles, *Antigone,* lines 951–54, translated by Robert Fagles, Penguin Classics, 1982.

Historical narrative: Thucydides, 5.26 (foretelling the end of the Peloponnesian War after twenty-seven years of fighting); Xenophon, *Hellenica,* book 2; Diodorus Siculus, 13.103.4–14.33.6; Nepos, *Life of Alcibiades, Life of Lysander,* and *Life of Thrasybulus;* Plutarch, *Life of Alcibiades* and *Life of Lysander;* Polyaenus, *Stratagems,* 1.45 (Lysander). Athenian maritime concerns in the spring of 405 B.C.: Aristophanes' comedy *Frogs.* The Spartan admiral Lysander believes in fooling boys with knucklebones and men with oaths: Plutarch, *Life of Lysander,* 8. Athenian generals at Aegospotami dismiss Alcibiades from their camp: Xenophon, *Hellenica,* 2.1, translation by Rex Warner (as is the following). The arrival of the *Paralos* at the Piraeus with news of the disaster at Aegospotami: quote from Xenophon, *Hellenica,* 2.2. The delegate from Phocis changes the mood of the conference in 404 B.C. by singing a chorus from Euripides' *Electra:* Plutarch, *Life of Lysander,* 15. The philosopher Socrates describes the *deuteros plous* or second voyaging that altered the course of his career: Plato, *Phaedo* 99D and *Statesman* 300B. Trial, imprisonment, and death of Socrates: Plato, *Apology* and *Phaedo;* Xenophon, *Apology;* and Diogenes Laertius, *Lives of Eminent Philosophers,* book 2, "Life of Socrates."

The reconstruction of the battle of Aegospotami that is presented in this book differs from previous interpretations. It is based on surveys of the Gallipoli peninsula that I conducted in 2006 with Muharrem Zeybek. Ancient sources imply that Aegospotami lay across the Hellespont from the city of Lampsacus, headquarters of the

Spartan fleet; that is, downstream from the port town of Gelibolu on the European shore. Based on that evidence, most modern historians have been forced to conclude that the battle of Aegospotami was decided by nothing more than Athenian folly and Spartan opportunism. Locating Aegospotami directly across from Lampsacus also makes nonsense of many details of action that are reported in the accounts of Xenophon, Diodorus, and Plutarch.

Standing on a rooftop in modern Lapseki on the site of ancient Lampsacus, it is possible to count the windows on buildings on the opposite shore using nothing more than the naked eye: there would have been no need for Lysander to send a scout ship to spy on the Athenians, let alone two or three (Plutarch, *Life of Lysander,* 10). The Hellespont may have been even narrower in antiquity, as it appears from the indentation on the European shore with its eroding cliffs that the current is cutting steadily into the northern bank. There are no long sandy beaches along this coast such as the Athenian generals would have required for their large fleet of triremes. Indeed, a rapidly flowing stream tends to deposit sand only at bends and corners, not along straightaways. On the shore opposite Lampsacus, near the traditionally accepted site of Aegospotami, I encountered a gang of diligent workers armed with shovels, who were attempting to enhance the value of their vacation homes by creating an artificial sandy beach where nature had failed to provide one. They were using a concrete embankment as a retaining wall for their efforts.

Four additional questions arise if Aegospotami is placed within the channel of the Hellespont. First, why were the Athenians short of supplies? They were closer to Sestos than Lysander and should have been able to set up a ferry service to bring food from the granaries there.

Second, how could Alcibiades have seen the Athenian camp from his fortress at Pactye? Xenophon, who rowed past the site of the great battle when homeward bound with the Ten Thousand in 399 B.C., states that Aegospotami was visible from Pactye, which lay on the isthmus of the Gallipoli peninsula (Xenophon, *Hellenica,* 2.1.25). Yet I found during a visit to Pactye that the inner reaches of the Hellespont were screened from view by the high ground inland from Gelibolu.

Third, how could Lysander have expected under any circumstances to take the Athenians by surprise? If Aegospotami lay directly across from Lampsacus, Lysander's movements would have been as easily visible to the Athenians as theirs were to him.

Fourth, how can we explain Conon's stop at the promontory of Abarnis if he started from a point farther downstream on the Hellespont? He was trying desperately to escape to the open sea, but would have had to row upstream toward Spartan-held Lampsacus to collect Lysander's cruising sails according to the traditional reconstruction of the battle.

The solution to these problems seemed apparent to me following a survey of the coastline between Pactye on the Sea of Marmara and the middle reaches of the Hellespont. North of modern Gelibolu stretches a sandy beach over a mile in length, cut by two small streams. This is the only beach on the European side long enough to accommodate the 180 Athenian triremes, and it is backed by a plain ideal for a camp. The beach is clearly visible from the site of Alcibiades' fortress, but is hidden from Lampsacus by a turn of the coastline and by a headland. Beyond the headland, and closer to Gelibolu, is a smaller sandy beach.

The topographical setting has led me to believe that the long beach was Aegospotami, taking its name from the two streams that empty into the Sea of Marmara midway along the strand. Lysander would indeed have needed two or three scout ships to see around the corner: one out in the Sea of Marmara with an oblique view of the beach and the plain behind it; the other one or two triremes would have been posted at the mouth of the Hellespont within sight of Lampsacus. From that position they could relay to Lysander the message flashed from the polished bronze shield on the leading scout ship.

Moreover, we can now understand the predicament of the Athenian generals in choosing a place for their camp. By beaching their ships at Aegospotami on the Sea of Marmara they could prevent Lysander from cruising eastward and taking Byzantium (which he in fact did immediately after his victory). At the same time, the Spartan fleet at Lampsacus now lay on the sea route between the Athenian camp and the food supplies at Sestos, forcing the men to desert the ships and go overland in search of provisions.

Let us now try to explain some of the crucial points in the battle. Once Lysander had decided to attack, he had to count on the possibility of fighting a naval battle. Accordingly, he landed at the low promontory of Abarnis near Lampsacus to unload his heavy cruising sails (and presumably masts as well). He cannot have placed them there earlier, or the Athenians would have seen them from their ships during their daily row between Aegospotami and Lampsacus.

From Abarnis, Lysander could then cross to a landing place on the European side that was still screened from the view of the Athenians at Aegospotami, namely the short beach south of the headland. I take this to be the maneuver lying behind Plutarch's otherwise inexplicable statement that as Lysander's ships attacked the Athenian camp, the Spartan land forces ran along the seacoast to capture a headland (Plutarch, *Life of Lysander,* 11). Lysander was showing that infinite capacity for taking pains that is the mark of a genius. Not only had he prepared for a naval battle, but he had also ensured that the Spartans would establish a beachhead near the Athenian camp even if his direct assault on Aegospotami from the sea failed.

In the event, however, there was no naval battle, and Lysander's assault did not fail. Only a few Athenian ships escaped, including the *Paralos* and Conon's little squadron. Plutarch's account of the battle makes it clear that Lysander was able to remain hidden from view until he was so close to the beach that the splashing oars of his ships were heard by the Athenians before they were seen. Once Conon had reached open water beyond the chaos on shore, his escape route to the Aegean would take him within sight of the Abarnis promontory, and provide him with an unexpected opportunity to supply his ships with cruising sails for the long journey ahead.

Can we explain the ancient statements implying that the beach of Aegospotami lay within the Hellespont? The most explicit ancient testimony about the location of Aegospotami comes from Xenophon and Strabo. The latter was an Asiatic Greek from a town south of the Black Sea who wrote a geography of the Roman world in the late first century B.C. at the time of the emperor Augustus. Strabo (7.331, fragment 55) noted that on a voyage up the Hellespont one would pass the ruins of Aegospotami before reaching the city of Kallipolis (modern Gelibolu) at the entrance to the Sea of Marmara. What are we to make of this testimony?

At the time of the battle in 405 B.C. there was no town at Aegospotami but only an open beach. I believe that the *polis* of Aegospotami was established by the Spartans in the years immediately following Lysander's great victory, much as Octavian (the future Augustus) established the city of Nicopolis in western Greece to commemorate his defeat of the fleets of Mark Antony and Cleopatra at Actium in 31 B.C. Aegospotami minted coins bearing the image of a goat, a pun on "Goat Rivers," but also the head of Demeter, indicating cultivation of grain. If the city was built inland, on the high ground to the north of the Hellespont, then its ruins could have been a landmark inside the channel even if the beach that inspired its name lay to the east, at the extreme end of the Sea of Marmara.

As for our other ancient source, Xenophon approached the battle site from the east, voyaging toward the mouth of the Hellespont across the Sea of Marmara in 399 B.C., as noted above. Seen from this direction, rather than from the bird's-eye vantage point of modern maps, one could indeed describe the long beach at Aegospotami as lying across from Lampsacus, and then go on (as Xenophon does) to state the width of the Hellespont at this point.

I believe that the details given by ancient historians about the action at Aegospotami outweigh the geographical testimony. Their accounts of Alcibiades' view of the beach, of the Athenian inability to get supplies from Sestos, and of Lysander's plan of attack all make it likely that ancient Aegospotami was the beach north of modern Gelibolu. It seems, however, that only the discovery of the meteorite or asteroid that is said to have fallen at Aegospotami in 468–467 B.C. (see Plutarch, *Life of Lysander*, 12, and the chronicle on the Parian Marble) will settle the question for good. Since it appears that the two streams have heavily sedimented the plain, the stone that fell from the sky may lie far below the modern surface.

Epigraph for Part Five, page 247: Pericles' speech to the Athenians in 430 B.C., in Thucydides, 2.64, translated by Rex Warner.

Chapter 17. Passing the Torch [397–371 B.C.]

Epigraph, page 249: Euripides, *Iphigenia Among the Taurians,* lines 114–17.

Historical narrative of the wars waged against the Spartans by the Persians and the Greeks, including the Athenians: Xenophon, *Hellenica,* books 3–6; Isocrates, *Panegyricus* and other orations; fragments on papyrus of the Oxyrhynchus historian or "P"; Diodorus Siculus, books 14 and 15; Nepos, *Life of Conon, Life of Thrasybulus, Life of Iphicrates, Life of Chabrias, Life of Timotheus,* and *Life of Phocion;* Plutarch, *Life of Phocion;* Polyaenus, *Stratagems,* 1.48 (Conon), 3.9 (Iphicrates), 3.10 (Timotheus, including battle of Alyzia), and 3.11 (Chabrias).

Conon urges Pharnabazos to injure the Spartans by sending ships and money to Athens in 493 B.C.: Xenophon, *Hellenica,* 4.8.9, translation by Rex Warner. The idea that walls should "slumber in the bosom of the earth": Plato, *Laws,* 778, adapted from the translation by Benjamin Jowett. Resurrection of Athenian naval power: Jack Cargill, *The Second Athenian League: Empire or Free Alliance?;* and Robin Seager, "The King's Peace and the Second Athenian Confederacy," in *The Cambridge Ancient History Volume VI: The Fourth Century B.C.,* ed. D. M. Lewis. Rebuilding the Long Walls, new construction in the Piraeus, and the monument to Themistocles: David H. Conwell, *Connecting a City to the Sea;* Robert Garland, *The Piraeus from the Fifth to the First Centuries B.C.;* and George A. Steinhauer, *Piraeus: Centre of Shipping and Culture.* Reconstruction of the shipsheds in the Navy Yard at Zea Harbor, including double shipsheds to house pairs of triremes end to end: Bjørn Lovén et al., "The Zea Harbour Project." The deforestation of Attica in the fourth century B.C.: Plato, *Critias,* 111, adapted from Jowett's translation.

In the *Life of Themistocles* by Plutarch, Themistocles' tomb quotation is attributed to Plato the comic poet, not the philosopher. Texts of King's Peace of 386 B.C. and Callistratus' speech of 371 B.C.: Xenophon, *Hellenica,* 5.1.31 and 6.3.14, translations by Rex Warner. Timotheus, the lobsters and the goddess Tyche or Fortune in the world's first known political cartoon: Aelian, *Historical Miscellany,* 13.43. Timotheus rebukes his superstitious steersman at Alyzia in 375 B.C.: Polyaenus, *Stratagems,* 3.10.2., adapted from the translation by E. Wheeler and P. Krentz. Iphicrates' quote, "Consider what I was, and what I now am": Aristotle, *Rhetoric,* 1.9, 1367B. Praise for Iphicrates' training cruise around the Peloponnese in 373 B.C.: Xenophon, *Hellenica,* 6.2.7–8. Ancient sources for the careers of Cephisodotus and Praxiteles as well as the marriage that linked the families of Timotheus and Iphicrates can be found in John K. Davies' *Athenian Propertied Families, 600–300 B.C.*

Chapter 18. Triremes of Atlantis [370–354 B.C.]

Epigraph, page 269: Plato, *Timaeus,* 25D.

Historical sources for the rise of Athenian maritime imperialism and the War with the Allies or "Social War": Diodorus Siculus, book 16, chapters 7, 21, and 22; also Nepos, *Life of Chabrias, Life of Timotheus,* and *Life of Iphicrates;* and Plutarch, *Life of Phocion.* Responses to the War with the Allies and to the Athenian financial crisis in the decade of the 350s: Isocrates, "On the Peace," 16, and Xenophon, "Poroi" ("Revenues"). For Periander's reform of the trierarchy see Vincent Gabrielsen, *Financing the Athenian Fleet.*

Plato's career, writings, and school at the Academy: Diogenes Laertius, *Lives of Eminent Philosophers,* book 3, "Life of Plato." Plato's maritime metaphors: excerpts from Plato's dialogues *Republic, Critias, Laws,* and *Statesman.* Athenian tribute payments to King Minos of Crete: Plato, *Laws,* 706, translation by T. J. Saunders. Negative assessment of Themistocles, Cimon, and Pericles: Plato, *Gorgias,* 518–19. Cosmic beam of light is like the girding cables of a trireme: Plato, *Republic,* 616, translation by Paul Shorey. Gods govern humans as steersmen guide ships: Plato, *Critias,* 109. Laying down the keel of a human soul: Plato, *Laws,* 803, translation by Saunders. Allegory of the true steersman: Plato, *Republic,* 488. The Atlantis myth: Plato's dialogues *Timaeus* and *Critias.* The Atlantis myth as an allegory of maritime and imperial powers, especially Athens: Pierre Vidal-Naquet, *The Atlantis Story: A Short History of Plato's Myth;* and Vidal-Naquet's "Athens and Atlantis: Structure and Meaning of a Platonic Myth," in his collection of articles titled *The Black Hunter.*

Chapter 19. The Voice of the Navy [354–339 B.C.]

Epigraph, page 280: Euripides, *Andromache,* lines 479–82, translated by John Davie, Penguin Classics, 1998.

Historical narrative: Diodorus Siculus, book 16; Demosthenes, *Philippics, Olynthiacs,* and other orations; Aeschines, *On the Embassy* and other orations; Isocrates, *To Philip* and other orations. A reconstruction of these decades is presented by J. R. Ellis in "Macedonian Hegemony Created," in *The Cambridge Ancient History Volume VI: The Fourth Century B.C.,* ed. D. M. Lewis et al.

The life and career of the orator Demosthenes: Plutarch, *Life of Demosthenes.* Evidence for the orator's family and early experience as a trierarch is presented in the entry for Demosthenes in John K. Davies, *Athenian Propertied Families, 600–300 B.C.* Aeschines and other contemporaries questioned the practical value of Demosthenes' opposition to Philip. The same negative view was expressed in the second century B.C. by Polybius, followed by a host of historical writers down to the present day. This book, taking Demosthenes' consistent championship of the navy as a starting point, attempts to offer a more positive view of his personality, politics, and patriotism.

Passages quoted from Demosthenes' orations to the Assembly: *On the Navy Boards,* 1 and 29, adapted from the translation of J. H. Vince; *First Philippic,* 15, 16, 29, 40, and 50, translation by R. D. Milns; *Third Philippic,* 51 and 69. Demosthenes reflects on Philip's advantages over a democratic leader such as himself, "First, he had absolute rule over his followers . . .": *On the Crown,* 235–36, translation by John Keaney.

Chapter 20. In the Shadow of Macedon [339–324 B.C.]

Epigraph, page 294: Isocrates, *Panegyricus* 21, adapted from the translation by George Norlin, Loeb Classical Library, 1928.

"If the lightning that struck us": Demosthenes, *On the Crown,* 194, adapted from translation by John Keaney. Historical narrative of Macedonian victories, the recognition by the Greeks of first Philip and then Alexander as their supreme war leaders, and Alexander's campaigns in Asia: Diodorus Siculus, books 16 and 17; Plutarch, *Life of Demosthenes* and *Life of Alexander;* and narratives of Alexander's expedition by Arrian, Quintus Curtius Rufus, and Justin (epitomizing the history of Pompeius Trogus). For a comprehensive history of Alexander's career see A. B. Bosworth, *Conquest and Empire: The Reign of Alexander the Great.*

New ships added to the Athenian navy, quadriremes and quinqueremes: John Morrison, "Hellenistic Oared Warships 399–31 B.C.," in *The Age of the Galley: Mediterranean Oared Vessels Since Pre-Classical Times.* Philo's Arsenal: Elvind Lorenzen, *The Arsenal at Piraeus.*

The philosophical school at the Lyceum: Diogenes Laertius, *Lives of Eminent Philosophers,* book 5, "Life of Aristotle" and "Life of Theophrastus." Excerpts from three treatises deriving from the school of Aristotle—*Problems, Meteorology,* and *Mechanics*—are quoted or adapted from the English versions in J. Barnes, ed., *The Complete Works of Aristotle: The Revised Oxford Translation.* Sources for quotations from the works of Aristotle are as follows: "From the collection of constitutions": *Nicomachean Ethics,* 1181B; "The constitution to which Aristides pointed and Ephialtes accomplished": *The Constitution of Athens,* 41, translation by P. J. Rhodes; "At Athens there is a difference between the dwellers in the city itself and those in the Piraeus": *Politics,* 5.3; "The large population associated with a mob of seaman": *Politics,* 7.6, the two translations from the *Politics* being by T. A. Sinclair and T. J. Saunders.

The monument of Lysicrates, with a frieze showing Dionysus transforming Etruscan pirates into dolphins, and the building projects of Lycurgus: John M.

Camp, *The Archaeology of Athens.* The colonizing expedition of 324 B.C. to the Adriatic led by Miltiades and including Lysicrates as a trierarch: Athenian inscription found in the nineteenth century at the Piraeus, inscribed on a broken marble slab, and numbered IG II², 1629. For translation and commentary, see P. J. Rhodes and Robin Osborne, *Greek Historical Inscriptions 404–323 B.C.* (Oxford, U.K., 2003).

Chapter 21. The Last Battle [324–322 B.C.]

Epigraph, page 311: Sophocles, *Oedipus Rex,* lines 68–69.

Historical narrative of Alexander's last years and Athenian leadership in the war against the Macedonians: Diodorus Siculus, books 17 and 18; Plutarch, *Life of Alexander, Life of Demosthenes,* and *Life of Phocion.* The opposition of upper-class Athenians to the war: Diodorus Siculus, 18.10. The Athenians call on the Greeks to follow their lead in making war on the Macedonians after the death of Alexander the Great in 323 B.C.: Diodorus Siculus, 18.10.1–2.

Naval battles of the Hellenic War (also known as the Lamian War) in 322 B.C.: Diodorus Siculus, 18.15, in which two naval battles and destruction of Athenian ships are mentioned; also Plutarch, *Life of Demetrius,* in which the false report of victory at the battle of Amorgos and the towing home of wrecks is described, and *Moralia,* 338A, where Plutarch refers to the light Athenian losses at Amorgos, in contrast to the glory that Cleitus claimed for his victory. Thucydides' verdict that the Athenians had lost the Peloponnesian War because of their own internal dissensions: Thucydides, 2.6.65.

The version of the naval war against the Macedonians presented in this book retains Diodorus' statement that Cleitus destroyed many Athenian ships near the Echinades Islands in western Greece (perhaps by catching them on shore, as Lysander had done at Aegospotami). It also equates Diodorus' two defeats that Cleitus inflicted on the Athenian fleet under Euetion with, first, the shadowy operation in the Hellespont referred to in a couple of inscriptions and, second, the famous battle at the island of Amorgos in the Cyclades. The battle of Amorgos is the only one of these naval actions listed on the ancient chronological table known as the Parian Marble, where it is entered under the year 323–322 B.C. Current scholarly views on how best to deal with this meager and scrappy evidence can be found in articles by Peter Green and Brian Bosworth, in *The Macedonians in Athens, 322–229 B.C.,* ed. Olga Palagia and Stephen V. Tracy (Oxford, 2003).

The breaking of Athenian democracy: Diodorus Siculus, 18.18, and Plutarch, *Life of Phocion.* The manuscripts of Diodorus, book 18, state that according to the terms of surrender to the Macedonians, twenty-two thousand Athenians lost their citizenship rights. Diodorus' figure is commonly emended to twelve thousand, to match the number given by Plutarch. Peter Green has suggested that twelve thousand was the number of Athenian citizens who actually went into exile, while the remainder stayed home despite abusive treatment. (Peter Green, "Occupation and Co-existence: The Impact of *Macedonians in Athens,* 323–307," in *Macedonians in Athens,* cited above.) The ancient evidence is also discussed by Lawrence Tritle in *Phocion the Good.*

The disharmony between upper and lower classes that appeared repeatedly in Athenian history was best described by Plutarch in his *Life of Pericles,* chapter 11: "Below the surface of affairs in Athens, there had existed from the very beginning a kind of flaw or seam, such as one finds in a piece of iron, which gave a hint of the rift that divided the aims of the common people and the aristocrats." (Translation adapted from Ian Scott-Kilvert.) Nicias reminds the Assembly that a trireme's crew can perform at its peak for only a short time: Thucydides, 7.14.

The Athenian navy ceased to exist in 322 B.C. following the Macedonian garrison's occupation of the Piraeus, when the Assembly allowed the onshore administrative organization of the fleet and the Navy Yard to lapse. After that watershed date, Athens occasionally launched ad hoc fleets of warships, just as any Mediterranean city might do to meet a crisis or fulfill a commitment to a hegemon or ally. In the decade following their loss of maritime autonomy, the Athenians several times sent out fleets at the behest of Macedonian rulers (Diodorus, 18.5.8). In 279 B.C. Athenian warships rescued Greeks who attempted to block an invading army of Gauls at Thermopylae, and some years later the Assembly sent five ships westward to aid the Romans in their war against Carthage (Pausanias, 1.4.3 and 1.29.14). Philo's Arsenal and the Navy Yard at the Piraeus endured until 86 B.C., when they were destroyed at the orders of the Roman general Sulla.

ANCIENT SOURCES

Aeschines (ca. 397–322 B.C.), Athenian actor turned orator. He was the principal political opponent of Demosthenes during the period of conflict with Macedon. Aeschines' three surviving speeches provide valuable insights into the range of public opinion at Athens, along with details about contemporary personalities, events, and policies.

Aeschylus (ca. 525–455 B.C.), Athenian playwright. A veteran of the battles at Marathon and Salamis, Aeschylus frequently alluded to maritime and military matters in his tragedies, of which seven survive. His *Persians* includes a poetic account of the battle of Salamis.

Androtion (ca. 410–340 B.C.), Athenian "atthidographer" or chronicler of the local history of Attica. Androtion served as governor of Amorgos during the time of the Second Maritime League. Almost seventy fragments of his work survive.

Aristophanes (ca. 450–385 B.C.), Athenian playwright. His surviving comedies— from *Acharnians* of 425 B.C. to *Plutus* of 388 B.C.—are an invaluable source for reconstructing the political, social, sexual, and maritime life of Athenians in the Golden Age. *Horsemen* of 424 B.C. and *Frogs* of 405 B.C. are particularly important for their references to the Athenian navy.

Aristotle (384–322 B.C.), philosopher, born at Stagira in northern Greece. His school at the Lyceum maintained Athens' place as the center of Greek philosophy. A pupil of Plato, Aristotle was famous for having tutored Alexander the Great and for his biological fieldwork in Lesbos with Theophrastus. His *Rhetoric* culls naval and maritime turns of phrase from contemporary orators, while his *Politics* shares his teacher Plato's negative view of the effects of naval power on a city-state. The corpus of works attributed to Aristotle or his school include treatises called *Mechanics,* *Meteorology,* and *Problems,* all of which contain material relating to ships and the sea. In the late nineteenth century, in a most important discovery in the field of classical papyrology, a copy of a *Constitution of Athens* attributed to Aristotle was found among the reams of ancient papyri in the British Museum. Amid its chronological review of Athens' changing political systems, this long-lost work provides many new details about naval history as well.

Ctesias (fifth century B.C.), Greek medical doctor from Cnidus in Asia Minor who served at the court of the Persian king Artaxerxes II. His history of the Persian Empire survives only in fragments but differs from the accounts of Herodotus and other writers especially with regard to numbers of troops and ships. References both to the expedition of Xerxes and to the Athenian expedition to Egypt in the 450s appear among the fragments of Ctesias.

Demosthenes (ca. 384–322 B.C.), Athenian orator and advocate of naval power. Posterity has remembered him best for his *Philippics,* brilliant speeches that attacked the Macedonian menace under Philip II.

Diodorus Siculus (first century B.C.), Sicilian Greek historian. His encyclopedic library of classical history provides alternative versions for events recounted by Herodotus, Thucydides, and Xenophon, drawing on such lost writers as Hellanicus of Lesbos, Ephorus of Cyme, and perhaps the Oxyrhynchus historian or "P" (see below). Diodorus' reputation has fluctuated more wildly than that of any other ancient writer, but for some events, such as the Peace of Callias and even entire battles, he remains an important source.

Diogenes Laertius (third century A.D.), Greek biographical writer. He did for philosophers what Plutarch had done for Greek and Roman men of action. Diogenes Laertius drew on more than two hundred ancient sources to create anecdotal *Lives* of Socrates, Plato, Aristotle, Theophrastus, and many others.

Eupolis (ca. 450–410 B.C.), Athenian playwright and contemporary of Aristophanes. The fragments of his comedies provide details about Athenian naval figures and maritime life. Ancient scholars claimed that Eupolis wrote the passage in Aristophanes' *Horsemen* in which the Athenian triremes discuss, like angry women, a proposal to send them to Carthage. Eupolis' comedy *Taxiarchs* brought the Athenian general Phormio onstage as a leading character.

Euripides (ca. 480–406 B.C.), Athenian playwright. He introduced many innovations into Attic tragedy through his ninety or so plays, of which nineteen survive. Many of them were parodied by Aristophanes. Though apparently lacking the direct contact that Aeschylus and Sophocles had with the Athenian navy, Euripides wrote detailed descriptions of ships and maritime exploits in *Helen, Iphigenia in Aulis,* and *Iphigenia Among the Taurians.*

Hermippus (fifth century B.C.), Athenian playwright. His comedies included scenes with rowers and other nautical subjects. Again, as with all poets of the Athenian Old Comedy except Aristophanes, only fragments of Hermippus' plays survive.

Herodotus (ca. 485–425 B.C.), Greek historian, born in Halicarnassus but in later life a citizen of the panhellenic colony at Thurii in southern Italy. Herodotus' historical work in nine books, often called *The Histories,* wove eyewitness accounts, oral traditions, and local chronicles into an epic account of the wars between Greeks and Persians. Herodotus is the indispensable source for the Persian Wars down to the capture of Sestos in 479 B.C. As Herodotus said himself, he considered it his mission to record the historical traditions of the Greeks—not necessarily to believe them.

Hippocrates (fifth century B.C.), medical pioneer, from the island of Cos in the Athenian Empire, who founded a school based on the careful recording of symptoms and their daily progress. Among the cases preserved in the immense Hippocratic corpus of writings (much or all of which was written by his followers) are some that deal with mariners.

Homer (ca. eighth century B.C.), Greek epic poet from Asia Minor and fountainhead of Greek literature. His works contain descriptions of ships and voyages: the "Catalog of Ships" in the *Iliad* purports to record the number of ships that Agamemnon levied from the different kingdoms of Greece for the expedition to Troy (Athens contributed fifty), while the episode in the *Odyssey* in which Odysseus builds a raft or vessel on Calypso's island remains the most detailed literary account of the ancient shipwright's art.

Isocrates (436–338 B.C.), Athenian patriot and teacher of rhetoric. Immensely long-lived, he was born while the Parthenon was still under construction and died shortly after the battle of Chaeronea. Isocrates circulated his "speeches" as political pamphlets and addressed such important issues as panhellenism, Athenian imperialism, and the rise of Macedon.

Nepos, Cornelius (first century B.C.), Latin writer. His short biographies of famous generals may have inspired Plutarch, more than a century later, to write more extensive *Lives* of Greek and Roman leaders. Like Plutarch, Nepos wrote biographical essays on Themistocles, Aristides, Cimon, Alcibiades, and Phocion. But Nepos also treated some important Athenian commanders ignored by Plutarch, such as Miltiades, Thrasybulus, Conon, Iphicrates, Chabrias, and Timotheus.

Oxyrhynchus Historian or "P" (fifth to fourth century B.C.), anonymous Greek historian whose work survives only in fragments. He picked up Greek history where Thucydides broke off in 411 B.C. and continued it down to 395 B.C., a decade after the official "end" of the Peloponnesian War. Passages from his work were recovered on scraps of papyrus in the ancient rubbish dumps at Oxyrhynchus in Egypt, west of the Nile. Correspondences between his history and the version preserved in the text of Diodorus Siculus suggest that Diodorus at times used "P" as a source. The Oxyrhynchus historian is often at variance with Xenophon, whose *Hellenica* is the principal surviving contemporary source for this period. Many identifications have been proposed, but none has won universal acceptance.

Pausanias (second century A.D.), Greek from Magnesia in Asia Minor. His *Description of Greece* provides historical background about hundreds of classical buildings and statues that were still standing during the time of the Roman Empire. Pausanias often quotes inscriptions that have now vanished and sometimes anecdotes from local guides as well. Among his passages most important for Athenian naval history are his descriptions of the tombs in the state cemetery along the Sacred Way, starting with those of Thrasybulus, Pericles, Chabrias, and Phormio next to the city gate and ending with those of Ephialtes and Lycurgus near the entrance to the Academy.

Plato (ca. 429–347 B.C.), Athenian philosopher and disciple of Socrates. Plato's dialogues contain numerous nautical images, along with anecdotes concerning such Athenian naval commanders as Nicias and Alcibiades. Many passages are harshly critical of the Athenian navy. Plato also wrote the myth of Atlantis as an allegory of the archetypal thalassocracy or naval power.

Plutarch (ca. A.D. 50–120), Greek biographer, philosopher, scholar, and essayist from Chaeronea in Boeotia. He also served as a priest of Apollo at Delphi. Such essays as "Were the Athenians more notable for war or wisdom?" reflect Plutarch's wide reading in historical sources, many of them now lost to us. His most important works for Athenian naval history are his famous *Lives*. Plutarch wrote biographies of Theseus, Solon, Themistocles, Aristides, Cimon, Pericles, Nicias, Alcibiades, Demosthenes, and Phocion. Passages in his biographies of such important non-Athenians as Lysander, Philip II, and Alexander the Great also shed light on Athenian naval history.

Polyaenus (second century A.D.), Macedonian writer on tactics. He dedicated his compilation of stratagems to the Roman emperors Marcus Aurelius and Lucius Verus. Athenian naval exploits are represented by entries on Themistocles, Aristides, Cimon, Tolmides, Pericles, Phormio, Diotimus, Nicias, Alcibiades, Aristocrates, Thrasyllus, Conon, Iphicrates, Timotheus, Chabrias, and Phocion. For some major battles, such as Phormio's "Battle of Fifty and Thirty" and Timotheus' victory at Alyzia, Polyaenus is the only surviving source. The entertaining trireme tactics of the Athenian naval commander Diotimus also appear only in Polyaenus. The final two sections in the Florentine codex's summary of Polyaenus are "Naval affairs" and "Capture of coastal sites and cities." Intriguingly, Polyaenus seems to have had access to an ancient pilots' manual: he describes several stratagems credited to specific steersmen on warships, including a Corinthian who faced the Athenian fleet at Syracuse.

Sophocles (ca. 496–406 B.C.), Athenian playwright. Sophocles also served his city as a naval commander during the Samian War in 440 B.C., as a treasurer of tribute money from the Athenian alliance, and as a proboulos or advisory councilor after the Sicilian disaster. His tragedies, including *Antigone* and *Oedipus Rex,* are permeated with nautical images and metaphors. Sophocles' evocations of the sea reach their climax in the romancelike rescue drama *Philoctetes,* which is set on the island of Lemnos.

Theophrastus (ca. 371–287 B.C.), natural scientist from Lesbos and follower of Aristotle. His monumental work *Enquiry into Plants* describes the species of trees used by shipbuilders for various parts of ships as well as for oars, masts, and other gear. Theophrastus' writings also preserve woodsmen's lore on the best seasons and locations for cutting trees and on methods for producing pitch. In a different vein, his comic sketches in the *Characters* depict contemporary Athenians from the period of Macedonian domination, many of whom are portrayed in maritime settings.

Thucydides (ca. 455–400 B.C.), Athenian historian of the Peloponnesian War. A naval commander himself, Thucydides was exiled from Athens following his failure to save Amphipolis from the Spartans in 424 B.C. During his years of banishment he devoted himself to writing a detailed history of the Peloponnesian War. His work in eight books reaches its overpowering climax in the account of the Sicilian expedition. Unlike Herodotus he avoids anecdotal and romantic elements, as well as variant versions of events from different sources. As an introduction to his history, Thucydides wrote a lengthy analysis of sea power in the Greek world, from the heroic age of the Trojan War down to the outbreak of the Peloponnesian War. His work is studded with public orations by such figures as Pericles as well as battle speeches delivered by generals. Some documents are quoted verbatim. Thucydides lived to see the end of the twenty-seven-year war in 404 B.C., but his year-by-year chronicle of events breaks off in 411 B.C. According to his ancient biographer Marcellus, Thucydides was murdered when he returned to Athens following the end of the war.

Timotheus (ca. 450–360 B.C.), poet of Miletus famous for his musical innovations. He wrote a long poem on the battle of Salamis that included a vivid scene involving a Greek and a captive Persian on the shore. The work survives only in fragments on papyrus.

Xenophon (ca. 428–354 B.C.), Athenian commander, historian, and essayist. His *Memorabilia* provide firsthand accounts of his teacher Socrates discoursing on generalship and other practical matters. In addition to "Revenues," in which he addresses some maritime matters, and extended naval descriptions and metaphors in the *Oeconomicus,* Xenophon provided vivid descriptions of voyaging in the Black Sea at the end of his *Anabasis.* His continuation of Thucydides' history of the Peloponnesian War, called *Hellenica,* ultimately took Greek history down to 362 B.C.

Xenophon the Orator, also known as Pseudo-Xenophon or the "Old Oligarch" (fifth century B.C.), Athenian writer whose important essay *Atheniaon Politeia* ("Constitution of the Athenians") purports to be an open letter written by an Athenian oligarch to correspondents outside Athens. In it he explains why good men like himself must put up with democracy in Athens. The writer was apparently an Athenian general or trierarch: at one point he refers to "my warships." The date of his composition is hotly debated, but seems to me to belong to the first year of the

Peloponnesian War in 431–430 B.C., after the first Peloponnesian invasion or invasions of Attica but before the outbreak of the plague. His views on the navy and sea power echo or prefigure those of Thucydides, while his appreciation of the commercial benefits of maritime empire recall lines by the playwright Hermippus. There was a wealthy Athenian citizen named Xenophon the son of Euripides, of the *deme* of Melite, who served as hipparch (or cavalry commander, a quintessentially aristocratic post) in the mid-fifth century. This Xenophon (not known to be related to the more famous historian of the same name) was elected regularly to the generalship from the time of the Samian War in 440 until his death in battle in 429. Xenophon the Orator (or the "Old Oligarch," as he has been nicknamed) spelled out the link between the Athenian navy and the political power of the thetes more clearly than any other surviving ancient writer.

BIBLIOGRAPHY OF MODERN SOURCES

THE ATHENIAN NAVY

Amit, M. *Athens and the Sea: A Study in Athenian Sea-Power.* Brussels, 1965.
Cargill, Jack. *The Second Athenian League: Empire or Free Alliance?* Berkeley, Calif., 1981.
Gabrielsen, Vincent. *Financing the Athenian Fleet.* Baltimore, 1994.
Jordan, Borimir. *The Athenian Navy in the Classical Period.* Berkeley, Calif., 1975.
Morrison, John, John Coates, and Boris Rankov. *The Athenian Trireme.* New York, 2000.
Welsh, Frank. *Building the Trireme.* London, 1988.

ANCIENT SHIPS, SEAFARING, AND NAVIES IN THE MEDITERRANEAN

Casson, Lionel. *Ships and Seamanship in the Ancient World.* Princeton, 1971.
Davies, M. I. "Sailing, Rowing, and Sporting in One's Cups on the Wine-Dark Sea." In *Athens Comes of Age: From Solon to Salamis,* edited by William Childs. Princeton, 1978.
Hale, John R. "The Value of Sea Trials in Experimental Archaeology." In *Naval History: The Seventh Symposium of the U.S. Naval Academy,* edited by William B. Cogar. Wilmington, Del., 1988.
———. "The Lost Technology of Ancient Greek Rowing." *Scientific American* 274, no. 5 (1996).
Lehmann, L. T. *The Polyeric Quest: Renaissance and Baroque Theories About Ancient Men-of-War.* Amsterdam, 1995.
Morrison, John S., and R. T. Williams. *Greek Oared Ships, 900–322 B.C.* Cambridge, U.K., 1968.

Morrison, John, ed. *The Age of the Galley: Mediterranean Oared Vessels Since Pre-Classical Times.* London, 1995.

Morrison, John, and John Coates. *Greek and Roman Oared Warships, 399–30 B.C.* Oxford, U.K., 1996.

Oron, Asaf. "The Athlit Ram Bronze Casting Reconsidered." *Journal of Archaeological Science* 33, no. 1 (2006).

Panvini, Rosalba. *The Archaic Greek Ship at Gela.* Regione Siciliana, Italy, 2001.

Polzer, M. E. "An Archaic Laced Hull in the Aegean: The 2003 Excavation and Study of the Pabuç Burnu Ship Remains." *Institute of Nautical Archaeology Quarterly* 31, no. 3 (2004).

Rodgers, William Ledyard. *Greek and Roman Naval Warfare.* Annapolis, Md., 1937.

Snodgrass, Mary Ellen. *Voyages in Classical Mythology.* Santa Barbara, Calif., 1994.

Spathari, Elsi. *Sailing Through Time: The Ship in Greek Art.* Athens, 1995.

Wachsmann, Shelley. *Seagoing Ships and Seamanship in the Bronze Age Levant.* College Station, Tex., 1998.

ATHENIAN WARS AND COMMANDERS

Adcock, F. E. *The Greek and Macedonian Art of War.* Berkeley, Calif., 1957.

Allen, Lindsay. *The Persian Empire.* Chicago, 2005.

Blamire, A. *Plutarch: Life of Kimon with Translation and Commentary.* London, 1989.

Bosworth, A. B. *Conquest and Empire: The Reign of Alexander the Great.* Cambridge, U.K., 1988.

Burn, Andrew Robert. *The Persian Wars: The Greeks and the Defence of the West, c. 546–478 B.C.* London, 2002.

Develin, Robert. *Athenian Officials, 684–381 B.C.* Cambridge, U.K., 1989.

Ducrey, Pierre. *Warfare in Ancient Greece.* New York, 1986.

Frost, Frank J. *Plutarch's Themistocles: A Historical Commentary.* Chicago, 1998.

Green, Peter. *Armada from Athens.* New York, 1970.

Hale, John R. "Phormio Crosses the T." *Military History Quarterly* 8, no. 4 (1996).

———. "General Phormio's Art of War." In *Polis and Polemos,* edited by Charles D. Hamilton and Peter Krentz. Claremont, Calif., 1997.

Hamel, Debra. *Athenian Generals: Military Authority in the Classical Period.* Leiden, 1998.

Hanson, Victor Davis. *The Wars of the Ancient Greeks.* London, 1999.

———. *Carnage and Culture: Landmark Battles in the Rise of Western Power.* New York, 2001.

Hignett, C. *Xerxes' Invasion of Greece.* Oxford, U.K., 1963.

Hunt, Peter. *Slaves, Warfare, and Ideology in the Greek Historians.* Cambridge, U.K., 1998.

Kagan, Donald. *The Outbreak of the Peloponnesian War.* Ithaca, N.Y., 1969.

———. *The Archidamian War.* Ithaca, N.Y., 1974.

———. *The Peace of Nicias and the Sicilian Expedition.* Ithaca, N.Y., 1981.

———. *The Fall of the Athenian Empire.* Ithaca, N.Y., 1987.

———. *Pericles of Athens and the Birth of Democracy.* New York, 1991.

———. *The Peloponnesian War.* New York, 2003.

Kallet-Marx, Lisa. *Money, Expense, and Naval Power in Thucydides' History.* Berkeley, Calif., 1993.

Lenardon, Robert J. *The Saga of Themistocles.* London, 1978.

Littman, Robert. "Dor and the Athenian Empire." *American Journal of Ancient History* 15, no. 2 (1990).

Pritchett, W. Kendrick. *Ancient Greek Battle Speeches.* Amsterdam, 2002.

Quinn, T. J. *Athens and Samos, Lesbos and Chios, 478–404.* Manchester, U.K., 1981.

Schreiner, Johan. *Hellanikos, Thukydides and the Era of Kimon.* Aarhus, Denmark, 1997.

Sheppard, Ruth, ed. *Alexander the Great at War.* Oxford, U.K., 2008.

Stadter, Philip A. *A Commentary on Plutarch's Pericles.* Chapel Hill, N.C., 1989.

Strauss, Barry. *The Battle of Salamis.* New York, 2004.

Tritle, Lawrence. *Phocion the Good.* New York, 1988.

Wallinga, H. T. *Xerxes' Great Adventure: The Naval Perspective.* Leiden, 2005.

Ward, Anne, et al. *The Quest for Theseus.* New York, 1970.

Wilson, John B. *Pylos 425 B.C.: A Historical and Topographic Study of Thucydides' Account of the Campaign.* Warminster, U.K., 1979.

THE PIRAEUS AND THE LONG WALLS

Cohen, Edward. *Ancient Athenian Maritime Courts.* Princeton, 1973.

Conwell, David H. *Connecting a City to the Sea.* Leiden, 2008.

Garland, Robert. *The Piraeus from the Fifth to the First Centuries B.C.* London, 2001.

Lorenzen, Elvind. *The Arsenal at Piraeus.* Copenhagen, 1964.

Lovén, Bjørn, et al. "The Zea Harbour Project." In *Proceedings of the Danish Institute at Athens.* Athens, 2007.

Nielsen, Mads M. "Three Pieces of the Piraean Puzzle." In *Proceedings of the Danish Institute at Athens.* Athens, 2007.

Schaldemose, Mette K. "The Zea Shipsheds." In *Proceedings of the Danish Institute at Athens.* Athens, 2007.

Steinhauer, George A. "Ancient Piraeus: The City of Themistocles and Hippodamus." In Steinhauer et al., *Piraeus: Centre of Shipping and Culture*. Athens,
2000.

ANCIENT ATHENS: HISTORY, ARCHAEOLOGY, AND CULTURE

Barnes, J., ed. *The Complete Works of Aristotle: The Revised Oxford Translation*. Prince-
ton, 1984.
Boedecker, Deborah, and Kurt Raaflaub, eds. *Democracy, Empire and the Arts in
Fifth Century Athens*. Cambridge, Mass., 1998.
Camp, John M. *The Athenian Agora: Excavations in the Heart of Classical Athens*.
London, 1986.
———. *The Archaeology of Athens*. New Haven, Conn., 2001.
Davies, John K. *Athenian Propertied Families, 600–300 B.C.* Oxford, U.K., 1971.
Flacelière, Robert. *Daily Life in Greece at the Time of Pericles*. New York, 1965.
Forsén, Björn, and Greg Stanton, eds. *The Pnyx in the History of Athens*. Helsinki,
1996.
Fredal, James. *Rhetorical Action in Ancient Athens: Persuasive Artistry from Solon to
Demosthenes*. Carbondale, Ill., 2006.
Goette, Hans. *Athens, Attica and the Megarid: An Archaeological Guide*. London,
1993.
Gomme, A. W. *The Population of Athens in the Fifth and Fourth Centuries B.C.*
Oxford, U.K., 1933.
Harding, Phillip. *Androtion and the Atthis*. Oxford, U.K., 1994.
Henderson, Jeffrey. *The Maculate Muse: Obscene Language in Attic Comedy*. New
York, 1991.
Hignett, C. *A History of the Athenian Constitution to the End of the Fifth Century B.C.*
Oxford, U.K., 1952.
Hurwit, Jeffrey M. *The Acropolis in the Age of Pericles*. Cambridge, U.K., 2004.
Krentz, Peter. *The Thirty at Athens*. Ithaca, N.Y., 1982.
Loomis, William T. *Wages, Welfare Costs and Inflation in Classical Athens*. Ann
Arbor, Mich., 1998.
McLeish, Kenneth. *The Theatre of Aristophanes*. London, 1980.
Meiggs, Russell. *The Athenian Empire*. Oxford, U.K., 1972.
Neils, Jenifer, et al. *Goddess and Polis: The Panathenaic Festival in Ancient Athens*.
Princeton, 1992.
Papadopoulous, John K., and Deborah Ruscillo. "A Ketos in Early Athens: An
Archaeology of Whales and Sea Monsters in the Greek World." *American Jour-
nal of Archaeology* 106, no. 2 (2002).
Parke, H. W. *Festivals of the Athenians*. London, 1977.

Roberts, Jennifer Tolbert. *Accountability in Athenian Government*. Madison, Wis., 1982.

Samons, Loren J., ed. *The Cambridge Companion to the Age of Pericles*. New York, 2007.

Seltman, C. *Athens, Its History and Coinage Before the Persian Invasion*. Cambridge, U.K., 1924.

Stockton, David. *The Classical Athenian Democracy*. Oxford, U.K., 1990.

Storey, Ian. *Eupolis: Poet of Old Comedy*. Oxford, U.K., 2003.

Tyrrell, William Blake, and Frieda S. Brown. *Athenian Myths and Institutions*. Oxford, U.K., 1991.

Vidal-Naquet, Pierre. *The Atlantis Story: A Short History of Plato's Myth*. Exeter, U.K., 2007.

THE WORLD OF ANCIENT GREECE

Badian, Ernst. *From Plataea to Potidaea: Studies in the History and Historiography of the Pentecontaetia*. Baltimore, 1993.

Broad, William J. *The Oracle: Ancient Delphi and the Science Behind Its Lost Secrets*. New York, 2006.

Camp, John M., and Elizabeth Fisher. *The World of the Ancient Greeks*. London, 2002.

Carpenter, Thomas H. *Art and Myth in Ancient Greece*. London, 1991.

Cartledge, Paul, ed. *The Cambridge Illustrated History of Ancient Greece*. Cambridge, U.K., 1998.

Detienne, Marcel, and Jean-Pierre Vernant. *Cunning Intelligence in Greek Culture and Society*. Chicago, 1991.

Gorman, Vanessa B. *Miletos: The Ornament of Ionia*. Ann Arbor, Mich., 2001.

Kagan, Donald. *Problems in Ancient History: The Ancient Near East and Greece*. London, 1966.

Koromila, Marianna. *The Greeks and the Black Sea*. Athens, 2002.

Lewis, D. M., ed. *The Cambridge Ancient History Volume VI: The Fourth Century B.C.* Cambridge, U.K., 1994.

Meiggs, Russell. *Trees and Timber in the Ancient Mediterranean World*. Oxford, U.K., 1982.

Rhodes, P. J., and Robin Osborne. *Greek Historical Inscriptions 404–323 B.C.* Oxford, U.K., 2003.

Roberts, John. *The Oxford Dictionary of the Classical World*. Oxford, U.K., 2005.

Varoufakis, George. *Ancient Greek Standards*. Athens, 1999.

Vidal-Naquet, Pierre. *The Black Hunter*. Baltimore, 1986.

ACKNOWLEDGMENTS

MANY BACKS WERE BENT AND ARMS STRAINED TO PROPEL *Lords of the Sea* across the finish line. Most of the heavy work was done by the crew from Team Viking, intrepid argonauts who launch their racing shells at the foot of Houston Street in Manhattan. For this particular effort the rowing cadence was set by the mighty stroke oar of Bruce Giffords, senior production editor, with copy editor Janet Biehl right behind him in the number 7 seat. Artists powered the boat's engine room: designer Carla Bolte at 6; cover designer Christopher Sergio at 5; mapmaker Jeff Ward at 4; while the most experienced oarsman, Sam Manning at 3, brought all his knowledge of Maine's wooden craft to the task of rendering the Athenian trireme in pen and ink. Publicists Meghan Fallon and Ben Petrone made a flashy bow pair, and the cries of coxswain and marketing director Nancy Sheppard drew the attention of crowds along the bank. In the coaches' launch, the editorial team of Liz Parker and Hilary Redmon gripped their stopwatches while Carolyn Coleburn recorded the session. Beside them, megaphone in hand, stood editor Wendy Wolf, the head coach, who had set all this activity in motion: a commanding yet encouraging figure with the steady gray eyes of Athena, the enigmatic smile of an archaic *kore* from the Acropolis, and an occasional rasp in the voice during moments of crisis. They have passed out of sight now down the broad and shining reaches of the Hudson, to tackle other books and other authors. It was my good fortune to row, for a little time, in their company.

Even before my friends at Viking set to work on the book's final version, a number of readers had worked their way through the manuscript and given helpful advice. Among them were Neville Blakemore, Eli Brown, Molly Bundy, Helen Darmara, Dan Davis, Sharon Heckel, Åsa and Håkan Ringbom, Camille Thomasson, Joan Vandertoll, and Tom Weil. I am particularly grateful to Matt Bahr of Pittsburgh, NFL placekicker supreme, who brought his keen eye for timing and strategy to bear on this story of the Athenian navy.

Many chapters began as lectures, and I thank the University of Louisville, the Archaeological Institute of America, and the Teaching Company (through a course titled "The Greek and Persian Wars") for sponsoring both lecture series and individual presentations. In 2003 the Louisville Collegiate School provided a hall where I talked my way through the entire history of the Athenian navy over thirteen hot July evenings. Research assistant Bess Reed coordinated the lectures, Elijah Pritchett taped them, Mary "Corky" Sachs transcribed the tapes, and Stephanie Smith wrestled the hours of discursive talk into edited and readable form. Generous funding from Daniel and Joanna Rose helped support the process and the research that accompanied it. To help me present the evidence in favor of a new site for the battle of Aegospotami, Captain Christopher Windisch of the United States Army Reserves superimposed ancient naval maneuvers onto modern satellite images of the Hellespont and the Gallipoli peninsula.

My travels and field surveys of sites in the Aegean and eastern Mediterranean have been supported by the American School of Classical Studies at Athens, the Association of Yale Alumni, Travel Dynamics, the trustees of the University of Louisville, my dear friends Bruce and Elizabeth Dunlevie, and VPRO Television Rotterdam, who flew me to Greece so that I could try out trireme-style rowing on a sheepskin pad at the Homilos Ereton rowing club in Zea Harbor. Welcome and enthusiastic traveling companions have been the Gunlicks of Virginia, the Regueiros of Pennsylvania, and the Ringboms of Finland. Muharrem Zeybek of Izmir provided indispensable guidance for my travels in Turkey, from the fast-flowing Eurymedon River in the south to the rainy coast of Cyzicus (modern Erdek) in the north. Where my own travels could not reach, Bob Brier and Pat Remler stepped in with vivid accounts of the Nile delta in Egypt. And to a kind invitation from the great archaeologist John Camp I owe my first glimpses of Halicarnassus, Miletus, Ephesus, Notium, Samos, Lesbos, the Hellespont, and other sites along the Athenian maritime empire's eastern frontier.

Over the years of research into Greek naval matters I have been educated by the conversations, correspondence, and critical comments of many great scholars, among them Lucien Basch, Jack Cargill, Lionel Casson, John

Coates, Philip de Souza, Victor Davis Hanson, Peter Krentz, Robert Littman, Sean McGrail, John Morrison, Bill Murray, Boris Rankov, Barry Strauss, Larry Tritle, Harry Tzalas, Hans van Wees, and H. T. Wallinga. Here at the University of Louisville I am indebted to my colleagues Bob Luginbill, who helped interpret the Greek text of Phormio's stratagems as recorded by Polyaenus; Bob Kebric, who took an interest in ancient rowing techniques; and astronomer John Kielkopf, who helped determine the positions of celestial bodies in the night sky at the time of the battle of Salamis. In Finland, Ville Aaltonen enlightened me about modern competitors who depend for their speed, as did the ancient Athenians, on rowing pads and leg muscles.

Among underwater archaeologists I have learned much about ancient ships from Bridget Buxton, Deborah Carlson, Susan Katzev, Paraskevi Micha, and Katerina Delaporta, ephor of underwater antiquities during the time of my research in Greece. I salute my friends and colleagues in the Persian Wars Shipwreck Survey—Shelley Wachsmann, Bob Hohlfelder, Dan Davis, Alexis Catsambis, Dana Yoerger, and the crew and scientific team of the Greek research vessel *Aegaeo*. I owe my understanding of the Navy Yard and the life of the Athenian trireme on shore to the amphibious heroes of the Zea Harbor Project, including Bjørn Lovén, Mads Nielsen, artist Ioannis Nakas, as well as the generous souls who joined the American Friends of the Zea Harbor Project.

Donald Kagan provided the original inspiration for this book. Years later, he also provided its title. On a snowy night in February 2006 I was sitting at the table in the Kagans' gleaming black-and-white kitchen. Myrna Kagan had already washed her hands of yet another obsessive discussion of the Athenian navy and retired to the upper regions. Don was staring at a long list of phrases, keywords, and rejected titles that had accumulated over half a decade in the quest to name the book. The only sound was the blizzard beating lightly on the windowpane. Suddenly Don raised his head, stared at me with a sort of visionary glow, and pronounced, in oracular tones, four words. I acknowledged at once that the phrase made a good title, and also had the benefit, if I remembered rightly, of being drawn from one of Pericles' speeches.

"Are you sure? Not the Funeral Oration, anyway. Bring me the book."

In the Kagans' house, a Greek text of Thucydides is never more than a few steps away from your chair. I fetched the nearest one. Don began to work his way through the last speech of Pericles, the defiant oration delivered after the plague had struck and the people had turned against their leader. As always, he held the page three inches away from his face and ran his finger along the lines, muttering as he read.

"If I did not see you discouraged . . . the world . . . land and sea . . ." The translating ceased. "Ha! It's better than you remembered. *Kyriôtatous!* The Athenians rule as supreme lords—*most* lords. So!" Don clapped the book shut and handed it back across the table. "Let it be *Lords of the Sea.*"

INDEX

Page numbers in *italics* refer to illustrations and maps.